THE HISTORY OF CIVILIZATION

ROME THE LAW-GIVER

THE HISTORY OF CIVILIZATION

General Editor C. K. Ogden

The *History of Civilization* is a landmark in early twentieth Century publishing. The aim of the general editor, C. K. Ogden, was to "summarise in one comprehensive synthesis the most recent findings and theories of historians, anthropologists, archaeologists, sociologists and all conscientious students of civilization." The *History*, which includes titles in the French series *L'Evolution de l'Humanité*, was published at a formative time in the development of the social sciences, and during a period of significant historical discoveries.

A list of the titles in the series can be found at the end of this book.

Spielhagen, Friedrich 59f., 169, 172–185, 225–231, 237
- *Clara Vere* 172–185
- *Die Sphinx [In der zwölften Stunde]* 225–231
- *Hammer und Amboß* 59
- *In Reih und Glied* 59
- *Sturmflut* 59
Sterne, Laurence 40
- *The Life and Opinions of Tristram Shandy, Gentleman* 40
Stifter, Adalbert 146, 149, 186, 189f., 192, 215, 247
- *Der Hochwald* 247
- *Der Nachsommer* 189, 192
- *Katzensilber* 190
Storm, Theodor 16f., 52, 67, 101, 143–145, 149, 156, 168, 186, 197–200, 215–223, 236, 246–254, 257
- *Am Kamin* 143f., 168
- *Aquis Submersus* 221
- *Beim Vetter Christian* 198–200, 215
- *Carsten Curator* 145, 156
- *Die Söhne des Senators* 16f.
- *Ein Doppelgänger* 67, 222f.
- *Im Schloß* 257
- *Immensee* 52, 101
- *Psyche* 186
- *Viola Tricolor* 215–220
- *Waldwinkel* 247–254

Tawada, Yoko 11
Tieck, Ludwig 56–60, 62, 67, 71, 75, 77, 80–82, 86–127, 130, 135, 137, 142, 156, 173f., 219, 222, 231, 234f., 241, 244–246, 248, 251f., 254, 256
- *Das jüngste Gericht* 82
- *Der blonde Eckbert* 56–58, 86–100, 102, 105, 109, 114–117, 119–121, 124, 170, 175, 219, 231, 246, 248, 250–252, 254
- *Der getreue Eckart und der Tannhäuser* 114, 121–123, 135
- *Der Mondsüchtige* 71
- *Der Psycholog* 81
- *Der Runenberg* 67, 75, 100, 103f., 105–114, 234
- *Die Elfen* 114–121, 156
- *Die Freunde* 80
- *Die Versöhnung* 256
- *Musikalische Leiden und Freuden* 80
- *Phantasus* 56f., 67, 114f., 121

Uexküll, Jakob von 6

Verbo 5
- *Heterotopia Lunar* 5
- *Injusticia Poética* 5
Virchow, Rudolf 1f.
- *Die Cellularpathologie in ihrer Begründung auf physiologische und pathologische Gewebelehre* 2
Vischer, Friedrich Theodor 39–52, 59f., 170, 216
- *Auch Einer. Eine Reisebekanntschaft* 39–52, 59f.
- *Das Symbol* 216

Walshe, Walter Hayle 2
- *The Physical Diagnosis of Diseases of the Lungs* 2
Werner, Zacharias 151f.
- *Der fünfundzwanzigste Februar* 151
- *Die Weihe der Kraft* 151, 154
Wilder, Thornton 8

DE GRUYTER

STUDIEN ZUR DEUTSCHEN LITERATUR

50 JAHRE FORSCHUNG IN MEHR ALS 200 BÄNDEN

Hrsg. v. Georg Braungart, Eva Geulen, Steffen Martus, Martina Wagner-Egelhaaf

Die Reihe *Studien zur deutschen Literatur* präsentiert herausragende Untersuchungen zur deutschsprachigen Literatur von der Frühen Neuzeit bis zur Gegenwart. Offen besonders auch für komparatistische, kulturwissenschaftliche und wissensgeschichtliche Fragestellungen, bietet sie ein traditionsreiches Forum für innovative literaturwissenschaftliche Forschung.

Alle Bücher sind auch als eBook und ePUB erhältlich.

Zuletzt erschienen:

Band 213
Stefan Tetzlaff
HETEROTOPIE ALS TEXTVERFAHREN
Erzählter Raum in Romantik und Realismus
2016. Ca. 313 S., 2 Abb.
Geb. € 99,95 [D]
ISBN 978-3-11-047192-2

Band 212
Dorothea Kliche-Behnke
NATIONALSOZIALISMUS UND SHOAH IM AUTOBIOGRAPHISCHEN ROMAN
2016. VIII, 225 S.
Geb. € 89,95 [D]
ISBN 978-3-11-047304-9

Band 211
Beatrix van Dam
GESCHICHTE ERZÄHLEN
Repräsentation von Vergangenheit in deutschen und niederländischen Texten der Gegenwart
2016. 366 S., 2 Abb.
Geb. € 99,95 [D]
ISBN 978-3-11-041963-4

Band 210
Zoë Ghyselinck
FORM UND FORMAUFLÖSUNG DER TRAGÖDIE
Die Poetik des Tragischen und der Tragödie als religiöses Erneuerungsmuster in den Schriften Paul Ernsts (1866–1933)
2015. 353 S.
Geb. € 99,95 [D]
ISBN 978-3-11-037171-0

Band 209
Hanna Klessinger
POSTDRAMATIK
Transformationen des epischen Theaters bei Peter Handke, Heiner Müller, Elfriede Jelinek und Rainald Goetz
2015. 292 S.
Geb. € 89,95 [D]
ISBN 978-3-11-037002-7

Band 208
Urs Büttner
POIESIS DES ‚SOZIALEN'
Achim von Arnims frühe Poetik bis zur Heidelberger Romantik (1800–1808)
2015. 492 S.
Geb. € 99,95 [D]
ISBN 978-3-11-031457-1

degruyter.com

ROME THE LAW-GIVER

J. Declareuil

LONDON AND NEW YORK

First published in 1927 by Routledge, Trench, Trubner
Reprinted 1996, 2000
by Routledge
2 Park Square, Milton Park,
Abingdon, Oxfordshire OX14 4RN
&
711 Third Avenue,
New York, NY 10017

Routledge is an imprint of the Taylor & Francis Group, an informa business

Transferred to Digital Printing 2008

First issued in paperback 2013

© 1996 Routledge

All rights reserved. No part of this book may be reprinted or utilized in any form or by any means electronic, mechanical, or other means, now known or hereafter invented, including photocopying and recording, in any information storage or retrieval system, without permission in writing from the publishers.

British Cataloguing in Publication Data

ISBN 13: 978-0-415-15581-6 (hbk)
ISBN 13: 978-0-415-86970-6 (pbk)
ISBN Roman Civilization (6 volume set): 978-0-415-15613-4
ISBN History of Civilization (50 volume set): 978-0-415-14380-6

Publisher's Note
The publisher has gone to great lengths to ensure the quality of this reprint but points out that some imperfections in the original may be apparent.

CONTENTS

	PAGE
FOREWORD (BY HENRI BERR)	xiii

PROLEGOMENA

CHAPTER

I. THE PLACE OF ROMAN LAW IN THE ANCIENT WORLD . **3**

    I. Rome's legal vocation, 3. II. The story of Law before the Romans, 4. III. The question of Rome's indebtedness to foreign legislations, 12.

II. THE FORMATION OR EXTERNAL HISTORY OF ROMAN LAW . **16**

    I. The sources of Roman Law, 16. II. Classification of legal matter according to its sources, 27. III. Byzantine Law and the compilations of Justinian, 30.

BOOK I

THE ANCIENT CUSTOMS AND THE FORMATION OF CLASSICAL LAW

I. THE GENS AND THE CITY . **37**

    I. LIFE IN THE "GENS" . **37**

        I. The autonomous *gens* and primitive customs, 37. II. The *jus gentilitatis*, 41.

    II. THE ORGANIZATION OF THE CITY . **42**

        I. The city. The *gens* within the city. The *jus civitatis*, 42. II. The growth of the city. The plebs, 44. III. Disappearance of the *gens* as an organic part of the city, 46. IV. The levelling legislation of the Twelve Tables, 48.

    III. LAW IN THE CITY . **52**

        I. The new conditions of the *jus civitatis*, 52. II. Legal relations with foreigners, 55.

II. ADMINISTRATION OF JUSTICE IN THE CITY. CIVIL PROCEDURE . **59**

    I. ADMINISTRATION OF JUSTICE ORGANIZED BY THE STATE. PROCEDURE AN ADVANTAGE DUE TO THE CITY . **59**

CONTENTS

CHAPTER	PAGE
II. THE STATUTORY PROCESSES	60

 I. The *legis actiones:* their origin and character, 60. II. Judicial organization and the distinction between *jus* and *judicium*, 62. III. The *legis actiones* for establishing a right, 63. IV. The *legis actiones:* modes of execution or coercion, 67.

 III. THE FORMULAR PROCEDURE . . . 70

 I. The appearance of the formulas. The Aebutian and Julian Laws. Judicial organization, 70. II. Summons and representation at law, 73. III. The procedure *in jure*, 75. IV. The composition of the formulas and the classification of the actions, 77. V. The procedure *in judicio* and the effects of the sentence, 83. VI. The modes of execution, 86.

 IV. USE OF THE "IMPERIUM" IN PROCEDURE . 88

 I. Use of the *imperium* in procedure, 88. II. The *cognitiones extra ordinem*, 89.

 V. THE WAYS OF RECOURSE . . . 91

III. THE LAW OF THE FAMILY AND ITS DEPENDENCIES . 93

 SECTION I. ORGANIZATION OF THE "DOMUS." . 93

  I. THE FAMILY GROUP 93

  I. Kinship. The family group or *domus*, 93. II. *Patria potestas* the foundation of the *domus*. The *paterfamilias*, 95.

  II. MARRIAGE 98

  I. The married woman, *uxor*. The various kinds of marriage. Marriages *cum* and *sine manu*, 98. II. The conditions of a marriage's validity, 104. III. The position of the wife in the *domus* and the obligations of marriage, 106. IV. The modes of dissolving a marriage, 108. V. The financial agreements between spouses. The dowry and its restitution, 109. VI. Free union or concubinage, 113.

  III. THE "FILIIFAMILIAS". . . . 114

  I. Legitimate children born in wedlock, 114. II. Fictitious filiations. Adrogated and adopted children, 117. III. Modes of acquiring *patria potestas* subsequent to marriage, 120. IV. The civil capacity of the *filiifamilias*, 121. V. Means of release from the *patria potestas*, 124.

  IV. THE SLAVES 126

  I. The *potestas dominica*. Causes of slavery, 126. II. The slave's social and legal position, 128. III. The restrictions imposed by law on the *potestas dominica*, 130.

  V. THE FREEDMEN 130

  I. The freedmen and the modes of enfranchisement, 130. II. Statutes restricting the power to enfranchise, 132. III. The condition of freedmen and the *jura patronatus*, 133.

  VI. THE CLIENTS 136

CONTENTS

CHAPTER	PAGE
SECTION II. PERSONS INCAPABLE "SUI JURIS."	137

I. GUARDIANSHIP 137
   I. The guardianship of women, 137. II. Guardianship of children under the age of puberty, 140.

II. CURATORSHIP 147
   I. Curatorships of madmen and spendthrifts, 147. II. Curatorship of persons under twenty-five years of age, 149.

IV. CORPORATIVE LIFE AND ARTIFICIAL PERSONS . 152
   I. Corporations and associations in the Law of the Republic, 152. II. The statutes and jurisprudence of the Empire, 153. III. Artificial personality: The *universitates*, 154.

V. THE LAW OF PROPERTY AND REAL RIGHTS . . 156

   I. THE PATRIMONY. DISTINCTIONS BETWEEN THINGS. RIGHTS TO THINGS OR ARISING OUT OF THINGS . 156

   II. THE RIGHT OF OWNERSHIP . . . 158
      I. Origin and nature of the right of ownership. Family ownership, 158. II. Ownership of moveables and ownership of land, 161. III. Provincial ownership, 163. IV. The sanctions of the right of ownership, 164.

   III. POSSESSION AND ITS VARIOUS TYPES . 165
      I. Possession: its legal value and its characteristics, 165. II. The possessory interdicts, 168. III. *In bonis habere*: bonitarian and prætorian ownership, 170.

   IV. MODES OF TRANSFER OF REAL RIGHTS . . 172
      I. The modes of acquiring ownership, 172. II. *Mancipatio. In jure cessio. Traditio. Adjudicatio*, 172. III. Usucapion; the *præscriptio longi temporis*, 177. IV. Assignations by statute, 181.

   V. SERVITUDES AND OTHER REAL RIGHTS . . 182
      I. The *jura in re aliena* : Servitudes and other real rights. 182. II. The prædial servitudes, 183. III. Usufruct, use, habitation, slaves' labour, 185. IV. The other real rights, 188.

VI. OBLIGATIONS OR PERSONAL RIGHTS . . 190

   I. THE CHARACTERISTICS OF PERSONAL RIGHTS . 190
      I. Personal rights. *Debitum* and *obligatio* defined, 190. II. The genesis and sources of obligation, 191.

   II. DELICTS 194
      I. Delictual obligation. Public and private delicts, 194. II. Private delicts and their sanctions in the Law of the Twelve Tables and in the Civil Law, 196. III. The prætorian reforms touching the ancient delicts, 200. IV. The prætorian delicts. Dissociation of the penal and recuperatory elements, 202. V. The part played by *interpretatio*. Private Law and penal Law, 208.

CONTENTS

CHAPTER	PAGE

III. CONTRACTS 209
    I. Agreements in the time of private justice, 209. II. The most ancient contracts of Roman Law. Formal contracts, 211. III. The contract *litteris*. The *mutuum* and the *pactum fiduciæ*, 218. IV. The consensual contracts: sale, hire, partnership, commission, 222. V. Contracts *re* of the second period: loan, deposit, pledge, 231. VI. The other synallagmatic agreements and the attempts of jurisprudence to sanction them, 232. VII. The pacts accessory to a contract and the prætorian pacts, 233.

IV. AN ATTEMPT TO CONSTRUCT A GENERAL THEORY OF CONTRACT 236
    I. Outline of a general theory of contract, 236. II. The capacity and consent of the contracting parties. Flaws in the consent, 236. III. The object and ground of obligations, 238. IV. Modalities affecting obligations, 239.

V. OBLIGATIONS ARISING NEITHER FROM DELICT NOR FROM CONTRACT 242

VI. EFFECTS OF OBLIGATIONS . . . 245
    I. Effects of obligations between creditor and debtor: voluntary and forced execution. Failure to execute and faults committed in the execution, 245. II. Effects of obligations as regards third parties. Absence of juridical representation: relaxations of this principle, 249. III. Inalienability of claims: how the principle was eluded, 252.

VII. EXTINCTION OF OBLIGATIONS . . 253
    I. Extinction of obligations: principal modes of the *jus civile*, 253. II. Set-off, 255. III. Prætorian methods of extinction, 256.

VII. THE ORGANIZATION OF CREDIT . . . 258

I. THE IDEA AND THE PRINCIPAL FORMS OF CREDIT 258
    I. The idea of credit: its principal forms, 258. II. The loan for consumption; loan at interest and its legislation, 258. III. Irregular deposit and the *receptum argentarii*, 262.

II. PERSONAL GUARANTEES . . . 262
    I. Personal guarantees: their antiquity, 262. II. Solidarity, 263. III. Security and its various forms: *sponsio, fidepromissio, fidejussio, mandatum pecuniæ credendæ*, 264.

III. REAL SURETIES 268
    I. The real sureties earlier than mortgage, 268. II. Mortgage, 268.

VIII. THE LAW OF INHERITANCE AND GIFTS . . 272

SECTION I. THE LAW OF INHERITANCE . . 272

I. PRIMITIVE LAW AND THE LAW OF THE TWELVE TABLES 272
    I. The law of inheritance and the social and political conditions, 272. II. The Law of the Twelve Tables: the *heredes sui*; wills; intestate inheritance, 273.

CONTENTS

CHAPTER	PAGE
II. TESTAMENTARY PRACTICE . . .	277

    I. Importance of the will. The creations of custom: will *per aes et libram*; extension of the *factio testamenti*, 277. II. Institution of an heir; contents of the will, 279. III. Nature of the inheritance: acceptance, repudiation, sanction, 283.

III. THE PRÆTORIAN LAW OF INHERITANCE . 287

    I. The prætorian reforms, 287. II. The prætorian will and *bonorum possessio secundum tabulas*, 288. III. *Bonorum possessiones ab intestato*, 288.

IV. THE RESTRICTIONS ON FREEDOM OF TESTATION 291

    I. Changed moral standards and restrictions on freedom of testation: new jurisprudence touching disinherison; *bonorum possessio contra tabulas*, 291. II. The *querela inofficiosi testamenti* ; the *quarta legitimæ partis*, 292.

V. THE IMPERIAL INNOVATIONS . . . 295

    I. The reforms of Augustus and the laws of escheat. The *jus liberorum*, 295. II. The Sc. Tertullianum and Orphitianum, 297. III. The *peculium castrense* and the law of inheritance for soldiers, 297.

VI. LEGACIES 298

    I. Legacies, burdens on the inheritance. Origin and utility of legacies, 298. II. The forms and modality of legacies. The Sc. Neronianum, 299. III. Capacity to acquire legacies. Modes of acquisition, 302. IV. Restrictions on freedom of bequest. The *quarta falcidia* ; the *leges novæ*, 303.

VII. TESTAMENTARY TRUSTS . . . 305

    I. Testamentary trusts; their causes; reform by Augustus. Their progressive assimilation to legacies, 305. II. *Restitutiones post mortem* and family trusts, 307.

SECTION II. GIFTS 308

    I. Nature and character of gifts, 308. II. Gifts *inter vivos*, 309. III. Gifts in prospect of death, 310.

BOOK II

THE LAW OF THE LOWER EMPIRE AND THE REFORMS OF JUSTINIAN

I. THE STATE AND THE INDIVIDUAL . . . 313

    I. Nationality and the status of persons, 313. II. The state and the social classes. The *collegia* and the *colonatus*, 315.

II. JUSTICE AND PROCEDURE 322

    I. Judicial organization, 322. II. General character of administrative procedure, 323. III. The suit. Modes of execution. Ways of recourse, 324.

CONTENTS

CHAPTER	PAGE
III. THE FAMILY AND ITS DEPENDENCIES	328

SECTION I. THE ORGANIZATION OF THE "DOMUS" . 328

    I. THE FAMILY 328
        I. Relationship, the *domus*, 328. II. The weakened *patria potestas*, 329.

    II. MARRIAGE 330
        I. The married woman. Modifications of the conditions and effects of marriage, 330. II. The financial agreements in regard to marriage, 332. III. Free unions; concubinage, 335.

    III. THE CHILDREN 335
        I. The *filiifamilias*. Modes of acquiring *patria potestas*, 335. II. The juridical capacity of the *filiifamilias*, 337. III. Grounds for extinction of *patria potestas*, 339.

    IV. SLAVES AND FREEDMEN . . . 340
        I. The *potestas dominica*. The condition of slaves, 340. II. The *jura patronatus*. Enfranchisement and the condition of freedmen, 341.

SECTION II. PERSONS INCAPABLE "SUI JURIS" . 342
        I. Guardianship, 342. II. Curatorship, 344.

IV. THE SYSTEM OF CORPORATIONS . . . 346

V. THE SYSTEM OF PROPERTY AND REAL RIGHTS . 348
        I. The chattels and the patrimony, 348. II. Ownership and possession, 348. III. The modes of acquiring ownership, 349. IV. Servitudes, 351. V. Extension of certain new real rights, 352. VI. The fate of mortgage and pledge, 353.

VI. OBLIGATIONS OR PERSONAL RIGHTS . . 354

    I. DELICTS, CONTRACTS AND AGREEMENTS . 354
        I. The spirit of the imperial jurisprudence and statutes, 354. II. The later history of private delicts, 354. III. The later history of contracts and agreements, 355. IV. General theory of contract: influence of social conditions, 359.

    II. EFFECTS OF OBLIGATIONS . . . 361
        I. Effects of obligations; transfer of claim and representation, 361. II. Execution and extinction: imperial reforms, 362.

    III. THE ORGANIZATION OF CREDIT . . 363
        I. Credit: its processes, 363. II. Personal and real guarantees, 363.

CONTENTS

CHAPTER	PAGE
VII. THE LAW OF INHERITANCE AND GIFTS	365
I. INHERITANCE	365

      I. Wills and codicils, 365. II. The new order of succession *ab intestato*, 367. III. Acquisition and division of inheritance, 368.

   II. LEGACIES AND TESTAMENTARY TRUSTS. THEIR AMALGAMATION UNDER JUSTINIAN . . 369

   III. GIFTS "INTER VIVOS" AND IN PROSPECT OF DEATH 371

CONCLUSION 373

BIBLIOGRAPHY 381

INDEX 395

FOREWORD

ROME AS ORGANIZER

THE INVENTION OF LAW

IN the preface to La Pensée grecque et les origines de l'Esprit scientifique, *we felt justified in making the following remark: " no universal history exists where the history of ideas has the place that it will hold in this work or has been made so essentially a part of it." At the beginning of this volume we can say as much as regards Law which, if it is a product of social life, is at any rate ultimately associated with the history of ideas.*

To devote a whole volume in the series to Roman Law is in strict accord with the nature of things. We need not insist here on the part played by Rome as organizer of human society in general, on what may be called quite literally the Roman " miracle :" see the preface to vol. xvi. It is the activity of Rome as conscious originator of Law that we must emphasize, that the present volume tries to make clear, as she elaborates its details and makes its general principles stand out in the full light of reflexion.

We know that, as societies become organized, the politico-juridic function—which, with the economic function, meets the needs of the group considered as such and forms the strictly social factor in history—gradually breaks up into various institutions. " Custom " is the undeveloped, or little developed, seed of all juridic development :[1] *morality and Law grow out of it. These institutions are distinguished from one another by the different nature of the sanctions by which they are maintained : an internal imperative in one case, coercion in the other. Law may be defined as the minimum of morality that is indispensable for life in society and is imposed by material sanctions.*[2]

[1] *Custom in the wider sense is imitation of the past by the present, the general principle of stability ; it is opposed to the imitation of fashion : see my* Synthèse en Histoire, *p.* 108. *In juridic sociology the sense is more restricted.*

[2] *A section in the* Année sociologique (*the third*) *is devoted to "* Juridic and Moral Sociology " (*a study of the juridic and moral rules considered in their*

FOREWORD

While we recognize the specific character of Law, which is properly social, we believe that from the very beginning the individual has had some influence in this sphere. If all individuals are elements of society, they are not all so to the same degree; there are some who feel the social needs more keenly than the rest, and these are society's agents.[1] *There are also social inventors, logical agents who are specially endowed with reason and transform the Law of Custom into a theoretical and applied science, " scientia juris civilis."*[2]

The part played by individual initiative will be clearly shown in this volume. Law by which public authority first establishes custom and then adds to it was at Rome formulated, adapted, corrected, extended, interpreted by the magistrates and by the jurists. These latter " organized and classified the means by which every legal problem could be brought to a solution which should at the same time satisfy the mind and the sense of equity;" they " raised a structure which later centuries were to regard as a sort of written reason " (p. 26). *This structure was enlarged and adapted for the use of foreigners, and thus the idea of a " jus gentium " appeared. " For the first time the conception of a universal reason arose, not in the books of the philosophers, but in the actual body of Roman jurisprudence "* (p. 29; cf. 31).

Nothing of this sort had really been seen in Greece; for if the Greeks created art and speculation, the jurist in their cities " was

---

origin). *This section contains the following divisions:* 1. Undeveloped societies based upon the totem clan; 2. Developed legal systems based upon the totem clan; 3. Systems of tribal Law; 4. National systems of Law and morals. *A critical Bibliography is given which, in some points, may supplement the excellent Bibliography of J. Declareuil.*

[1] *" Custom, or at any rate each of its elements, always has an author, whether known or forgotten."—Declareuil, p.* 17.

[2] *See Declareuil, p.* 6.—*" The intuition that binds the individual to his environment, the need that he shares with this environment but feels more keenly and, on the other hand, the rational labour in which social invention properly consists are intermingled to various extents. But it is precisely the part played by reflective invention that becomes more and more important and more and more obvious. Apparently evolution tends to make society—which is already within individuals—ever more present to the consciousness of an increasing number of individuals. . . . According to the Durkheim theory it is claimed that the more complicated civilization becomes, the more the individual feels the ' transcendent ' relationship of society to himself, until ' each member of a little Australian tribe carries within himself the whole of his tribal civilization.' But the civilized man reflects upon this transcendent society, recognizing it more and more clearly as something objective; and thus he either adapts himself to it or seeks to modify it in accordance with reason." See the* Synthèse en Histoire, *pp.* 175-6 *and the Preface to vol. vi.*

FOREWORD

not distinguished from the philosopher or the statesman" (p. 10).[1] *Those realists the Romans were born jurists. They were so anxious to maintain just relations between living beings that they early adopted a legal attitude towards the gods themselves : it was not necessary to love the gods, but to give them their due of worship and observe the contract which binds them no less than the worshipper. " In many cases the forms used in prayer may be compared with legal formulas."*[2] *To Publius Scævola is attributed the saying " Fiat justitia, pereat mundus." It expresses the legal principle in its extreme form ; but it ignores the flexibility of this work of the jurists, which has been compared with casuistry.*[3]

The Romans achieved their legal work slowly and empirically, and yet it has a logical basis that never loses its validity. They have created " a body or, more accurately, several bodies of doctrine and of rational forms for almost all the situations and for many aspects of social life " (p. 4 ; cf. 6 and 379-80) ; and " to the work accomplished during a particular period at a particular point on the earth's surface whole centuries and, within those centuries, millions of human beings have been indebted " (p. 1). That is the glory of the Roman genius and its chief legacy to posterity.

The sources and the formation of Roman Law ; its evolution ; the establishment of a public order where greater independence is gradually allowed to the individual, but where the rights of the individual are reconciled with the various social interests ; then, later on, the loss of equilibrium owing to exaggerated individualism on the one hand and the establishment of State Socialism on the other : all this is luminously set forth in the following volume.

J. Declareuil possesses in the highest degree the historical spirit which animates Romanists to-day and involves that critical sagacity, that philological mastery, of which Frenchmen like Cujas, Antoine Favre and Jacques Godefroy first set the example. Sound learning, important personal researches and

---

[1] See the *Prefaces* to vols. *xi.* and *xvi.*
[2] See A. Grenier, vol. *xvii.*
[3] " *The Roman jurists who were admirable casuists admitted neither 'a priori' theses nor cumbersome generalizations, relying on their subtle genius to discover in each case the adequate or, as they called it, the 'elegans' solution* "
—J. Declareuil, Le quatrième centenaire de Cujas (1922), *p.* 9.

a very wide knowledge of the literature of the subject lie at the foundation of this book, where, without the dryness of a severe treatise, the results acquired are presented in vigorous epitome.

The synopsis of Roman Law contained in the present volume is, at the same time, an appropriate element in our general Synopsis. J. Declareuil has taken very great care to connect Roman Law with the general course of legal, sociological and historical evolution; and his endeavour will undoubtedly be appreciated, being as it is the work of a jurist who unites unbounded historical curiosity with the interests of the specialist and the qualifications of the expert, and addresses himself to all historians, to all devotees of history in the widest sense of the word.

HENRI BERR.

PROLEGOMENA

PROLEGOMENA

I

THE PLACE OF ROMAN LAW IN THE ANCIENT WORLD

I. Rome's Legal Vocation

WHEN the peoples rise above the condition of barbarism in which the bare necessities of existence are supplied by rudimentary institutions that are practically the same everywhere, their racial characteristics become more clearly contrasted and their distinctive powers are revealed. Their individuality emerges and each section of humanity is found to have a special mission and vocation. The vast number of ideas of which humanity is capable and the material advantages to be derived from them provide a larger field than any one nation can occupy in its entirety; and were any nation presumptuous enough to make the attempt, its story would be in danger of ending before the work was accomplished. The peoples who have left the deepest trace in history accepted this division of labour without demur and were content with the task of giving utterance to a few partial truths and adapting them to the service of life. This co-operation in the work of civilization, varying in importance according to the intellectual power, the physical and moral worth of each people, is sometimes very trifling in its results, but sometimes of such vast and far-reaching importance that to the work accomplished during a particular period at a particular point on the earth's surface whole centuries and, within those centuries, millions of human beings have been indebted.

In this division of labour Rome's mission was war and her vocation Law. She raised military science to the highest level that it reached in antiquity, but this acquisition was only used as a means to secure self-discipline in every sphere of thought by invariable obedience to rules, and the rules that govern individuals in their dealings with one another and with the associations to which they belong are what we call Law.

The Romans not only conquered men and took possession of their lands; they organized them too; and it was the first time that such a thing had been done with the same measure of success. Earlier conquerors, with the exception perhaps of Alexander, wanted only tribute; when that had been paid, they governed the vanquished from a distance and left them to their fate. Rome took seriously the task of governor and guardian which was hers by right of conquest. She considered her own Law good for the subject peoples and gradually, by constant suggestion, induced them to submit to it; and because her laws, always introduced by the same sure method, held sway for a long time over very large and diverse regions and became insensibly adjusted to the most varied conditions of life that arose while her empire lasted or could arise in the future, she bequeathed to the world a body of Law and of Jurisprudence by which a section of the human race has lived ever since; a body or, more accurately, several bodies of doctrine and of rational forms for almost all the situations and for many aspects of social life. She was aware of the fact herself. At the beginning of the fifth century, when the tide of barbarism was already sweeping over Western Europe, a poet of Roman Gaul sang over the ruins the immortal triumph of her laws:

> "Porrige victuras romana in sæcula leges,
> Solaque fatales non vereare colos."[1]

II. THE STORY OF LAW BEFORE THE ROMANS

The statement that Rome organized Law does not only mean that she possessed a large number of statutes. Great legislative activity is no proof of perfection in this matter but may be the reverse.

Among the nations who preceded her in power and renown more than one may have possessed as many statutes as she did, and there is hardly a single modern State whose legal armoury is not more abundantly stocked.

If it were merely a question of the number of statutes, she would have appeared somewhat too late to play the part of initiator. About the time of her foundation the power of

[1] Rutilius Claudius Namatianus, *Itiner.*, 20, 133-4.

Assyria which had seemed to be tottering made a sudden recovery, annexed the ancient kingdom of Chaldæa and brought under her hegemony almost all the small peoples between Nineveh and the sea. Egypt had reached her 23rd and 24th dynasties and laid claim to three great legislators of earlier days. A fourth, Bocchoris, was about to impose a series of reforms upon her that were very disturbing to her ancient constitution, but these were to be far surpassed by the revolutionary audacities of Amasis about two centuries later, when Rome was still hidden in the mists of her legendary kingship. She had hardly emerged from them when the Persian tide swept over the whole Eastern world. Now, Chaldæa, Egypt, Assyria and Persia had been blessed for centuries with systems of legislation that research is making clearer to us every day through the discovery of inscriptions and papyri.

The Law of Crete still retained something of the celebrity that clung to the name of Minos and to the enactments of a thalassocracy less mythical than was recently supposed. Sparta had prided herself for one or two centuries on the constitution inflicted upon her by Lycurgus; while the most famous legal systems of Athens and of some other Greek cities first saw the light of day at a time when Rome had as yet shown no distinct sign of her vocation or of any legal activity whatever.

It was not then by the possession of statutes, or of any particular statutes, or by their use to maintain the complex machinery of social relations that Rome acquired this priority; it was rather by the definition, arrangement and classification of those relations and of the forms that she adapted to suit them, by distinguishing them according to their origins or their causes, by analyzing them, by determining their effects and in some cases foreseeing and skilfully combining these latter; by the construction, in short, out of scattered and incongruous elements derived from all these sources, of a Science and an Art of Law. I mean to say that she created a frame of mind and methods of procedure capable of referring all legal data to a single norm; and this was so skilfully achieved that the life was neither crushed out of them nor distorted, but on the contrary gained that fulness and vigour which the jurists meant when they said of a solution: *elegans est.* This Science, *juris civilis scientia*, with certain reservations that must be taken for granted, and especially this art, *ars boni et æqui*, with the good sense, *prudentia*, and the methods, *disciplina*, that they require are essentially Roman. Nowhere else can they be found so highly developed, either because their memory, if they ever existed, has perished or more probably because they had never been conceived elsewhere.

As a matter of fact Rome's first steps in the domain of Law did not differ from those of the civilizations which had preceded her; it was the subsequent development that differed. In the remote periods that history is gradually bringing within her sphere human societies seem to have been generally ordered in imitation of the divine world as they conceived it. Law takes shape from the precepts of Theology, or its obsolete rules serve to meet the immediate needs of everyday life. Imitation of the gods in order to conciliate them and gain their favour, preservation of the society's existence, those are the two guiding ideas in primitive legislation.

To this end were directed the ancient theocratic and feudal constitutions of Egypt and also, though with a more rapid tendency towards individualism, those of the industrious, money-loving and evidently very mixed populations who inhabited the alluvial plains of the Tigris and the Euphrates. The customs of Israel and of the neighbouring peoples were closely bound up with ritual requirements and governed by religious ideas. Of all these, as of the Romans, it may be said that their " civil Law was for a long time kept secret among the mysteries and sacraments of the immortal gods and was known only to the priests."[1] Their short, clear commands, lacking all suppleness and adaptability, were as decisive as an oracle or as the few statements of fact which in those days formed the rudiments of the other branches of knowledge. Law at that date had neither autonomy nor specialized organs. Every omission or obscurity necessitated recourse to the fountain of origin, i.e. to the god or to his representative or at least to some privileged person favoured with his confidence or clever enough to set himself up as his interpreter.[2]

[1] Liv. 9, 46; Val. Max. 2, 5. [2] **CXXIV**, 39 et s., 83 et seq.

But if the origins were similar, we must not suppose that the body of Law put off its swathing-clothes and advanced to a foreseen destiny by a line of development that was always and everywhere the same! The comparative method of studying Law and history remains valuable, but the quasi-infallibility which was recently attached to it by evolutionary theories vanishes when it is confuted by the facts. Racial bias, promptings of environment, historical contingencies and also the interaction of diverse tendencies that we call chance —this whole mass of incalculable influences hastens, retards or arrests the progress of the nations along their common primitive way and, at certain critical periods, either diverts them from it altogether or causes them to deviate more or less. In the map of history streams of influence cut across each other or intermingle; but although no scene of the mixed drama which pre-Roman antiquity presents to us was without importance for Latin civilization, in the strictly defined sphere with which we are concerned it was Rome who found and supplied the deficiency.

The other civilizations left nothing behind them. Neither Chaldæa nor Assyria nor any of their neighbours has done so, notwithstanding a highly developed commercial instinct, a family organization with bonds becoming ever more relaxed and thus rendering the relations between individuals ever more complex, a system of private ownership not always absolute but long established and permitting various divisions of the soil and conditions of tenure, a wealth of contracts freed from the paralysis of excessive formalism and made very reliable by the regular use of writing, and finally a well advanced understanding of the laws of credit. Neither has Egypt in the bondage of her many kinds of socialism— hieratic, feudal, guild—where the condition of groups and of individuals, the division and tenure of the soil was ordered in accordance with a political design which maintained, over and above the statutes themselves, certain institutions of great antiquity that were constantly re-established by the violent reactions of the people, in spite of foreign infiltration and the continuous undermining of usurpers, against individualism and its economic consequences: viz. disruption of the old kindred associations, enfranchisement of the soil, freedom of contracts. Neither has Persia, who only brought a religion and a Law, assuming that it already existed, to the swathing-clothes of dogma and ritual, and derived her legal apparatus from Babylon and the Ionians.

We do not know what future discoveries may have in store for us; our documents may be multiplied tenfold; but we must apparently give up hope of extracting from the Mesopotamian soil any legal monument that differs very widely from those already known. We possess collections of royal edicts, one from 2100 B.C., for the " Code of Hammourabi " is no more than that; but although it is certainly a great work of classification, it is not a methodical epitome of Chaldæan Law. We have also charges, rescripts and an abundant supply of judicial acts, some going back to 4000 B.C. and others bringing us down to the last days of the second Babylonian Empire.[1] The collection of Assyrian statutes or, more accurately, customs derived from the excavations of Kalaat Shergat, although less ancient (1400–1200 B.C.), shows no progress but rather a condition of lower development, and might be compared sometimes with certain *Leges barbarorum*, sometimes with those ordinances which the historians of ancient Rome have been pleased to call *Leges regiæ*.[2]

The legal literature of Egypt does not reveal any different characteristics. What was that code in eight volumes which was placed before the Tribunal of Truth ? Probably a customary where moral and religious precepts were mingled with the rudiments of procedure and of Ecclesiastical Law. The title of code is also given to each legislator's collection of innovations, but none of them ever thought of drawing up a systematic corpus of either the whole or a part of Egyptian Law, however bold their innovations might be—those of Bocchoris, for example, in favour of loan at interest, of mortgage and of sale for money. These codes were summaries, more or less complete, of the reigning prince's edicts, and the very clear and curt directions which these administrative methods produced—the only form that the Law assumed —left no room for deductive interpretations or for legal constructions. The rudimentary ideas which inspired them

---

[1] Cf. Oppert-Menant, *Docum. jurid. de la Syrie et de la Chaldée.* L. P. Scheil, *La Loi d'Hammourabi* (2000 B.C.); **XIII**, 27, 5.

[2] L. P. Scheil, *Rec. de lois assyriennes, texte assyrien avec la trad. franç. et index*, Paris 1921. Ed. Cuq, " Un recueil de lois assyriennes " (*Rev. d'Assyriologie*, 1922).

remained static. The judgments of Horemheb, preserved for centuries after him, bore no closer resemblance to our collections of famous decisions, nor did the compilations of sentences assigned to Bocchoris or to Amasis, of which the first had the advantage (if it is one) of being put into verse by an Alexandrian poet of the time of Hadrian. They were sometimes ingenious or shrewd solutions of an unusual or striking sort, sometimes hard and fast precepts that were all the more valued because they left no room for speculation. The litigants contented themselves with little books of practical advice in which the ethical aspect was as prominent as the legal.[1] There was no work of doctrine, no attempt at classification or analysis, no evidence of any desire to make a standard of the general principles that were latent in the mass of particular cases. It is true that certain formularies may be pointed out in Chaldæa and in Egypt; but of the triple function of the Roman jurists, *respondere*, *cavere*, *agere*, only *cavere* was seriously practised by the lawyers of Babylon, Nineveh, Memphis or Thebes, as if the predominance of the scribe had already reduced Law to a dull and meticulous notarial practice.

Even the Greeks, whose instinct it was to make an art of every form of intellectual activity, i.e. to make it the object of a science, and whose rapidly developed stock of legal material provided many elements for theory to work upon, produced no true monument of jurisprudence. Law in Greece remained an appendage to rhetoric and ethics, even Civil Law forming no separate branch of study. Their most ingenious ideas about the basis of Law and its modes of formation are scattered through their metaphysical or ethical treatises.

The most natural method of Greek thought was always to proceed by reference to an ideal. The earliest societies were organized after the model of the divine world of their dreams, and the Greek city of the philosophers strove to reproduce the divine city as nearly as possible within its bounds, i.e. to establish among men Justice as it is conceived in the mind of God. This was a transition from the theological plane to that of metaphysics and also of ethics, for the object of the

[1] Révillout, *Cours de droit égyptien*, 47-51; **XX**, 77, 5; 80, 5, 583; Maspéro *Hist. des peuples del Orient classique*, 3, 245, 502, 578.

latter, the Good, was attained by obedience to the data of the former.

Thenceforward the individual was subordinated to the city which held his whole life at its disposal, since he could not reasonably refuse to make his contribution to the rule of Justice or to obey the laws of conduct which found their only basis and explanation therein. Thus Law seemed to be no more than the broker or sergeant of ethics. The most ancient constitutions, drawn up in accordance with these ideas by priests or philosophers, aimed at placing power in the hands of the best citizens; but at length it appeared that this ideal of the ancient law-givers, which had found its highest expression in the work of Plato, was beginning to fade. History gave a new direction to Greek philosophy, which turned its eyes from heaven and sought to secure within the city and for the benefit of its inhabitants the greatest possible sum of happiness. From the collection and study of constitutions and of the statutes which they had inspired, Aristotle, Theophrastus and their pupils endeavoured to derive a body of maxims and processes hitherto empirical but capable of providing the elements of a political science that would assure this happiness. In these successive aims the Greeks were intent above all on the organization of the body politic. The legislators did not concern themselves with private institutions except to adapt them more perfectly to their conceptions of the city, whether aristocratic, plutocratic or democratic; and the lawyer was not distinguished from the philosopher or the statesman.[1]

But in the majority of Greek cities two important legal strata have been noted. The first consisted of the ancient customs of the clan which were brought into the city at its foundation and long determined the family organization, the system of ownership of the land, and the methods of transferring real rights, but were shaken more often and more seriously than elsewhere by political revolutions, by the schemes of legislators and by the movements of the peoples. The second was the product of these revolutions and of these legislations, and was less deeply rooted in men's brains and hearts. First plutocracy and then complete democracy shattered what was left of the clan and family organizations,

[1] **CXXIII**, 3 et seq.

and gave a power to money that the earlier legislators had kept from it by restricting commerce and sometimes forbidding their citizens to take part in it. The whole system of contracts invaded the sphere of practice, procedure was simplified, Law threw off the trammels of the philosophical constitutions, collected importations from the East, and developed in the direction of a sort of *jus gentium*, except in certain sections of the penal and civil Law which remained fixed at a comparatively low stage of development. After democracy had wrecked the primitive institutions, endless disturbances deprived the whole body of Law of that comparative stability which is essential to any scientific formation. Law was too often identified with the caprice of the mob, and the extralegal sentences of the popular tribunals rendered as impracticable as it was useless any doctrinal work, which would have had no chance of success except through the restoration of peace to the agoras either by Macedonian domination or by incorporation in the Roman Republic. But the initiative in such matters does not lie with the conquered. So far as the whole body of relations determined by contract was concerned, unification proceeded slowly in the eastern part of the Roman domains; and in other cases many old institutions were recast in the crucible of the Provincial Edict, thus forming a sort of parallel, even within the imperial boundaries, to the Law of the sovereign city.[1]

Our basic documents consist of certain laws mutilated by the chance of quotation or by the fate of the inscriptions in which they are recorded, some pronouncements on famous legislations, some rare passages in the grammarians and philosophers, and an important series of pleadings rendered specially valuable by the legal fragments and the types of contract included in them, for the logographers who were not always professional lawyers were accustomed to state the fact, to which the legal text would be applied automatically without, as in Roman advocacy, undergoing any learned distortions or tendencious interpretations. Study of the papyri has contributed a large number of particular acts to the subject, especially from the hellenistic or Roman period. The materials for a scientific legal structure that were scattered

[1] CI, 4-9, 31-32; **XXIV**, 28, 319 et seq. De Francisci, *La Papyrologia nel systema di studi di storia giuridica*, 1920, 9 et seq.

through the Eastern world in the time of Alexander and became for the most part the common property of the nations he had thought to bring under his rule, are no substitute for the structure itself which remained unbuilt. It is not maintained that Rome derived no benefit from any of them; on the contrary, she profited by more than one happy and fertile idea; but it was she alone who gradually erected the building in which they were incorporated.

III. THE QUESTION OF ROME'S INDEBTEDNESS TO FOREIGN LEGISLATIONS

This organization of Law was the work of Rome's maturity from the end of her sixth century to the third century of the Christian era. As the civilized world was then conquered and the Romans were able to profit by the world's experience, we should like to know whether their legal creations were entirely original, whether at the beginning of this period they were already to some extent indebted to the nations they had first conquered or annexed, and whether they drew thenceforward upon the legal magma which was gradually revealed to them by the progress of their conquests in the East, for it is clear that they derived nothing from any other source.

The ancient city was isolated by its self-sufficiency; but as the customs and social systems of peoples of the same line of descent are originally similar, the populations of central Italy lived at first in accordance with traditions and a type of social organization that were widely distributed without the necessity for any one of them to borrow from the others. These traditions, which were introduced into the city by the clans that founded it, provided its private Law and the lower strata of its public Law; such usages being conventionally called the laws of King Italicus. The Etruscans show no marked differences and it is not necessary to suppose that the revolution generally connected with the name of Servius Tullius was influenced or precipitated by analogous social movements in the cities of lower Italy. In any case we must reject the idea that more distant originals were copied, though some have sought them as far off as Egypt.[1] Defined by certain pontifical rulings and by the decrees of the *gentes*,

---

[1] Cic., *de Rep.*, 2, 36; Liv., 3, 9-57; D., 1, 2, 2, 3-4-24.—**CCXXXVIII**, 16, 10, 19.

the old Law of custom was for a long time the only source of nurture for Rome's judicial life. In spite of the legend and of two or three possible but doubtful borrowings from the Law of Solon,[1] the whole legislation of the Decemvirs on all essential matters contained only what might or indeed must have been conceived in a Latin environment. The nature and form of the enactments which jurists and grammarians trace back to it show that it was a collection and focussing of national customs rather than a scientific legislation overburdened by a long past; and the rare legal texts of the following period do not contradict these data. The infatuation of a part of the nobility during the sixth century for everything Greek does not seem to have had any serious effect upon Law. The increased intercourse with foreigners which led to the creation at Rome of the Prætor Peregrinus and the conception of the *jus gentium* was not marked by any direct importation of legal practice or forms from abroad. If some were suggested thereby, they were thought out anew by the jurists and so completely assimilated that no trace of the original elements could be recognized in them. Even the use of a Greek term is no decisive proof and the origin of Roman mortgage is an open question. It was rather in the disuse of obsolete forms inadequate for the new conditions of life inspired by foreign ideas that the influence of these latter showed itself.

But the general culture and the philosophical schools of Greece were not without influence on the development of Law towards the end of the Republic and under the Empire. The neo-platonism and stoicism in the eclectic treatises of Cicero[2] made an impression on the jurists and impelled them to introduce into certain juridical organisms the elements of morality which they lacked. The idea of a written Law composed by a human legislator and contrasted with the unwritten laws revealed by conscience which constitute divine or natural Law, the distinction of Law from Equity and the recognition of their interdependence, with the consequent amendment or abolition of old customs and venerable but obsolete statutes which will figure so prominently in the work of the Edict, the extension of certain consequences of kinship to all degrees of consanguinity, the relative or paramount

[1] Cic., *de Leg.*, 2, 23-25; D., 10, 1, 13.   [2] CIX, 1, 9-34.

importance assigned to intention in the spheres of delict and contract, a certain anxiety to discover the real wishes of testators, a distinction, though an imperfect one, between the ideas of legal and moral responsibility, between penalties and damages, and on the other hand a latent distrust of practices favouring the development of credit—all these were most probably derived from this source. Cicero also connected the origins of legal science with the art of the Greek rhetoricians and the superiority of Servius Sulpicius to the jurists of his time with his use of their dialectic.[1] Hence the clear, easy and finished style of the majority of classical lawyers. Several of the greatest of them were of Eastern origin; but at bottom even the most daring proved to be Romans of the most conservative type. The peculiarities of Gaius, the daring ventures of Ulpian and above all of Papinian in adopting various solutions from provincial Law do not involve neglect of details that are not always easy to grasp. We are even surprised by so much disdain for, or at least disregard of, more advanced, more highly developed institutions which could at any rate be more quickly and easily put into practice: the validity of pacts and freedom of agreements, the place and authority of writing in legal acts, methods of transferring real estate by transcription and of registering acts, etc. There were two parallel practices governed by the Urban Edict and the Provincial Edict respectively, the former rarely borrowing from the latter. Even important institutions in the social life of the Empire were practically ignored in the scientific development of classical Law, for instance the system of administering the great landed estates as we find it recorded in African and oriental inscriptions. Perhaps in the third century the attention of the legislator was somewhat distracted, but at that date doctrine begins to cease, for classical Law has been brought to perfection.

After Diocletian judicial activity, apart from the increasing production of statutes, retains a certain amount of vigour only in the East, where the schools continue to exist with some distinction. For two centuries almost all the imperial constitutions aim at imposing a political system which may

[1] Cic.. *Brutus*, 41, in f. 42; Wenger, *Orientalisches Recht im Recht der Griechen u. der Römer*, 1914.

reincorporate the individuals who have been released by classical Law from the grip of primitive associations, direct their activities with sovereign authority for its own advantage and lead the way to the most complete and the most scientifically promoted experiment in Socialism that the world has ever seen. This was undoubtedly suggested by the oriental conception of the Divine State, at once feeble and superfluous, and by its old system of a population hereditarily attached to the soil or to a profession, which the imperial power used and extended. But this piecemeal borrowing of institutions, which had never before been put in practice with such consistency of purpose and had nowhere produced similar results, does not detract from the originality of the Lower Empire's social arrangements. Then the centre of Empire was changed. Constantine and his successors legislated primarily for the East and set ever greater store by the Law that was made there: hellenistic Law, Roman Law corrupted by provincial usage. In the fifth century everything tended in this direction. Then Justinian thought to effect the union of these elements with the traditional Roman Law either by means of interpolations and amendments in his compilations or by giving countenance to modern or oriental theories in his Novels. His work is not so much the crown of the Roman legal structure as a building wherein the Roman materials play a large part, like the columns, capitals and dressed stonework of earlier monuments in the fortresses of his time. An adjustment of jurisprudence to the racial environment, the social arrangements, the conditions of life, whether spiritual or material, in the sixth century; an elimination of everything in the Roman science which had failed to take root or had fallen into disuse in the East, and a substitution of hellenistic equivalents; an attempt to secure system by the introduction of abstract conceptions in the place of Rome's empiricism: such in appearance was the work of the compilers which gave rise to the first synthesis of Byzantine Law.[1] But the alloy which was as yet little recognized kept enough resemblance to Roman Law and a sufficient number of Roman elements to deceive observers, so that it has long been regarded as a compendium of Rome's legal system. Indeed it contained enough of the original to exercise a beneficial influence on

[1] CI, 1; XXXII, 1, 50.

subsequent civilizations, bequeathing to them all that has retained its vitality in the ancient Law that was systematized by the most Roman of the Eastern emperors.[1]

II

THE FORMATION OR EXTERNAL HISTORY OF ROMAN LAW

I. THE SOURCES OF ROMAN LAW

Law at Rome took many forms. The classical jurists used to say that it was derived from statutes, plebiscites, senatus-consulta, imperial constitutions, magisterial edicts and lawyers' interpretations.[2] They omitted the source that was originally most fruitful, namely custom. Among those they quoted, the last two, for which it would be vain to search elsewhere, gave Roman Law its most original characteristics and explain at the same time its fertility and its flexibility. All these sources were not simultaneously effective; they appeared successively in the course of history, some being almost exhausted when others began to show themselves. But their contributions to the body of Law survived them and preserved their special qualities. A classification had to be made, but it was late and its results are not always clear to us.

The most ancient Law was entirely customary. Legislations which have retained custom among their modes of creating Law derive its authority from its antiquity and from the tacit consent of the people: an artificial conception that has nothing primitive about it. Custom is originally a fact. It is established by the institutions that a group of men have adopted and by the rules which those men observe in their dealings with one another, although neither the former nor the latter can be connected with any superior and constraining will. It does not postulate an organized State although, when such a State has been established, it can subsist within it and command its respect by continuing to exercise its special creative power in regions which the State avoids or neglects. Historians define it as the spontaneous product of the popular conscience, using the word "conscience" in its psychological

[1] **CXXXV**, 247-269. [2] G., 1, 2; I. J., 1, 2, 3; D., 1, 1, 6.

sense and understanding by it that judicial habit of mind which adapts itself instinctively and continuously to the necessities of individual and social life. Hence it sees therein the most perfect means of producing Law, since it is the most natural and free from artifice. But as a matter of fact there is no more a case of spontaneous generation here than anywhere else: custom, or at any rate each of its elements, always has an author, whether known or forgotten. Many incidents indeed combine to produce it, i.e. to suggest its formula to the man who first proposes and applies it, thus establishing the precedent by which it is brought into being. Apart from chance and imitation, there is the part played by climatic, geographic or economic necessities, by religious ideas, by the occasional conventions of individuals and families, by the reforms suggested by experience, whether sought or not, by the discoveries or caprices of individuals, which have proved alluring or striking owing to the prestige of their authors, and finally above all by the solutions proposed in cases of disagreement by arbitrators or wise men.[1] The origin of custom is in most cases a decision taken on a certain day by a chief, or a verdict pronounced by him, whether recognized as such or not. It is obeyed because it seems good and venerable; its antiquity, when it has any, being only appealed to as an additional proof of its worth. The idea of sanction by popular consent is foreign to these often very limited societies, where there is hardly any equality between individuals.

Rome owed to custom the essential part of her clan and family organization, her first system of land-ownership, her old methods of transfer and guarantee, her primitive procedure, i.e. practically the whole of her system of private relations up to the time of the Twelve Tables. Many of these customs went back to the remote past of the race. Others were formed in its final dwelling-place, some by contact with the new-born State. All Law created in this way tends to translate juridical acts and situations into a rigid formalism, an exceedingly concrete symbolism: words and gestures to which a meaning is arbitrarily attached that nothing else would be allowed to express. The conservative spirit of the Romans found satisfaction in these formalities which became one of the characteristics of their legal science, for formalism

[1] **CXXIV**, 10-19; 39-46; **CLXXXII**, 1, 55 21-24.

has a twofold justification, one psychological and the other social. In the first place, men of little refinement have great difficulty in making up their minds and even in recognizing the moment at which their decision is reached. It is fitting that some material sign should make this objective and detach it, so to speak, from themselves, whereupon their mind is set at rest and accepts the accomplished fact; and it is also fitting that this sign should have so precise a meaning that no doubt or dispute can arise as regards the nature and object of the accomplished act. Then in primitive times public opinion and, later on, public authority refuse to recognize rights or allow their enforcement, unless the act which created them has been performed with such publicity and formality as may strike the attention of the society and leave no possibility of doubt as to its existence. It should be noted that for a long time Law was not separated from religion, being entirely a matter of ritual, and that the priests who were the first regulators of custom and procedure maintained in it this ritual and symbolical character.

As legal relations grow more complicated and the social group increases in size, the content of custom and even its existence become uncertain and hard to prove; and its obscure origination, which is the work not of the masses but of the aristocracy, whose authority diminishes in proportion to the development of the State, seems henceforward a matter of chance. When the State monopolizes power it aims at a single, all-embracing legislation, whereas the sphere of custom is always restricted, almost parochial. While sanctioning the customary Law that already exists, the State reserves to itself as a matter of principle the right of making Law in future; and then follows the ascendency of written Law, *jus scriptum*, i.e. the organization of Law by public authority in the form of statute, plebiscite, edict, senatusconsultum or imperial constitution.

The statute, *lex*, was a written enactment made on the proposal, *rogatio*, of a magistrate (king, consul, prætor) who had obtained favourable auspices and was authorized by the comitia of the people to publish it under his own name provided that it was ratified by the Senate. It was in some sort a religious act inspired or at least permitted by the gods, and there is no need to see in it, as has since been supposed, any exercise of popular sovereignty. At first the mass of customary Law already in existence left little scope for legislative activity. Although there is mention of *leges regiæ* or of *leges curiatæ*, we do not know of any statutes within the sphere of private Law before those of the Twelve Tables. The most ancient known to us were, like those, voted by the comitia in their centuries.[1]

The plebiscite, *plebis scitum*, which was at first a particular decision made by the plebs on the proposal of a tribune and binding the plebs alone, became a variety of statute and took that name after the *rogationes* addressed to the *comitia tributa* had been assimilated to those addressed to the *comitia centuriata* by virtue of certain obscure laws (*Valeria Horatia, Publilia Philonis, Hortensia*) of doubtful import which rendered preliminary and finally set aside the *auctoritas patrum*. But towards the end of the Republic the Senate claimed the right to declare a statute null by reason of some formal defect. The statutes of which we possess any important fragments were due to the *comitia tributa*.[2]

In none of the *comitia* was voting either individual or direct. The votes were taken by groups and the assemblies were distinguished according to the kind of groups composing them: *quum ex generibus hominum suffragium feratur, curiata comitia esse ; quum ex censu et ætate, centuriata ; quum ex regionibus et locis, tributa*. The opinion of individuals only counted within the groups to which they were successively assigned; and the successive predominance of the *comitia curiata* in which the people were grouped according to *gentes*, the *comitia centuriata* in which they were grouped according to their wealth, and the *comitia tributa* where place of residence alone was taken into account, marked the three stages of Roman society—aristocratic, plutocratic, socialistic, though the part taken by the masses in the creation of Law was not sensibly changed or increased. The veto (little regarded) on introducing complex statutes, the obligation to publish and lay down their text in advance, the colonial vote by correspondence in the time of Augustus, some slight changes in the manner of describing the people's part in creating Law, which were counteracted by certain cunningly devised methods

[1] CCXXXVIII, 6¹, 359; 16, 19 et seq.
[2] Aul. Gel., 15, 27; T. G., 24-108; G., 1, 3.

of taking the vote within the comitia so as to assure the preponderance of certain tribes—all this served only to emphasize the decline.[1] The comitia fell into disuse between the reigns of Tiberius and Nerva.[2]

The statute could govern every political and judicial activity of the citizens and of other persons dependent on Rome's sovereignty; and yet it advanced but slowly in the sphere of private relations, since for a long time it regarded individuals merely as members of clan or family groups. Even in the relations between man and man or between different groups it was sometimes slow to intervene. Hence perhaps the strange distinction that we find between various legal prescriptions calculated to determine the worth of a juridical act; namely *leges imperfectæ* which prohibit the act without sanctioning their prohibition, *leges minus quam perfectæ* which allow the act to produce its effects but impose a penalty on the man who avails himself of it, and no doubt *leges perfectæ* which finally annul it. No rational and final explanation of the system has yet been given, but it seems likely to have been due to progressive daring on the part of the legislator in these matters.[3]

The senatusconsultum remained for a long time outside the sphere of private Law. On the decline of the Republic the Senate sometimes intervened indirectly either by requiring a magistrate to use the *jus edictale* in a prescribed sense or by ordering him to suspend the application of a statute for the time being; but when the comitia fell into disuse in the first century of the Christian era, it inherited their legislative power, notwithstanding a sharp controversy, and exercised it, at least from Hadrian's reign, on the motion, *relatio*, of a magistrate who had the right to preside at its meetings and gave his name to the act. As a matter of fact the *relatio* was very soon reserved to the Emperor alone, who made it in the form of an *oratio* or statement of grounds which was invariably approved by the assembly.[4] In time he came to use it as the means of making a direct statement of his commands or prohibitions; and in the third century he published the act without reference to the Senate.

[1] Liv., 1, 43; 9, 46; 45, 15; Dion. Hal., 4, 20; Cic., *pro Cn. Planc.*, 20.
[2] Tac., *An.*, 1, 19.
[3] **CXI**, 1, 462-464; **CLXXXI**, 19, 1; **CCLXXIX**.
[4] Liv., 39, 19; Tac., *An.*, 12, 53; 13, 26; 16, 27; T. G., 128-136; G., 1, 4, 84.

Custom and statute are the normal methods of creating Law which are to be found among all peoples. During a very considerable period of Roman history the magistrates' edict, *edictum magistratuum*, shared with these to an extent which could not be paralleled elsewhere. Public authorities everywhere have the right to make regulations and communicate them, verbally or in writing, to their subordinates; and this right, common to all magistrates and called at Rome the *jus edicendi*, underwent a special development there and acquired a very peculiar character in the case of the judicial magistrates: the city and alien prætors, the ædiles, the provincial governors and the quæstors. By means of edicts published during their tenure of office but especially when they entered upon it, they became accustomed to regulate certain matters within their competence and to indicate how they proposed to meet certain difficulties. At first their initiative was limited by the rigidity of the statutory processes and was rarely exercised except by the adoption of certain methods of constraint: *missiones in possessionem*, interdicts, prætorian stipulations or other measures of public order taken in virtue of their *imperium*. But from the time of the *Lex Æbutia* this power, according to Gaius, was remarkably extended. While introducing or generalizing a procedure by means of formulas, this statute required the magistrate to fix and publish the latter, so that he became the official interpreter of existing Law, *viva vox juris civilis*, which could only be invoked by means of formulas of his own devising, whose adequacy or inadequacy to the claims of the litigants he was free to decide, permitting or forbidding their use in a way that would hardly have been possible in the days when procedure was directed by the litigants alone.

Henceforward who would fail to recognize the scope allowed him *adjuvandi vel supplendi vel corrigendi juris civilis gratia ?*[1] Theoretically he could neither make nor abrogate the Law; in practice the Law only became effective when he said *judicium dabo* and remained inoperative when he said *judicium non dabo*. Insensibly things came to be understood in this sense. *Jus honorarium*, especially that of the prætor, extending, correcting, supplementing custom and statute, became the most fruitful and best adjusted source of Roman

[1] G., 1, 6; 4, 30; D. Cas., 36, 23; D., 1, 2, 2; 2, 2, 1; Cic., *ad Att.*, 6, 1.

Law, and in the sphere of Private Law statutes became exceedingly rare. Although they had full power to issue occasional edicts, *edicta repentina*, the judicial magistrates caused a white tablet to be set up in the forum when they entered upon office showing the cases in which they would grant or refuse an action or any other benefit, the method of procedure or of enforcement, and the legal formulas established either by statute or by their own edicts. These dispositions remained valid for the duration of their magistracy (whence the name *lex annua*), during which period a *Lex Cornelia* of 687 A.U.C. forbade any change being made in them; they were for the most part taken over by succeeding magistrates under the name of *edictum translatitium*, thus remaining operative longer and allowing ever less scope for *edicta nova*, and they were imitated by other judicial magistrates,[1] so that their sphere of operation was also extended. Finally this body of Law, so far at any rate as the edicts of the urban prætor and the curule ædiles were concerned, was officially collected and classified under the title of *Edictum perpetuum* by C. Salvius Julianus at the command of Hadrian between 129 and 138 A.D.[2] A senatusconsultum required its observation by all new prætors and ædiles without depriving them of the *jus edicendi* when new circumstances arose; but there seems to have been no addition to the prætorian Law from this time forward. Since the beginning of the Empire, the prætor's initiative had been of necessity very much restricted.

Perhaps even more important than the edict in the development of Roman Law were the works of exposition, *interpretatio*, of which no other examples can be found in antiquity. To the legal science of the jurists Roman Law was above all indebted for its originality and its greatness. Even customary Law could not dispense with a practitioner. The priests were the first to give a fixed form and meaning to the creations of custom, to direct their development and to give guidance to the litigants in their uncertainty and confusion; and this was the task of the Roman pontiffs so long as religion and Law remained unseparated. It is probable that they often played

---

[1] For the forms and dispositions of the urban edict cf. **CLX**, 1, 117-203; **XIII**, 44, 391-447.
[2] **XIII**, 35, 731; **CXI**, 21; Cpr. **CLX**, 1, 249, 305; **XXIV**, 20, 19; **XXXIII**, 30, 490

the part of arbitrators and that their rudimentary science exercised a regulative influence on procedure. As they alone knew the whole of the Law and could adapt it to particular suits, men trusted in their guidance, and every year the college appointed one of its members to give consultations of this kind; but after the Law of the Twelve Tables, when the formulas and the calendar had been made public, Law became secularized and legal science was no longer their exclusive property. At first the new practitioners seem to have followed the beaten track: *respondere*, to give consultations, *cavere*, to draw up forms for acts, *agere*, to direct procedure and compose legal formulas. But their subtlety in drawing up formulas and conducting processes was immediately creative in its effect, supplementing and extending the rules of custom, making them more flexible and extracting from them all the good that they contained. In Rome's fifth century Ti. Coruncanius inaugurated a form of instruction by means of consultations given in public. The sixth and seventh centuries saw the appearance beside the formularies of customaries such as the *Tripertita* of Sextus Ælius Pætus, the books on Civil Law by Junius Brutus and the two Scaevolas, father and son, expositions of the Law of the Twelve Tables and of the comment already made upon it and upon custom, and at the same time manuals of procedure whose type was perpetuated in the series of *libri ad Sabinum*. Finally the development of the edict led to the inauguration by Servius Sulpicius Rufus and Aulus Ofilius in the seventh century of the long succession of *Commentarii ad edictum*. The prestige of the lawyers increased their number. Study of the Law—and it was the edict that attracted most of their attention—came to be regarded as an actual obligation upon members of the nobility;[1] and at length, in the time of Augustus, Alfenus set the fashion of a sort of general expositions of the Law which went by the name of *Digesta*.

At the beginning of the Empire the jurists were divided for no apparent reason into two schools: on the one hand the Proculians led by Labeo and Proculus who were supported by Pegasus, Neratius and the Celsi; on the other the Sabinians who recognized Aetius Capito and Massurius Sabinus as masters and were also called Cassians after one of their adepts,

[1] Cic., *de Rep.*, 1, 5.—CCXXXVIII, 16, 55, 18-27

PROLEGOMENA

C. Cassius Longinus, being further supported by the younger Sabinus, L. Javolenus Priscus, Aburnius Valens, Tuscianus, Salvius Julianus and Gaius.[1] The former seem to have been more inclined to make innovations, the latter more observant of tradition. Some have supposed that this schism was merely due to the existence of two more or less rival places of instruction. Perhaps as much political as legal, it had almost disappeared by the middle of the second century. The great names of Ulpius Marcellus, Q. Cervidius Scaevola, Tryphoninus, Paul, Papinian, Ulpian, Modestinus do not belong to any school. Most of them were members of the imperial council and all collaborated with the Emperor to establish a unified system of jurisprudence.[2]

At first, in whatever form their activity showed itself, the work of the jurists was of a private nature. Their influence on the formation of Law was due to their knowledge and personal prestige. But Augustus gave some of them the *jus publice respondendi ex auctoritate principis*,[3] i.e. the right of giving written and sealed consultations whose solutions were binding upon the judge in the suit for which they had been invoked, unless the litigants had obtained contradictory rulings on the same point. This made a monopoly for the profit of certain individuals of a practice which had long been growing up owing to the usual incompetence of the judges. Gaius seems to say that a rescript of Hadrian allows any doctrine on which the jurists possessing *permissio jura condendi* are unanimous to be binding on the judges, whose opinion only remained free in cases where the jurists disagreed. The meaning of this text has been disputed, although a statute of Constantine (321) which destroys the authority of Paul's and Ulpian's notes on Papinian and, on the other hand, confirms Paul's *Sententiæ ad filium* shows that the legal force of the jurists' writings extended beyond their *responsa*.[4] In 426 Theodosius and Valentinian enacted by the so-called law of citations that henceforth only the opinions of Gaius, Paul, Ulpian, Papian and Modestinus, and of authors quoted by them whose original text could be produced, might be appealed to in court. In case of disagreement the opinion of

---

[1] Cf. Lenel, *Das Sabinussystem*, 1892.
[2] D., 1, 2, 2-47-53; Tac., *An.*, 3, 75.—**LXXI, XCVII; CXVI,** 132 et seq.; **CCLII,** 1, 7-100; Fitting, *Alter und Folge der Schriften römischer Juristen von Hadrian bis Alexander*, 2nd ed., 1908.
[3] Gaius, 1, 7; I. J., 1, 2, 8. **CCXXX,** 189. [4] G., 1, 7; C. Th., 1, 4,

the majority constituted the Law; in case of equal division, that of Papinian.¹

During five hundred years the work of the jurists continued almost without interruption, and as their genius differed from that of the Greeks, it was less a science than an art that they created: *ars boni et æqui*. No people have drawn a clearer distinction than the Romans between the absolute and the relative, or better understood that every legal solution belongs to the sphere of contingency. Their endeavour was to make apparent in each particular case what appeared to them to be Law, and then, better still, what with greater moral refinement they called Equity. They were quite at liberty to do this in the great majority of cases, notwithstanding the apparent inflexibility of the *jus civile*. This Law was to a great extent customary, therefore very supple and capable of being moulded in accordance with the shifting forms of society; and since the creative power of custom in its primitive forms had been exhausted, they took its place.² It was continued by their *sententiæ, opiniones* and *regulæ ;* and they rather than the prætor, who was more its adapter, were the *vox viva juris civilis*. The small number of statutes and the vast amount of legal matter which they left untouched allowed no room for the fiction that they contained the whole of the Law, even epitomized in its most general form. On the contrary they were exceedingly concrete and narrowly restricted in application, so that there was no necessity for, or even possibility of, forced or logical interpretations in order to find the solution of particular cases among them. For a century and a half our contemporaries have placed the source of Law in the region of metaphysics; but when the jurists set aside the majority of the old customs (*mores majorum*) or statutes, they went no further than ethics, which can easily be combined with practice. Their object was to suppress or smooth away the obstacles which arise in the path of human intercourse. To define the particular case, to make a skilful diagnosis of the problem contained in it, to solve that problem, i.e. to bring it under the rule of Law by means of a subtle dialectic learnt from the Greek rhetoricians which made use of hardly any other instruments than analogy, extension on utilitarian grounds and social expediency, and yet was always satisfying to the mind and therefore elegant—for this there was needed a certain sleight

¹ C. Th., 1, 4, 3.   ² **XIII**, 29, 536 and 1110.

of hand, a genius rather for versatility than for mathematical precision. Law was always a living thing to them: only the names of the litigants are missing from their expositions and often even those are stated. In their books with significant titles: *Digesta, Responsa, Res quotidianæ*, when they are not mere manuals (*Institutiones, Regulæ*), even in their commentaries on the statutes or the edict, they state no general principles, except in vague and flexible terms; it is a succession of *casus* that passes before us. We should not hesitate to compare them with casuists, who have been foolishly abused. Both alike strive to meet human problems with human solutions whose rationale is derived only from actual possibilities and from common sense. Thus they raised the structure which later centuries were to regard as a sort of written reason, although it has only reached us in the form of fragments mixed with the interpolations and distortions of the Byzantine compilers. But we can see that they did something which had never been done elsewhere, namely organized and classified the means by which every legal problem could be brought to a solution which should at the same time satisfy the mind and the sense of equity, without ever ignoring what was demanded or rejected by their garnered experience.

This great work was finished about the second quarter of the third century. The Lower Empire saw no more original works but only compilations, of which the *Fragmenta vaticana* and the *Consultatio veteris cujusdam jurisconsulti* are typical, or else works of annotation or paraphrase like the *Interpretatio* which has been preserved for us in the Roman Law of the Visigoths. Law fell into the hands of ignorant and unlicensed practitioners; instruction seems to have ceased in the West, and the only source of Law that survived was the imperial constitution.

The imperial constitution, *constitutio principis*, was regarded as equivalent to a statute by Pomponius and Gaius as early as the second century. As a matter of fact the Emperors had at first declined the *cura legum* and did not invent a new method of making Law for their own special use; but it was within their competence to use every method hitherto practised except the statute. They had the *jus edicendi* on the same conditions as the curule magistrates; by their *decreta*, judgments without appeal, they determined or created jurisprudence; by their *rescripta*, replies in the form of letters, of *adnotatio* or of *subscriptio* to the consultations required of them, they shared the privilege of the authorized lawyers whom they finally supplanted; by *mandata* or *epistulæ* they gave the provincial governors instructions or orders which, being renewed without alteration, established an administrative custom. The Emperor's Council became the only source of Law and of justice. Moreover the *Lex Regia* which invested them with power to do anything necessary for the public order and welfare was regarded in the second century as a delegation of legislative power in their favour.[1] In order to make one of their acts universally applicable they required it to be posted up publicly in Rome and entered in the *Liber rescriptorum*. Finally the publication of their will was the only formality required, by whatever name the act containing it was qualified. From the second century the Emperor had complete legislative power; from the third no one any longer shared it with him.[2]

II. CLASSIFICATION OF LEGAL MATTER ACCORDING TO ITS SOURCES

The jurists classified the various divisions of the Law according to their sources, and on this subject the texts show certain variations that can be explained historically.

We must at once set aside certain philosophical distinctions of Greek origin: that between *jus ex scripto* meaning actual Law and *jus ex non scripto* in the sense of the universal moral Law, although later on these same terms were used to contrast custom with the other sources of the national Law; also that which opposed positive Law under the name of *jus civile* to a *jus naturale* common to all living beings.[3] Then we must note that the Roman classification does not affect *jus publicum* which is considered from the point of view of the means by which it is created or the beings to which it applies, the distinction between *jus publicum* and *jus privatum* being determined by the adage: *privatorum conventio juri publico*

---

[1] G., 1, 5; D., 1, 2, 2-11-12; 4, 1-pr.—**CCXXXVIII**, 5, 185 et seq.; 16, 142; T. G., 106, cf. Suet., *Calig.*, 34.
[2] I. J., 1, 2, 6; C. Th., 1, 2, 11; C. J., 1, 14, 12.—**CXVI**, 428 et seq.
[3] D., 1, 1, 1-3, 6; I. J., 1, 2 pr., 3. **CIX**, 1, 9-34.

non derogat, the Roman version of the idea of public order.¹

Within the sphere of private Law almost the only distinction drawn by lawyers of the time of the Severi was that between *jus civile* and *jus honorarium*. This way of regarding the matter was of recent development. Originally *jus civile*, *proprium jus civile*, was custom; but in the last centuries of the Republic this name was transferred to the *interpretatio prudentium* which maintained and developed custom, and indeed had long replaced it. Thus *jus civile* was opposed to *leges*. As late as the second century Pomponius, giving a short historical summary of the sources of Law, said: " Civil Law properly so called consists of the jurist's exposition alone "; "*proprium jus civile quod, sine scripto, in sola prudentium interpretatione consistit.*"² Cicero in the works of his youth already held this doctrine, and traces of it may be found up to the end of the classical period; but as the work of the jurists extended successively from the original content of custom, of which a part was summed up in the Twelve Tables, to *leges*, to *senatusconsulta* (in so far as they affected private Law) and, later, to the acts of the Emperors, the terminology became looser and *jus civile* included both the commentary and the thing commented on. The two sources at first opposed to one another were covered by the same title; and as in fact they reacted upon one another in the creation of Law at this period, *jus civile* often meant for the lawyers of the Empire the whole body of private Law then in force and the science of Law itself. The *interpretatio* was developed to such an extent that the majority of the statutes, especially the antient statutes, were overwhelmed by the mass of comment to which they had given rise.

But other distinctions drawn by the jurists between the sources of Law preserved some comparatively limited meanings for the phrase *jus civile*. It was successively opposed to *jus gentium*, *jus honorarium* and a certain *jus naturale* which was very imperfectly defined.³

At first the self-sufficiency of the city-state allowed no dealings between the *proprium jus civile* and foreign Law which, for the Roman, did not exist. Nothing that we should

---

[1] CXL, 1, 199-200.   [2] D., 1, 2, 2-3.
[3] CXL, 17-84; XIII, 27, 540 et seq.

describe as international private Law was conceived of in those days. Rome recognized no rights of foreigners except those which she conferred upon them by one-sided treaties or concessions; and the *jus gentium* only comprised the accepted usage in regard to ambassadors. But as early as Cicero the term acquired another sense: that of legal institutions common to various peoples; and afterwards it was used by the jurists to describe the whole body of legal relations which Rome recognized as valid either between foreigners or between Roman citizens and foreigners within the bounds of the Empire, in accordance with the gradual decrease of national or municipal particularism. Soon many rules and practices governing these relations were found to be good and useful and were incorporated in the Law of the citizens; and these innovations became so numerous that in the first quarter of the second century we find them grouped together by the lawyers under the title of *jus gentium*,[1] though we cannot infer from the silence of the earlier texts that the phrase was not used in this sense before. This broader, more flexible *jus gentium*, adapted to certain particular matters, was itself of Roman creation; for even if it was suggested by foreign practice and applied to foreigners, it had been recast in the mould of Roman thought and had no validity except as an institution imposed or tolerated by Rome. Such undoubtedly was the earlier conception, but Gaius substituted another, at once less legal and less true historically, according to which *jus civile* was Law created for each people alone and not to be met with elsewhere, while *jus gentium* was Law revealed by natural reason and therefore observed among all peoples. For the first time the conception of a universal reason arose, not in the books of the philosophers but in the actual body of Roman jurisprudence, and this was the work of a lawyer of oriental origin. Almost at the same time the idea of a *jus naturale*, clearly connected with the *jus gentium* thus understood, began to appear in certain doctrinal works, notably those of the last Sabinians, of Salvius Julianus and of Gaius himself. These ways of regarding the sources of Law were prominent until the time of the Severi, including under the term *jus civile* all Law peculiar to Roman citizens as opposed to *jus gentium* and *jus naturale*.[2]

[1] CXL, 84-101; XIII, *l.c.* [2] G., 1, 1. CXL, 92 et seq.; XIII, *l.c.*

On the other hand *jus civile*, this time including *jus gentium*, was further contrasted with *jus honorarium* of which the prætor's edict was the chief source, whence its other title of *jus prætorium*. This antithesis had already been made by the jurists of the Republican period; but apparently it was not until much later that the habit arose of dividing all Law into two parts, one the product of the edict, the other comprising all that was not derived from that source. Gaius ignores so broad a classification. No doubt he always regarded the work of the edict as piecemeal, fragmentary, confined to certain favoured spheres, although, whatever may have been said to the contrary, no source of Law escaped the judicial magistrates' power of amendment, whether it were custom, *interpretatio* or actual written Law. As a matter of fact the division of all Law into civil and prætorian is clearly stated for us in a passage of Papinian.[1] The tendency both in teaching and comment to set up two parallel series of works, one (growing ever more lengthy) on the edict, the other on all that was contrasted with it under the now generic title of *jus civile*, prepared the way for this; but in my opinion the determining factors were the cessation of the prætors' activity and the codification of Salvius Julianus, part of which had its canon fixed, so to speak, by the *Edictum perpetuum*, that part namely which gave the tone to the rest of the *jus honorarium*. As a result of this, the latter seemed henceforward to be fixed and acquired a character of its own within bounds that could not alter.[2] The importance of these classifications was diminished under the Lower Empire.

III. Byzantine Law and the Compilations of Justinian

The antithesis of *jus civile* and *jus honorarium* is found once more in the imperial constitutions in reference to certain subjects, e.g. the Law of Inheritance; but for several reasons it became more and more rare. First of all the Byzantines substituted their logic and their abstract conceptions for the empirical classifications, the practical and traditional methods of the Romans. The form in which Roman thought had expressed itself was not maintained, except in so far as the compilations provided an asylum for ancient formulas robbed

[1] D., 1, 1, 7-pr.   [2] **CXL**, 101-149; **XIII**, 29, 547.

of their original authority and value. After the Severi the era of scientific creation came to an end. There are no more great jurists. Mere practitioners make collections in which extracts from doctrinal works and from imperial constitutions are mixed together, the typical western example being that to which the *Fragmenta vaticana* belong. The humble labours of annotators and scholiasts, of which a few oriental samples probably due to the schools of Berytus and Alexandria have come down to us, the composition of manuals consisting chiefly of compilation and paraphrase, such as the *Syro-Roman Law-Book* published in several languages, must have had their unknown fellows.[1] But in the schools of the Orient, at Constantinople, at Alexandria, at Berytus,[2] where there was an endeavour to maintain a certain level of thought, the adulteration of the Roman tradition is clearly revealed by the tendency to submit its content to the categories of a philosophy that was shallow enough in itself. In particular the conception of *jus gentium* reappears as contrasted with *jus civile* but conveying the hitherto tentative and secondary idea of *natura, jus naturale*, and assuming or reassuming the sense of universal reason which had already been given to it in some philosophical passages of Cicero and Seneca.[3] In the second place, although a part was still assigned to custom in the creation and abrogation of Law,[4] the imperial constitution had now become the only effective source, absorbing the earlier Law by determining what parts of it should be valid as statutes and what methods of interpretation should be used, as in the constitutions of 321 and 426 and, later, in the Institutes and Digest of Justinian.[5] Having thus been made a part of the emperor's creation, *jus civile* came to mean the more ancient Roman legislation as distinguished from the *leges* or *leges edictales* promulgated by the more recent emperors. Henceforward legislative authority, the power to create Law, was concentrated in the Emperor's will alone and expressed in the form of *edicta* which had permanent validity and were addressed either to the people or to the Senate or to some high official, generally a prætorian prefect.

This dissemination of legislative texts made their study and even their knowledge a matter of difficulty; and Theo-

[1] T. G., 511-635; **XXXIII**, 1925, 494-514.   [2] **CII**, 2.
[3] I. J., 1, 2-pr., 1, 2.   [4] D., 1, 3, 32, 35; C. J., 8, 53, 2.
[5] C. J., 1, 14, 12-pr.; 17, 2-18; C. Th., 1, 4, 1, 2, 3; I. J., 1, 2, 6.

dosius II determined in agreement with his western colleague Valentinian III to order a codification of all imperial constitutions since the time of Constantine. Two compilations due to private initiative—the Gregorian Code, drawn up about 291, which contained the essential part of all imperial legislation since Hadrian, and the Hermogenian Code, composed in 295—had anticipated this proceeding so far as the earlier periods were concerned. A commission was invested with authority to review, abridge and even correct the constitutions of the fourth and early fifth centuries, and the Theodosian Code which was the result of this labour began to be published on the 1st January 439. It was divided into sixteen books subdivided into titles, each of which contained a larger or smaller number of fragments or abridgments of constitutions arranged in chronological order. A series of *Novellæ* published by the same Emperors in the two divisions of the Empire, *The Novels of Theodosius II and Valentinian III*, continued and completed this body of Law, which became the foundation of the Lower Empire's political, social and legal organization, and consequently gave application to remarkably different principles from those which had governed the creation of Law during the classical period. State Socialism was especially subversive of the old-established conditions governing personal status and landed estates. Until the reign of the last of the Severi, legislation, jurisprudence and doctrine had confined themselves to the gradual increase, perfection and amendment of legal institutions which, although constantly improved, had never undergone any revolution; but under the Lower Empire there was a revolution and most social values were then reversed. The constitutions included in the Theodosian Code bear witness to this change in the social order, when they are not themselves the cause of it.

This imperial Law—ancient Law taken over by the emperors, new Law created by them—was summed up in the famous work of Justinian which consisted of three compilations: the first devoted to the constitutions from the reign of Hadrian to that of Justinian; the second to the *interpretatio*, as it appeared in the works of the jurists that had been given authority by the Emperor's will and by the *permissio jura condendi* ; the third a manual akin to each of the other two

EXTERNAL HISTORY OF ROMAN LAW

since, although to a large extent composed of borrowings from the *Institutes* of Gaius and from certain other works of the jurists, it also contained epitomes of the constitutions of Justinian.

The Code, *Codex repetitæ prælectionis*, was drawn up by a commission appointed on the 15th February 528 which recast the Gregorian, Hermogenian and Theodosian Codes, combining their methods of arrangement, and published its work on the 7th April 529. The *Codex Justinianus* which we possess is a new edition of this, completed by the *Quinquaginta decisiones* addressed during the interval to the prætorian prefect, John the Cappadocian, in order to determine certain points of Jurisprudence, and by some constitutions published on the observations of the men who drew up the Digest. It was divided into twelve books which were subdivided into several titles on the model of the ancient *Digesta* and contained under each title extracts from or epitomes of the imperial statutes from the time of Hadrian until 534 arranged in chronological order and often rehandled or interpolated. It was published on the 29th December 534.

The Digest, *Digesta, Pandectæ*, after some preliminary revision of which the *Quinquaginta decisiones* seem to have been one of the chief elements, was announced by a constitution of the 15th December 530 which appointed a commission consisting of imperial officials, professors from Constantinople and Berytus, advocates of the prefecture of the East, and presided over by Tribonian, the *Quæstor sacri palatii*. It only took three of the ten years which the Emperor allowed it for the completion of its task, and the Digest was published on the 16th December 533. It contained fifty books, all except books XXX to XXXII being divided into titles; and under each title there was a varying number of fragments from the jurists, often modified or interpolated and always adapted to the Law of the period, to which the Emperor officially gave the name of statutes, *leges*. These fragments, derived from works selected in accordance with a programme that had been marked out beforehand, are generally arranged in three groups drawn respectively from the *libri ad Sabinum*, the *libri ad edictum* and the works of Papinian, probably because the annual courses of study in the Eastern schools of Law, especially in that of Berytus which was the most famous, were based upon the *libri ad Sabinum* of Ulpian, the *libri ad edictum* of the same author and the *Responsa* of Papinian, in this order, although a fourth course consisting of various elements was sometimes added to these. The distribution of the fragments within each group is very confused. Study of the interpolations which has already been carried very far, often so far as to become hypercritical, has made it possible to distinguish the solutions of classical Law from the tribonianisms in a considerable number of texts.[1]

The Institutes, *Institutiones*, are an elementary manual drawn up by Tribonian, Dorotheus and Theophilus in four books according to the plan of the *Institutiones* of Gaius but divided into titles and paragraphs. Their contents are borrowed from the *Institutiones* and *Res cottidianæ* of Gaius, from the *Institutiones* of Florentinus, Ulpian and Marcian, and from certain other works whose authors are not stated,[2] but with the modifications needed to adapt these borrowings to the Byzantine legislation. A constitution of the 20th November 533 gave the force of law to this manual on the same date as it was given to the Digest.

The constitutions of Justinian later than the Code, which are known by the name of *Novels*, have come down to us by three lines of descent: in the *Epitome* of Julian, professor at the School of Law at Constantinople, which is a latin abridgment of 124 of them and was the only collection of this kind known in the West during the early Middle Ages; in the *Authentica* or *Authenticum novellarum corpus* which contains 134 latin novels or rather greek novels translated into latin (*versio vulgata*), and in a *Greek Collection* of 168 novels of which seven are later than Justinian and four are edicts of prætorian prefects.

[1] LVI, CLXII. [2] CCCIV.

BOOK I

THE ANCIENT CUSTOMS AND THE FORMATION OF CLASSICAL LAW

CHAPTER I

THE GENS AND THE CITY

I

LIFE IN THE " GENS "

I. THE AUTONOMOUS " GENS " AND THE PRIMITIVE CUSTOMS

THE Roman State was formed by the aggregation of pre-existing associations, the *gentes*. Identical with the Greek γένος, the *gens* was, in the ninth century before our era, the only social institution of the Italian peoples who were not yet established in cities, and to a great extent it dominated the others within the bounds of the city itself. It preceded the State and contributed towards its foundation. From the beginning it was a complex organism because of the number of human beings which it contained, the diversity of their conditions, the religious, economic and legal ideas in accordance with which it moulded their life. Our information on the subject is rare and scattered, but enough has survived to enable us to reconstruct its essential characteristics.[1]

It appears to have been an association of families united by blood, i.e. who believed themselves to be descended from a common ancestor. The proof of this origin, the ancestor's name, *nomen gentilicium*, was borne by all the *gentiles* and served as title for the association: *gens Julia, gens Claudia*. The *gentiles* were distinguished from one another by *prænomina* which were few in number and often peculiar to certain *gentes*; sometimes only two were used alternately from generation to generation. At first the *gens* differed little from the patriarchal family, but succeeding generations extended the bounds of the family association more or less quickly. It was divided into several branches, each of which added to the *nomen gentilicium* a surname, *cognomen*; and in the historical period men were called *Claudius Pulcher, Claudius Centho*,

[1] CLVII, 110-130; CCV, 103 et seq.; CCVII, 2, 383; CCLXVIII, 1, 229 et seq.; Cpr. XVII, 3, 385.

Claudius Nero, Cornelius Scipio, Cornelius Sylla, etc.[1] The little group of relatives by the male side, governed in regal fashion by the eldest, was succeeded by an aristocratic society in which the emancipated junior branches formed so many distinct families or *domus* within the *gens*. This revolution, which Plato noted in the case of the γένη, seems to have been effected in the Latin and Sabellian *gentes* by the time of the foundation of Rome.[2]

In order to belong to the *gens* it was necessary not only that one should be a descendant by the male side of the eponymous ancestor, but also that connexion with the *gens* should never have been broken either in the person of the claimant to admission or in that of any of his ancestors; i.e. that in this unbroken line of freeborn ascendants no case of what will later be described as *capitis deminutio* can be shown to have occurred—a disqualification which in those days could only be the result of slavery or of sentence of expulsion pronounced by the *gens* on very serious grounds.[3] These free-born members, the more or less distant posterity of the eponymous ancestor who remained the god and centre of his line, were the true *gentiles*, his *genus ;* but other families lived beneath the sovereignty of the *gens*.

These client families also bore the *nomen gentilicium*, as a sign not of origin but of dependence. In contrast with them the *gentiles* were termed *patricii, patroni*. The client (from *cluere*, to listen, obey) was a man placed with his family under the protection of a powerful association which defended him and gave him maintenance. In the absence of an organized State to provide the individual with help and security, the poor, weak and irresolute seek the protection of the strong and daring. It is not granted to all to possess the power, energy and intelligence which daily life in such circumstances requires. The man who has them founds a *gens* and becomes its eponymous ancestor and god; the man who lacks them becomes his humble and obedient partner. In this partnership, which is profitable to both, the rights of each party will be in inverse ratio to his interest in the association. The client received a piece of land, doles, protection, and an assured existence; the *gens* gained cultivators, and, when

---

[1] **CCXXXVII**, 1, 1-68; **XXIX**, 19, 469-481.   [2] **CXXIV**, 5 et seq., 14, 45.
[3] Cic., *Top.*, 4; Varro, *de Ling. lat.*, 8, 4; Festus, s.v., *Gens, Gentilis*.

THE GENS AND THE CITY

necessary, soldiers. In return for protection and gifts, which they could withdraw, the patrons or patricians exacted certain prestations which custom at length made regular and definite: to help the patron dower his daughters; to pay his ransom in war and that of his children; to accompany him in the field; to avenge him (so long as private justice lasted) or help him compensate his victims or their avengers in order to restore peace; not to marry outside the *gens*; to render the patron all services included under the name of *obsequium*.[1] In the city these obligations, which moreover were reciprocal, were perpetuated by forbidding patron and client to prosecute each other, to give evidence against each other, or to vote on different sides, and by requiring them to help each other, especially in court, where the patron directed his client's case, and also in the payment of debts, penalties and fines.[2] Religious Law, *fas*, punished the violation of these rules by its anathemas, and it was echoed by the Twelve Tables when they repeated after it: *Patronus, si clienti fraudem fecerit, sacer esto;*—"Cursed be the patron who has defrauded his client of his protection!"[3] By patron we must understand every *gentilis*, for the bond of clientship was originally formed between the client and the *gens*.[4] It was perpetual and considered to be closer than the bond of agnate relationship, and the passage of centuries was required to break it.

Both patricians and clients owned slaves: prisoners of war, foreigners carried off and sold by land- or sea-pirates, servants born to the house. They were few in number and became a part of the household, being treated with consideration, associated with the domestic cult, and given a place in the family tomb. Enfranchisement gave them and their descendants a place within the *gens*, whose name they then took, beside the client families; but they were burdened with a special *obsequium*, clients of free origin being bound by obligations only to the *gens*, whereas freedmen were further bound by obligations to the *domus* of their old master.

Every *gens* was associated with a larger or smaller piece of land. In the first centuries of the Republic a piece of land was still the indispensable appanage of a *gens*, and when the

---
[1] Dion. Hal., 2, 10.—**CXXIV**, 46 et seq.
[2] Dion. Hal., 2, 10; Aul. Gel., 20, 1; Cic., *de Orat.*, 3, 33.
[3] Aul. Gel., 20, 1.—**XIII**, 26, 147.
[4] Plut., *Marius*, 5; Cic., *de Orat.*, 1, 39; *in Verr.*, 1, 45.

Sabine Atta Clausus claimed Roman citizenship, he was given an estate on the banks of the Anio for his *gens* and his five thousand clients.[1] The *gentes* of the conquered cities who were admitted to the patriciate kept their rural estates, *agri gentilicii*. Being all devoted to the settled life of agriculture, the *gentes* still clung to their agrarian collectivism, not in obedience to economic ideas, but simply because the *gens* had at first been a single family living at the hearth and table of a single chief. After a time separate hearths were created but not separate estates.[2] We know nothing of the manner in which these lands were cultivated or apportioned. It seems that when allotments were discontinued, each portion was confirmed in the possession of the *patresfamilias* who cultivated it by hereditary right: hence the insensible appropriation of this land. The abeyant right of the *gens* was no longer asserted except when a *domus* became extinct or its head proved incapable of cultivating its portion: hence, later on, the right of succession escheated to the *gentiles* in default of the nearest agnate, at any rate from the time of the Twelve Tables, and probably still earlier in default of *heredes sui*; hence also the nature of primitive guardianship and curatorship which allowed dispossession of the incapable owner.[3] A considerable fraction of the *agri gentilicii* was granted to the clients on a precarious tenure, which however was rarely cancelled.[4] A gradual consolidation also worked for the advantage of the client families and ended in the establishment of an agricultural plebs which long continued to be the reserve of the Roman armies. Patricians and clients cultivated their lands with the help of their children and their slaves; the clients working perhaps without enjoying the fruits, and being also obliged to give their labour. The holdings, which were of moderate size, so that an average family could cultivate one of them without neglecting such other labours as the life of that time and those circumstances required, must have varied between eight and twenty acres.

[1] Liv., 6, 20. [2] **XIII**, 26, 180, 317.
[3] Cic., *de Inv.*, 12, 50 (XII T., 5, 4, 7).
[4] Festus, s.v. *Patres, Patronus, Patrocinia*.

THE GENS AND THE CITY

II. THE " JUS GENTILITATIS "

The *gens* could contain several thousand persons. It was a State in miniature, and the body of rights that it recognized and guaranteed to its members constituted the *jus gentilitatis*. Its head, *princeps*, *dux* or *princeps generis*,[1] was priest, judge and military leader. On his motion the *patres* made decrees which were binding upon the whole association. In remembrance of the time when the *gens* was only a single family, the family régime retained its force, pronouncing on the celibacy of its members, the exposure of children, marriage, etc.[2] There was no limit to its judicial powers. Sentence of death, interdiction of fire and water cut off the guilty person from its protection and its cult, and heavy punishments were imposed by its sentences. But the ties of blood were so strong that the heads of the *domus* generally made a friendly settlement of their differences or referred them to an arbitrator who reached his decision by the aid of precedent, of the disputants' oaths or of certain mysterious methods such as ordeals or the drawing of lots. Private warfare was thus restricted to litigants of different *gentes*, but then the solidarity of the *gens* involved the whole association in the dispute.[3]

Being a religious community, the *gens* had a cult in which *gentiles*, clients and even slaves took part. The *sacra gentilicia* had for their centre a temple and the tomb of the eponymous ancestor, and worship was offered to the Manes, the spirits of all the deified ancestors, to the Hearth kindled by the founder, and often to local divinities of the countryside as well. The *gens* connected its survival with this Hearth and tomb where the succeeding generations came to take their place. Only the male descendants of the common ancestor were qualified to preserve the continuity of rites and sacrifices, to draw near to the Hearth and the altar: therefore the *gens* rejected strangers. It was impossible to belong to it and to another, and women who left their *domus* to marry elsewhere ceased to be recognized as members.

It only recognized agnate relationship; and the *domus*, a fraction of the *gens*, will recognize no other.[4]

The autonomous *gens* once had its own army, but was no

---

[1] Festus, s.v. *Familia*; Suet., *Tiber.*, 1; Dion. Hal., 2, 7; 9, 5. **CXXIV**, 6-7.
[2] Liv., 6, 20; Suet., *l.c.*   [3] **CXXIV**, 16-20, 47.   [4] Liv., 5, 46.

longer suffered to retain it when it was absorbed by the Roman State. It retained, however, a memory of tragic times, and knew how to reconstitute its army in order to undertake some perilous expedition for the advantage of the city.[1]

II

THE ORGANIZATION OF THE CITY

I. THE CITY. THE " GENS " WITHIN THE CITY. THE " JUS CIVITATIS "

In the course of time various sorts of intercourse were established between neighbouring *gentes* and between their dependants. Now, there was no conception of legal relations existing between any but members of the same religious society, so these *gentes* united in a common worship under a common head. This new grouping, whether curia or tribe, had its distinct centre apart from those of the confederate associations; and these larger confederacies joined together to form another yet vaster one, namely the city.

This process, which has been described for us in the case of Athens, was repeated at the foundation of all ancient cities except colonies immediately established in their entirety, though they too were modelled upon this preexisting type. Rome was at first an aggregate of *gentes* or a federation of tribes which were themselves composed of *gentes*.

When they entered the city, the *gentes* did not modify their internal régime or give up their independence in their *pagi*. They only consented to obey in specified circumstances one common head who was king, priest, supreme judge and commander-in-chief. They formed themselves into a religious community and united their forces about a common citadel which was the seat of government, the dwelling-place of the city's gods, a market and a defence in time of war. The *jus civitatis* was the whole body of rights which the *gentes* recognized as binding between themselves, whose observance they guaranteed for the benefit of each *gens* and its members. It comprised, in the political sphere, the *jus suffragii*, right of voting, the *jus honorum*, right of election to magistracies, the

[1] Liv., 2, 47-48.

THE GENS AND THE CITY

jus militiæ, right of serving in the legion; in the religious sphere, the *jus sacrorum*, membership of the city's cult, the *jus aupiciorum*, right of taking the auspices, the *jus sacerdotii*, right of occupying the national priesthoods; in the sphere of private intercourse, *dominium*, absolute and exclusive ownership by the *gentes* of their lands, *conubium*, the right to contract a legal marriage, *commercium* or guarantee of the legal agreements that might be entered into between members of different *gentes*, and finally the right to enforce recognition of the obligations that might result from these and to secure their sanction at the supreme court of the king by means of a procedure which was determined by certain fixed forms, the *legis actiones*.

As the city authorities had originally no jurisdiction in the *pagi* of the *gentes*, the rights thus acquired were exercised for the most part in the federal territory and presupposed a place of residence there. Hence this territory had been divided into thirty curias among which the *patresfamilias* were distributed, each having received within his curia two acres of land in order that he might establish a city residence there for himself and his family. Exercise of the *jus civitatis* was dependent on this hereditary possession or *heredium* which could not be alienated under penalty of *infamia*.[1] This is what the texts refer to when they speak of an original distribution of estates, or of grants made from the territory of the *Urbs* to populations that had emigrated to Rome or had been transported thither, such as the *gens Claudia* which received *heredia* there for its *patres*.[2]

For several generations the *heredium* remained the common property of all descendants by the male line of the head of the *domus* to whom it had originally been allotted. Residence there was not continuous, for the town was hardly visited except for political meetings, religious festivals and the markets on every ninth day.[3] Over and above the protection afforded by the old associations, the State offered its own; its army, its police and its courts of law. In addition to their time-honoured administrative machinery, which began to grow obsolete, it offered its own new and better adjusted methods. The *gentes* lived independently at home, i.e. on

---

[1] Festus, s.v. *Heredium* ; Varro, *de r. r.*, 1, 10-2; Pliny, H.N., 18, 2-7; Dion. Hal., 2, 7; Cic., *de Orat.*, 2, 55; *pro L. Sul.*, 20.
[2] CXII, 243.   [3] Varro, *de r. r.*, pr., 2.

their *agri gentilicii;* but within the city the State had immediate contact with the *domus* which it had organized in the curias. All the *patres* and also their sons of full age were equal before the civic Law: a fact which continually prompted them to break away from the old organization and entrust themselves to the new one.

II. THE GROWTH OF THE CITY: THE PLEBS

Other elements, of disputed origin, were very soon introduced. Immigrant tradesmen and artisans, refugees from near or distant cities or tribes, inhabitants of conquered towns who were either transported to Rome or deprived of political and civil rights and left on their own territory, clients perhaps escaped from the association of the *gens* were all alike distinguished from the people of the *gentes*, the *populus romanus*, under the vague title of *plebs*.[1] This formed a second society by the side of the normal one, a confused mass of people differing in manners, customs and perhaps dialects, who were placed outside the framework of the State but enjoyed some of its privileges and occupied important strategic points in its economic life. At one time apparently an attempt was made to incorporate them in the city by distributing them as clients among the patrician *domus* inscribed in the curias;[2] but quite different methods of arrangement determined by trade and place of residence were finally adopted, people of the same occupation having generally a common origin and dwelling in the same quarter. Later on Numa was credited with the institution of nine trade bodies which were at the same time religious associations and included all the artisans.[3] Besides these, *sodalitates* were formed either for religious purposes, for mutual aid or for pleasure. The kings, except the last few, favoured them and moreover invited the plebeians to share in the *assignationes viritanæ*, grants of conquered territory to individuals, which they frequently made.[4] Hence the State took upon itself the protection of the poor, the weak, the isolated, and all of whom the federal charter took no account. Customs borrowed from the *populus* or brought from their

[1] **CXXVI**, 5-6; **CLII**, 275 et seq.; cpr. **CCXLIII**. [2] Plut., *Rom.*, 19.
[3] Plut., *Numa*, 29; Dion. Hal., 2, 62.—**CCXXXIV**, 1, 182; **CCXXXV**, 5 et seq.; **CCLXXVI**, 2, 734; **XXI**, 32, 276-278.
[4] Dion. Hal., 4, 7, 4, 3; Plut., *Numa*, 16; Liv., 1, 33; 2, 6.

countries of origin gave a comparative order to their legal relations, a certain degree of validity, subject to the disciplinary power of the king; and the authority of the State owed its development especially, at first, to these relations between the king and the plebs. Being henceforward attached to the Roman soil, the plebeian houses aspired to a share in the city; and the reform attributed to Servius Tullius advanced the plebeians of some competence still further in this direction. After division into four urban tribes according to place of residence, the patricians and plebeians were enrolled together at the Census and distributed, according to their wealth, among the *equites* or in one of the five classes. The army and the *comitia centuriata* were open to the rich whose influence there was proportionate to their wealth, whoever they might be and whatever the nature of their patrimony, for there is no authority for saying that the term *assiduus* applied to members of the five classes meant the dweller on an estate.[1]

The innovation here was that in some ways patricians and plebeians became members of the same community, while in others they continued to be sharply divided. The creation of the tribunate (A.U.C. 260) and of the plebeian ædile, the separate meetings or *concilia* of the plebs were not calculated to secure harmony. By the unconditional veto and the criminal jurisdiction of the tribunes and, later, by the transference of their election from the centuries to the tribes (A.U.C. 283), the State was in danger of being thrown out of gear and destroyed. But economic circumstances became inextricably involved and interests were shared in common. The agrarian law of Spurius Cassius (A.U.C. 268) affected the patricians and the rich plebeians alike, and threatened them both with the danger of Latin claims. A compromise was made, and the year 297 A.U.C. saw the number of tribunes doubled. The only Law common to both orders, within the sphere of private Law, was the acts comprised under the title of *commercium* ; and it was for their sake and for the sake of the economic advantages derived from them that the *populus romanus* had already made such large concessions in the political sphere on the occasion of each secession of the

---

[1] Cic., *de Rep.*, 2, 2; *Top.*, 1, 10; Aul. Gel., 16-10; Festus, s.v. *Assiduus;* Varro, *de Ling. lat.*, s.v. *Proletarius.* Cf. **CCXXXVII**, 1, 178.

plebs. Within ten years the plebeians ceased to be contented and demanded legislation to secure equality. Something of this sort was agreed upon in the year 300 A.U.C., and three years later its working out was entrusted to certain legislators invested with consular powers, *decemviri consulari imperio legibus scribendis*. The result of their work was the Law of the Twelve Tables.

III. Disappearance of the "Gens" as an Organic Part of the City

Henceforward the victories of the plebs increased in number. Moreover the régime of the *gens* was rapidly coming to an end; the remembrance of blood-relationship within it was disappearing, and the *patresfamilias* began to desire more complete independence. Once a means of protection, the *gens* no longer seemed anything but an encumbrance, since the State now offered similar advantages on a much wider plane of evolution. Except in regard to the *ager gentilicius* and in the sphere of private Law, it had no further part to play. The rights which the city granted to its members directly became every day more important. The legislative activity of the gentile assembly and its disciplinary power were no longer shown, except on rare occasions. A long prescription insensibly transferred to the actual occupiers of the land the *dominium* itself and led them in the direction of individual, or at any rate family, ownership, of which the *assignationes viritanæ* had already set the example. On the other hand there was no addition to the number of clients, which was gradually exhausted, since the plebs with its hope of *assignationes* attracted the poor and weak in another direction. The old client families broke away, or else long possession confirmed in their hands the tenure that had once been precarious.

Then the exercise of sovereignty over the *pagi* of the *gentes* changed its form. On the day when the *domus* repudiated the authority of the *gens* over its land, the State had to apply its powers of police and recover the land-taxes from the occupiers of the soil without intermediary. From the point of view of the State, the *gens* ceased to exist, and its influence only survived in purely personal relations. From this two

THE GENS AND THE CITY

consequences followed. First, in public Law, there was the more or less rapid creation of seventeen rural tribes, sixteen of which bore the names of *gentes* and thus showed their connexion with the old *agri gentilicii*.[1] Hitherto individuals had not been controlled and ordered by the State except on the land of the *Urbs*, because outside those bounds the *gens* intervened. Now the administrative authority of the city was extended to cover the whole *ager romanus*, and there was no longer any urgent need to have a dwelling in the town. The territories became united like the nation, and inscription in the register of a tribe became the warrant of nationality. But all the *gentes* did not suffer this dethronement simultaneously; the first to be affected was, according to Varro, the powerful *gens Romulia* at the very gates of the *Urbs*.[2] Secondly, in private Law, the State granted to the *patres-familias* the same *dominium* over the appropriated lands as it had originally granted to the *gens* over its *pagus*. The *dominium ex jure Quiritium* continued to be the right by which the members of the city secured the possession of their land under the sole condition of one year's peaceful occupation, the original period for usucapion.[3] We have no evidence concerning the average area of these private estates.

This revolution took place between the expulsion of the kings and the legislation of the decemvirs. The view which places it before the Servian reform[4] is inadmissible, because this reform ignores the rural tribes,[5] and the tradition which fixes the coming of the *gens Claudia* at a later date shows that it was established in accordance with the strictest and fullest requirements of the *gens* system.[6] The fact is that the transformation of the *agri gentilicii* into administrative districts took place gradually;[7] hence the uncertainty of tradition about its date. That which is proposed, namely 258 A.U.C., is quite imaginary.[8]

What survived of the *jura gentilicia* concerning inheritance, guardianship, curatorship and legal or financial assistance could no longer impair either political or civil equality. Certain magistracies or offices of religious jurisdiction remained

---

[1] CCXXXVII, 1, 106; CCXXXVIII, 6¹, 504 et seq.; CLVIII, 273; CLIX, 1, 294 et seq.
[2] CCXXXVIII, 6¹, 186, n. 3. [3] CXLVI, 172 et seq. [4] CCXXXIV, 1, 252.
[5] Festus, s.v. *Urbanas*. [6] Liv., 4, 3. [7] CCXCVIII, 54-55.
[8] Liv., 2, 21; Dion. Hal., 4, 15; 7, 68.—CCXXXVII, 1, 188.

for a time the perquisite of the patrician houses, just as the tribunate and the plebeian ædileship were confined to the plebs; but the latter surmounted one by one the various stages of the *jus honorum*, and the *transitio ad plebem*, of whose forms we are ignorant, allowed patricians sometimes to occupy the plebeian magistracies. Towards the end of the Republic adoption was allowed between the two orders. The patricians retained the prestige of their cancelled greatness, and vanity led some plebeian families to set themselves up in the manner of *gentes*.

IV. THE LEVELLING LEGISLATION OF THE TWELVE TABLES

Civil equality between the *populus romanus* and the plebs was inaugurated by the legislation of the decemvirs. Certain police regulations affecting the family, the sanctions grouped together under the name of royal laws (*leges regiæ*), are only an echo of the royal jurisprudence exercised with special regard to the plebs. The collection which was made of them under the name of *Jus Papirianum*, annotated and probably composed by Granius Flaccus, was only a contribution to the movement inspired by the Emperor in favour of tradition. The source of private Law was originally custom, and the *mores majorum* which governed the *gentes* contained a core that was common to all the social groups of central Italy as well as usages peculiar to the Latin or Roman confederation or to each *gens*. The heterogeneous elements that formed the plebs had also established for themselves a common Law of custom by eliminating such practices as were too foreign to blend with the mass and returning to those which were associated by their primitive nature with the oldest habits of the race and had most chance of universal acceptance.

The liberation of the patrician *domus* and the establishment of plebeian families in legally organized *domus* opened the way for an aggregate of regulations that could be applied to both alike and could bring the heads of houses and the persons and things in their power under a more or less uniform régime. Common rights and the enforcement of those rights by methods of procedure that were known and open to all, such was the object of the legislators (303-305 A.U.C.).

However, the Law of the Twelve Tables was neither a

complete code nor even a work of coherent and methodical structure. The attempts to reconstruct it have nothing in common. This venerable monument has not escaped the criticism that has been aimed at the traditional account of Rome's first centuries. Owing to resemblances and a sort of parallelism between the story of its composition and promulgation and that of the publication of the *jus civile* or the formulas by Cn. Flavius a century and half later, some have regarded the first of these stories as a legend assigning an earlier date and the form of positive Law to a doctrinal compilation belonging to the middle of Rome's fifth century.[1] Further, because the fragments attributed to the Twelve Tables only appear in the literature of the fifth century and even the phrase *Lex XII Tabularum* is not found before the seventh, it has been assumed from the dissemination of these texts, from their concise style, their resemblance to proverbs and brocards, the marked modernity of their language, that they are merely a number of popular sayings or rules of custom collected by some lawyer, perhaps by the Sextus Ælius Pætus Catus, Consul in 556 A.U.C., whose *Tripertita* are offered to us as the most ancient edition known and at the same time the oldest commentary on the Twelve Tables.[2] Rejecting the evidence of the Fasti concerning a decemviral legislation in 303 and 304 A.U.C., it is maintained that this jurist or somebody else did for this part of the customary Law what Gr. Flaccus did later on for the *Jus Papirianum*. But these arguments are met by the following facts. Ever since there had been such a thing as Latin literature, there had been allusions in it to the Law of the Twelve Tables and to their contents. Through Cicero, Polybius and Fabius Pictor we go back to the beginning of the sixth century. Already Sextus Ælius Pætus and perhaps L. Acilius have commented on it, and in course of time special books will be written on the subject by Servius Sulpicius, Labeo and Gaius. The historicity of the decemvirs is based not only on the Capitoline Fasti but also on the Fasti in general whose genuineness is guaranteed by the absence of rhotacism and by the obscurity of the ancient consuls who would not have been invented

[1] **CCXLV**, 1, 550 et seq.; 2, 546 et seq., 631 et seq. Ettore Pais has since changed his opinion and admitted the authenticity of the Twelve Tables: *Studi historici per l'antichita classica*, 2, 3.

[2] **XIII**, 26, 149 et seq.; **XVII**, 1902, 385, 481; 1903, 15; **XLII**, 1, 501-626.

thus. It is not all in the form of proverbs or brocards, and the large proportion of it that was based on custom explains those that occur. Although some fragments have been modernized, the archaic terminology and grammatical forms show that it is older than the sixth century. The institutions that it implies carry us back to the environment of a small agricultural society of very low development, which is only just beginning to experience the need of a monetary system.[1] All that we know of earlier Roman history tends towards this work; all that we know of later history is explained by reference to it.

And yet the labour of discovering and co-ordinating the fragments of this Law that are scattered through Roman literature has only led to an incomplete reconstruction and an arbitrary arrangement. There was not a separate table devoted to each class of subject-matter, but only twelve oak panels set up in the forum, on which the Law was written without arrangement under general headings or distinction of paragraphs or any other kind of subdivision except the purely material one between the different panels. The arrangement adopted after Dirksen is merely probable and convenient.[2]

The first object of primitive legislations is procedure: the conditions and forms of summons, of remittal of causes and appointment of witnesses; the limitation of time for appearance in court; the ritual of the suit, evidence and inquiry; the means of execution. All this engaged the special attention of the decemvirs. As a rule primitive Law merely follows the practices of private justice while making them harmless: hence its requirement of strange gestures, its brutality, whether feigned or real, and its singularities. Now the fragments brought together in the first three tables are echoes of these methods of procedure, no detail of which could be omitted or perverted under pain of losing the case, whoever the litigant might be—whether patrician or plebeian.

The decemvirs also had in view a family régime common to the *populus* and to the *plebs*. The paternal and marital power which had been increased when the authority and regulations of the *gens* disappeared, and which may have been

[1] **XIII**, 26, 351 et seq.; **CLIX**, 1, 15 et seq.; **XXXIII**, 26, 408-524; **XI**, 1902, 599 et seq.; **XVI**, 1907, 201 et seq.
[2] **CXXXVII**; T. G., 12 et seq.

THE GENS AND THE CITY 51

already granted to plebeians by the kings, the condition of persons incapable *sui juris* and of freedmen, the question of intestate succession—all these became the object of State regulation; and as the power of the head of a *domus* extended to things, some essential rules were formulated concerning the right of ownership, *dominium*, and its modes of transfer, and a rudimentary system of real servitudes was sketched out.

A series of penal dispositions aimed especially at rustic offences, at acts of magic directed against the cultivators or the fruits of the soil, betray the superstitions of a peasant society with its prejudiced, vindictive and credulous mental attitude. Though originally townsmen and artisans, the plebs had quickly spread beyond the ranks of the merchants and free workmen, and had been diverted in some measure to the life of agriculture by the *assignationes viritanæ* or the purchase of estates. The Roman masses continued to be countrymen.[1]

Various sumptuary dispositions imposed by a wise economy; a few dispositions of public Law, such as the prohibition of *privilegia*, i.e. of statutes made to meet a particular case (*jussa de singulis concepta*),[2] the restriction of capital sentences to the comitia centuriata (*jus provocationis*) or the establishment of a right of appeal to them from the sentences of the consuls, the introduction of the death penalty for judges who take bribes—all these measures show a care to promote equality. Nevertheless, in the second year of the decemvirate, the refusal of *conubium*, i.e. of the right to contract a legitimate marriage between patrician and plebeian, maintained two separate societies in spite of their political communion; but this obstacle was removed six years afterwards by the *Lex Canuleia* (311 A.U.C.).

It is improbable that the Law of the Twelve Tables contained the judicial Fasti. Traditions differ on the point. They were no more efficacious than our own codes in enabling litigants to find their way among the formalities of procedure, and thus the patrician jurists retained a powerful influence, for they knew the *verba*. The composition of formularies was always one of the jurist's objects. A jurisprudence, a rich growth of doctrines gathered about the dry and concise terms of the Law, and a commentary was added to it. We

[1] CCXLV, 1, 409, 527; CCLXXVII, 8 et seq.　　[2] Aul. Gel., 10, 20.

can easily imagine the work of Cn. Flavius in the fifth century, taking the form of a more or less annotated formulary or custumal. It gave rise to the enormous work of the *interpretatio prudentium*. This *Jus Flavianum* won for its author the curule ædileship (450 A.Ú.C.), which seems to have enabled him to publish the judicial calendar.[1]

The Law was made public. The *Tripertita* of Sextus Ælius Pætus Catus: the text of the Twelve Tables with the whole of the existing *interpretatio* and the *legis actiones* subjoined; a *Jus Ælianum*, probably the *Æliana studia* of which Cicero speaks,[2] whose nature is not precisely known, whether it was a custumal, a style-book or a part of the preceding work; the general formulary of M. Manilius; the ten books of *Jus Civile* by P. Mucius Scævola resumed and continued by his son Quintus;—all these works, but especially the last, provided the most complete exposition of the Law during the period which elapsed between the decemvirate and the appearance of the edict.[3]

III

LAW IN THE CITY

I. THE NEW CONDITIONS OF THE " JUS CIVITATIS "

The *jus civitatis* was originally enjoyed through the medium of a *gens* ; but when the association of the *gens* was broken up, the elements which had been contained within it were allowed to spread freely throughout the State, which became their natural sphere. Composed of a number of very exclusive earlier associations, the city possessed the same characteristics.

The disorganization of the *gentes* and the advance of the plebs caused the State to define the particular conditions on which this right depended. It was acquired either by birth or on subsequent grounds: *ut sit civis aut natus oportet aut factus*.[4] In the former case the condition of the parents was alone of consequence. If he was born *ex justis nuptiis*, i.e. of a legal marriage, the child's status was that of the father on the day of conception; otherwise it was that of the mother at the moment of delivery, though some amendments were

---

[1] Cf. **CCCV** ; **CLIX**, 1, 223, 2. [2] Cic., *de Orat.*, 1, 46.
[3] D., 1, 2, 2-6.—**CCXXXVII**, 16, 29-40; **CXII**, 150-151.
[4] Quint., *de Inst. Orat.*, 8, 10, 65.

THE GENS AND THE CITY

made to this system: e.g. a *Lex Minicia* (?), earlier than the Social War, declared of inferior, i.e. non-Roman, status a child born of parents of whom one was not a Roman; while certain senatusconsulta of Hadrian's time conferred citizenship upon the child born of a marriage between a Latin father and a Roman mother, and upon the child who was conceived before and born after the naturalization of his parents.[1]

Citizenship could be obtained subsequent to birth: (i.) by enfranchisement *jure civili* in various different ways;[2] (ii.) by the gift of citizenship, *donatis civitatis*, bestowed upon an individual or a group either by the people, or by the Senate or a magistrate with the people's consent, or later by the Emperor.[3] If it was granted individually, each recipient had to be proposed by name;[4] if collectively, it was assigned to a city or a people or sometimes a body of auxiliary troops. Though rare at first, this became more frequent later on. From the political point of view it was either more or less complete: there were *civitates cum* and *sine suffragio*, i.e. with or without political rights. In the last century of the Republic Roman Citizenship was extended by a series of concessions to the whole of Italy. The Emperors sometimes bestowed it grudgingly, sometimes lavishly. By an edict of 212, whose scope is somewhat doubtful, Caracalla seems to have granted it to all inhabitants of the Empire except the *dedititii*.[5]

From an early date (659 A.U.C.) until a certain *Lex Licinia Mucia* the *Latini veteres* and *colonarii* had been able to claim the right of citizenship if they had settled in Rome and left a child in their country of origin, if they had secured the conviction of a Roman magistrate of peculation, or if they had occupied a municipal magistracy.[6] Under the Empire the cities of *minus Latium* were those whose magistrates enjoyed this favour, the cities of *majus Latium* those in which it was extended to the *decuriones*.[7] The Junian Latin freedmen also secured a number of opportunities of acquiring citizenship, which are noted by Gaius and Ulpian;[8] among them the *causæ probatio* and *erroris causæ probatio*, which were also open

---

[1] G., 1, 55-56, 78-92; Ulp., 5, 8-10. [2] See p. 131 et seq.
[3] G., 1, 93, 94; T. G., 61. [4] Plin. mi., *Epist.*, 10, 6; D., 1, 5, 17.
[5] Dion Cas., 77, 9; D., 1, 5, 17.—**CLVIII**, 121-3; **XXV**, 16, 475; 27, 257; **CXCII**, 351-358.
[6] Liv., 41, 8; Cic., *pro Balbo*, 24; Appian, *de b. c.*, 2, 26. [7] G., 1, 96
[8] G., 1, 32-4; 3, 72; Ulp., 3, 1, 4, 5, 6.

to Latins and aliens, the second even to children of *dedititii*.[1]

The right of citizenship was lost by naturalization in a foreign city, for Roman Citizenship could not be simply resigned, at any rate after the last century of the Republic. Neither double nationality nor absence of nationality—such was the rule in classical Law.[2] It was also lost by legal forfeiture of citizen's status (slavery, outlawry, surrender to the enemy;)[3] and afterwards, under the Empire, by a sentence that made the convicted person an alien of no fixed nationality, *peregrinus sine certa civitate* (deportation, condemnation on public works).[4]

The municipal organization of the Mediterranean world in its subjection to the empire of Rome, which made the Roman State an aggregate of cities under the sovereignty of one of them, caused the dwellers in towns enjoying the *jus civitatis* to possess two countries: Rome and their city of origin, which was called the *origo*. The latter was determined by rules analogous to those on which the right of citizenship depended, except that certain *cives Romani* could have two *origines*, e.g. the freedman of two patrons whose *origines* differed, the person adrogated who retained his own *origo* while acquiring that of the adrogator.[5]

Every citizen, whether *paterfamilias* or *filiusfamilias*, who had attained his political majority, counted in the State and on the registers of the Census as a *caput*, i.e. as a human being capable of receiving rights from the city. His disappearance from that city involved the erasure of his name, or *capitis deminutio*, whereby he lost all his rights. Originally this was the result of slavery alone: *justa servitus*, of which the effect could not be cancelled by any *jus postliminii* or by the handing over of a child of the family *in mancipio* to a third party by the head of the *domus*. It involved loss of liberty and loss of nationality at the same time.[6] But treaties and friendly intercourse with other peoples from Rome's fifth century onwards and, towards the end of the Republic, the half legal, half philosophical idea of a *jus gentium*, as well as

---

[1] G., 1, 29-32, 67-75; **CXII**, 103, n. 1.
[2] G., 1, 131; Cic., *pro Balbo*, 11-14; *pro dom.*, 30. Cf. C. Nepos, *Vit. Attici*, 3.
[3] Cic., *pro Cæc.*, 43.   [4] D., 48, 19, 2-1.
[5] Cic., *de Leg.*, 2, 1; D., 50, 1, 1-2, 6-3, 7-pr., 15-3, 17-9, 22-pr., 27, pr., 37-1.
[6] G., 1, 158-163; Ulp., 11, 13.

THE GENS AND THE CITY

the order of precedence recognized among the dependants of the Roman State—citizens, Latins, aliens—led to a distinction between liberty and citizenship. It was recognized that some free men were not citizens and that citizenship could be lost without loss of liberty.[1] *Capitis deminutio* was divided into *maxima* (slavery) and *minor* (loss of citizenship). This latter term originally meant loss of citizenship by the acquisition of another nationality and also, later on, forfeiture of Roman citizenship as a penalty without acquiring any other, so that those who underwent it remained Roman subjects while ceasing to be citizens.[2] But from a period earlier than Cicero, the child who had been sold retained his liberty and citizenship *in mancipio* and was only said to be *in loco servi*, in the position of a slave. In the time of Gaius he no longer lost even his free-born condition; and yet the term *capitis deminutio* continued to be applied to his case, so that, under the Empire, a third type appeared, *capitis deminutio minima*, which referred merely to changes of civil status among the citizens.[3] *Intestabilitas*, incapacity to serve as a witness, *nota censoria*, a public reprimand pronounced by the censor, *infamia*, the consequence of some sentences, did not cancel or limit the *caput*, but affected the *existimatio*, the citizen's good name, and involved the forfeiture of certain political and legal rights.[4]

II. Legal Relations with Foreigners

At first the city was wrapped up in itself and ignored foreigners. The Roman recognized no right belonging to the *hostis* and possessed every right against him: murder, capture, plunder were quite blameless when he was concerned.[5] It was not until after the time of Sylla, who wanted to deprive certain towns of the right of citizenship, that it was conceived that the condition of alien or of citizen could become a subject of legal dispute and a *quæstio perpetua* was established to take cognizance of such cases.

[1] D., 4, 5, 3-pr., 15; I. J., 1, 16, pr., 5. Cf. Cic., *Top.*, 4, 18.
[2] Festus, s.v. *Cap. demin.*—**CCXXXVIII**, 5², 200 et seq.; **CXXXIV**, 2.
[3] G., 1, 159-163, 216; Ulp., 11, 13. Cf. **CXLII**, 160 et seq.; **CC**, 1, 5 et seq.; **CXXXIII**, 1.
[4] Cic., *pro Cluen.*, 42-43; Aul. Gel., 15, 13; D., 28, 1, 18-1, 26. **CCXXXVIII**, 4, 101; 17, 991.
[5] D., 49, 15, 5-2. Cf. Cic., *de Off.*, 1, 12.

For a long time it was impossible to reside on the territory of another city without the patronage of one of its citizens, which was obtained by means of a compact, *fœdus amicitiæ* or *hospitalitatis*, entered into with the host, *hostis*.¹ But although *hospitalitas* appeared to be sacred and guaranteed by the gods, it became at length insufficient, and the making of agreements was taken over from the individual by the State. Rome and some other peoples allowed each other reciprocal privileges under the names of *conubium* and *commercium*. The *jus conubii* had reference to the ability of dependants of the two States to contract a legitimate marriage, *justa nuptia*.² *Commercium* is defined by Ulpian as " the right to buy and sell to one another " according to the forms of Civil Law, which included sale by *mancipatio*, formal sale for cash, the power to become creditor or debtor by the *nexum*, the most ancient form of contract known at Rome, and the power to plead usucapion. To this was added later the *factio testamenti* or capacity to make a will, probably in consequence of the *testamentum per œs et libram*.³ *Commercium agrorum*, the right to acquire real estate in the *ager romanus*, was only slowly conceded and was made the subject of a special stipulation that is found among almost all the peoples of Greece and of Italy.⁴ These concessions implied a jurisdiction to guarantee them, and the right of appeal thereto was the *jus reciperationis*. " *Reciperatio* takes place," said Festus, " when there is a treaty between the Roman people and foreign kings, nations and cities to determine how captured property shall be restored and recovered, and how private suits shall be adjudicated."⁵ The treaty prescribed the method of nomination and the number of the judges or *recuperatores*. The Prætor Peregrinus was created in 512 A.U.C. to organize these suits.⁶ In course of time the number of legal acts included under the head of *commercium* was increased by all those of the *jus gentium*. *Conubium* and *commercium* could be granted together or separately, and without any political right.⁷

Roman imperialism, like that of modern nations, brought

---

¹ Festus, s.v. *hostis* ; Varro, *de L. l.*, 5, 3 ; D., 50, 16, 284-pr.
² Ulp., 5, 3, 4.—**CCXXXVIII**, 6², 290.
³ Ulp., 19, 4, 5 ; Festus, s.v. *Sanates*.
⁴ Cic., *in Verr.*, 3, 40 ; Liv., 35, 7.—**CCXXXVIII**, 2, 111.
⁵ Festus, s.v. *Recuperator* ; *Lex Acilia* ; T.-G., 33.
⁶ G., 1, 6.   ⁷ Ulp., 5, 4 ; 19, 4.—**CCXXXVIII**, 6², 182.

THE GENS AND THE CITY

into being various classes of subject peoples; but as the differences of race, religion and civilization were less marked, a gradual assimilation took place. When the power of Rome was declining, Sidonius Apollinaris wrote that only slaves and barbarians were excluded from this city which embraced the whole world; but it had not always been so. For a long time Rome distinguished the peoples under her hegemony according to the value of the rights which she had conceded to them: the right of Roman citizenship either with or without a vote, the Latin right, the right of aliens, the right of *dedititii*. The Latin right (*Latinitas* or *jus latinitatis*) was the status gradually conceded to the Latin allies and involved *conubium*, at least as a general rule; *commercium*, even *commercium agrorum ;* power to adopt and to be adopted; *factio testamenti ;* judgment by the Urban Prætor; opportunities for acquiring Roman citizenship; admission to the army as *socii ;* and, finally, a vote in the *comitia tributa*.[1] The Latins became citizens in 664 A.U.C.,[2] but their old status did not disappear: it was subsequently granted as a privilege to cities, peoples or classes of individuals that Rome desired to honour without the gift of full citizenship. Except for *conubium*, it had been the status of the colonies founded by the Latin confederation up to 416 A.U.C. or by Rome up to 486: whence the term *Latini colonarii*. Under the Empire it was granted lavishly.[3]

The right of aliens (*jus peregrinum*) varied with different peoples according to the terms of the treaty, *fœdus œquum* or *inæquum*, which bound them to Rome. It was generally based upon the alien customs or statutes which the conquered peoples retained by agreement with the Romans or at their good pleasure. The legal acts of the *jus gentium* were held to be valid between Romans and aliens.[4]

The right of *dedititii* (*jus dedititiorum*) was the status imposed upon peoples who had surrendered to the Roman people at discretion according to the formula of *deditio*.[5] Their own Law was taken from them and they were made subject to police regulations established by the authority of Rome.

This variety of statuses, this subtle distinction between

---

[1] Liv., 25, 3; Appian, *de b. c.*, 1, 2, 3; *Lex Malacitana*, T. G., 113; **CCXXXVIII**, G¹, 457.
[2] Cic., *p. Balb.*, 8; Aul. Gel., 4, 4.
[3] **XXV**, 16, 458-463; Gaius, 1, 29; Plin., *H. N.*, 3, 4.
[4] G., 1, 86; *Lex Antonia de Thermessibus* (683); T. G., 68.
[5] Liv., 1, 38; 36, 28; G., 1, 14.

subjection, annexation and incorporation, enabled the Roman Government to gather a vast number of various peoples beneath its empire without violating their customs or their social habits, but also without being compelled to admit them immediately and unconditionally to its own political organization—a proceeding never free from danger, which it was wise enough to avoid. On the other hand it clearly showed that its privileges would be granted in proportion to the loyalty of the subject peoples and the desire for assimilation that was noted in them.

CHAPTER II

ADMINISTRATION OF JUSTICE IN THE CITY. CIVIL PROCEDURE

I

ADMINISTRATION OF JUSTICE ORGANIZED BY THE STATE. PROCEDURE AN ADVANTAGE DUE TO THE CITY

MOST of the advantages due to the city are outside the scope of this work. Within its sphere, that of private Law, the immediate gain is not so much a legislation supplemented by custom as the establishment of a judicial procedure which puts an end to the disorder inseparable from private justice. Procedure brings order and clarity into the administration of justice. Its technique is a strict logic translated into acts, a series of moves defined by analysis, steps to be taken in order to discover the legal truth and secure the triumph of the Law. Its forms are so essential that they have preceded in order of time every legislative activity. In newly formed societies procedure is born of collaboration between the litigants and the chief legal authorities.

From the very first the city of Rome adopted certain practices and put into force a small number of regulations which were for the most part common to all the populations of central Italy. Some of them required no legal organization; others, being amended and adapted to a technique that was due beyond doubt to the college of pontiffs, gave rise to a State administration of justice. As a rule the State first offers recourse to Law and finally makes it compulsory. At Rome the king was also the supreme judge, and there is nothing to show that his judicial authority was supplementary or limited by any individual initiative.[1] It was only in the internal development of procedure that any remembrance was retained of the methods of private justice which, except in the interests of self-defence, was now suppressed.[2] With its

[1] CLIX, 36. [2] LXX, 2¹, 20.

symbolical gestures reminiscent of the incidents of private warfare, this procedure conducted the litigants, under the control of the State, to a less hazardous issue.[1] It became adapted by usage to suit the national life and acquired in course of time the special characteristics which distinguished it as Roman procedure from any other, exchanging the rigid primitive forms first for a more flexible system suggested by the inevitable simplifications of practice, and then for another which was still better suited to governmental and administrative action. This last was used in addition to the earlier systems, at first in rare cases and afterwards more frequently, until at length it invaded the whole field of procedure—in certain provinces from the beginning of our era, throughout the Empire during the course of the third century.

II

THE STATUTORY PROCESSES

I. The " Legis Actiones ": Their Origin and Character

The most ancient Roman procedure is known by the name of *legis actiones*. This title does not mean that it had been created by the statutes which afterwards brought it to completion, for in essentials it was customary and older than the city itself; but that these legal means could not be used, at least after the Twelve Tables, except in the cases where it allowed their use and, under penalty of being nonsuited, in the exact terms which it employed in authorizing them. If the statute had not foreseen the litigation, there was no legal formula that could be pronounced at law and consequently no action.[2] According to Gaius these forms of procedure were 5 in number: *sacramentum, judicis postulatio, condictio, manus injectio, pignoris capio ;* and this text must be strictly adhered to, notwithstanding a theory which tends to swell their number.[3] The lawyer attributes common characteristics to all of them: (i.) the use of formal gestures and words, the latter reproducing the exact letter of the statute: thus one had to

[1] **CXXIV**, 11 et seq., 47 et seq., 99 et seq.; **CLXXXII**, 1, 78; 3, 168, 332.
[2] G., 4, 11.—**CLIX**, 1, 69; **XIII**, 21, 253; **CLXXXII**, 3, 312-320; **XXXVIII** s.v. *Legis actio*.
[3] G., 4, 12; D., 1, 2-6.—**CXI**, 1, 407-408.

ADMINISTRATION OF JUSTICE   61

beware of saying *vites*, even if vines were in question, when the word *arbores* was written in the statute—a verbal formalism that is common to all primitive legislations;[1] (ii.) the presence of the parties, since the statutory process did not allow either judgment by default or representation at law, except in a few very rare cases;[2] though there is some doubt about the antiquity of the *cognitor*, i.e. judicial mandatory, and the extent of his capacity after this period;[3] (iii.) the necessity to take action on a *dies fastus* ; (iv.) the presence of the magistrate, although, since the parties conducted their own case within the lines laid down by the statute, this impartial magistrate could no more depart from these in granting or refusing an action than he could divert the litigants from the result to which they were brought by their correct or clumsy employment of the necessary formalities. He then ascertained and pronounced the Law.[4]

Pignoris capio, however, being merely the taking of a pledge, required neither the intervention of the magistrate, nor a *dies fastus*, nor even the presence of the distrainee; and Gaius says that, on these grounds, there was some hesitation whether to regard it as a statutory process. It might have been left among the other extrajudicial procedures which custom hedged about with strict formalities: e.g. search *lance licioque*, conducted by the person robbed carrying a dish and wearing a girdle; report of *nova opera*, etc. Perhaps it was reckoned among the statutory processes after the Law of the Twelve Tables because it was only allowed in cases authorized thereby.

Even after the passing of this Law the art of adapting the methods of procedure to the various legal requirements was not known to all, and every year the college of pontiffs appointed one of its members to guide the litigants in this matter. Probably in the long run this led to definition of the procedure which had to be followed in each class of case. A canon was drawn up and published by Cn. Flavius, a sort of style-book called the *Jus Flavianum*, and then, as the kinds of litigation became more complicated, it was necessary later

---

[1] D., 47, 7, 1.—CLIX, 1, 15, 38, 59.
[2] *Pro populo, pro libertate, pro tutela, ex lege Hostilia:* CXI, 1^2, 138; CCXXXI, 1, 284; CLXXVII.
[3] G., 4, 29, 82, 87; D., 50, 17, 122-pr.—CLIX, 1, 70, 192; CXLII, 91.
[4] G., 4, 29.—CLIX, 1, 42 et seq., 69 et seq.

on to publish an enlarged edition, which was probably the *Jus Ælianum*.¹

II. JUDICIAL ORGANIZATION AND THE DISTINCTION BETWEEN " JUS " AND " JUDICIUM "

The office of presiding at a statutory process and pronouncing the Law, i.e. civil jurisdiction, originally belonged to the king alone and then to the consuls. In 388 A.U.C. it devolved upon a new magistrate, the prætor, who at first had to be a patrician, this being a means of reserving for the *populus romanus* the largest possible share in the administration of Justice, though only for a time, because later on this magistracy too became open to the plebs. In 512 A.U.C. it was divided, and besides the city prætor, competent in cases between citizens alone, an alien prætor was appointed who was at first competent in cases between aliens only, and afterwards in cases between aliens and citizens. We must also note the jurisdiction of the curule ædiles, which was of uncertain date and limited to certain civil matters. At a very early date the city prætor had delegates in Italy, the *præfecti jure dicundo*, who disappeared after the extension of the right of citizenship to the Italians.²

In the provinces governors and quæstors took the place of prætors and ædiles, and the governors might have legates to hold their assizes in civil suits.³

At first the procedure was conducted from beginning to end in the presence of the king;⁴ but from an early date the statutory process was divided, when its object was the verification of a claim, into procedure *in jure* and procedure *in judicio*. The magistrate contented himself with organizing the process and sent the parties before a judge whose duty it was to decide the dispute. This has been ascribed to a reaction against the absolute authority of the king and a partial reestablishment of the primitive right to choose one's own judge.⁵ Originally there was always one judge alone, and after the Law of the Twelve Tables there continued to be one only in all suits, *lites*, which admitted of solution by a

¹ D., 1, 2, 2-7.—**CCCV**.   ² **CLX**, 1, 211, 396.
³ D., 1, 2, 2-16, 27-28.—**CLIX**, 1, 218, 295.   ⁴ Cf. **CLVIII**, 1044.
⁵ Cic., *de Rep.*, 5, 2; *pro Cluent.*, 43; Dion. Hal., 4, 25; 38, 10.—**CXI**, 1, 4, 79; **CXI**, 1², 134; **LXXVII**, 8, 234; **CCCII**, 1, 249.

ADMINISTRATION OF JUSTICE

bare affirmative or negative; but disputes, *jurgia*, involving the verification or establishment of a situation of fact, which required a more elastic power of decision, were decided by one judge or by several.[1] *Recuperatores* varying in number were appointed to decide suits between aliens or between citizens and aliens.[2] There were also permanent tribunals—*decemviri stlitibus judicandis, centumviri*—only known from Rome's seventh century, whose origin and history is still a matter of dispute and of whose competence we shall speak in due course.[3]

Failing selection beforehand by the parties, the judges were chosen from a list of senators whose names were proposed one after the other by the plaintiff until one was accepted by the defendant. If the latter refused to accept any of them, he rendered himself *indefensus*. Later on, this system was replaced by the drawing of lots combined with the right to a certain number of challenges. The *recuperatores* were also chosen by lot from lists whose methods of composition are unknown. Members of the permanent tribunals were chosen by the comitia. The centumvirs were originally three for each tribe (505), but under Trajan their number was increased to 180 and they formed several chambers presided over by a *prætor hastarius*, so called because of the spear, *hasta*, which was set before the tribunal.[4]

This divided procedure bore the name of *ordo judiciorum privatorum*, being thus distinguished not only from the *judicia publica* properly so called,[5] but also from all suits, whatever their origin, in which the whole process was conducted before the magistrate, these latter being called *judicia extraordinaria, cognitiones extraordinariæ*.[6]

III. THE "LEGIS ACTIONES" INVOLVING VERIFICATION OF A CLAIM

The statutory processes involving verification of a claim were the *actio sacramenti*, an old adaptation of custom in

---

[1] Cic., *pro Rosc.*, 4, 11; *pro Mur.*, 12, 27.—**CCCII**, 1, 31; **XXXVIII**, s.v. *jurgium*.
[2] Festus, s.v. *Reciperatio*.—**XXXIII**, s.v. *Recuperatores*.
[3] **CLIX**, 1, 4, 83, 159; **CLVIII**, 1057, 1; **XIII**, 29, 577 et seq.; **XXXIII**, 29, 170; **XLVII**, 1, 147.
[4] Festus, s.v. *Centumviralia judicia*; G., 4, 16, 31.
[5] **CXI**, 1, 403, 484.
[6] *Ibid.*

which all the violent deeds of private justice had been reduced to an expressive but harmless mimicry, the *judicis postulatio*, connected by the jurists with the Twelve Tables, and the *legis actio per condictionem*, created by the Silian and Calpurnian Laws.

The first was adapted for all suits, though the corrupt manuscript of the *Institutes* of Gaius only reveals its employment for the recovery of movable property, *actio sacramenti in rem*. It has been conjectured that the *actio in personam*, by which a claim was maintained, was not very different from it.[1]

For the *actio sacramenti* the Law of the Twelve Tables adopted a customary method of summons. Any person met outside his house (which was inviolable) who disobeyed the order *in jus te voco* without a lawful excuse was seized in the presence of witnesses and carried before the magistrate,[2] unless he found a *vindex* or surety who guaranteed his appearance on the stated day.[3] If there was an adjournment or the case was not finished on that day, the defendant had to furnish fresh sureties called *vades* before he was allowed to go free.[4]

Both parties being present, the procedure *in jure* was conducted before the judicial magistrate in the manner of a pantomime in which each party, armed with a rod (*festuca*), seized the object in dispute to tear it away from the other and asserted his right of ownership. This was the contest (*manuum conjectio, vis festucaria*). If a piece of land was involved, this mock contest originally had to take place on the disputed ground, for, in the time of private justice, the conflict ended in the violent ejection of the occupier; but in course of time it sufficed for the magistrate to arrange a sham conveyance to the spot, or else a clod of earth or a tile represented the field or the immovable, and the litigants joined battle over it. Then the magistrate, like the voluntary arbitrator of earlier days and as if the disturbance of order in the city could alone justify his intervention, invited them to let go and explain matters. In a calmer tone, the party who had brought the

---

[1] G., 4, 13, 15, 16.—**CLX**, 1, 476 et seq.; **CXCI**, 49 et seq., **XXXVIII**, s.v *Sacramentum*.
[2] XII T., 1, 1, 2, 3, 4; D., 2, 4, 18, 20, 22; Festus, s.v. *Portum*.
[3] **XXXIII**, 24, 279; 26, 285, 295; **XIII**, 14, 601.
[4] G., 4, 184.—**CLIX**, 1, 73; **CL**, 10 et seq.; **XIII**, 34, 521 et seq.

ADMINISTRATION OF JUSTICE 65

action asked the other why he opposed his claim, and the defendant had either to admit its validity, thus establishing his adversary's right by his admission (*confessio*) and opening the way for him to make execution, or else to assert his own right in a counter-claim which placed the litigants on an equal footing and regularized the situation. Public authority had to be constrained by some means to decide between them, and each litigant had to estimate the other's degree of conviction in his claim.

The *sacramentum*, which served both these purposes, was a sort of wager whereby each party in turn pledged himself to pay a considerable stake, which the Law of the Twelve Tables fixed at 50 or 500 asses according as the subject of dispute was worth less or more than 1000 asses,[1] if the claim which he made under oath was found to be contrary to the truth. It involved on the part of one if not of both parties an act of perjury liable to bring down the vengeance of the gods upon the religious community to which they belonged. Thus it was the magistrate's office to discover either personally or through his agents which was the guilty party, in order to impose upon him an expiatory sacrifice formerly consisting of the cattle handed over to the pontiffs, which, in the days before the use of money, had constituted the stakes.[2] In this roundabout way the case was brought to an end. It was known who had falsely affirmed his right to the thing in dispute, and the stage of execution had been arrived at, unless the judge had declared both *sacramenta injusta* and found both litigants guilty of perjury.

After the separation of *jus* from *judicium*, the task of deciding which party had made a false oath and wager was entrusted to the judge. The magistrate henceforward only presided over the agreement between the parties as regards the choice of the judge and the nature of the question to be submitted to him, and occasionally over the grant of interim possession of the object in dispute to one of the parties, who had to guarantee its restitution and that of its fruits by sureties which on this occasion were termed *prædes litis et vindiciarum*.[3] As the litigants called the persons present to

[1] G.,4,16,17; Aul. Gel.,20-10; Festus,s.v. *Sacramentum;* Varro, *de L.l.*,5,180.
[2] **CXX**, 51-221; **CXLII**, 218; **CLIX**, 40, 55, 84; **CXCI**, 20; **CXCVI**, 1, 14-33.
[3] D., 1, 2, 2-24; Festus, s.v. *Vindiciæ*.—**CLIX**, 1, 740; **CXI**, 1², 88; **CCLXXXVIII**.

witness all this, this decisive moment in the procedure was termed *litis contestatio*. By a solemn engagement (*vadimonium*) they bound themselves reciprocally to appear before the judge on the appointed day.[1] At an uncertain date, when the process had become secularized and no longer involved either oath or expiation, a *Lex Pinaria* postponed the nomination of the judge until 30 days after the judicial contract entered into between the litigants. The payment of the stake, now a mere penalty imposed on the rash litigant, was no longer made in the temple but was postponed until the conclusion of the case and guaranteed by sureties.[2]

We know nothing of the procedure before the magistrate in the two other statutory processes, except that the *judicis postulatio*, which some believe to be a simplification of the *actio sacramenti*, though it may have originated in a different conception, involved, as its name implies, an application to the magistrate by one of the litigants to nominate a judge or arbitrator according to the nature of the suit.[3] With its formalities similarly curtailed, the *legis actio per conditionem*, which was framed as a means of recovering the money debts of the *Lex Silia* or the definite and certain things, other than money, referred to in the *Lex Calpurnia*, began with a requisition made by the plaintiff on the defendant to appear to have a judge appointed on the expiry of 30 days. Gaius says that it merely doubled the previous procedures. It had disappeared before the end of the Republic.[4]

All had this character in common: viz. that when once completed, they made a new suit impossible between the same persons concerning the same right; whence the rule *bis de eadem re ne sit actio*, two actions may not be brought concerning the same dispute.[5]

As regards the appearance before the judge, the essential rules were laid down by the Twelve Tables. On the third day after his appointment, having taken an oath to judge in accordance with the statutes, he had to repair to the *comitium* or the *forum*, and the parties were required to appear

[1] G., 4, 108; Festus, s.v. *Contestari litem, Superstites*.—CXII, 699, 717, 989; CCCI, 69-79; XIII, 32, 529.
[2] G., 4, 13-15; Festus, s.v. *Res comperendinata*.—CLIX, 87, 178; CL, 27 et seq.
[3] G., 4, 17; Val. Prob., 4, 8; Cic., *de Orat.*, 1, 36.—CLX, 1, 127; XLIII, 319; XXXIII, 2, 145; 25, 54 et seq.
[4] G., 4, 17a, 20, 33; Fest., s.v. *Condicere*.—CLIX, 1, 87; CXCI, 59 et seq.
[5] CXII, 397, 885, 892.

ADMINISTRATION OF JUSTICE

before him before mid-day, failure of one of them to appear by that time, without legal excuse, causing the suit to be adjudged in favour of the other.[1] When both had appeared, they made a brief statement of their claims, and then followed the pleading and the marshalling of evidence. It is remarkable that Roman Law never had any theory concerning the nature of evidence, so that none was either preferred or excluded. At the conclusion of the pleading, except when the suit could not be ended before sunset, which involved adjournment, the judge (or the tribunal) pronounced his sentence, the reply to the question which had been put to him. That exhausted his powers, since, being merely a private individual without interest in the dispute, he had neither the right nor the means to execute his judgment. It was the successful litigant's task to bring that about, and he had not always a direct means of doing so. In real actions his only means, unless he was interim possessor, may have been his recourse against his adversary's sureties; but it does not appear that anything could prevent the magistrate, to whom he reported the judge's sentence, from lending him the support of public authority in compelling the loser to carry it out.[2]

IV. The "Legis Actiones" Modes of Execution or Coercion

Two other statutory processes, modes of execution or of coercion, were of the type that is common, except for a few details, to all rudimentary societies, and recall, within the framework of a rigid technique, the most violent deeds of the old private prosecution, when each individual enforced his own rights or at least endeavoured to compel his adversary to make terms or accept arbitration. Their utilization was now limited to cases strictly defined by statute.[3]

Manus injectio was the violent seizure of the debtor by the creditor in order to take vengeance on him or compel him to right a wrong. In the days of unrestricted private justice there was nothing to prevent a man, if he was the stronger,

---

[1] XII T., 1, 7, 8, 9; G., 4, 5; Fest., s.v. *Insons, Status dies*; D., 2, 11, 2, 3; 50, 16, 254-pr.—CLIX, 1, 88, 103.
[2] LXXVII, 122; LX, 1-2, 149; CXCI, 1, 20; CCXXX, 1, 30; CXII, 909.
[3] CXXIV, 108-112; CLXXXII, 1, 251-260; 3, 323.

from doing this to anyone; but in a State that is organized or beginning to be organized custom or statute prohibits this act of violence except in cases of undoubted debt and with the permission or at least under the control of the judicial authority. This was the system of the Twelve Tables which allowed it only against the *damnatus* and the *judicatus*, i.e. against the man who owed a sum of money either in consequence of a *damnatio* (a word originally meaning an order to pay under the threat of a magic or religious sanction) pronounced by statute, by a judge or by a private individual, or else in consequence of the establishment of the debt in court as a result of the judge's decision or the debtor's admission.[1] At first this was not the effect of every judicial sentence. The sentences of the kings and afterwards of the consuls or other judicial magistrates very soon acquired, if they did not always possess, the force of final judgments. Cicero explains that the king was requested to pronounce the Law and that, when he had done so, his sentence was equivalent to a statute;[2] but this does not seem to have been the case at first with the sentences of judges or arbitrators. At all events, since the power of execution depended on the certainty and the liquidation of the debt, if the second of these conditions was not brought about by the sentence, there was an opportunity of realizing it, before execution, by means of the procedure called *arbitrium litis œstimandœ*, which involved assessment by an arbitrator of the value of the award or *judicatum*.[3] Compulsory execution then followed; but it might also result from other acts. If in classical Law the final judgment was the type of legal certitude to which other kinds were assimilated, it had not always been so. The condemned debtor to whom the Twelve Tables allowed 30 days in which to make his submission was not the first debtor liable to *manus injectio* : we shall find others who had preceded him.

The picturesque archaism of this procedure should be noted. Declaring in a loud voice the value and the cause of the debt, the creditor seized the debtor by the throat and dragged him then and there into the magistrate's presence in order to get permission to keep him in private confinement at first and

---

[1] Val. Prob., 4, 10; *Lex Acilia repetundarum*, 1, 58 et seq.; T.-G., 41.—**CXII**, 808, 846, 850.
[2] Cic., *de Rep.*, 5, 2; Liv., 1, 40; Dion. Hal., 2, 56; 4, 25.
[3] **CXI**, 1, 142.

ADMINISTRATION OF JUSTICE

to dispose of him later. When this permission had been obtained, he was bound within the following 60 days to bring forward the debtor at three consecutive markets in order to proclaim the amount of the debt there. The conditions of this detention were meticulously prescribed by statute. From the actual moment of arrest until the expiry of this period of respite, the debtor could be saved from the consequences of compulsory execution either by payment of his debt or by the intervention of a solvent third party, called in the circumstances a *vindex*, who disputed the existence of the debt and the legality of the arrest. This intervention, which is explained by the bonds of family, clan and patronage, gave the debtor his freedom; but if it was wrongly made, it constituted an offence which exposed the *vindex* to a penalty of twice the original debt. Failing payment or a *vindex*, the debtor was handed over by the magistrate to the creditor, who could sell him to a foreigner as a slave or kill him. If he had several creditors, they were authorized to cut him up among them.[1] The meaning of *partes secanto* has been disputed; but as there is no doubt that he could be killed or sold, it was surely necessary for the creditors to divide among themselves in the first case his body and in the second his price. Nothing could be more agreeable to primitive Law; and analogous solutions were admitted by the customs of other peoples, in particular by Scandinavian customs. Such was the law; but there was room for compromise, and thanks to this the great majority of debtors escaped death and slavery, and remained in the work-shops of their creditors until their labour had discharged their debts.[2] In course of time these severities were abated. The *Lex Pœtelia Papiria* (428 A.U.C.) abolished the right of death or sale; and new cases of *manus injectio* introduced by various statutes no longer required the appearance of a *vindex* as defendant: the presumed debtor could himself dispute the legality of the violence done to him. This was *manus injectio pura*. A *Lex Vallia* of the sixth or seventh century A.U.C. made this type of procedure applicable in all cases except two: those of *manus injectio judicati* and *depensi causa* ; the first when executed against a judgment debtor, the second when executed by a surety against the debtor for whom

[1] XII T., 3, 5, 6; cf. the Fragments of Autun, 4, 81 et seq.; T. G., 366 et seq.—**CXI**, 1², 143.
[2] Quintil., *Inst. orat.*, 5, 10, 60; 7, 3; G., 4, 44.

he had paid. The *Lex Coloniæ Genetivæ Juliæ* gives us a description of *manus injectio judicati* in its final form.¹

Pignoris capio corresponded to the private distress of movables that was practised in all primitive legislations as a mode of coercion or reprisal. In the Roman texts not only is it disallowed except in a limited number of cases prescribed by custom or statute, but its employment, which was reserved in principle to the public authority, is almost confined to the spheres of administrative or religious Law, and is not granted to private individuals except by delegation from the State.² Most legislations have limited its use betimes by bringing it under the control of the public authority. The Roman State abolished it altogether.

III

THE FORMULAR PROCEDURE

I. THE APPEARANCE OF THE FORMULAS. THE ÆBUTIAN AND JULIAN LAWS. JUDICIAL ORGANIZATION

Gaius says that the formalism of the statutory processes, which involved many cases of formal invalidity, had made these methods of procedure detested.³ No doubt other causes helped to bring about their disuse, and the increasing complexity of legal relations required more flexible processes which the magistrate could adapt to meet new needs. Hence the invention of the formulas.

Both the time and the manner of their first introduction is disputed. Many conjectures have been made in the attempt to find a precedent for the *Lex Æbutia*. Was it the practice of the Prætor Peregrinus in suits between aliens and citizens,⁴ although statutory processes could be brought before him; the already increased activity of the Prætor Urbanus in the nomination of judges in *judicis postulatio* and *condictio*;⁵ the imitation of foreign models;⁶ or a last stage in the evolu-

---

¹ G., 4, 22-25; *Lex Col. Gen. Jul.*, 61; T. G., 91.—**XXXIII**, 22. 144.
² G., 4, 26-29, 32; Aul. Gel., 6, 10; *Sc. de pago Montano*: T. G., 150.—**CLIX**, 1, 142; **CI**, 34-78; **CXXIV**, 108-115. ³ G., 4, 30.
⁴ *Lex Alicia* (631), 1, 28, 58-60; T. G., 91 et seq.—**CXI**, 1, 284; **CCXLII**, 1, 42; **CLX**, 1, 116, 3; 121, 1.
⁵ **CCXXIV**, 573; **XXXIII**, 30, 426; **XLIII**, 319.
⁶ **CLVIII**, 1053 et seq.; **CV**, 22; **CCL**; **XXXIII**, 26, 530; **XXXVIII**, s.v. *Ord. judic.*

ADMINISTRATION OF JUSTICE 71

tion of statutory processes, when the conditions of the judicial contract were fixed in writing at the moment when the proceedings *in jure* terminated ?[1] It seems that their first employment must have been by the Prætor Peregrinus, since the statutory processes were only exceptionally allowed in favour of aliens, and the *recuperatores* must in most cases have received exact instructions as regards the conditions of the treaty which conferred the right of *reciperatio*. Perhaps the Prætor Urbanus adopted a similar method in the case of processes intrusted to an arbitrator, since it would be an advantage to give him full details of the program which he would have to carry out or of the problem submitted to him. But Gaius and Aulus Gellius ascribe the origin of the reform to the *Lex Æbutia* alone, which was afterwards supplemented by two *Leges Juliæ* ascribed to Augustus. The result is that some Romanists suppose this *Lex Æbutia*, between 605 and 628 A.U.C., to have authorized formular procedure between citizens for the first time, while others suppose that it merely extended its application to every class of suit, in particular to those which were submitted to a single judge and were termed *lites*.[2] As a matter of fact the Agrarian Law of 643 A.U.C. and the *Lex Rubria* of 702 show the system in full use, and Cicero reckons among the rights consecrated by their antiquity those which were conferred by the edict. But the *Lex Æbutia* did not abolish the statutory processes: at first the litigants had the choice between the two methods of procedure,[3] and history provides other examples of this parallelism. The litigants' right of choice gave the magistrate a more active part to play, for by authorizing the chosen procedure he must of necessity refuse them the alternative, and his directions must often have influenced their choice.

Towards the end, apparently, of the year 737 A.U.C. a *Lex Julia judiciorum privatorum* introduced some important amendments. It finally abolished the statutory processes, except in actions against the owners of dangerous buildings (*damnum infectum*) and suits brought before the centumvirs,

---

[1] **LXX**, 2-1, 216.
[2] Aul. Gel., 16, 19, 1; G., 4, 30.—**CLIX**, 1, 195; **CLX**, 1, 67 et seq.; **CXII**, 851; **CCXXXVI**, 28, 583. A new theory, published by Nap, dates the *Lex Æbutia* as late as 64 or 63 B.C., and assumes that it merely brought into general use the formular system already established in the case of money debts by the *Lex Valeria* (86) and the *Lex Cornelia* (87): **XIV**, 2, 447.
[3] **LXVII**, 1, 89; **CCCII**, 1, 62, 85, 103; **XXXVIII**, s.v. *Lex Æbutia*; **XIII**, 29, 16.

or again in cases where their forms were adopted by voluntary jurisdiction (enfranchisement, adoption, etc.).[1] Further, it contained certain regulations concerning the *album judicum* or list of judges, their capacity and grounds of exemption and those of the *recuperatores*, as well as concerning adjournment or dimittal of causes; and it fixed the pendency of *judicia legitima* at 18 months.[2]

The new procedure maintained the distinction between *jus* and *judicium*; and the prætors, both urban and peregrin, as well as occasionally the ædiles, continued to preside over the former. Under the Empire a series of prætors appeared with limited jurisdiction: the *prætor hastarius* who directed procedure before the centumvirs, the *prætor de liberalibus causis* and the *prætor fideicommissarius* who were competent in questions of freedom and of testamentary trusts, etc. Hadrian placed the greater part of Italy under the jurisdiction of four legates, *consulares per omnem Italiam judices;* and afterwards Marcus Aurelius confined the jurisdiction of the urban prætor to the *urbica diœcesis*, i.e. to the precincts of Rome, and divided the rest of Italy between the *juridici*, important magistrates who to some extent usurped the jurisdiction of the municipal duumvirs or quatuorvirs. Finally jurisdiction at Rome passed to the Prefect of the City, while in the provinces where the formular procedure had been introduced it remained with the governors and their legates; but it is doubtful whether this procedure was ever used in the imperial provinces.[3]

Procedure *in judicio* was always at Rome intrusted to judges, and the privilege of providing them was a matter of dispute between the senators and the knights. We know of the conflict between the two orders in the seventh century concerning the exclusive or divided right (*Lex Aurelia*, 684 A.U.C.) of constituting the lists of these *judices selecti* that were drawn up by the prætor. At some time or other the *tribuni ærarii* and certain persons of note were associated with them in this privilege. Under the Empire, when they were drawn up by the Emperor, these lists were still further increased in the interests of democracy and comprised first

---
[1] G., 4, 30, 31; D., 39, 3, 11-3; 4, 1, 14-1.—**XXXIII**, 33, 295 et seq.
[2] G., 4, 104.—**XXXIII**, 33, 367 et seq. For *judicia legitima* see p. 76.
[3] *L. agraria* (643), 1. 37-39; T. G., 53.—**CCXXXVIII**, 1^1, 320; 6^2, 463; **XXXIII**, 2, 36 et seq.; **CXXV**, 258 et seq.

ADMINISTRATION OF JUSTICE 73

4, then 5 decuries, the last being recruited from citizens whose wealth only amounted to half the equestrian census. In the provinces they were drawn up either by the Emperor or by the governor.[1] The *recuperatores*, generally 11 in number, were also chosen by lot from a list drawn up in some way that is now unknown, and each litigant had the right of making four challenges. As regards the permanent tribunals, the *Lex Julia* probably introduced the decemvirs *stlitibus judicandis* into the tribunal of centumvirs with the right of summoning its meetings.[2]

II. Summons and Representation at Law

The method of summons (*in jus vocatio*) was a little complicated. The plaintiff had to give his opponent notice of the kind of action which he proposed to bring against him (*editio actionis*).[3] If the defendant neither obeyed the summons nor provided a *vindex* or surety, he could be compelled to appear by force or by means of a penal action, granted by the prætorian Edict, which was equally available against the man who wrongfully opposed arrest.[4] Contumacy or default, which made it impossible to continue the suit at law, was penalized by giving the plaintiff a right of entry on the defendant's property.[5] But apart from these complications, the parties were free to guarantee their appearance by means of a solemn engagement called *vadimonium*, whose voluntary usage finally replaced the old form of summons, which was deemed brutal. This engagement, reinforced sometimes by sureties, sometimes by an oath, was sanctioned by a penalty equal in principle to the sum in dispute.[6] Perhaps summons by writ, which was then authorized by the magistrate, was used in certain cases from the classical period onwards.[7]

Procedure, at any rate before the magistrate, still required the presence of the parties; but thanks to a transposition of names in the formula, the mechanism of which will be explained later on, a sort of representation at law was arrived

[1] I, 12, 4333.   [2] **CCXXII**, 278.
[3] G., 4, 46, 183; D., 2, 4, 2, 6; Val. Max., 2, 1; Ed.-P. 1, 168.
[4] D., 2, 4, 19, 21. **XXXIII**, 25, 232.   [5] D., 2, 4, 7, 1.
[6] G., 4, 184-187; D., 2, 8, 15, 16; 11, 2, 3; 5, 1, 2, 6; Aul. Gel., 6, 1.—**LXX**, 2-1, 225; **CL**, 104 et seq.; **XXII**, 1910, 143.
[7] **XXIV**, 1896, 152; **LXXXIII**, 20 et seq.

at, first by a *cognitor*, a mandatory appointed by a set form of words in the presence of the other party, and then by a *procurator*, a mandatory appointed without any formality and even without the opponent's knowledge, who could only act as an agent. The consequences of the sentence (rights or obligations) were binding on the *cognitor*,[1] so that his solvency had to be guaranteed to the adverse party (*cautio judicatum solvi*); and this naturally led to the requirement that he should cede his rights, especially the *actio judicati*, a means of procedure against the condemned defendant who failed to satisfy the judgment, which was granted to his principal unless the controvertible right had been transferred to him personally.[2] The employment of a *procurator* became common in the first and second centuries of the Empire. When representing the plaintiff, he had to guarantee the defendant beforehand against the non-ratification by his principal of the issue of the suit (*cautio de rato*), and by way of compensation he was not required to cede his *actio judicati* to the latter until after this ratification had been made. When representing the defendant, he was bound to meet this *actio* and had no power, if he was only an agent, to compel his principal to take his place.[3] The differences between these two kinds of judicial mandatories were due to the latter's uncertain position in relation to his principal. Even when the representatives' position was certain and statutory, as in the case of a guardian, a curator, a syndic of an artificial person, a *procurator* appointed by a person present who declared him to be such, the jurisprudence of the second century under the influence of oriental practices regarded them all in the same way. Antoninus Pius enacted that execution of the sentence should be granted directly to the ward or against the ward for whom the guardian had pleaded; and this was afterwards extended, under the Severi, to all *procuratores* whose mandate was certain. Henceforward they were exempted from giving security[4] and the *cognitor* disappeared.

[1] G., 4, 83-84, 97-98; *Fr. vat.*, 317-325; P.-L., 734.
[2] G., 4, 101; *Fr. vat.*, 317, 331.
[3] G., 4, 98, 99, 101; *Fr. vat.*, 331, 332.
[4] D., 26, 7, 2-pr., 23; C. J., 2, 12, 10; *Fr. Vat.*, 331, 332.—**CXLIV; CCXCVI,** 28 et seq.

III. THE PROCEDURE "IN JURE"

Here we have no more symbolical gestures, no more set forms of words, but an immediate statement by the plaintiff of the action he wishes to bring and a request to the magistrate to authorize it (*editio* and *postulatio actionis*.)[1] Based upon the Civil Law or the edict, the actions were enumerated and their formulas were stated in the album where the edict was written and exposed to public view. There one made one's choice;[2] but at first the magistrate seems to have gone so far as to improvise formulas for particular cases that had not been anticipated, this being the probable origin of the actions *in factum*, i.e. with an issue of fact.[3]

The parties stated their case with the magistrate's guidance and could modify their claims so long as they were before him.[4] The magistrate and the plaintiff had the right of questioning the defendant on facts capable of influencing the authorization or the nature of the action, and in such cases his answer was final, just as the consequences of his silence were definitely fixed.[5] In certain cases the edict authorized the plaintiff to proffer an oath to the defendant concerning the truth of his claims, and the latter must then, under penalty of losing the case, in some cases either take it or throw it back on the plaintiff, in others take it without alternative.[6] Otherwise, when the plaintiff's claims were decisive, the defendant either acknowledged them to be well-founded or failed to make the defence required of him by law; and he was then held to be *judicatus*, i.e. in the position of a judgment debtor—immediately, if the object of the suit was a clear and definite sum of money; after an *arbitrium litis æstimandæ*, if it was not[7]—as we have seen was already the case in the time of the statutory processes. He might, however, make a defence by denying his adversary's right (*defensio*) or by opposing to it a rival and counteractive right (*exceptio*).

[1] Cic., *pro Cæc.*, 3; *in Verr.*, 2-3.—**CCXCV**, 117 et seq.; **XXVII**, 22, 253-259.
[2] Cic., *pro Rosc. com.*, 8; G., 4, 104-106.
[3] D., 19, 5, 1-pr.—**XXXIII**, 13, 202.
[4] D., 11, 1, 11-1-4; 22, 3, 18-2; Ed.-P., 1, 164, 180.—**CCXCV**, 127-130.
[5] D., 11, 1, 1-6, 9-pr., 20-pr., 21-2, 22-4; C. J., 4, 31-11.—Ed.-P., 1, 163.—**XXXVIII**, s.v. *Interrogat. in jure*.
[6] D., 12, 2, 1-3, 5-10, 14, 17-pr.; 9, 4, 21-2, 22-4, 25-1; C. J., 4, 1-9.—**CXXIX**, 57 et seq.; **XXXVIII**, s.v. *jusjurandum*; **XIII**, 32, 125, 344, 437.
[7] Paul, 2, 1-5; 5, 5a; 2-5; D., 42, 1, 56; 2, 1, 3, 4, 6-pr., -1; 50, 17, 52; C. J., 6, 31, 4; Ed.-P., 2, 144-149.—**CLVII**, 225; **XIII**, 29, 171, 449.

It was at this point that the magistrate who, from the beginning of the procedure, could have stopped it either on the ground of the parties' incapacity or of the improbability of their claims, declared whether he would authorize or refuse the action. He refused it if it could not lead to a more complete result than that already attained, if the defendant availed himself of a certain and peremptory *exceptio*, if the edict contained no formula corresponding to the plaintiff's claims, or if the parties refused to comply with certain conditions imposed upon them by statute or by the edict, e.g. to give security for satisfaction of judgment.[1]

If he authorized it, the appointment of the judge and the drawing up of the formula, to which he then proceeded, constituted the terms of the judicial contract by which the parties pledged themselves to accept the judge's sentence, and one of the original characteristics of procedure was thus perpetuated. It continued to be contractual; there was *lis incohata, judicium acceptum*.[2] The formula delivered by the magistrate was the written instrument of this contract, and no change could be made in it by the contracting parties without another sovereign intervention on the magistrate's part. Their agreement to go before a judge nominated therein, in order to have the content of this formula verified, was always the critical moment of the *litis contestatio* which, although it retained this title, no longer required the presence of witnesses. The use of writing supplied their place.

The process before the judge, the *judicium* thus organized, was termed *judicium legitimum* when both litigants were Roman citizens and there was one judge only, and it had to be litigated in Rome or within the first milestone from the city. In all other cases it was termed *judicium imperio continens*. The first was not limited in time until the *Lex Julia judiciorum privatorum*, which caused the suit to lapse for non-prosecution at the end of 18 months; the second, which derived its validity from the sovereign decision of the magistrate, only retained it until the end of his term of office.[3]

The judicial contract substituted for the original right,

[1] G., 4, 88, 89, 91, 102.—**XXXII**, 4, 383 et seq.; **XIV**, 1925. 467 et seq.; **XXXIII**, 16, 1, 137; 24, 197, 344; **LXX**, 2-1, 295-300.
[2] D., 2, 13, 1-1; 9, 4, 22-4; 15, 1, 3, 11; 45, 1, 83-1.—**CCXCV**, 123; **XIII**, 26, 543; **XXIV**, 17, 149-190; **XXXIII**, 15, 189.
[3] G., 4, 103-109; cf. 1, 183; 3, 83; Ulp., 11, 24, 27; *Fr. vat.*, 47.—**XXXIII**, 12, 267; **CXI**, 1, 757; **CXXXVIII**, 29.

ADMINISTRATION OF JUSTICE

which had served as basis for the prosecution, a new obligation: viz. to submit to the judge's sentence, according to strict law in the first kind of *judicia*, by means of an *exceptio* in the second. This extinction of the original right, which alone justified the action, placed an obstacle in the way of its renewal. This new obligation to submit to the sentence was clearly binding on all persons present who had made the judicial contract, therefore, in some cases, on the *cognitor* and the *procurator*; and at the moment when this contract was made, the judge had to take his seat in order to estimate the amount of the condemnation. But the *litis contestatio* allowed interest to run on, cancelled neither *mora* nor mortgage, and did not interrupt usucapion: it merely operated as if the sovereign magistrate had required the plaintiff to abdicate all his subjective claims in exchange for the support of public authority, and to rely upon objective Law whose ascertainment and declaration had been intrusted by the State to the judge.[1]

IV. THE COMPOSITION OF THE FORMULAS AND THE CLASSIFICATION OF THE ACTIONS

The drawing up of the formulas was a delicate task, and the conception of this mechanism was one of the most original discoveries of the Roman legal genius. Throughout the period of the edict's creative activity it dominated procedure and the whole body of Law, since through these formulas the laws were methodically classified and received the forms best adapted to the various types of case that could arise. To a careless observer they would seem to be mere accessories, but in fact they were essential: an ever available machine enabled by its series of interchangeable parts to give shape to the innumerable matters which, in accordance with the requirements of social life, must be endowed with legal force and form.

They were all entered in the album of the prætorian Edict, those based upon the Civil Law (*actiones juris civilis*) without any addition, the rest (*actiones honorariæ*) preceded by the edict which authorized them and proclaimed their conditions.

---

[1] G., 3, 180, 181; 4, 107; *Fr. vat.*, 263; D., 45, 1, 83-1; 46, 2, 29; 50, 17, 39-pr.—**CCCI**; **XXXIII**, 31, 371; **XXIV**, 21, 139.

The latter were sometimes an extension of the former, under the name of *actiones utiles*, to cases where the Civil Law did not permit their use; and occasionally, in order to grant them, the edict assumed the fulfilment of a condition imposed by the Civil Law when in point of fact it had not been fulfilled, in which case they were termed *actiones ficticiæ*.[1] Sometimes they were devised by the prætor to meet new circumstances or interests and to secure the triumph of equity, when they had an issue of fact and were distinguished by the title of actions *in factum conceptæ* from all the rest, which were *in jus conceptæ*.[2] The actions of the Civil Law were permanently available; but many *actiones honorariæ* lapsed within one year from the day on which they could have been brought, sometimes in a shorter period.[3]

It was not necessary for all the regulations contained in the formula to be used in every suit, and when they were all used, they were not always applied in the same way. Hence there was very great variety and many different categories of actions.

The appointment of judge, arbitrator or *recuperatores* was stated at the beginning. Then followed a series of propositions with technical names—*demonstratio, intentio, adjudicatio, condemnatio*—and, as accessories, *præscriptiones, exceptiones,* replications, duplications.[4]

The *demonstratio* announced the cause of the dispute by its technical name or by a description of the fact which gave rise to the suit.[5] It was only used in uncertain personal actions.

The *intentio*, the essential part of the formula, set forth the plaintiff's claim in the form of a question to be decided by the judge. Most of the distinctions between different kinds of actions were derived from the content of the *intentio*.[6] It revealed the nature of the object in dispute, which led to the division of all suits into personal actions, by which one claimed to be the creditor of some person whose name was in principle stated in the *intentio*,[7] and real actions, in which

---

[1] G., 3, 219; 4, 34-38; D., 4, 5, 2-1; 9, 2, 11-10.—**LXXXV**.
[2] G., 4, 45-47, 110-112; D., 19, 5, 1-1, 2, 3, 11.—**XIII**, 24, 260; **XVII**, 20, 527; **XXXIII**, 19, 261; 23, 445; 16, 7; 20, 99; **XIV**, 1925, 183 et seq.
[3] G., 4, 110-111; D., 44, 33, 1; I. J., 4, 2-pr.   [4] G., 4, 39-44.
[5] G. 4, 40, 46.—**XLIV**, 1, 58 et seq.
[6] G., 4, 41.—**CXI**, 2, 736; **XLIV**, 1, 35-65; **CXCV**, 2, 1332.
[7] Also called *condictiones* : G , 4, 5, 18; Ed.-P., 1, 270.—**CVLIII**, 644-647.

both parties claimed the same right over a thing. They were and have continued to be mutually exclusive, because as a general rule one cannot claim to be at once owner and creditor in respect of the same thing.[1]

On the *intentio* also depended a group of actions called *in rem scriptæ*, because they were the means of establishing an absolute right against all other legal persons, which involved the absence of the defendant's name. These were the real actions, certain personal actions in which the person of the debtor was not determined absolutely but depended on circumstances,[2] actions of prætorian origin devised to establish a legal situation concerning persons or things without drawing immediate consequences therefrom, and *actiones præjudiciales* or *præjudicia*, whose formula was generally limited to the *intentio*.[3]

Personal actions were termed *certæ*, certain, when the *intentio* showed that the plaintiff laid claim to a determinate thing, a definite sum of money or a number of objects whose quality was determined, and *incertæ* when the value of the object in dispute had to be assessed by the judge. Real actions were *certæ*, except claims to a share in a thing to be apportioned by the judge.[4] This was an important classification, because in *actiones certæ* a claim for more than was due (*plus petitio*) involved the loss of the suit,[5] whereas this was impossible in the other actions, in which it was the judge's office to say what was due. It was also by the *intentio* that the claim was shown to have been brought into court, so that it could not be the ground for a second action. If less than was due had been claimed, the surplus was not lost, but a new action could not be brought to obtain it until the expiry of the term of office of the prætor who had granted the first.[6]

From the time of Q. Mucius Scaevola and of Cicero there was a class of actions distinguished by the words *ex bona fide* inscribed in their *intentio* and called for that reason *judicia*

---

[1] G.,4, 1-5; D., 44, 7, 25-pr.; 50, 16, 178-2; I. J., 4, 6-1; Ed.-P., 1, 220.—**XXVII**, 30, 322.
[2] G., 4, 44; D., 4, 2, 9-8; 10, 5-pr.; 39, 3-12; 43, 24, 5, 13.—**XL**, s.v. *Azioni in rem scriptæ*.
[3] G, 3, 123; 4, 44; Paul, 5, 9-1; I. J., 4, 6-13.—**XXXVIII**, s.v. *Præjudicium;* **CLVIII**, 1081; **CXII**, 856.
[4] G., 4, 41, 43; D., 10, 1, 10; 2, 2, 3; 3, 2-1; D., 5, 4, 1-5; 45, 1, 74, 75-pr.-7; G., 4, 37, 60.
[5] G., 4, 53-53d. [6] G., 4, 56.

80 FORMATION OF CLASSICAL LAW

ex bona fide—personal actions of Civil Law *in jus conceptæ*. The lists of them given by Cicero, Gaius and Justinian are slightly discrepant.[1] They were opposed to actions of strict law, *judicia juris stricti*, in which the judge was bound by the letter of the formula, because in these actions *bonæ fidei* he estimated the amount due on his own authority, took account of the acts or omissions of the parties, and had power to acquit the defendant or soften the condemnation.[2]

The *adjudicatio*, which Gaius places next in the formula for actions for division of property and regulation of boundaries, was merely the original *intentio* of actions for division and was only occasionally used in actions concerning boundaries. It gave the judge power to assign ownership or another real right to one of the litigants.[3]

The *condemnatio* contained, strictly speaking, the *munus judicandi*, the authority to judge, i.e. to condemn or acquit, according as the *intentio* has been found true or false. One of the most curious characteristics of the formular procedure was that every condemnation was reckoned in money. If the subject of dispute was a determinate thing or a prestation in kind, the judge condemned the loser to pay its estimated value:[4] a proceeding which after all had much in its favour, for it had the advantage of immediately fixing the amount of the damages due in case of non-performance, without the need for recourse to a second suit, and of putting all adversaries of the same judgment debtor on an equal footing, whatever the nature of their claim, by reducing all claims to a common denomination. The drawback to it was that no one received what he wanted; but this drawback was diminished in two ways—by the discretionary actions, and by the late-established rule that all actions involve free power of absolution, *omnia judicia sunt absolutoria*. Suits were also distinguished by the Romans in different categories according to the structure of the *condemnatio*.

Discretionary actions were those, whether real or personal, in which a clause made the judge's power to condemn conditional upon the defendant's failure to provide the satisfaction (restitutions, exhibitions, etc.) which the judge had decided

[1] G., 4, 61-63, 114; I. J., 4, 6, 28-30.—**XXXIII**, 11, 165; **XXVII**, 24, 55.
[2] D., 8, 5, 3; 45, 1, 53, 119, 121.—**XXIV**, 16, 244, 255.
[3] G., 4, 42; I. J., 4, 41, 44; Ed.-P., 1, 236-241.—**XIII**, 28, 275; **XLII**, 1, 32.
[4] G., 4, 48.

ADMINISTRATION OF JUSTICE 81

to be due to the plaintiff and had ordered him to hand over.[1] As a matter of fact it was to the defendant's interest to obey, for otherwise he exposed himself to a very heavy condemnation assessed by the plaintiff himself on oath, which sometimes involved *infamia* or payment of fourfold damages, etc.[2] In course of time it was admitted that the defendant could in all actions, either spontaneously or on the judge's invitation, offer to satisfy the claims of the plaintiff in kind, so long as final judgment had not been passed. The Proculians opposed this admission in actions of strict law, but the opposite opinion of the Sabinians finally won the day.[3]

The result of the condemnation was either the reparation of a wrong (*actiones rei persequendæ gratia*), or the recovery of a penalty which could be once, twice, thrice or four times the value of the object in dispute (penal actions), or both these things together (mixed actions).[4] Actions of the first kind, and of the last in so far as their character was reparative, continued to lie against the debtor's heirs after his death and were not merged into one in the case of concurrent actions or of joint-debtors.[5] The opposite was the case with the penal actions and the mixed actions in so far as their condemnation was a penalty: they lapsed at the death of the debtor, if they had not already been brought into court, and also by simple agreement. Often they were restricted to one year; but change of civil status (*capitis deminutio*) had no effect upon them. Some, whose special object was to satisfy the anger of the person outraged (*vindictam spirantes*), also lapsed at his death and could not be transmitted by him.[6]

The condemnation was called certain (*condemnatio certa*) when the formula fixed its amount, uncertain (*incerta*) when the judge was authorized by the formula to assess the amount without limitation, and uncertain in a restricted sense (*incerta cum taxatione*) when he was directed to make an assessment not exceeding a maximum stated in the formula.[7] Even when *incerta*, it imposed a criterion on the judge which was some-

---

[1] The clause was: "Nisi arbitratu tuo restituetur, exhibeatur...condemna."
[2] G., 4, 163; I.J., 4, 6, 31; Ed.-P., 2, 740.—**XXXIII**, 24, 238; **XLIV**, 2, 151; **CLVIII**, 1084.
[3] G., 4, 114; I. J., 4, 12, 2.—**LXI**, 94.
[4] G., 4, 6-9; I. J., 4, 6, 16; 12, 1.
[5] D., 2, 10, 1, 4; but cf. D., 4, 7, 4-6, 5-7.—**CLVIII**, 416; **XXXIII**, 32, 313.
[6] G., 4, 112; Paul, 1, 19, 2; D., 25, 6, 1-3; Cic., *ad fam.*, 7, 22; D., 2, 4, 24; 9, 3-5, 5. **CCXCIX**, 2, 530.
[7] G., 4, 43, 49-52.

82 FORMATION OF CLASSICAL LAW

times the intrinsic value of the thing in dispute (*quanti ea res est*), sometimes the value of its possession to the plaintiff (*quod interest*)—two ideas which were not for a long time separated by legal analysis[1]—sometimes, in a small group of penal actions of prætorian origin, a sum to be equitably determined in accordance with the nature and circumstances of the case (*quod æquius melius erit*), these last actions being termed *actiones in bonum et æquum conceptæ*.[2]

Such were the original components of the formula, those into which the new procedure had condensed the rough and ready methods of its predecessor; but more were added. In order to avoid mistakes on the part of the judge, the ancient formalism required that in each suit a single very simple question should be submitted to him. The defendant could dispute the plaintiff's claims but could not avail himself of a rival right or of a fact that made them fraudulent. In order to do so, he had to bring another action. The clarity and stability of the written formulas made it possible to do this in the original action.[3]

Originally the prætor allowed a demurrer or *præscriptio* to be entered in the formula after the appointment of the judge, first in favour of the plaintiff, then of the defendant; and its solution by the judge involved either a total or partial reservation of the former's claim, contrary to the principle that the same dispute could not be the subject of two actions,[4] or the total or partial acquittal of the latter,[5] or the determination of the quality in which one of the parties should plead,[6] or the preliminary verification of some assertion made by one of them:[7] all matters which must of necessity affect the judge's answer to the question contained in the *intentio*.

After a time the prætor transposed the demurrers in favour of the defendant and the *intentio*, which they tended to weaken and which ought logically to be proved first; and the defendant then proved his statements after it. A maxim which has continued in use until our own time summed up this obligation: *reus in exceptione actor fit*, the name of exception (*exceptio*) having been given to this additional part

---

[1] D., 47, 8, 2, 13; 50, 16, 179, 193.
[2] Cic., *Top.*, 17; D., 11, 7, 14, 6; Ed.-P., 1, 188, 194; 2, 21, 132.—**XIII**, 25, 541-564; **CCXIX**, 210 et seq.
[3] G., 4, 108.—**XXXVIII**, s.v. *Præscriptio*. [4] G., 4, 130, 133.
[5] D., 5, 3, 52; 45, 1, 76-1; G., 4, 133-137. [6] G., 4, 134-137.
[7] D., 22, 3, 18-2.—**XIII**, 11, 427, 447.

ADMINISTRATION OF JUSTICE

of the formula. The plaintiff could meet it with a replication, which was sometimes answered by a rejoinder, etc.[1] It is a matter of dispute whether a well-founded exception always led to the defendant's acquittal or in certain cases left the judge free to reduce the condemnation.[2] The number of exceptions was limited, and each had a very restricted field, the widest being that of *exceptio doli*. All had their origin in the edict, even if some were inspired by the Civil Law or suggested by the Senate or the Emperor.[3] Based upon an original flaw in the claim or upon a subsequent fact, some of them were dilatory, others peremptory, some prompted by the facts of the case, others by the quality of the persons (*rei* or *personæ cohærentes*).[4] They had to be alleged before the magistrate under penalty of exclusion, with the following exceptions: (i.) in actions *bonæ fidei*, the *exceptio doli* and a few others; (ii.) some which had been established in order to secure respect for certain statutes or senatusconsulta and could be alleged at any point in the proceedings; (iii.) the peremptory exceptions, which were available even after the delivery of the formula, but only by way of *restitutio in integrum*, i.e. by decree of the sovereign magistrate.[5]

V. The Procedure "In Judicio" and the Effects of the Sentence

The procedure before the judge remained public and oral, and failure of one of the parties to appear always involved his loss of the suit.[6] After the pleading, the proofs furnished by the litigants (testimonials, written evidence, presumptions, oaths tendered or offered, avowal, etc.)[7] were arranged in order and weighed by the judge alone[8] who, if he could not arrive at a decision, was allowed to swear that the case was not clear to him (*sibi litem non liquere*).[9] This occurrence and some others affecting the person of the judge (death, legal impediment, incapacity, loss of status) or of the litigants (death,

---

[1] G., 4, 107, 116, 126, 133; *Fr. vat.*, 259.
[2] D., 44, 1, 22; 16, 1, 17-2.—**CLVIII**, 1096-1; **CCLII**, 2¹, 261; **LIV**, 67 et seq.
[3] I. J., 4, 3, 17.   [4] *Fr. vat.*, 266; D., 14, 6, 11; I. J., 4, 14, 4.
[5] G., 4, 120-125; I. J., 4, 13, 8-11.
[6] **CCLVIII**, 28, 35, 134; **XXXIII**, 93, 160.
[7] C. J., 4, 20: the witnesses did not take an oath: D., 4, 2, 23-pr.; 22, 4, 5.—
CXI, 2, 759; **CXCIX**, 63-70; **XIII**, 30, 500; 32, 135 et seq.; **XXX**, 14, 238.
[8] **XXIV**, 12, 400; **CCLII**, 2¹, 240; 3¹, 264.   [9] Aul. Gel., 14, 2

change of state or of *procurator*) made it necessary to return to the magistrate in order to get the formula altered (*translatio judicii*).¹

While basing it upon the formula, the judge had to draw up his sentence in conformity with the statutes and the principles of Law, under pain of making the suit his own and becoming responsible for the damages caused.² It was no more than a reply to the question raised in the *intentio*, and it was modelled on the *condemnatio*, whatever mistake, whether flagrant or trivial, might have been made by the magistrate or the parties. The formula was the judge's law.³ The most dangerous mistakes were those of *plus* and *minus petitio*, i.e. claim by the plaintiff of more or less than his due. If he claimed too much, or made his execution at another time or in another place or manner than had been determined, he received a negative reply and so lost the action without possibility of reopening it.⁴ If he claimed too little, the judge was obliged to condemn his opponent only in the amount of his claim, and the balance could not be recovered by a new action until the next magistrate entered upon office.⁵ Mistakes made in the condemnation bound the judges as well. All these difficulties were avoided by asking the magistrate for a *formula incerta* and leaving the judge to assess the amount due. A mistake in the *demonstratio* left matters as they were and did not prevent the reopening of the suit, since the *demonstratio* was at first framed in regard to a legal act or a fact that was not the true ground of action.⁶

The sentence pronounced by the judge or by the majority of the *recuperatores* was often made heavier by accessory penalties: the amount of the *sponsio pœnalis*, by the undertaking to pay a fine in case of loss of the action,⁷ by ignominy,⁸ or, in certain actions, by duplication of the damages in case of false denial (*infitiatio*).⁹ On the other hand the plaintiff who lost his suit might incur them himself as the result of a special action (*judicium calumniœ* or *contrarium*).¹⁰

---

[1] D., 5, 1, 18-pr.; 32, 46, 57, 60.—**XXXIII**, 26, 524; 32, 459.
[2] D., 50, 13, 6; I. J., 4, 5, pr., 1.
[3] Cic., *in Verr.*, 2, 2, 12; G., 4, 52-60; Paul, 1, 10; *Fr. vat.*, 53.
[4] D., 21, 1, 43-9; I. J , 4, 6, 33.   [5] G., 4, 56, 122; Ed.-P , 1, 142
[6] G., 4, 58-60.—**LXX**, 2-2, 183, 186.
[7] G., 4, 171-181.   [8] G., 4, 182; D., 3, 2, 1
[9] G., 4, 171; Paul, 1, 19-1.—**XIII**, 27, 579 et seq. Cf. **XXXIII**, 22, 114.
[10] G., 4, 171-180.

ADMINISTRATION OF JUSTICE 85

The sentence, pronounced by the judges in a loud voice, put an end to their authority and had two immediate effects. In the first place it made the existence or non-existence of the controvertible right a matter of certainty, final judgment being held to be true.[1] A suit could not be reopened. After the distinction of *jus* from *judicium* the interdiction against reopening the suit had been made part of the judicial contract which terminated the proceedings before the magistrate. It was forbidden by strict law in personal actions, if the *judicium* was *legitimum*, and by way of exception (*exceptio rei in judicium deductæ*) in all other cases.[2] In course of time jurisprudence evolved a broader principle—that of the final judgment sanctioned by the *exceptio rei judicatæ* which, besides reopening the action, did away with the scandal and trouble caused by contradictory legal decisions.[3] The respective spheres of these two principles (which some confound together)[4] and the origin and cause of the second are matters of dispute. Some Romanists think that, from the time of Gaius, the two exceptions were combined and became one only,[5] being distinguished by name according as they were invoked before or after the sentence;[6] others believe that they were always distinct.[7]

A more subtle doctrine deprived the final judgment of the absolute character which it always had in the time of the kings and may have retained in the sentences of the magistrates. It was no longer recognized as valid except in regard to the parties in the case,[8] and afterwards its application was extended to cover not only the same action, but the same subject of dispute (*eadem res*).[9] It required identity of question, i.e. a plaintiff claiming a satisfaction already obtained or judged not to be due to him,[10] and identity of legal persons.[11] The absolute authority of the final judgment was maintained however in suits concerning personal status and family rights.[12] Moreover there were cases in which, after having been tried over with the principal party concerned,

---

[1] **CLIX**, 1, 42; **XLIII**, 242 et seq.; **CCXXX**, 134.
[2] D., 44, 2, 9-1, 17; 20, 1, 16-5.   [3] D., 44, 2, 5, 6, 7-4-5.
[4] Ed.-P., 2, 254 et seq.—**LXX**, 2-2, 66-4; **CXXX**, 1, no. 162; **CXLI**, 111.
[5] Arg. G., 3, 181; 4, 106, 107, 121.   [6] Arg., *Fr. d'Autun*, 110.
[7] **CXLI**, 3 et seq.; **XXIV**, 21, 143.   [8] D., 42, 1, 63; C. J., 7, 56, 2.
[9] D., 44, 2, 5, 12, 13, 14-pr. **XXXIII**, 29, 378; 30, 6.
[10] D., 44, 2, 3, 14-3, 81.   [11] D., 44, 2, 3; 11, 10
[12] **XLIII**, 242; **XLIV**, 1, 350

e.g. the heir, the process was acquired by a whole group, e.g. by all the beneficiaries under the will.¹

In the second place the sentence once more transformed the plaintiff's claim which had already been changed after a fashion by the judicial contract at the *litis contestatio*, the object of the new claim being the amount of the condemnation (*judicatum*).² But although assessed in money, a certain and liquid debt, the condemnation was not equivalent to a writ of execution. It created an obligation sanctioned, like all the rest, by an action, the *actio judicati;* and in case of non-performance, it was necessary to request the magistrate to grant this action.³

VI. THE MODES OF EXECUTION

But the magistrate did not grant it unless the debtor undertook to guarantee the payment of a new condemnation (*cautio judicatum solvi*). Moreover, in case of false denial (*infitiatio*) by the defendant, this condemnation was twice the amount of the first.⁴ As a result of these two conditions the defendant in most cases admitted his debt (*confessio certi*) or made no defence (*indefensio*), so that there was no ground for granting a formula and the magistrate pronounced a decree of execution.

In the formular procedure there were two modes of execution, one against the body of the debtor and the other against his property.

In the first the defendant, arrested by the magistrate's authority, was kept in private confinement by the creditor until he had paid his debt or compensated for it by his work.⁵ This was a normal proceeding until the time of the Emperor Zeno, who forbade private prisons. But the surrender of property (*bonorum cessio*) was very soon admitted, which gave the debtor, together with the *beneficium competentiæ*, a means of escaping imprisonment and ignominy.⁶

After the *Lex Æbutia*, perhaps about the year 636, the prætor organized an execution against property: at first for cases in which it was impossible to execute against the body of the debtor, and then for any case in which the plaintiff

---

[1] D., 30, 50, 1.   [2] G., 3, 180.
[3] **CXLI**, 125 et seq.; **CCXCV**; cf. **LXVII**, 2, 200 et seq.
[4] **CCXCV**, 27 et seq.; **XXVII**, 22, 242; 26, 258
[5] Quint., *Inst. Orat.*, 5, 10; 7, 3; Aul. Gel., 20-1; *Lex Rubria*, cc. 21-22:— T. G., 76; Ed.-P., 142 et seq.
[6] G., 3, 76; D., 42, 3, 1-7; *Lex Julia munic.*, 116-122: T. G., 87

chose to use it. This became the usual mode. It was a sale of the entire property of the debtor (*bonorum venditio*),[1] copied from that (*bonorum sectio*) which the State already practised in regard to its own, and it involved announcement by posters (*proscriptiones*) and sale by auction (*auctio*).[2] At the request of any one of the creditors, the prætor ordered a precautionary distress[3] in the interests of all, which they had to advertise publicly and follow by the appointment of a curator of the property:[4] then, in default of execution, confirmation of distress was granted at their request with a view to sale.[5] Thirty days after the public advertisement of the sale, if the debtor was alive, fifteen if he was dead—the advertisement involving ignominy and incapacity to appear in court as defendant[6]—a decree called upon the creditors to appoint a liquidator (*magister bonorum*), who drew up a schedule of the charges, caused extracts from it to be published,[7] and finally proceeded to sell the whole of the distressed property to the bidder who offered the largest dividend to the creditors.[8] This bidder (*bonorum emptor*) acquired prætorian ownership of the corporeal objects and, in order to guard his possession, the right to one of those means of defence called interdicts (*interdictum possessorium*).[9] Actions outstanding either for or against the debtor were made over to him *utilitatis causa*: if the debtor was living, by means of a transposition formula (*formula rutiliana*) where the name of the debtor inserted in the *intentio* was replaced by his own in the condemnation; if the debtor was dead, by a fiction of heredity (*formula serviana*).[10] The debtor could not be prosecuted anew for debts incurred before the sale, even after a return to prosperity, except within the measure of his means and after the delay of a year.[11]

Certain senatusconsulta substituted for the *bonorum venditio*, in the case of persons of high rank, a sale by lots (*bonorum distractio*) which the magistrate charged the curator of the property to carry on, after distress had been made, until the debts were met. The surplus was restored to the debtor.[12] This system was applied to persons incapable *sui juris*.[13]

[1] G., 3, 77-81; D., 7, 72, 1. [2] **CCXXXVIII**, 1, 203, 253; 4, 251.
[3] G., 3, 79; D., 41, 2, 10.—**CXCVI**, 115-140. [4] G., 3, 79.
[5] D., 42, 7; Ed.-P., 2, 175. [6] D., 42, 6, 1. [7] G., 3, 79.
[8] G., 3, 79; Ed.-P., 2, 163.—**XXI**, 72, 461. [9] G., 3, 80-81; 4, 145.
[10] G., 4, 35, 65, 68; Ed.-P., 2, 166, 173.—**CLX**, 1, 91.
[11] G., 155.—**CXI**, 2, 769. [12] D., 27, 10, 5. [13] **XXIV**, 11, 89.

IV

USE OF THE "IMPERIUM" IN PROCEDURE

I. USE OF THE "IMPERIUM" IN PROCEDURE

The magistrate came to use in the interests of his jurisdiction the sovereign powers which he held by right of *imperium*.

In order to guarantee certain situations without an action, to guard against apprehended damage, to insure the execution of interlocutory judgments, he ordered the parties, or one of them, to pledge themselves by a verbal contract to make the execution or compensate for the damage, should the circumstance arise. These were prætorian stipulations, either simple (*cautio*) or guaranteed by sureties (*satisdatio*), which he compelled them to make by the threat of distress or of refusal or authorization of actions, according to the nature of the case.[1]

On other occasions he granted one of the litigants, as a means of coercion, the right of entry on all or part of the other's property (*missiones in possessionem, in rem, in bona*), sometimes as a precautionary measure, sometimes with a view to the sale of the goods or the patrimony distressed; and he safeguarded the situation thus created either by actions *in factum* or by interdicts.[2]

Further, when custom and statute gave no help, he met the case by making ordinances (*decreta*) or issuing prohibitions (*interdicta*), a specific title that afterwards became general.[3] In civil matters the orders or prohibitions issued on the occasion of a dispute between two persons and at the request of one of them constituted the law in their case. Originally the prætor had secured the observance of his interdicts by means of coercion.[4] Under the formular procedure they were on principle inscribed in the edict, and their causes and conditions were defined.[5] If a litigant applied for one of them, the magistrate granted it in the presence of his opponent, whose failure to appear was equivalent to assent.[6] On the

---

[1] G., 4, 31, 99; D., 46, 5, 1-2; I. J., 8, 18; Ed.-P., 1, 52; 2, 265.
[2] D., 25, 5, 1-2; 36, 4, 5, 27; 42, 4, 217-1; 1, 43, 4, 3-pr.
[3] G., 4, 139-141. [4] CLVIII, 1127.
[5] Ed.-P., 2, 188-248. [6] D., 44, 29, 3-14.

ADMINISTRATION OF JUSTICE

other hand, if he disputed the plaintiff's right to avail himself of the interdict, there was ground for an action to verify it. In case of flagrant violation of the magistrate's order or prohibition, the procedure remained so complicated that classical Law tended to replace it by prætorian actions of the kind termed, for reasons stated above, *actiones in factum*. Gaius describes two forms of this procedure.[1] Interdicts in private Law were classified according to their objects as prohibitory, restitutory or exhibitory; and as double or simple according as the parties in the suit were both claimants or not. The best known group is that of possessory interdicts.[2]

More original and important was the magistrate's assumption of authority to cancel on the ground of their injustice certain normal effects of the statute or the Civil Law.[3] This was the full restoration of rights (*restitutio in integrum*). At first sight nothing would appear more arbitrary, and it was only resorted to in the absence of any other means of attaining the same end.[4] Moreover a special branch of jurisprudence was concerned with the occasions for and the conditions of these restitutions. By incorporating them in the edict, the prætor voluntarily limited his own powers; for instead of being decretal they became edictal and also restricted to one year of validity.[5] Paul gives six grounds for their employment: violence, fraud, *capitis deminutio*, pardonable error, necessary absence and minority.[6] Their effect was to restore to the beneficiary the right or advantages of which the rescinded act had deprived him, and to authorize him to bring the action which guaranteed his possession. It was either restitutory or rescisory.[7]

II. THE "COGNITIONES EXTRA ORDINEM"

The principle of separating *jus* from *judicium* was imperative,[8] but certain matters escaped it, i.e. those, increasing in number every day, for which there was no action. In the old times, when Rome was republican and aristocratic, many private or social relations had been governed exclusively by

---

[1] G., 4, 141, 161-170; Ed.-P., 2, 188-195.
[2] G., 4, 142-160; I. J., 4, 15.
[3] Paul, 1, 7.
[4] D., 4, 1, 3, 4, 16-pr.—**CXI**, 2. 763.
[5] Ed.-P., 1, 127.
[6] Paul, *l.c.;* D., 4, 4, 7-4, 29-1, 45-1; 42, 1, 33.
[7] D., 3, 3, 46-3; 4, 6, 26-5-6.
[8] **CLIX**, 1, 69-71.

90 FORMATION OF CLASSICAL LAW

what was called the usage of honest men; but with the advance of democracy which marked the end of the Republic and the beginning of the Empire they had to be defined and provided with legal sanctions. A more complex but proportionately less regulated state of society led to a more meticulous interference of public justice in relations which had once depended exclusively upon morals and opinion: e.g. in relations between ascendants and descendants (the obligation to provide dowries and alimony) or between masters and slaves, in the matter of fees for the liberal professions and of testamentary trusts,[1] etc., all of them matters on the verge of the *ordo judiciorum privatorum* over which the State found it desirable to exercise not merely control, but a freer and more flexible authority in the legal sphere. It then became possible to address plaints (*persecutiones*) to the magistrate, whose decision was final, and these were the *cognitiones extra ordinem*.[2] Not being closely connected, they were divided among the jurisdictions of several curule magistrates or high imperial officials; and in course of time, especially after the Severi, suits which had hitherto been a matter for ordinary procedure either could be or had to be brought before them (e.g. questions of status). This State control of justice seems to have been more quickly developed in the provinces, not, as some have said, because the governors insensibly perverted the formular system by combining for their own advantage *jus* and *judicium*, but because tradition here was less of an obstacle to the substitution of administrative forms for the old legal formalism of the sovereign City.[3] The magistrates could delegate their powers to inquisitors or mandatories (*judices dati*) from whom appeal lay to them.[4] Their judgments, termed *decreta*, condemned the defendant in the thing itself. The sanction took the form either of an *actio judicati* brought before them,[5] or of a direct and violent execution.[6] The taking of a pledge (*pignus ex causa judicati captum*) in accordance with regulations laid down by Marcus Aurelius seems to bear reference to these processes.[7]

[1] G., 2, 278; D., 50, 13, 1, 5. [2] **XXXIX**, 4, 206, 215.
[3] **LXXXIII**, 18. [4] D., 49, 1, 1-3, 3-3.—**CCXXXVIII**, 2, 944.
[5] **CCXCV**, 247 et seq. [6] Ed.-P., 2, 150, 187.—**CXLI**, 176.
[7] D., 42, 1, 31.—**CXI**, 2, 645; **CCXCV**, 228-247; **CXXXVI**; **LXXXIII**, 17-22.

V

THE WAYS OF RECOURSE

The sovereign authority of the magistrate and the private character of the judge, whose powers lapsed on the pronouncement of sentence, made very difficult (for opposite reasons) any way of recourse in the formular procedure against legal decisions.

Against the acts of the magistrate the parties could invoke the *par majorve potestas* of a magistrate of equal or superior rank, or the *auxilium* of the tribunes of the plebs, though the latter was only available in Rome. These interventions, which were very rare in practice, only suspended or annulled the act without substituting another in its place; moreover they were of no avail against the judge.[1]

Full restoration of rights could undoubtedly be requested of the magistrate against a judge's sentence as against any act that established an unjust situation; but the concrete cases that we find in the texts of the restitution of actions consumed by having been brought into court all refer to mistakes in the formula, never to the judge's sentence.[2]

In practice the defendant could, as a rule, only avail himself of the prohibitions or exceptions allegeable against the *actio judicati*, and the loser, whoever he was, of penal proceedings against the judge who had made the process his own.

But from the time of the Republic there was permitted, in the case of a *cognitio extraordinaria*, a kind of recourse described by the term *revocare in duplum*, which probably refers to the possibility of submitting again to the same judge, within a prescribed period, a question already judged by him, on the ground of the nullity or error of the first decision. The judge in virtue of his *imperium* either retracted, or condemned the applicant in a penalty of twice the value of the object in dispute.[3]

With the Empire the practice of appeal (*appellatio*) was introduced, in which some have seen the effect of the Emperor's tribunician power, others that of his right of control

---

[1] **CCXXXVII**, 1, 304 et seq.; **CCXCVIII**, 294.
[2] Ed.-P., 1, 136, 142.
[3] Paul, 5, 5a, 6a, 7, 8; C. Gr., X, 1, 1; cf. Ed.-P., 2, 186.—**CXI**, 2, 723; **CXLI**, 159 et seq.

92 FORMATION OF CLASSICAL LAW

over his legates.[1] Developed at first in the administrative sphere,[2] in regular gradation through the hierarchy of imperial agents, it remained foreign to the formular system.[3] It was open to both parties and was lodged by means of a request addressed, within a period of 3 to 5 days, to the first judge, who made a report on it to his superior (*litteræ dimissoriæ, libelli apostolici*).[4] It was accompanied by an undertaking to pay a penalty in case of failure and was suspensive, devolutive and reformatory.[5] It could be renewed from stage to stage as long as there existed a superior judge; but usually the Prætorian Prefect judged *vice principis* in the last resort.

[1] **CCXXXVIII**, 2, 265; 5, 267; **CXCV**, 1, 499.   [2] **CXXV**, 22 et seq.
[3] Cf. **CCLIII**.   [4] Paul, 5, 33, 34-1, 37-1.
[5] D., 49, 1, 3-3; 7, 1-pr., 1, 4-15, 11, 12.—**CCXXXVIII**, 5, 267 et seq.

CHAPTER III
THE LAW OF THE FAMILY AND ITS DEPENDENCIES

SECTION I
ORGANIZATION OF THE "DOMUS"

I
THE FAMILY GROUP

I. KINSHIP. THE FAMILY GROUP OR "DOMUS"

THE word *familia*, when it refers in the texts only to ties of blood, means sometimes the whole body of related persons, sometimes the family group properly so-called, the *domus*.

Civil kinship was exclusively agnate. According to the Civil Law, all descendants by the male line of a common ancestor were relatives, so that there was merely a difference of degree between *gentiles* and *adgnati*, though in the classical period this degree was not determined. Ulpian has preserved an ancient definition of agnation which only included those who had actually lived together under the power of the same *paterfamilias*.[1] That was how it was regarded in the *gens*, when the bond of a common clan extended relationship by the male line beyond the *domus*; but after the dissolution of the *gentes*, *adgnatio* meant relationship by the male line only in so far as the Law of the State recognized its effects, which was apparently in cases where it could be proved.[2] Moreover agnation could be fictitious and purely legal in cases of adrogation or adoption or marriage *cum manu*. The system lasted, with successive relaxations, until the time of Justinian.

These relaxations were to the advantage of cognate relationship which included of equal right kinsmen by the male and by the female line. At all times this had been recognized to have certain effects as an impediment to marriage, and

[1] D., 50, 16, 195-2. [2] T. G., 503.

for a long time the cognates had sat at the family tribunal, *tribunal propinquorum*. They were treated with favour by the statutes; and the prætorian, as afterwards the imperial, Law of Inheritance, the regulations concerning private assistance, and certain innovations in the internal economy of the family assured to them, especially under the Empire, a place of ever-increasing importance.[1]

To these two relationships, agnate and cognate, was applied our method of reckoning by lines and by degrees.[2] We derive it from Roman Law.

The family or *domus* was originally a group of persons and things over which a *paterfamilias* exercised authority. It included two sorts of persons: (i.) the *paterfamilias* who was alone *sui juris*, dependent on no one but himself; (ii.) the persons *alieni juris*, whether free or not, who were subject to his authority. Free persons were his wife *in manu*, his children and his other descendants by the male line; unfree were his slaves and the free persons sold to him, who were assimilated to slaves, termed *servi* and said to be his *in mancipio*.[3] Also included in the *familia* were the freedmen, over whom the head of the *domus* possessed *jura patronatus*, rights of patronage, which originally meant very strict subjection.

Like the *gens* out of which it sprang, the *domus* was a religious society. It had its cult and its festivals, *sacra privata*, over which the city pontiffs had only a right of supervision: a worship addressed to the *Di Penates*, protectors of the house, to the *Lar domesticus* or *familiaris*, sometimes identified with the founder of the line, to the *Di Manes*, spirits of ancestors and of other deceased members of the group (whence the common tomb), and finally to the Hearth where fire burned in the atrium. The *paterfamilias* was the priest of this cult and was responsible for the constant performance of its rites.[4]

The family was also a civil society. Its autonomous, monarchic constitution invested the *paterfamilias*, who was the domestic magistrate in virtue of a private right respected and guaranteed by statute, with absolute authority in his

---

[1] **CXI**, 2, 78-80.
[2] D., 38, 10, 10; Paul, 5, 11; T. G., 502.
[3] D., 50, 16, 195-2, 198; Festus, s.v. *Familia*.
[4] Cic., *de Leg.*, 3, 21.—**CCXXXVIII**, 12, 159, 173

THE LAW OF THE FAMILY

own house, whither the public authority did not penetrate.[1] His magistracy involved a judicial power shown by the judgments which he pronounced either alone or assisted by the *propinqui*, according to circumstances—judgments sanctioned by the penalties of exclusion from the *domus*, imprisonment, scourging or death;[2] and also an administrative power embodied in his decisions as magistrate and administrator, which were binding not only while he lived and ruled, but also during the period that followed his decease.[3]

The family had a common patrimony under the control of the *paterfamilias* and his descendants. He alone disposed of it and administered it with absolute freedom during his lifetime; and his right, though gradually controlled and somewhat restricted in this connection, was likewise shown in his dispositions in prospect of death.

II. "Patria Potestas" the Foundation of the "Domus." The "Paterfamilias"

The word *pater* did not suggest the idea of generation but that of protection and authority.[4] The *paterfamilias* was the citizen *sui juris*, i.e. dependent on himself alone, whatever his age might be and whether he was married or single, for he was the man who *in domo dominium habet*. Without him there was neither *familia* nor *domus;* but he without anyone else could constitute a *domus*. Over all the persons or goods that it could contain he possessed not a right, *jus*, derived from custom or statute, but a power, *potestas*, of which he alone was the source.[5] Originally this power over the whole of the *familia* had been summed up in the single word *manus;* but as a result of nascent legal analysis and above all of the need to distinguish between the different rights that were or were not guaranteed to him in various ways by the State, the term *manus* was restricted to mean his power over his wife. *Patria potestas* signified his power over the descendants by the male line, *potestas dominica* his ownership of the slaves, and *dominium* his ownership of the goods and chattels. *Mancipium*, though often used in a very general sense, meant in

[1] Cic., *pro domo*, 51. [2] Dion. Hal., 2, 25, 26; Val. Max., 5, 8; 6, 1.
[3] Cic., *de Orat.*, 1, 40; Suet., *Aug.*, 65.
[4] Bréal and Bailly, *Dict. étym.*, 351.
[5] Cic., *pro domo*, 29; Aul. Gel., 5, 19; D., 50, 16, 195-2.

particular the quasi-servitude of free persons sold to the *paterfamilias*, and *jura patronatus* were his rights over freedmen.

The nature of his authority over the persons *alieni juris* was indicated in their own names, that of the wife *in manu* being preceded by the husband's prænomen in the genitive case, and those of the others being supplemented by the title of son, daughter, slave or freedman of such and such a father, master or patron, who was described in their case also by his prænomen.

For a long time power over persons and power over things were considered to be of the same nature and the Law provided them both with the same sanctions. The *paterfamilias* could kill, mutilate or eject from his house the persons *alieni juris* just as he could break, destroy or abandon the things that belonged to him. He could sell them and, as late as Cicero's time, give them in pledge. Until the reign of Augustus a *filiusfamilias* could be stolen.[1] In primitive economy the power to dispose of persons *in potestate* was confounded with the real right over things, for both alike had a pecuniary value.[2] The same means of acquisition or alienation were used in each case, the same procedure to secure their recognition at law. The original sanction of the right of the *paterfamilias* over a free person *alieni juris* was an action for ownership (*vindicatio*), and it was only under the Empire when, as Ulpian says, suits of this kind came within the *notio prætoris*, that this was replaced by a *cognitio extraordinaria*.[3]

The head of the *domus* was so absolutely master of these persons that they were only members of the *domus* at his will and pleasure. He was responsible to his ancestors for the continuance of his line, and no legal check could restrict the means that he used to insure it. He composed his family in the way that seemed best to himself and assigned what place he pleased to the persons admitted into it; his power in this respect being increased when the old authority of the clan disappeared. This absolutism was confirmed by the city in its earliest days, since it saw therein the guarantee of its own greatness.[4]

---

[1] Cic., *pro Cæc.*, 34; *de Orat.*, 1, 40; G., 1, 134; 3, 199; Paul, 5, 11, 1; *Coll. leg. mos.*, 4, 18; Dion Cass., 2, 26-27; C. J., 7, 7, 16-1.
[2] **LXIX**, 175; **CXI**, 1, 171.
[3] G., 1, 134; D., 43, 30. 3-6.—**CLIX**, 37; **XIII** 21, 442.   [4] **CXXVI**, 6-11.

THE LAW OF THE FAMILY

This power was perpetual, whatever age the persons *alieni juris* might have reached, and was only extinguished by death or *capitis deminutio*, which struck the name of the *paterfamilias* off the list of citizens *sui juris*.[1] The effects of enslavement as prisoner of war were cancelled by return to Roman or Latin soil, since the *jus postliminii* restored all his rights to the captive as if he had never lost them. In the case of the person *alieni juris, potestas* could only be extinguished on the same grounds and subject to the same reservation; while, as regards dominical power and *dominium*, the effects were the same in the case of slaves or chattels which had been carried off by the enemy, as soon as they were brought back to Roman or allied territory.[2] Except in these circumstances, exclusion from the *familia* could only take place at the pleasure of its head.

But although this power was so great, it could not, when exercised within the city, for ever escape the city's control. A day came when the manner in which it might be used by the *paterfamilias* was subject to regulation by the censors; and with the growth of individualism certain restrictions, few at first but afterwards more serious, were imposed upon it by statute.

In the case of offences endangering the safety of the State or merely public order, the judicial authorities had from the earliest times a competence concurrent with that of the domestic judge. The power of the State could not be limited or kept in check by that of an individual citizen, and the guilty person could be removed from his family by sentence of the magistrate.[3]

In civil matters an ancient pontifical prescription had forbidden the sale of sons married *cum manu*. The Twelve Tables freed the son who had been sold three times in succession.[4] The Julian Law *de adulteriis* abolished the husband's power of life and death over his wife, while maintaining that of her father;[5] and the right of pledging children *in potestate* was suppressed.[6] Paternal power was restricted above all by the Emperors. Certain rescripts reduced the domestic jurisdiction to a right of chastisement; Trajan compelled a

[1] G., 1, 55.   [2] Paul, 3, 4a, 8; D., 24, 3, 10-pr.—**CXI**, 1, 573.
[3] Liv., 1, 26; 3, 13; 4, 29, 39; Aul. Gel., 11, 18; G., 3, 189; *Sc. de bacch.*: T. G., 129.   [4] G., 1, 132; Ulp., 10, 1.
[5] *Coll. leg. mos.*, 4, 2, 3; D., 48, 5, 22-1.   [6] Paul, 5, 2, 1.

father who maltreated his son to emancipate him; Hadrian condemned a father who killed his son to deportation, reserving to the State judges alone the power to pronounce capital sentences;[1] Caracalla forbade the sale of children except in cases of extreme poverty.[2]

The same limitations were gradually imposed upon the dominical power. Under Augustus the *Lex Petronia* forbade the exposure of slaves to the wild beasts of the arena without a magistrate's authorization. Claudius enfranchized sick slaves who had been abandoned. Masters who abused the right of chastisement were compelled to sell their slaves; and exercise of the power of life and death was made equivalent to murder.[3] The powers of the patron over his freedmen were also limited.

The *dominium* over things was strictly regulated; and the absolutism of the head of the *domus* was further affected by the legislation concerning inheritance, by the creation of *peculia* which constituted distinct patrimonies for certain persons *alieni juris,* and by certain protective guarantees of dowries, etc. But the gravest blow that it received was without doubt the disappearance of the ancient principle that he could compose his *domus* in accordance with his own wishes. The second century of the Christian era saw this essential rule of old Roman society give place to the modern system of the legal family.

II

MARRIAGE

I. THE MARRIED WOMAN, "UXOR." THE VARIOUS KINDS OF MARRIAGE. MARRIAGES "CUM" AND "SINE MANU"

Marriage insured the perpetuance of the family and of its *sacra privata.* Some of the *gentes* had forbidden celibacy; and in the city the censors sometimes reprimanded unmarried citizens, while certain statutes punished them with loss of privileges.[4]

In every period the Romans were monogamists. In order to secure the continuance of his line and his family cult, the

[1] D., 37, 12, 5; 48, 8, 2; 9, 5.
[2] G., 1, 117, 118; Paul, 5, 1, 1; C. J., 4, 43, 1; 7, 16, 1.
[3] G., 1, 53; D., 1, 6, 2. [4] Val. Max., 2, 9; Festus, s.v. *Uxorium.*

THE LAW OF THE FAMILY 99

paterfamilias acquired the right to take a woman and allot her as wife, *uxor quæsendorum liberorum causa*, with a view to offspring, either to himself or to one of the males placed under his paternal power. Among the *populus romanus* marriage was from the first conceived of as a sacred association involving community of all temporal and spiritual goods, consecrated (at least in certain cases) by the State religion, and in principle indissoluble. Among the plebs, although perhaps less sacred in character, it retained more resemblance to the old customs of the race. But the Twelve Tables held these unions to be equally valid and in conformity with the Civil Law, intitling them *justæ nuptiæ*.[1]

Such marriages required the *conubium* or *jus conubii*, i.e. the right of the parties to wed one another or, more generally speaking, the enjoyment of family rights. This right, which the members of the *gentes* had possessed, was recognized by the *Lex Canuleia* (311 A.U.C.) as belonging to all freeborn persons, whether members of the plebs or of the *populus*. Under Augustus the *Lex Julia* and the *Lex Papia Poppæa* recognized it between freeborn persons and freedmen, except in the case of senators and their descendants of either sex, who were forbidden marriage with freedmen and with some other persons of low condition.[2] Some cities enjoyed it as early as the fifth century;[3] and from that time onwards it was more freely bestowed, first in central Italy and afterwards further afield, by grants of the *jus civitatis cum* or *sine suffragio*. The emperors granted it to particular individuals, e.g. in the veteran's certificates.[4] In the absence of *conubium* the union of the spouses had no civil effect; but if they were aliens of the same city, it produced results according to the Law of that city. Between Romans and aliens it originally had no effect; but later on such unions were regarded as legal marriages, and opportunities were given for transforming them into *justæ nuptiæ*.[5]

Most peoples have used different forms of marriage simultaneously,[6] and the Romans recognized *justæ nuptiæ cum manu* and *justæ nuptiæ sine manu*.

By the former the woman entered the agnate family of her husband, being placed under his power or under that of his

[1] D., 23, 2, 1; I. J., 1, 9, 1   [2] Ulp., 5, 3, 4; G., 1, 67.
[3] Liv., 1, 26, 49.   [4] CCXXXVIII, 3, 550 et seq.; CV, 43 et seq.
[5] G., 1, 29-32, 67-71.   [6] CXXVI, 8-10.

paterfamilias. We know that the word *manus* did not connote any different kind of power from that which the head of the *domus* exercised over his descendants, and in this sort of union the woman was said to be *in loco filiæ mariti* and counted as such. The acquisition of this power over the woman with a view to marriage involved certain legal acts which have sometimes been wrongly confused with the marriage itself. They were however quite distinct from it. Gaius does not say that the marriage was realized by these acts, but only that the *manus* was acquired thereby. They were three in number: *usus*, *confarreatio* and *cœmptio*. The *manus* was always acquired by the *paterfamilias*, but the marriage was sometimes his own, sometimes that of a person *alieni juris*. *Coemptio* might have another end than marriage;[1] and, finally, a marriage contracted before the establishment of the *manus* involved its acquisition at the end of one year. It is generally allowed that in *confarreatio* the marriage and the transfer of power over the woman were accomplished simultaneously by means of the same formalities, but nothing could be more uncertain.

Confarreatio, an institution of the *populus*, was governed by the mystical relations that existed between *gentes* united in a single religious community. As nothing that concerned the internal life of each *gens* was a ground for State intervention, the ceremonies which it involved seem only to have been required at first when the marriage necessitated the transference of the woman from one *gens* to another. They severed the religious bonds between the future wife and her original clan, and gave her a share in the cult of the new one. In the presence of the Pontifex Maximus and the Flamen of Jupiter, with 10 witnesses who must be Roman citizens, the parties offered a sacrifice to Jupiter, in which a loaf made of spelt, *farreus panis*, was prominent, and accompanied it with ritual prayers. The woman could then be admitted to community of water and fire in the house of the *paterfamilias* under whose power she passed. This rite, which was less and less practised after the dissolution of the *gentes* and the passing of the *Lex Canuleia*, was still required under the Empire to enable a child of the marriage to become one of the major Flamens or *rex sacrificiorum*. Also the Flamen of Jupiter

---

[1] CXII, 158, 221

THE LAW OF THE FAMILY

was bound to have acquired the *manus* over the *flaminica* by this process, but Tiberius decided that she should no longer be under his power except for the *sacra*. By *confarreatio* the woman was indissolubly united to her husband's *domus* and cult, and could only be detached from it, under conditions that are obscure to us, by the opposite rite of *diffareatio*.[1]

Coemptio and *usus* carry us back to more ancient customs of humanity. Purchase and abduction were at first the simplest means of acquiring wives. *Coemptio* was purchase of the woman by way of *mancipatio*, an ancient type of sale. The father, who had the right to make profit out of his children, sold his daughter to whoever had need of her in order to procure descendants,[2] and in course of time the purchase became symbolical: one no longer bought the woman, but the power over her, which amounted to the same thing.[3] *Usus* was akin to the ancient practice of abduction by force, now adapted to suit a more civilized society in which possession was not transformed into rightful ownership until after the lapse of a certain period. The *manus* was acquired by undisturbed possession of the woman for one year. The Law of the Twelve Tables allowed it to be cancelled by the wife's absence from her husband's house on three consecutive nights other than the three last nights of the year. This was the *usurpatio trinoctii*.[4] *Coemptio* and *usus* were evidently practised by the plebeians who enjoyed the right of *commercium*. It is not known whether the patricians did in fact make use of them in early days, but in any case the Twelve Tables made them common to both orders.

There is some doubt about the origin and antiquity of the *justæ nuptiæ sine manu* which enabled the *paterfamilias* to obtain the children he desired without adding to his family the woman who consented to provide them or was handed over to him for this purpose. The principle that he composed his family as he liked explains this contrivance, which is very ancient.[5] With the growth of individualism there came a day when the old community of rights between spouses was felt to be a burden. The *usurpatio trinoctii*, the

---

[1] G., 1, 112, 113; Ulp., 9, 1; Tac., *An.*, 4, 16; Festus, s.v. *Diffareatio.*—I, 10 6002; **CCXXXVIII**, 12, 365; **XXI**, 57, 3; **CXCVI**, 1, 154; **CXCVII**.
[2] G., 1, 113; Servius, *ad Æn.*, 4, 103 —**LXXXVI**, 1, 50.
[3] G., 1, 14; *Col. leg. mos.*, 4, 2, 3-7-1.   [4] G., 1, 111; Aul. Gel. 3, 2.
[5] **XIII**, 11, 17 et seq.; **CXXVI**, 8 et seq.; cf. **CLVIII**, 161; **CV**, 16.

102 FORMATION OF CLASSICAL LAW

rule that *usus* could not procure the *manus* over a woman *sui juris* without the consent of her guardians, and the agreements made with the *patresfamilias* of the others caused the entry of the wife into her husband's family to become more and more rare.

It is true that *coemptio* was maintained, at least in theory, until after classical times; but the common practice was marriage *sine manu*. The woman then remained in her original family and in the pecuniary position which she had occupied before marriage, either *sui juris* or *in patria potestate*. In the latter case her father retained all his rights over her, and as he could legally exercise them to subvert the *de facto* position of the woman thus married, unions of this kind, which finally became the commonest, remained for a long time precarious. We can see how insecure the domestic hearth would then have been, if the *patria potestas* which was the cause of its disturbance from without had not been its solid foundation within. It was not until the reign of Antoninus Pius that a rescript showed disapproval of the wife's father separating the spouses against their will, the husband being provided with an *exceptio* against the interdict *de libera ducenda* on which the father relied to recover his daughter. Towards the end of the third century the interdicts *de uxore exhibenda, vel ducenda*, allowed the husband to recover his wife if the *paterfamilias* had regained possession of her without just grounds.[1]

When the *manus* had been acquired, the marriage could only take place at the pleasure of the head of the *domus*.[2] If he was to be the husband, the woman, being under his power, had only to obey him; if one of his descendants, obedience was due to him from both spouses. In the absence of *manus* its place was supplied by an agreement between the contracting parties—between the future spouses if they were *sui juris*, otherwise between their *patresfamilias*.[3]

But religion required the consummation of the marriage to be preceded by charming and picturesque ceremonies. A woman marrying for the first time proceeded to the joining of hands (*dexterarum junctio*), and a sow was sacrificed to

[1] Paul, 5, 6, 15; D., 43, 30, 1-5, 2; C. J., 5, 17, 5.—**VII**, 2, 237.
[2] For the betrothal that might precede the marriage see **CXII**, 155; **CV**, 51-55.
[3] Varro, *de R. r.*, 2, 4, 9; Plut., *Quest. rom.*, 80; Serv., *in Æn.*, 3, 136.

THE LAW OF THE FAMILY

the gods of generation and fertility. On the night itself three young persons whose fathers were still living simulated a rape and conducted the bride to her husband's dwelling (*deductio in domum*). The husband carried his wife into the house in order that her feet might not touch the threshold; and in the atrium she was presented with water and fire, and said: *Ubi tu Gaius ibi ego Gaia.* On the next morning she made a sacrifice to the Lar and the Penates. For a long time these religious ceremonies and some others, which were the same whether the union of the spouses took place *cum* or *sine manu*, were regarded by conscience and morality as the true marriage: a fact which explains the equal dignity of the wife in both cases. This has left its trace in the meaning attributed to the *deductio in domum* which some modern Romanists regard as a real element in the formation of the marriage,[1] although for the Jurists it was no more than one of the proofs. But the civil authority only took account of the decision of the *paterfamilias* which had given the bride this place in the *domus*. The religious rites were in its eyes of no more significance than the private cult, for in the domain of Law the will of the head of the *domus* sufficed.

Later on, when the Civil Law intervened in the forms of marriage, the Jurists gradually advanced from this idea to the late doctrine of Paul that marriage depended on the consent of the spouses and of their *patresfamilias*, this consent being alone sufficient. The Emperors defended the Roman idea that consent sufficed against oriental practice which recognized no marriage that had not been consummated.[2] A Roman woman could be a widow and virgin simultaneously; while, on the other hand, physical cohabitation did not imply marriage.

No official certificate was drawn up. As is generally the case where marriage is a mere matter of consent, proof of it could only be furnished by the avowal of the parties or by the ordinary means of written agreements or depositions. Sometimes the *instrumentum dotale*, the *tabulæ nuptiales* containing the financial agreements, the memory of the religious celebration were appealed to as evidence and served to distinguish marriage from concubinage.

[1] **CLVIII**, 162; **CCLXXXII**, 102; Paul, 2, 9, 8; D., 23, 2, 5.
[2] Ulp., 5, 2; D., 23, 2, 21; 35, 1, 15.

II. THE CONDITIONS OF A MARRIAGE'S VALIDITY

For a long time the conditions of a marriage's validity were fixed by the *paterfamilias*, subject to the authority of the *mores majorum* and, later, to the censor's supervision. The State did not intervene until the day came when, in this matter, families no longer followed of their own free will a course in conformity with its superior interests. Then the right of citizenship involved certain impediments of private import, while others of public import were imposed by various statutes—impediments that we should describe as nullifying, for legislation that required neither publicity nor the intervention of a public officer could hardly be called prohibitive. But breach of the rule forbidding a widow to remarry during the period of mourning for her husband involved only certain penalties and not the nullity of the marriage.

The only impediment that could be traced back to the oldest strata of custom was that of proximity in blood—in the direct line *ad infinitum*, in the collateral line first of all to the sixth degree, later to the fourth degree only, and finally, under the Empire, between relatives of whom one was parted by only a single degree from the common progenitor, though from the time of Claudius marriage was permitted between a paternal uncle and his niece.[1] Within these various limits cognate relationship (and this shows that we have here a matter of physiological prejudice) was an obstacle to marriage whether it resulted from *justæ nuptiæ*, from marriage according to the *jus gentium*, from concubinage, from *contubernium*, or from mere *stuprum*. Since all agnates were cognates, the impediment based upon kinship alone, whether civil or fictitious, held good in the collateral line as long as it lasted, and in the direct line even after it had ceased.[2] Relationship by marriage, *affinitas*, had the same effects, according to the doctrine of the Empire, in the direct line. Decency also forbade marriage between a father and his son's fiancée, a husband and his wife's daughter. Non-observance of the impediments due to kinship by blood or by marriage constituted the crime of incest, which was punished by the same penalties as adultery.[3]

[1] G., 1, 59-63; Liv., 42, 84; Tac., *An.*, 12, 6.—**XVII**, 3, 372.
[2] Cic., *pro Cluent.*, 12.   [3] G., 1, 63.—**XLIX**, 1, n°. 90.

THE LAW OF THE FAMILY

By fixing the age of presumed puberty (14 for boys, 12 for girls), the Civil Law limited the freedom of the *paterfamilias*, whose estimate in this matter had long been final. In vain did the Sabinians defend the ancient practice of recognizing only actual puberty against the Proculian doctrine of legal presumption.[1] No eunuch could contract a marriage.[2]

The consent of the spouses, which became the actual form of marriage, had to be supported by that of the male ascendants when the contracting parties were *in potestate*.[3] But the *Lex Julia de maritandis ordinibus* (736 A.U.C.) had already authorized the magistrate to exact the consent of the *paterfamilias* to the marriage of children *in potestate*, and sometimes to grant it in his place. Absence and captivity justified the spouses in dispensing with this consent, nor could the *jus postliminii* be invoked by the ascendant against the completed marriage.[4] In the case of persons *sui juris* who were less than 25 years old a constitution required that the father or mother or, in the case of their death, the next of kin should consent to undertake their protection.[5]

With a view to the reform of public morals the same *Lex Julia* created other impediments. Freeborn persons could not marry persons branded with *infamia* by their profession or by a condemnation; senators, their daughters and their descendants by the male line were forbidden to marry such persons and also to marry freedwomen or their daughters, promotion to senatorial rank dissolving a previous marriage with these persons.[6] Marriage was also forbidden between an adulteress and her paramour, a ravisher and the woman he had carried off.[7] Successive enactments prohibited marriage between guardians or their sons on the one hand and their wards on the other; between curators or their sons and the girls less than 25 years old who were under their charge; between high officials or their sons and the women of their provinces.[8]

The civil sanction of these prohibitions was the nullity of the marriage.[9] The disappearance of a temporary impediment regularized the union but had no retrospective

---

[1] G., 1, 196; Ulp., 11, 28; C. J., 5, 60, 3.—**XIII**, 24, 366.
[2] D., 23, 3, 39-1. [3] D., 23, 2, 2, 16-1; I. J., 1, 11, 7.
[4] D., 23, 2, 19; 49, 15, 13-3. [5] C. J., 5, 4, 1.
[6] Ulp., 13; 16, 2; D., 23, 2, 44. [7] D., 48, 5, 41-pr.
[8] D., 23, 2, 36, 38. [9] I. J., 1, 10, 12.

effects.[1] There were certain rescripts in favour of the woman who deemed herself to be a wife, but they never led to a theory of presumed marriage.[2]

III. THE POSITION OF THE WIFE IN THE "DOMUS" AND THE OBLIGATIONS OF MARRIAGE

Except for her position in regard to her husband's family, most of the effects of marriage were the same for the wife *in manu* and the wife married *sine manu*. Naturally enough the former had once taken her husband's gentile name, but later on she retained her own followed by that of her husband in the genitive case. This may have been the custom also for wives *sine manu*. Finally most of them kept their original family name.[3] At one time the plebeian woman and the freedwoman could not become patrician or freeborn by marriage; but under the Empire it was held, first in the case of senators' wives and then in all cases, that the woman acquired the rank of her husband.[4] By her marriage she either rose or sank in the social scale.

But we must not exaggerate the dependence of the wife *in manu* (*materfamilias, matrona, domina*), who was the equal of her husband within doors, directed the children's education and left the house to do business outside it, or on the other hand the freedom of the wife *sine manu*, on whom the same restrictions were imposed, since her home was that of her husband in consequence of the physical cohabitation to which she had given her consent. The Roman wife gained by the gradual advance of individualism. Family life gave her a dignity, a social importance, which the Greek wife soon lost when she was shut up in the women's apartments and left public life to the courtesan. It is true that a moral change was visible in the last centuries of the Republic; but the moralists and historians, who are given to noting only what is abnormal, have gravely exaggerated it. Not all wives gave occasion for the *Lex Julia de adulteriis* or dated the years by the names of their husbands.

The wife owed respect and fidelity to her husband, as he owed her protection and kindness,[5] and the sanctions of these

---
[1] D., 1, 5, 11.   [2] D., 23, 2, 57.
[3] **CCXXXVIII**, 6¹, 234; 14, 10.   [4] D., 1, 9, 1-1; C. J., 11, 1, 13.
[5] D., 24, 3, 14-1; 47, 10, 12.

THE LAW OF THE FAMILY

obligations were enforced whether she was or was not *in manu*. Before 763 A.U.C. only the wife's adultery was punished, on account of the confusion which it might introduce into the family tree and the family *sacra*. If the husband caught her in flagrant delict he was authorized to kill her; otherwise she was condemned to death or exile by him or by her own father at the tribunal of the *propinqui*. After the *Lex Julia* the adulterous husband could be sued for immediate restitution of the dowry; while, as regards the adulterous wife, the right to kill was restricted to her father catching her in flagrant delict at his own or her husband's house, killing by the latter being no longer justifiable homicide. The right of bringing a criminal prosecution against the adulterous wife before the *quæstio perpetua* was restricted for sixty days to her father or the divorced husband. If at the expiry of that period neither of them had taken action, she could for four months be prosecuted by any citizen over 25 years of age. In case of the husband's death before the expiry of the period of privilege, the *privilegium patris* also disappeared and the action became public, remaining open for 6 months. But Juvenal said: *Ubi nunc lex Julia? Dormis;* and in vain did Domitian and Septimius Severus promulgate it anew. The *quæstio perpetua* gave place to a *cognitio extra ordinem*, and its penalties (banishment, confiscation of the dowry or of half the *parapherna*) were replaced by arbitrary punishments. The death penalty was imposed more often.

According to the *Lex Julia* the civil consequences of adultery were as follows: an obligation on the husband to repudiate his wife, in case of flagrant delict, under pain of incurring the penalties for *lenocinium;* interdiction of the wife who had been condemned in the criminal court from marrying again or serving as a witness; and an *actio de moribus* or *retentiones propter mores* of the dowry by the husband, this action, because inspired by the desire for vengeance (*vindictam spirans*), being merged in the *judicium publicum* or criminal prosecution.[1]

[1] D., 48, 5.—**CXLVI**, 71-169.

IV. THE MODES OF DISSOLVING A MARRIAGE

A marriage was dissolved by the death of one of the spouses, by *capitis deminutio* or by divorce.[1]

The widow could remarry at once; but a very ancient rule of propriety, due at first to fear of the dead and later to fear of *turbatio sanguinis*, imposed upon her a period of mourning amounting to one lunar year, which religion had sanctioned by the obligation of making an expiatory sacrifice, and which the edict afterwards sanctioned by branding with ignominy all who gave their hands in marriage before its expiry.[2] In the classical period, although this impediment was maintained even in cases where the widow was not obliged to wear mourning for a husband who had been condemned as a criminal, it was cancelled if she gave birth to a child before the expiry of the prescribed interval.

Slavery within the meaning of the Civil Law dissolved marriage. Captivity, which may not have had this effect at first, came to possess it later on, at any rate in the case of the wife *in manu*, subject to the proviso of the *jus postliminii*. On loss of citizenship a marriage ceased at any rate to be *justum*, i.e. sanctioned by the Civil Law; and *capitis deminutio minima*, which had no effect on a marriage *sine manu*, caused in the opposite case loss of the *manus*, which could be recovered by *usus*.[3]

The old religion authorized the husband, in some very rare cases which historical Law seems to have ignored, to dissolve a marriage by *confarreatio* by repudiating his wife; this repudiation being generally followed by the death penalty.[4] The Twelve Tables seem to have left an arbitrary power in the hands of the *paterfamilias*, supported more or less by near relatives; but on the other hand the *paterfamilias* of a woman married *sine manu* could recover his daughter. The more frequent practice of divorce and repudiation, till then unknown on the woman's part, was dated by tradition from the middle of the fifth century. In the seventh century divorce at the mere caprice of one of the spouses became a thing of custom. All that was necessary was to send a freedman to the other with a *libellus repudii*, or for the

---
[1] D., 24, 2, 1.   [2] *Fr. vat.*, 320; D., 3, 2, 1, 11-1.
[3] D., 23, 2, 67-3; 48, 20, 5-1; C. J., 5, 17, 1.—**XXXIII**, 9, 46.
[4] Plut., *Rom.*, 22.

THE LAW OF THE FAMILY

husband to order his wife to leave the house: *Tuas res habeto; bœtito foras.*[1] "Take your belongings; depart hence." Any wife, whether *sui juris* or not, could avail herself of this mode, except the freedwoman espoused by her patron. Some people divorced each other without any ground or ill-feeling and with an exchange of presents. Even the *Lex Julia de maritandis ordinibus*, which claimed to bring about a renascence of ancient morality, required no other legal form for divorce than the presence of seven witnesses when the freedman delivered the *libellus*. Classical Law remained firm on this point. If it once be admitted that the continuance of a marriage, like its contraction, is due solely to the spouse's consent, and that the good of the State and order in families must yield to individual caprice, any enactment tending to restrict this liberty of the spouses by putting obstacles in the way of divorce, as was often done in the East, in Egyptian or Greek Law, must be regarded as illegal. The Law protected the freedom of the individual even against voluntary surrender.[2]

V. The Financial Agreements between Spouses. The Dowry and its Restitution

Since marriage involved expense, it gave rise to certain financial agreements.[3] The wife helped to meet this expense by contributing a dowry, no less in marriages *cum manu* (though some have denied the fact) than in marriages *sine manu*.[4] If it was provided by the wife's *paterfamilias* on whom, in the eighth century, the *Lex Julia de maritandis ordinibus* made its provision obligatory, the dowry was said to be profectitious; in all other cases it was called adventitious.[5] It always became the property of the husband and a part of the common patrimony administered by the *paterfamilias*. In marriages *cum manu* it included all that the woman *sui juris* possessed at the moment when the *manus* was acquired; but the woman *sui juris* who was married *sine manu* could reserve a fortune of her own—the *parapherna*.[6] Although it was generally settled beforehand, conditionally

[1] Aul. Gel., 4, 3; Val. Max., 2, 1, 4; 9, 2; Festus, s.v. *Diffareatio*.
[2] G., 1, 115, 118, 127; D., 24, 2, 2-1; C. J., 8, 38, 2.
[3] D., 23, 3, 76; 49, 17, 16-pr. [4] **CXCVII**, 499 et seq.
[5] Cic., *Top.*, 4, 23; *Fr. vat.*, 115. [6] D., 23, 3, 9-3.

upon the marriage taking place, the dowry could be settled or increased after marriage.[1]

Classical Law had collected together three modes of settling the dowry:[2] (i.) the *datio dotis*, an immediate transfer of the dotal goods to the husband; (ii.) the *dictio dotis*, a solemn verbal undertaking that could only be made by a woman *sui juris*, by her debtor at her order, or by her paternal ascendants[3]; (iii.) the *promissio dotis*, which could be made by anyone in the form of a stipulation or verbal contract. If the marriage did not follow in due course, the contributor of the dowry had a *condictio sine causa* against the beneficiary of the *datio*—a personal action to oblige him to retransfer the goods received; while the verbal engagements, *dictio* and *promissio*, were annulled by the non-fulfilment of the condition.[4] If the marriage took place, the contributor was held to his guarantee, but only vis-à-vis the husband. In the case of *datio*, since no guarantee was required for fictitious sales, there was a special stipulation, unless there had been a valuation of the dowry, which was equivalent to sale. In the case of *promissio* the husband demanded and could finally exact an express promise of guarantee against dispossession.[5]

Having been definitively acquired for the patrimony of the husband's *domus*, the dowry was for a long time perpetual, like the expenses which gave rise to it.[6] At the most, the domestic tribunal sometimes decreed a partial restitution to the repudiated wife. Further, there was an ancient custom that the husband should bequeath a considerable legacy to his wife to enable her to live honourably after his death, and this was generally equal in value to the dowry.[7] But the spread of divorce led to a stipulation that the dowry or its equivalent should be restored in order that the relict might not be left without resources and might be able to remarry, this being the *dos receptitia*.[8] It is uncertain, however, what was involved in the earliest times by this promise of restitution or *cautio rei uxoriæ*: whether it was the dowry itself, or its equivalent in value, or a compensation to be estimated by the judge according to the circumstances of the case.[9] The nature of the action for restitution which was established a

[1] Paul, 2, 21*b*, 1; *Fr. vat.*, 110; D., 23, 3, 18, 21, 43.
[2] Ulp., 6, 1; 11, 20. [3] G., 3, 96. [4] D., 23, 3, 8, 43.
[5] **XIII**, 19, 5-17. [6] Aul. Gel., 4, 3; 10, 23; Val. Max., 2, 9, 2.
[7] **CXLVI**, 43 et seq. [8] Aul. Gel., 4, 3. [9] **CXLVI**, 146-149.

THE LAW OF THE FAMILY 111

little later would suggest this last meaning. In any case the *cautio* opened the way for a personal action in the interests of the stipulator and his heirs. About the seventh century, failing a *cautio*, the prætor introduced an action (*actio rei uxoriæ*) authorizing the divorced wife to reclaim her dowry in compensation for the wrong done to her by a divorce on more or less insufficient grounds.[1] It was a penal action framed *in factum*, one of those that were termed *actiones in bonum et æquum conceptæ*. The *filiafamilias* could bring it in person, and it was not rendered void by the *capitis deminutiones media* and *minima*. Its condemnation was fixed at what was reasonable (*quod æquius melius*); but the husband enjoyed the *beneficium competentiæ*.[2] At length this restitution lost its penal character and had only a social and economic object, being thenceforward always a result of the husband's predecease. The action resembled the civil actions *bonæ fidei*, and in the time of Gaius it was one of them.[3]

But by the end of the Republic a distinction was already drawn between the profectitious dowry, which was repayable not only to the wife but, in case of her predecease, to the ascendant who had furnished it, with deduction in favour of the husband of a fifth part for each living child, and the adventitious dowry, in respect of which the action for restitution could only be brought by the surviving wife, if she was *sui juris*, or by the *paterfamilias* proceeding *adjecta persona filiæ*, if she was *in patria potestate*.[4] After a divorce the action did not pass to the wife's heirs, unless she died while the husband's restitution was still in arrears. In principle a dowry consisting of fungible things was repayable in three annual instalments; but it was repayable immediately in case of the husband's adultery, or in six months if less serious offences on his part had occasioned the divorce. Failing a valuation equivalent to sale at the moment of settlement, which made him debtor for a sum of money, the husband was responsible even for slight negligence in the administration of the dotal goods.[5]

But in determining the conditions for restitution of dowry, jurisprudence allowed the husband certain deductions (*retentiones*) which secured the results formerly obtained by means

[1] **XIII**, 17, 146-177.　　[2] Cic., *Top.*, 17; D., 42, 1, 20.
[3] G., 4, 62; D., 4, 5, 8; Ed.-P., 2, 221-225.
[4] Ulp., 6, 4, 6; D., 24, 3, 3; *Fr. sinaica*, 10, 12.　　[5] Ulp., 6, 7, 8, 13.

of actions against the wife: e.g. *actio de moribus*, a prætorian and penal action involving a condemnation proportionate to the wife's guilt; *actio rerum amotarum*, an action granted in consequence of the wife's removal of her husband's property.¹ These deductions were allowed *propter mores* and *propter liberos* (one sixth for each child up to the amount of half the dowry) in cases of divorce and in favour of the husband alone; *propter res amotas* and *propter impensas* (cost of maintenance of the dotal goods) in all cases and in favour of the husband's heirs as well as himself.²

At the same time, from the beginning of the Empire, guarantees were introduced to secure the preservation of the dowry. The *Lex Julia de fundo dotali*, a chapter of the statute *de maritandis ordinibus*, forbade the husband to alienate dotal land in Italy without the consent of his wife, while usucapion in respect thereof was only possible if it had begun to run before the settlement of the dowry.³ But jurisprudence excepted immovables received by the husband on a valuation equivalent to sale (if there was no clause to the contrary), necessary alienations (allotments, auctions, etc.), and alienations of the whole patrimony *en bloc*, in which however the purchaser took over the immovables burdened with their charges.⁴ On the other hand, by its interpretation of the Sc. Velleianum which forbade wives incurring obligations for their husbands, it prohibited any mortgage on the dotal land even with the wife's consent, or at least required that the effect of the mortgage should not take place unless the immovable remained the husband's property after the dissolution of the marriage.⁵ During the marriage the husband alone could reclaim dotal land in Italy that had been illegally alienated; after its dissolution the wife alone could do so, if the dowry had been restored to her, for if it had not been restored and the husband had alienated the land before the guarantee was given, the alienation was confirmed.⁶ Later on, the wife's claim to restitution of dowry was favoured in another way. She was given a position of privilege copied from Egyptian Law, and the dowry had to be returned before payment of debts guaranteed by the husband's note of hand.⁷

[1] G., 4, 102.—**XIII**, 17, 153.
[2] Ulp., 6, 9, 10, 12, 14-17; *Fr. sin.*, 8, 9; D., 23, 5, 18; 25, 1.
[3] Paul, 2, 21*b*, 2; D., 50, 16, 28-pr. [4] D., 23, 3, 1-pr., 11, 16.
[5] D., 23, 8, 4; I. J., 2, 8-pr. [6] D., 4, 4, 3-5. [7] C. J., 7, 74, 1.

THE LAW OF THE FAMILY

Gifts between husband and wife, which had long been permitted, were rendered absolutely null by jurisprudence, except when they did not impoverish the donor (e.g. when an inheritance or a legacy was declined in favour of the other spouse), when they were merely customary, or when they were made on the occasion of holding a magistracy, of divorce, of exile, or in anticipation of death. But the principle was not rigorously applied, and the Law was content so long as one of the spouses was not enriched at the expense of the other. Moreover, in the reign of Caracalla, the *oratio Antonini* (206) declared these donations valid and confirmed when the donor died in the course of the marriage without having revoked them, and they were ever more closely assimilated to donations in anticipation of death, although the assimilation never became complete.[1]

VI. FREE UNION OR CONCUBINAGE

Free unions, which had doubtless at all times been more or less practised at Rome, increased in number towards the end of the Republic to such an extent that some have seen in them a form of legal union inferior to marriage, which was sanctioned by Augustus, the moral reformer, by way of compensation to those persons who were forbidden by his statutes to intermarry.[2] At any rate they suppose that he exempted them from the penalties imposed by the *Lex Julia de adulteriis* on *stuprum* committed with women and girls of honourable condition, provided that the unions did not violate the principle of monogamy or the regulations concerning kinship or puberty which governed all sexual intercourse.[3] If he did so, which is doubtful,[4] that was all he did. But certainly the statutes seem to have remained indifferent to unions of this kind, which custom alone tolerated or required until the beginning of the Lower Empire. The children of these unions, who in law had no connection with their fathers, were termed *spurii, liberi naturales, filiastri*, and had no relatives except their maternal cognates, differing in no respect from other children born out of wedlock.[5]

[1] Paul, 5, 11, 6; *Fr. vat.*, 304; D., 24, 1, 1, 2, 3, 10.
[2] CV, 1, n° 100; XI, 4, 549; CCXXVIII, 29.
[3] Paul, 2, 20, 1; D., 23, 2, 56.—XIII, 4, 377; XXIV, 11, 233; CLVIII, 193.
[4] XXIV, 27, 55 et seq.; CCLIX, 69-84.
[5] XIII, 16, 15; XLVIII, 149; CCXLIV, 2, 695; CCLIX, 60 et seq.

The duty of fidelity and the obligation not to leave her patron without his consent, which bound the freedwoman who was a concubine, were part of the *obsequium* due to the patron and had no reference to the legality of their union.

III

THE " FILIIFAMILIAS "

I. LEGITIMATE CHILDREN BORN IN WEDLOCK

The end of marriage was to perpetuate a line, a name and a family cult; but the *paterfamilias*, who was absolute master of his *domus*, introduced into it at his pleasure either children born of his wife or strangers whom he had adrogated or adopted.

Modern legislations declare the child legitimate who is born under conditions prescribed by them, and take no account of the parents' wishes. It is the Law, not the parents, that determines his civil status. But the ancient city did not, originally, intervene either in the composition or the internal organization of the family. The *gens* and the *domus* were closed against it, and it held each of the members of these associations to be what his head affirmed him to be. In order to rank as a legitimate child it was not sufficient to be born in wedlock; it was necessary, above all, to be acknowledged by the *paterfamilias*. The supposed statute requiring all the sons and the eldest of the daughters to be brought up, and the analogous decrees of the *gentes*, were obsolete traditions if not legends. The head of a *domus* who has taken a wife with a view to obtaining children is not obliged to accept all that she bears him. He can order abortion which, until a very late period, was only punishable when practised against his will or without his knowledge.[1] If he has not done so, the child is presented to him immediately after birth and laid at his feet, and if he turns away from it (*liberum repudiat, negat*), it is exposed, sold or put to death. Even if it survives, it is excluded from the family and from the city, and whoever finds it can make it his slave as if it were an alien. On the other hand, if he lifts it from the ground and accepts it

[1] Dion. Hal., 2, 15; 9, 22.—**CXXVI**, 11 et seq.

THE LAW OF THE FAMILY

(*liberum tollit, suscipit*), the acknowledged child is submitted 8 or 9 days later to the *lustratio*, presented to the gods of the house and given a prænomen.[1] It is now capable of continuing the domestic cult, and becomes *heres suus et necessarius* of its father. According to the Civil Law the child born in wedlock has the status of its father; but this assumes previous acceptance of the new-born child by the head of the *domus*, for until that has taken place, the decision of the city is suspended.[2]

As a result of this old Law the posthumous child born *sui juris*, who had neither a father nor a grandfather to grant him admission to the family, was *de facto* excluded from it, being not even an agnate of his own relatives; and this was a serious mishap for the family line, if the *paterfamilias* left no other male descendants.

Legislation afterwards connected by the Jurists with the Twelve Tables and ascribed to humanitarian feeling, but more probably due to the desire to obtain someone to carry on the family cult and meet the claims of creditors, finally regarded as *heres suus* the posthumous child born within 10 months of the husband's death who, if the latter had lived, would have been under his immediate power at the hour of its birth.[3] This solution of the problem seems to belong to the seventh century, a period when the dispositions of the edict created a complicated procedure for making the legitimacy of the posthumous child apparent to the other heirs and securing him certain privileges.[4] This was the first essential article of the family code which the State imposed with sovereign authority; for anticipatory disinheritance, which certainly prevented the posthumous child from inheriting, did not rob him of his legitimacy. On this point the magisterial power of the head of the family died with him.

Something very different was seen in the first 25 years of the second century of the Christian era. Two senatusconsulta *de partu agnoscendo*—the *Sc. Plancianum* of Trajan's reign and another assigned to Hadrian's time but without a name— which were suggested by economic considerations and by the desire to establish on a legal presumption the obligation to

[1] **CCXXXVIII**, 12, 99; cf. **LXII**, 2, 85 et seq.
[2] Ulp., 5, 6; Liv., 4, 4.
[3] D., 5, 4, 3-pr.—**CXXVI**, 14 et seq.
[4] D., 25, 4, 1-10-15, 6-1; 37, 9, 1-24.

provide maintenance for children in the direct line, marked the beginning of a real revolution.

The first established a method of procedure by which a wife who was with child at the moment of divorce could debar her husband from his right of disavowing the child, provided that he had been informed of her condition and had not submitted to certain formalities.[1] The second instituted a method of procedure to secure recognition of children born while the marriage lasted. These senatusconsulta were only concerned with children born under the father's or grandfather's power, and took no account of those born *sui juris*, for whom they were of no value; but the idea of the Senate was to make the legitimacy or illegitimacy of the child depend on the working of these procedures.[2] Later on, a rescript of Marcus Aurelius and of Verus completed the system by guarding against the risks of concealment of birth by the woman who had been divorced when with child.[3] The ancient right *suscipere vel negare liberum* disappeared;[4] but since jurisprudence had reduced the effect of the senatusconsulta to a mere presumption of filiation permitting the establishment of a right to maintenance between the fathers and the presumed children, the question of the children's status became the object of a special *præjudicium* inserted by Julian in the perpetual edict. This dissociation of the objects of the senatusconsulta—recognition of the child's legitimacy and obligation to provide maintenance—was confirmed by Antoninus Pius. The *præjudicium* took over all questions, principal and accessory, concerning the child's status, the determination of which thus passed out of the control of the *paterfamilias* into that of the State. The formula, which was very flexible, seems to have varied according to the fact by which legitimacy was established; the judge's decision was final, and there was no special system of proof as there is in our Law to-day. No register of civil status existed, and the registration of births, which was practised in the East and extended to the whole Empire by Marcus Aurelius, only constituted one of the ordinary means of proof.[5] There were none of those presumptions with which we are familiar concerning duration of pregnancy or responsibility for conceptions

[1] D., 25, 3, 1, 3; Paul, 24, 5-10.   [2] D., 25, 3, 3; 4, 1.
[3] C. J., 8, 47, 9.   [4] D., 25, 3, 1-14.—**CXXII**, 22 et seq.
[5] **XIII**, 30, 495; **XVII**, 18, 416; **CV**, 76; **CXC**.

THE LAW OF THE FAMILY

while the marriage lasted. The adage *pater is est quem nuptiæ demonstrant*, when once included in the texts, is no more than an empirical means to enable the prætor to refuse action to a descendant against his ascendant when the question of status is not in dispute.[1] With these reservations, the Law of the third century, the Law of the Severi, defined a legitimate child as a child begotten of a married woman by her husband.[2]

II. Fictitious Filiations. Adrogated and Adopted Children

In the early centuries *adrogatio* affected the economy of the city. Through it the head of a family passed under the power of others; a *domus*, a cult, a patrimony ceased to exist; the balance of power among the *gentes* might be upset. Accordingly it required the approval of the pontiffs, a *rogatio* addressed to the people, and that the adrogator should be without hope of having children of his own. Later on, the statutes of escheat required that he should also be 60 years of age.[3] The pontiffs inquired into the condition of the gentile and domestic cults and into the position, rank and fortune of the families concerned. If their decision was a negative one, no more could be done; if not, the president of the comitia inquired, in the people's presence, of the adrogator whether he accepted such and such a *paterfamilias* as his legitimate son, of the adrogatus whether he submitted himself to the adrogator's power of life and death, of the Quirites whether they ordered this to be done. When the statute had been voted by the curias, the pontiffs proceeded before the Comitia Calata, who acted as witnesses, to conduct the *detestatio sacrorum* which cancelled every bond between the adrogatus and his ancient *gens*.[4]

When the city began to deal with individuals instead of associations, the *rogatio* no longer took place except, for form's sake, before the thirty lictors of the curias, and the pontiff's inquiry was limited to the *sacra*, the moral propriety of the act, and its consequences for third parties.

[1] D., 1, 5, 8; C. J., 4, 21, 6. [2] D., 1, 6, 6-pr.
[3] Cic., *pro domo*, 13, 29.—**XIII**, 17, 363.
[4] G., 1, 99, 102; Ulp., 8, 2; Tac., *An.*, 12, 26; *Hist.*, 1, 15; Aul. Gel, 5, 19; 15, 27.

It was no longer necessary that adrogator and adrogatus should be capable of appearing in the Comitia. Antoninus Pius allowed the adrogation of children under the age of puberty by the decree of a magistrate acting on the advice of the pontiffs and of a family council.[1] Women also could be adrogated.[2] Claudius required the consent of the curator in the case of persons under 25 years old; but, on the other hand, classical Law forbade the adrogation of wards and minors by their guardians and curators, who would have found thereby a means to avoid giving any account of their administration.[3]

The adrogator gave the adrogatus the rank of son or of some more distant descendant, whence followed all the consequences, political, social and domestic, that this position involved. The patrimony of the adrogatus became an integral part of that of his new *domus*; but in the seventh century the pontiffs guarded against the risks which this absorption involved for third parties by refusing to authorize adrogation until the debts of the adrogatus had been paid or their payment had been guaranteed by the adrogator in person; moreover, in cases where the adrogator did not meet an action arising out of debts incurred before adrogation, the prætor authorized *bonorum venditio*, sale of the adrogator's property in bulk, up to the amount of the adrogated person's original contribution plus any subsequent additions made through his agency.[4]

Antoninus Pius enacted that, after the adrogation of children under the age of puberty, the adrogator should promise under surety to restore to its heirs the patrimony of an adrogated child who died without reaching puberty. After reaching puberty the adrogatus could have the adrogation cancelled and recover his property, if it seemed to his interest to do so. He also recovered it if he was emancipated on grounds recognized by the law before attaining puberty; and if he was otherwise emancipated or disinherited, he had a right to the *quarta antonina*.[5] Adrogation thus conceived ceased to be the last means of saving a *domus* and became instead a benevolent institution for orphans.

[1] Ulp., 8, 5. [2] C. J., 8, 48, 3.
[3] C. J., 8, 48, 8, 17; 5, 59, 5.—**CCLII**, 1, 230.
[4] G., 3, 80, 1; I. J., 1, 11, 3.—**XIII**, 17, 363 et seq.; **CXXXIII**, 52-53.
[5] I. J., 3, 10, 2.

THE LAW OF THE FAMILY 119

A closely related legal act, adoption by testament, which must not be confused with the appointment of an heir on condition that he takes the name of the testator, was borrowed at some time or other by Roman practice from Greek Law.[1] The testamentary disposition was submitted, at any rate in certain cases, to the approval of the pontiffs and announced before the fictitious assembly of the curias.[2] This adoption had no effect until after the testator's death, the adoptee being put in the position of a *heres suus* of the latter. The most famous case of adoption in this form was that of Octavius by Cæsar, and some other instances of it are known.

Roman *adoptio* was a purely private matter: the handing over of a child by one *paterfamilias* to another to take rank as his descendant made no change in the city. Hence it was possible to adopt children under the age of puberty and even women, although there was less advantage to be gained by adopting them, since they did not perpetuate the family cult or name.[3] In the form known to us adoption could not have been practised until after the breaking up of the *gentes* and the establishment of civil equality between *populus* and *plebs*. The lawyers based it upon the Twelve Tables, whose rule they observed: *si pater filium ter venum duit, filius a patre liber esto*. Three successive sales freed a *filiusfamilias* from the *patria potestas*, one alone sufficing for a daughter and for grandsons. These sales, performed according to the rite of *mancipatio*, placed the child under the *mancipium* of the purchaser, who could either resell it or not to the *paterfamilias*; whereupon the adopter brought an action against one or the other of them in claim of paternal power (*vindicatio filii*).[4] In case of their admission or failure to make a defence, the magistrate awarded the child to him as his son or daughter. By this procedure of *in jure cessio* it was long possible to adopt slaves or aliens.[5]

The original purpose of adoption implied that power to adopt should be restricted to a *paterfamilias* only, and its legal form required no other qualification. It was only gradually, under pretence of copying nature, that eunuchs

---

[1] Cic., *Brut.*, 58; Appian, 3, 14.—**CCXXXVIII**, 6¹, 42 et seq.; **XIII**, 21, 721; **CXCV**, 2, 246. [2] **CV**, 65, 3.
[3] For the primitive customs concerning adoption see **CCVII**, 1, 466.
[4] XII T., 4, 2; G., 1, 98, 99, 134; D., I, 7, 3-4; Aul. Gel., 5, 19.
[5] I. J., 1, 11, 12.

came to be forbidden to adopt and that the adopter was required to be older than his adoptee.¹ Moreover celibates and impotents could thus procure descendants. Sometimes too, by a procedure of which we are ignorant, women created a posterity for themselves; but this was an anomaly.²

The adopted person went out of his original family and even lost certain advantages of *cognatio*. Passing under the *patria potestas* of the adopter, he took the latter's gentile name followed by that of his own original *gens*, usually in adjectival form, as in the case of the adrogatus.³ He became *heres suus* of the adopter if he was adopted as a son, or of one of the adopter's descendants if he took rank in the *domus* as a grandson. There are indications however that custom no longer allowed in classical times so complete a separation of the adoptee from his family of origin as legal logic required, thus preparing the way which the legislators of the Lower Empire followed later on.⁴

III. Modes of Acquiring "Patria Potestas" Subsequent to Marriage

The *paterfamilias*, who composed his family as he pleased, could on occasion introduce into it his own children born out of wedlock. Such birth involved neither advantage nor disability, the surname of *Spurius* being borne quite openly. *Vulgo quæsitus*, the child without a legal father was born *sui juris* with no relations but his mother's cognates. Adrogation and testamentary adoption were then open to the father as means of joining the child to his own *domus*;⁵ but we know of nothing before the time of the Lower Empire that resembled what we call legitimization.

It was only permitted by certain statutes, in the case of a marriage that was invalid or did not carry with it the *patria potestas* through lack of *conubium* between the spouses, to claim this *potestas* over children already born when, for certain defined reasons, the union was transformed into *justæ nuptiæ*: e.g. in the case of a Latin with the right to claim Roman citizenship; of a Roman citizen proving that he had married

---

¹ G., 1, 106; 4, 79; Paul, 3, 4a, 2; I. J., 1, 11, 4, 9.
² Cic., *ad Att.*, 7, 8; Suet., *Galba*, 4.
³ I. J., 1, 11, 8; D., 1, 7, 35.—**CCXXXVII**, 1, 123, 480. ⁴ **CV**, 62, 63.
⁵ D., 1, 5, 23; 2, 4, 5; 23, 2, 14-2.—**I**, 6, 7304, 7788, 8420; **CLVI**, 543; **XIII**, 9 1.

THE LAW OF THE FAMILY

a Latin or an alien in error (*erroris probatio*); of a Latin-Junian who had married a Roman or a Latin wife in the presence of seven witnesses, and had a son aged one year (*causæ probatio*). By claiming the right of Roman citizenship, as the statutes authorized them to do, these *patresfamilias* transformed their marriages into *justæ nuptiæ* and acquired *patria potestas* over their children without retroactive effect.[1]

IV. THE CIVIL CAPACITY OF THE "FILIIFAMILIAS"

The authority of the *paterfamilias* gave the children under his power a limited capacity which moreover, during the classical period, differed in degree for sons, *filiifamilias*, and daughters, *filiæfamilias*, respectively.

The *filiifamilias* acquired a civil and political capacity on reaching an age which seems for a long time to have been left to the discretion of the *paterfamilias* and was identical with that at which they began to bear arms. This attainment of majority was fixed by the Servian Constitution at 17 years and was marked by the exchange of the toga prætexta for the toga virilis and by the inscription of the prænomen, the symbol of adult personality, in the registers of the census, where the child had hitherto had no place except in the total of persons *alieni juris* and under age who belonged to the *domus*. Later on, the name was inscribed in the *tabularium* of the tribunes.[2] Under the Empire there was a tendency to lower the age of civil majority, and the Sabinian doctrine, which held by the actual fact of puberty, was opposed by that of the Proculians, who fixed the legal majority at 14 for boys and 12 for girls. In their preoccupation with questions of moral psychology the Jurists, and perhaps first among them Julian, distinguished between the *infans* who was altogether incapable and irresponsible, the *proximus pubertati* who was responsible for his delicts and frauds, and the pubescent who was in theory as capable as a person *sui juris*.[3]

But this capacity, which was originally less complete, had to be measured by its effect upon the family's collective

---

[1] G., 1, 31-32; 67, 68, 95.   [2] CCXXXVIII, 12, 154; CXXVI, 3.
[3] G., 3, 104, 208; D., 44, 4, 4-26.

122 FORMATION OF CLASSICAL LAW

interests and must be compatible with the unique ownership of the patrimony by the *paterfamilias* and his exclusive power of administration. The *filiusfamilias* could acquire real rights and claims for the common patrimony. As *adstipulator* he acquired a claim in his own person.[1] He could be liable for his delicts or, if it was so desired, render his *paterfamilias* liable, who was responsible for the doings of his *domus* and could choose between repairing the damage and surrendering the delinquent to the victim of the delict. This was called the noxal surrender.[2] It is not certain whether he could bind himself by his contracts, for voluntary execution would have affected the patrimony and execution against the body of the debtor would have affected the *patria potestas*. When this capacity was admitted, probably in the early days of the Empire, the *filiusfamilias* could be sued at law, but the creditor could not execute the condemnation until the debtor had become *sui juris*, and even then the latter enjoyed the *beneficium competentiæ* if he had not received the paternal inheritance. No other act capable of burdening the family patrimony was allowed him without an order from the head of the *domus*.[3]

He was authorized however to bring an action for *injuria* if he was personally injured, the interdict *quod vi aut clam* if he had been the victim of a violent dispossession, and the actions *commodati*, provided that the *paterfamilias* was absent or prevented from appearing. The first of these was finally granted to him when the *paterfamilias* was present but took no action, since it belonged to the rights of personality.[4] For the same reason the prosecution of his wife for adultery and the *querela inofficiosi testamenti* belonged to him in his own right.[5] In cases of urgency, when the father was prevented from appearing, Julian granted him an *actio utilis*, and in other cases a *judicium extra ordinem;* but the *judicatum* was always acquired for the common patrimony, and all actions except those belonging to the son in his own right became void at the father's death.[6] Finally Ulpian taught that, in case the father was prevented from appearing, the

---

[1] G., 2, 86-90. For *adstipulatio* see p. 215.
[2] G., 4, 76; I. J., 4, 8, 3; XII T., 8, 9, 14; Aul. Gel., 11, 8.
[3] D., 14, 5, 2-pr.; 17, 2, 58-2.—**CXLII**, 118.   [4] D., 16, 3, 19; 44, 7, 9.
[5] D., 5, 1, 18-1; 12, 1-17. For the *querela inofficiosi testamenti* see p. 293.
[6] **CXI**, 2, 123; **LXXXI**, 351-361.

THE LAW OF THE FAMILY

son could always take action as well in civil as in criminal cases;[1] but he could never be the plaintiff in a real action, since it was impossible for him to assert his own possession of the right sanctioned thereby.[2]

The *filiafamilias*, whether a spinster or married *sine manu*, and the wife *in manu*, who was held to be her husband's daughter, while rendering the *paterfamilias* liable *noxaliter* by their delicts and acquiring property only for the common patrimony, remained incapable of binding themselves by a civil obligation until the end of the fourth century of the Christian era.[3]

Under Claudius or Vespasian the *Sc. Macedonianum* requested the prætor, in consequence of several scandals, to refuse moneylenders the action for recovery of a loan for consumption against persons *alieni juris*, unless their *paterfamilias* had ordered them to borrow the money or had profited by it, or the moneylender had been the victim of a fraud.[4]

Thus the legal individuality of persons *alieni juris* slowly emerged from the family group and acquired substance. By the edict, the jurists' doctrine or the statutes, hypothetical cases were conceived in which the right was so closely attached to the individual that no forbear intervened and it seemed just that he should exercise it himself. Among family rights, his marriage, the adoption of young children to a place in his line, and the emancipation of his own children required his consent; and there was a tendency to see a division of *manus* between the *paterfamilias* and the husband still *in patria potestate* over the wife of the latter, who also had his share in the settlement and restitution of the dowry.[5]

Under Augustus this personality was affirmed or rather enhanced by the institution of the *peculium castrense*[6] comprising property acquired while on military service or in consequence of it, to which the son had all the rights of a *paterfamilias* except, after his discharge, that of disposing of it by will. But Hadrian gave him this too, and also the rights of patronage over the freedmen of the *peculium*. Failing a will, this property reverted to the father[7] as *pecu-*

[1] D., 5, 1, 18-1.   [2] G., 2, 96; 3, 124.
[3] G., 2, 86-90; 3, 104; *Fr. vat.*, 99; D., 13, 6, 3-4.—**LXXXI**, 370-380.
[4] D., 14, 16.   [5] D., 3, 3, 8-pr.; 18, 10, 17, 18.
[6] Ulp., 20, 10; D., 14, 6, 2.   [7] D., 38, 2, 22; 49, 14, 11.

lium, i.e. as if it had been a part of the family patrimony entrusted to the son's administration.¹ Under the Severi, Paul and Ulpian admitted natural obligations between members of the same *domus*.²

V. MEANS OF RELEASE FROM THE " PATRIA POTESTAS "

Since the *patria potestas* was perpetual, it was not brought to an end by the attainment of any majority. Chance occurrences sometimes made its exercise impossible: e.g. the death of the child; capture by the enemy, either of the child or of the *paterfamilias*, subject to the reservation of the *jus postliminii* which re-established it in such a manner that it was long regarded in principle as if it had never ceased;³ selection by the pontifex maximus as a flamen of Jupiter or a vestal virgin, whose family rights were suspended during the period of priesthood and were not recovered except by the ritual of an *exauguratio*;⁴ loss of citizenship by the father or the child *in potestate*, since the Civil Law took no account of aliens. But within the scope of this Law the rule was that no one escaped from *patria potestas* except at the will of the head of the *domus*; while on the other hand he excluded from it whom he would, either permanently or temporarily. It was not until very late, after the State had assumed the right of organizing the family régime, that this power of the head of the family could be reduced, or that he could be constrained to exercise it in a particular way.

Roman Law did not recognize what the Greeks called ἀποκήρυξις (*abdicatio*). Originally no doubt the *paterfamilias* could expel an unworthy member from the family group and simultaneously from the city, for membership of the city depended upon membership of a *gens*; but at a very early date political rights were recognized to be independent of the family régime, so that the domestic sentence could not take them away except by means of the death penalty. Every other means fell into disuse,⁵ and this state of affairs was confirmed by the Law of the Twelve Tables.

From the time of that Law the *paterfamilias* who wished

¹ D., 38, 17, 10-pr.; I. J., 2, 12-pr.—**CXI**, 2, 123; **LXXXI**, 362.
² D., 44, 7, 14, 43.   ³ G., 1, 127, 129, 131; Ulp., 10, 2, 3; Paul, 2, 25, 5.
⁴ G., 1, 130; Aul. Gel., 1, 12, 13, 15.—**CCXXXVIII**, 3, 60; **CV**, 102; **XIII**, 28, 40 et seq.   ⁵ C. J., 8, 45, 6.—**CXI**, 1², 46; **CV**, 101.

THE LAW OF THE FAMILY 125

either to punish or to reward a child by detaching him from the *domus* used no method except that of emancipation, a procedure built up by the lawyers upon one of its prescriptions. After three sales by mancipation in the case of a son, or one only in the case of a daughter or grandson, the *patria potestas* was lost and the child was placed under the *mancipium* of the purchaser, who generally resold it to the father. By enfranchising the child, one or other of them acquired the rights of patronage over it, so that its independence was not complete—a fact which explains why emancipation was at first used especially as a form of punishment. This act of voluntary jurisdiction (*emancipatio*) was accomplished by a fictitious suit for recovery of freedom, whence the enfranchisement followed.[1] The only ties which still connected the emancipated person with his old family were those of *cognatio*.[2] Originally emancipation depended upon the *paterfamilias* alone, but classical Law required at least the tacit consent of the person emancipated, and admitted that a child who had been ill-used by the head of his family, or had been given some gift on condition that he became emancipated, might claim emancipation.[3] Henceforward it was only regarded as a favour, since the Law of Succession provided more flexible and more appropriate sanctions for a child's misdoings.

The *patria potestas* was also extinguished by adoption (*datio in adoptionem*) which, as we have seen, involved a preliminary emancipation, and by *conventio in manum*,[4] both of which depended upon the will of the *paterfamilias* alone.

The *paterfamilias* could sell his dependants *alieni juris*, and originally without doubt this sale made the child the slave of his purchaser;[5] but by the Law of the Twelve Tables he remained free, although he was inscribed in the census as *servus* of the latter, who disposed of his services and benefited by his earnings.[6] By this procedure children could also be given in pledge. The sale was accomplished by *mancipatio*[7] and had no permanent effects except in the case of daughters and grand-children. In the case of sons, enfranchisement after the first two sales re-established the *patria potestas*.[8]

[1] G., 1, 132; Ulp., 10, 1. [2] G., 1, 163; D., 38, 10, 4-10
[3] Paul, 2, 25, 5; D., 1, 7, 31; 30, 114-8; Pliny mi., *Ep.*, 4, 2.
[4] G., 1, 134, 136.
[5] Cic., *de Orat.*, 1, 40.—**CCLXXVI**, 3 et seq.; **CCXXX**, 358.
[6] Paul, 5, 1, 1, 2; C. J., 7, 16, 1.   [7] G., 1, 117-119.
[8] XII T., 4, 2; G., 1, 132; 4, 79, 138.

The texts do not give us the ancient Law as regards the condition of persons *in mancipio*.[1] Such a situation, which from the beginning of the Empire was very rare, except when the parents were exceedingly poor, was generally the result of a noxal surrender.[2] It seems that political rights were merely suspended and were restored by enfranchisement.[3] The *mancipium*, which placed the child in the purchaser's *familia*, could belong to a woman. It was rather a matter of value than of power, at least in classical times. It was acquired through the medium of the person who submitted to it.[4] The *mancipatus* did not permanently lose either citizenship or *ingenuitas* or *conubium*, and he retained the right to bring an *actio injuriarum* in his own name even against his master. His children followed his condition.

IV

THE SLAVES

I. THE "POTESTAS DOMINICA." CAUSES OF SLAVERY

Slaves formed a part of the *familia*. Introduced into the *domus* by their master, they were presented to the Lar and the Hearth, given a share in the lustral water and the family cult, where on occasion they took the place of the head of the house, buried in the family tomb and counted among the *di manes*.[5] At first few in number and natives of the surrounding countries, they lived on terms of intimacy with their master and were well treated.[6] The *potestas dominica* hardly differed from the *patria potestas*. It involved rights of punishment, of life and death, exercised more often by acts of magisterial authority than in virtue of ownership, although it was the latter that explained them;[7] a right of disposal that was not subject to the same limitations as the other kinds of *potestas*; and the same sanction, a real action for recovery of ownership (*vindicatio*).[8] By giving one class of persons

---

[1] **CXCV**, 2, 233 et seq.   [2] G., 1, 141; 4, 79.   [3] G., 2, 86; 3, 104, 163.
[4] G., 1, 138, 141, 162.—**CXCV**, 2, 240 et seq.; **CCXXXVII**, 3, 5 et seq.; **CCLXXVI**.
[5] Varro, *de L. l.*, 6, 24; D., 11, 7, 2-pr.—**CCXXXVIII**, 12, 23 et seq.
[6] Liv., 2, 22; Pliny, *H. N.*, 33, 6; Macrobius, *Sat.*, 1, 11.
[7] G., 1, 9, 48, 52; I. J., 1, 3, pr.; cf. Cic., *in Cat.*, 4, 6; *in Verr.*, 5, 4.
[8] Dion. Hal., 20, 13.

THE LAW OF THE FAMILY

alieni juris a place in political society, the State had prepared the way for their gradual and partial emancipation from the authority of the *paterfamilias* and given shape to their legal personality, while by excluding the rest it had increased their dependence and made them once more an important element in the patrimony (*res mancipi*), as they had been in the ancient agricultural system.[1] Hence the *potestas dominica* passed with the *dominium* into the possession of women and of aliens who had the right of *commercium*.[2] But no fiction deprived the slaves altogether of their natural personality. The division of mankind into free persons and slaves went back to an early period. The condition of a free man (*status libertatis*) was established or disputed by the procedure of the *causa liberalis* which was brought under the form of the *sacramentum*, fixed at 50 asses in specie, first before the *decemviri stlitibus judicandis*, the judges in questions of status, later before the *centumviri*,[3] and in the provinces before the *recuperatores*.

Since the object of the suit could not himself take action, he was represented by an *assertor libertatis*; and for fear his defence might be badly conducted, this sort of process could, as an exception, be renewed several times. After Gaius the suit took the form of a *præjudicium* or a *cognitio extra ordinem*.[4]

The most ancient causes of slavery at Rome were connected with the Law of Nations: (i.) capture of a foreigner either in time of war or of peace, for a foreigner was always fair game;[5] (ii.) birth of a mother who was a slave on the day of delivery; though, later on, classical Law maintained the *ingenuitas* of a child whose mother had been free at any time during pregnancy.[6] These kinds of slavery were a misfortune, not a disgrace.

It was otherwise with those arising at a later period out of the action of the Civil Law, for they were all penal forfeitures. According to the old Law the citizen who failed to have his name inscribed in the census and was sold for the profit of the people, the insolvent debtor and the thief caught red-handed, who were awarded to the creditor and the person

---

[1] G., 2, 13, 14*a*; Ulp., 19, 1; D., 1, 5, 4-1-2; 50, 16, 195.
[2] G., 1, 52-54.   [3] G., 4, 14; D., 40, 7, 5.
[4] Cic., *pro domo*, 27, 78; Paul, 5, 1, 5; D., 40, 12, 24-pr., 25-2; C. J., 7, 16, 17, 1-pr.
[5] D., 49, 15, 5-1; I. J., 1, 3, 4.   [6] G., 1, 83-86; D., 1, 5, 5-2, 3.

robbed, were sold *trans Tiberim*, i.e. to an alien, since in those days a citizen might not be a slave on Roman territory.[1] But some later acts did not trouble themselves on that account: (i.) a senatusconsultum of the republican period ordered that anyone over 25 who dishonestly caused himself to be sold to a citizen by a third party, in order to share in the price, should be awarded to that citizen as his slave; (ii.) the *Sc. Claudianum* ordered that a free woman who refused to break off her relations with a slave, after being thrice required to do so by the slave's master, should by a magistrate's decree be awarded to this master as his slave, provided that he was neither her son nor her freedman; (iii.) Claudius re-enslaved the freedman who called his patron's civil status in question, and Commodus made this rule general in all cases of ingratitude, when the enfranchisement had been spontaneous on the part of the patron.[2] In many other cases of slavery as a form of punishment the condemned persons, *servi poenæ* or without a master, were debarred from forming any legal relations in the sphere of private Law.

II. THE SLAVE'S SOCIAL AND LEGAL POSITION

Deprived of any legal personality, even of a name, the slave had no family.[3] For him there was no marriage but only a *de facto* union (*contubernium*) which had no other consequence than a vague *cognatio servilis*.[4] The children of the *ancilla* were counted as fruits accruing to the master's patrimony.[5] But as regards the customs of slaves, the documents reveal to us sometimes disorderliness amounting almost to promiscuity, sometimes permanent unions and families held together by the bonds of affection for several generations.[6] The *ancilla* often bears the name of *uxor* in epigraphical texts; and in these households the children did in fact know their father and sometimes several of their paternal and maternal ascendants, having family relations with them analogous to those in free families.

Though incapable of acquiring property on his own account,

---

[1] Cic., *de Orat.*, 1, 40; Liv., 1, 44; Dion. Hal., 4, 55; XII T., 3, 5; G., 3, 189.
[2] Paul., 2, 21a; D., 40, 22, 7-pr., 1.
[3] Called *puer*, *puer Marci*=*Marcipor*, he has in fact only a prænomen, followed sometimes by that of his master in the genitive case: **LI,** 149; **XCV,** 79.   [4] D., 23, 2, 36-6; 2, 8; I. J., 1, 10, 10.
[5] D., 6, 2, 12; 15, 1, 57-2.   [6] For the sources see **CV,** 131-135.

THE LAW OF THE FAMILY

the slave, like the wife *in manu* and the *filiifamilias*, was an instrument whereby the master could acquire it. It has been said that he borrowed his master's personality, but, speaking more exactly, this was because the heads of *domus* had established the custom of substituting one of their slaves for themselves in acts of this kind, and third parties knew that the master would assume responsibility for the act, although the criterion of the operation was the slave's will alone.[1] Having his master's authority he bound him too. Thanks to these customs, the slave was used for the exploitation of the family patrimony in all manner of ways, especially by the constitution of *peculia*, which were separate fractions of it entrusted to his free administration.[2] Other slaves, *vicarii*, were often included in these *peculia* whose head was the *servus ordinarius*.[3] Sometimes the whole but generally a part of this *peculium* was left in his possession when he was enfranchised. We shall describe elsewhere the part played by slaves in commerce, industry and finance, which often made them important or influential personages, living in comfort and luxury unknown to many free men.

The slave could not put himself personally under an obligation or put others under an obligation to him. He could never do so by his contracts; but the Roman conception of responsibility, which was not dissociated from that of imputability, authorized the victim of his delicts to avenge himself on his body: hence the noxal action against his successive masters, constraining them either to deliver up the wrongdoer or to make satisfaction in his place, and, after enfranchisement, the ordinary penal action against the former slave himself.[4] But it was especially in regard to slaves that the idea of natural obligation was introduced in the second century of the Christian era, though it was afterwards extended to other cases; and obligations of this kind could be contracted not only between slaves and third parties but also between master and slave. This was, to a lesser extent, the consequence of the enhanced importance given by jurisprudence at this period to the personality of all those who were *alieni juris*.[5]

[1] G., 1, 52; D., 50, 17, 133.—**CXXXIV**, 2, 34 et seq.
[2] D., 15, 1, 5-4.—**XCII**, 131 et seq.; **CCLII**, 1, 113 et seq.
[3] Erman, *Servus Vicarius*, p. 425 et seq.
[4] G., 4, 74-77.—**CXI**, 1, 112; **XCII**, 261 et seq.; cf. **CCLXXXVI**, 22.
[5] Seneca, *Ep.*, 47, 95; *de Ben.*, 3, 38.—**CXII**, 368; **CLXV**, **XCII**, 296-312.

III. THE RESTRICTIONS IMPOSED BY LAW ON THE "POTESTAS DOMINICA"

Towards the end of the Republic and especially under the Empire in the second century, the multiplicity of human beings of every condition in town and country establishments (*familiæ urbanæ* and *rusticæ*) gave rise to humanitarian ideas. The Emperors checked abuse of the dominical power. A *Lex Petronia* forbade the exposure of slaves to the wild-beasts of the arena without the judge's sentence. Masters who ill-treated their slaves were compelled to sell them; and the sick or aged slave who had been abandoned was enfranchised as a matter of course.[1] The domestic judge's power of life and death was transferred to the magistrate;[2] and the clause in sales forbidding prostitution of the slave was made obligatory.[3]

At the same time the slave's indeterminate personality was reconceived or strengthened. It was the Law, not nature, that had deprived him of it. Then arose the idea of natural obligation, with the results that we have already described. The *actio injuriarum* was allowed to the master on behalf of the injured *ancilla*, and slanderous denunciation of a slave gave rise to a criminal prosecution.[4]

V

THE FREEDMEN

I. THE FREEDMEN AND THE MODES OF ENFRANCHISEMENT

Slavery was ended by enfranchisement (*manumissio*) or, in the case of prisoners of war, by escape and by the effect of the *jus postliminii*. In this latter case the brand of slavery ceased to have any further effect in the sphere of Roman legal relations; but the sole effect of *manumissio* was, originally, to make the freedman a citizen. It was held that by enfranchising him his master gave him birth as a citizen, bestowing on him his own name and political status; but every bond of subjection was not broken. The dominical power was replaced by the rights of patronage, which were at first per-

---

[1] G., 2, 53; 3, 218; D., 1, 12, 18; 40, 8, 2; 48, 8, 11-2; Aul. Gel., 5, 14.
[2] D., 1, 6, 2; 29, 5, 3-1; Spart., *Vit. Hadr.*, 18.
[3] D., 18, 7, 6-pr.; C. J., 4, 56, 1.   [4] D., 47, 10, 25.

petual. The freedman, *libertinus*, remained attached to the *domus* and dependent on the *paterfamilias*;[1] but just as the dominical power could, through its analogy with the *dominium*, belong to a woman *sui juris*, so too and on the same conditions could she possess the rights of patronage resulting from a *manumissio* which she had herself effected.

According to the Civil Law, enfranchisement was effected: (i.) *per vindictam*, a fictitious process in which the magistrate declared the slave free on the affirmation of an *assertor libertatis* and the admission of the master or his failure to plead; (ii.) *censu*, when by his master's order the slave claimed and obtained his enrolment as *sui juris* in the registers of the census on the day of *lustratio* ; (iii.) *per testamentum*, either directly, in which case the freedman, *libertus orcinus*, was considered to be the testator's freedman, or by an obligation to enfranchise him imposed upon the heir, who was then the *manumissor*. If the testator had made the *manumissio* subject to a suspensive term or condition, the slave remained in the interim *statuliber*, i.e. free *de facto*.[2] Jurisprudence always showed itself in favour of freedom and interpreted acts capable of conferring it in that sense. On several occasions various statutes had to react against this tendency.

Thus when a master had declared his slave free by word of mouth, *inter amicos*, or in writing without using one of the three legitimate modes, the enfranchisement was null; but the prætor opposed any re-enslavement, and the slave remained free *de facto* without even being subject to the rights of patronage. If the master only possessed the slave *in bonis*, which was equivalent to ownership allowing usucapion and guaranteed by an action, the *manumissio* produced similar incomplete results, so that there was a population of uncertain status whose condition was irregular and equivocal. A *Lex Junia Norbana* (727 or 772 A.U.C.) gave these people a definite status by assimilating them to the Latin colonists, and they were called Latin-Junians after it.[3] The *Lex Ælia Sentia* (757 A.U.C.) assimilated to the *dedititii* freedmen who, when

[1] **XCV**, 79-85.
[2] G., 1, 12-17; Ulp., 1, 6-9; 2, 1-12; *Fr. Dosith.*, 17; Festus, s.v. *Manumitti* ; D., 40, 2, 1-7.—**XXXIII**, 13, 225; 28, 149. Julian authorized enfranchisement by oral trust: D., 40, 5, 20.
[3] G., 1, 22; 3, 56; Ulp., 1, 10-11; *Fr. Dos.*, 5-7. Cf. C. Th., 9, 24, 1-5.—**XXXIII**, 26, 1. For the date of the Lex Junia see **CXII**, 101, 4.

they were slaves, had been subjected to degrading punishments, branded with red-hot iron, etc.¹

Formerly, owing to the small number of slaves and consequently of enfranchisements, there had been little danger in this direct introduction of former slaves into the ranks of the citizens, although elsewhere, e.g. at Athens, it had never been tolerated. But towards the end of the Republic, aliens and barbarians made captive in the wars, crowded together on large estates and in private prisons, distributed among all the various grades of service in the great houses, threatened, thanks to the scant political intelligence of their democratizing masters, to overrun the State as a result of legally authorized enfranchisements. In order to prevent this irruption of undesirables, due no less to the misplaced generosity of the masters than to the compliant jurisprudence of the prætors, freedom to enfranchise slaves was restricted in several ways by legislation.

II. STATUTES RESTRICTING THE POWER TO ENFRANCHISE

First of all, conditions were imposed upon enfranchisements *inter vivos*. The tax, *vicesima manumissionum*, based of old on the value of the slave enfranchised (397 A.U.C.), in order to protect free labour, no longer sufficed as a restriction. The *Lex Ælia Sentia* (757) prohibited enfranchisement on the one hand by a master under 25 and, on the other, of a slave under 30, unless there existed in either case a just cause for enfranchisement that had been weighed and recognized by a *concilium manumissionis* consisting, at Rome, of 5 senators and 5 knights under the presidency of the prætor; in the provinces, of 20 *recuperatores*, who must be Roman citizens, presided over by the governor. It was further stipulated that the enfranchisement must take place immediately afterwards *per vindictam*.² The same statute declared null and void all enfranchisements made by a master to defraud his creditors;³ but a minor could legally renounce his real right over a slave, in order to allow the master to enfranchise him.⁴

[1] G., 1, 12-15, 22; Paul, 4, 12, 1-8; cf. 1, 11.—On the *favor libertatis* see **XCII**, 228-261.   [2] G., 1, 17-22; Ulp., 1, 12; *Fr. Dos.*, 17.
[3] D., 40, 9, 10; C. J., 7, 16, 7; I. J., 1, 6, pr.—**LXXXI**, 240.
[4] G., 1, 38-41; I. J., 1, 6, 5.

THE LAW OF THE FAMILY

It was at their death above all that masters flooded the city with freedmen of all kinds, who at last became so numerous that their distinctive dress was forbidden, in order that they might not realize their own number.

The *Lex Fufia Caninia* (752 A.U.C.)[1] enacted that, without ever exceeding 100 enfranchisements, testators should not be allowed to enfranchise their slaves by legacy or trust beyond half the total number, if this was from 2 to 10, one third if it was from 10 to 30, and one quarter if it was from 30 to 100. When these proportions were exceeded, the enfranchisement was null and void in the case of the last to be named, and it was null for all alike if the testator had written their names in a circle.[2] The *Lex Ælia Sentia* applied to enfranchisements in anticipation of death, but excepted the slave under 30, even if condemned and branded, who had been enfranchised by will and appointed sole heir by an insolvent master.

There were also some other obstacles due to the requirements of public order or of the penal Law or to lack of *dominium* over the slave.[3]

III. THE CONDITION OF FREEDMEN AND THE "JURA PATRONATUS"

In classical Law there were then three kinds of freedmen (*liberti, libertini*): *l. cives romani, l. Latini-Juniani, l. dedititii.*

The citizen freedmen took the gentile name, the prænomen, the dwelling-place, *origo* and nationality of the *manumissor*, and enjoyed a limited right of citizenship, having neither *jus honorum* nor, in principle, *jus militiæ*, and being deprived *de facto* of their *jus suffragii* by distribution among the urban tribes and even, at one time, by exclusion from the tribes. They had no right of *conubium*, until the reign of Augustus, with freeborn persons or, after his reign, with the *clarissimi*. They were forbidden to bring an action unless they had a son or a fortune of 30,000 sesterces; they were liable to be put to the torture as witnesses, and their incapacity to occupy municipal magistracies was confirmed by the *Lex Visellia*.[4]

Their civil condition was no less limited by the rights of

[1] **III**, 1907, 16.   [2] G., 1, 42-46; Ulp., 1, 24; Paul, 4, 14.
[3] Paul, 4, 12, 1; Ulp., 1, 18, 19; D., 40, 1, 3; C. J., 7, 7, 1.
[4] C. J., 9, 21, 1.—**XCV**, 79 et seq.; **CCXXXVIII**, 6², 1 et seq.

134 FORMATION OF CLASSICAL LAW

patronage belonging to their patron or to his heirs *ab intestato*, even if these had been disinherited or were willing to forgo them, for the *paterfamilias* could not detach these rights from the family or from the *gens*.[1] Cicero says that freedmen were not very different from slaves. The freedman was called *servus, por*, and remained for a long time subject to the domestic magistracy.[2] He also resembled the clients among whom he had occupied the lowest position in the *gens*. He owed *obsequium* to the patron and to his agnate descendants, who retained a right of guardianship over him, and, failing legitimate offspring, a right of inheritance, which the edict protected by means of two actions, *fabiana* and *calvisiana*, granted against alienations *inter vivos* in violation of this right.[3] He could not summon his patron before a magistrate without the magistrate's authorization and without allowing him the *beneficium competentiæ*.[4] It was his duty to support and succour the patron and his family in all their needs: a duty which, in the second century of the Christian era, was commuted into a simple obligation of maintenance.[5]

On the day of enfranchisement, the patrons caused to be defined by a sworn agreement (*juramentum liberti*) the services or forced labours (*operæ*) that would be due to them, and these were often so burdensome that on several occasions edicts were issued to abolish or at least restrict them.[6] In classical Law the rights of patronage, which had formerly been sanctioned by a *judicium domesticum* and guaranteed against the rival claims of third parties by a *vindicatio*, were made the subject of a *præjudicium* established by the edict.[7]

On the other hand, the duties of the patron—to support his freedman in court, to give him material assistance and maintenance, to refrain from bringing any capital charge against him and from bearing witness against him, to show moderation in his exaction of the *operæ*—were only at a very late date sanctioned by loss of the rights of patronage and made the subject of a *cognitio extra ordinem*.[8]

---

[1] G., 1, 194; D., 37, 14, 9-pr.; but the *paterfamilias* could divide among his sons the *jura patronatus* over his own personal *liberti*: D., 38, 4, 1-pr.
[2] Cic., *ad Quint.*, 1, 1; G., 4, 46; D., 30, 7, 15-1-3.
[3] G., 3, 45, 46; D., 44, 38, 2; Ed.-P., 2, 78; T. G., 454-458.
[4] G., 4, 46; I. J., 4, 6, 38.   [5] Paul, 2, 32.
[6] D., 28, 1, 2-1, 8-pr. Their surrender was forbidden by the Lex Ælia Sentia: D., 38, 1, 25; 37, 14, 61.—**XXXIII**, 23, 143.
[7] D., 40, 14, 6; I. J., 4, 6, 13; Ed.-P., 2, 264.   [8] D., 38, 2, 14.

THE LAW OF THE FAMILY

The status of freedman was at first perpetual and unalterable, but it was limited in the fifth or sixth century A.U.C. to the second generation, and afterwards to the first. The grandson of the former slave was born free, and this was later the case with any child of a free father.[1] Moreover, as a result of the levelling tendency that grew up under the Empire, freedmen of the equestrian census and afterwards, by the Emperor's grant, others as well were given the *jus aureorum annulorum*, which relieved them of their political and civil disabilities, subject to reservation of the patron's rights; while finally, with the patron's consent, the *restitutio natalium* cancelled the rights of patronage and gave them the status of freeborn men.[2]

The Latin-Junian freedmen were assimilated to the Latin colonists, having neither *jus honorum* nor *jus suffragii* nor *conubium* with citizens; but they enjoyed the *jus commercii* and *factio testamenti* in the passive sense, though without the right to take under a will (*jus capiendi*) unless they became citizens within 100 days of the opening of the inheritance. Testamentary trusts were open to them, but they could not make a will. At their death their patrimony returned to the patron as *peculium*, so that, strictly speaking, they died slaves.[3] But they were helped to acquire the right of citizenship in all sorts of ways, and it might be said that the legislator strove to introduce them by various subterfuges into the city from which he had excluded them by means of the *Lex Julia* and the *Lex Ælia Sentia*.[4]

The dedititian freedmen had neither nationality nor *origo* nor *jus commercii* nor *jus conubii*. Roman citizenship was for ever closed against them, and they could not come within a hundred miles of Rome without relapsing into servitude. This was a kind of prohibition of residence. They could not take under a will, even by trust.[5] Originally their condition was hereditary, but a son of a dedititian could escape from it later by invoking the *erroris causæ probatio*.[6]

[1] Quintil., *Inst. orat.*, 5, 10, 60.
[2] D., 40, 10, 6; 11, 2; *Fr. vat.*, 226. Cf. **XCII**, 314 et seq.
[3] G., 1, 23; 3, 56-58; Ulp., 5, 4, 9; 20, 14; 27, 1; 22, 3; *Fr. vat.*, 226
[4] G., 1, 24, 28, 35, 67-75; 3, 172; Ulp., 3, 1.
[5] G., 1, 13, 26, 27
[6] G., 1, 67, 68.

136 FORMATION OF CLASSICAL LAW

VI

THE CLIENTS

Remembrance of the old client system had more or less survived the disappearance of the *gens*. From time to time, on the occasion of an inheritance or a lawsuit, old patrician families managed to recall this dependence to the memory of some chief family which had forgotten it sooner than they had.[1] But clients of a new and very complex character gathered about the powerful families of the republican nobility: clients sometimes of high rank, who sought the support of a great man able to make them a large fortune or advance them to positions of honour; needy or ambitious clients anxious for preferment or alms or both; fawning parasites who went to salute their patron and pay court to him every day; devoted electors and handy men;[2] aliens or subject cities or municipia that required a protector among the great personages of the sovereign city.[3] Though this subjection had no legal significance, it nevertheless involved certain symbolic formalities. The client put himself in fealty (*commendare, tradere in clientelam, in fidem*) to a patron who accepted him (*in fidem suscipere*).[4] He had to honour (*colere*) his patron and, to a great extent, obey him (*observare*); and the patron had to protect his client and help him in his physical or moral needs.[5] The client could, however, leave his patron. Persons of all conditions became clients and, in the case of great patrons, they were finally arranged in a hierarchy according to the degree of favour or distinction which they received: *amici, comites, convivæ, familiares* or mere *salutatores*. Sometimes there were two or three classes of *amici* or of *comites*. Under the Empire the most powerful patron was the Emperor, and the occupation of a high position among his clients constituted a title.[6]

In order to complete the picture of this little world, sometimes considerable enough, over which the Roman *pater-*

---

[1] Cic., *de Orat.*, 1, 39.
[2] Plautus, *Menœchmi*, 4, 2; Seneca, *de Benef.*, 6, 84; Tac., *Hist.*, 1, 4; Juvenal, *Sat.*, 1, 99 et seq. [3] Cic., *pro Plancio*, 41.
[4] *Lex Acilia*, 10; T. G., 34; Cic., *pro Rosc. Am.*, 33, 37; *ad Att.*, 8, 1; *ad Fam.*, 7, 17, 20; Aul. Gel., 5, 13; 20, 1.
[5] Plautus, *l.c.*; Cic., *de dom.*, 21.
[6] Suet., *Tib.*, 46, 56; Capitolinus, *Vita Mar. Aur.*, 22.

familias ruled with more or less sovereign authority, we must add to these voluntary subjects the throng of men who had been subjected at various periods of the past or were still being subjected to the head of the *domus*, whether his power was great or mediocre, by misfortune or the operation of statutes: *nexi, redempti*, persons *in mancipio, alumni*, etc.

SECTION II

PERSONS INCAPABLE "SUI JURIS"

Under the régime of the *gentes* incapable persons not *in patria potestate* were placed under the control of the group, which was represented by the heads of families, so that the authority and influence of each *paterfamilias* was thereby extended. This right of control constituted a power analogous to that which he exercised over persons *alieni juris*, and was termed *vis ac potestas*. It was established in the interests of the whole group. When the clan system was almost broken up, the Law of the Twelve Tables still assigned this power to those who, as heirs to it in his default, had most interest in conserving the incapable's patrimony; but from this time forward in the history of incapacity there is a steady evolution, promoted by the State, from the collectivist to the individualist point of view, according to which the interests of the person deemed incapable are more and more exclusively considered.

The distinction between guardianship and curatorship had been recognized as early as the Law of the Twelve Tables, and both followed the same line of evolution. Curatorship of persons under 25 years of age began much later and developed on individualistic lines only.

I

GUARDIANSHIP

I. THE GUARDIANSHIP OF WOMEN

The guardianship of women, which was still termed *potestas* by Cicero and *manus* by Livy, originally presupposed a right to dispose of both person and property.[1] It was bestowed

[1] D., 26, 1, 1-pr.

by the Twelve Tables on the heirs *ab intestato* of the freeborn woman in the order of their succession—agnates, *gentiles* ; and, in the case of a freedwoman, upon the patron and his heirs *ab intestato*.[1] As it was one of their rights, it belonged to them whatever their age and their personal capacity might be; but they were free to transfer it for the duration of the legal personality both of the transferer and of the transferee (*tutor cessicius*).[2]

But the development of the domestic magistracy of the *paterfamilias*, consecrated by the Law of the Twelve Tables, assigned a supplementary position to the statutory *tutela* thus organized, and gave the first place to the testamentary *tutela*, which was based upon the will and choice of the head of the *domus*. The testamentary guardian was no less required to watch the interests of the family; but as it might happen that those interests were not his own, he was allowed to resign the guardianship but not to dispose of it by transfer.[3]

A woman was not incapable *de facto*. If she was in ward by reason of her light-mindedness and natural ignorance, as was sometimes said in classical times, this was only in so far as those defects might cause injury to her heirs; so that the guardianship gave rise to no obligation on the part of the guardian towards the woman. His task was to help her in her legal acts, which became rarer in course of time, by giving or refusing his *auctoritas* according to their likelihood of success or failure: e.g. in statutory processes, *judicium legitimum*, *aditio hereditatis*, enfranchisement by the Civil Law, alienation of *res mancipi*, *negotia civilia*, consent to the *contubernium* of her freedwoman with someone else's slave.[4] If there was no guardian or the guardian was prevented from being present, these acts were impossible. Until Hadrian's time the woman *sui juris* could not make a will unless she had left her agnate family as a result of *capitis deminutio* : if she was authorized to do so later, it was because the family rights were thereby cancelled.[5]

Towards the end of the Republic the growth of individualism and the relaxation of family bonds led to practices which

[1] Cic., *pro Mur.*, 12; Liv., 34, 2; 39, 9.
[2] G., 1, 144; 168-170; Ulp., 11, 3, 6-8, 19.
[3] Liv., 39, 19; G., 1, 145-149, 151-154; Ulp., 11, 17. BGU, 1113; **XIII**, 43, 455.
[4] G., 1, 179, 191, 192; 2, 47, 79, 81, 85, 118; 3, 108; Ulp., 11, 17, 20-27.
[5] Cic., *Top.*, 4; G., 1, 115a.

THE LAW OF THE FAMILY

made Cicero say that the guardians had now passed under the guardianship of the women.

Some husbands, infatuated by newfangled ideas, devised to their wives *in manu* the choice of their guardian (*optio angusta*), or even the right to change him at their pleasure (*optio plena*).[1] Some aged and compliant statutory guardians authorized women to place themselves under the *manus* of a third party (*coemptio fiduciæ causa*), who pledged himself to enfranchise them and thus to become a complaisant fiduciary guardian (*senex coemptionalis*.)[2] When restoring the woman's patrimony at the moment of enfranchisement, he generally retained the charges on it.

The Atilian (sixth century), Julian and Titian Laws directed the magistrate to appoint a guardian for women who were without one, in order that they might be able to perform the acts requiring *auctoritas*; and a subsequent senatusconsultum made the same provision in case of a guardian's absence or incapacity.[3]

Finally the magistrate went so far as to compel the guardian to grant his *auctoritas*, except when he was the woman's patron or the ascendant who had enfranchised her, in which case he was always free to refuse it to a will and often to a *mancipatio* or a contractual engagement.[4]

Except for the acts which they could not validly perform without the help of the guardian, women either administered their patrimony themselves or, more commonly, intrusted its administration to a friend, a *curator* who was altogether distinct from the guardian. Even when regarded as an institution for the woman's protection, this guardianship seemed every day more troublesome and old-fashioned. The statutes of escheat exempted all women with the *jus liberorum*.[5] A *Lex Claudia* (46 A.D.) abolished the statutory guardianship of the agnates. Little by little the institution fell into disuse, but traces of it may still be found in some papyri until the sixth century.[6]

[1] Cic., *pro Mur.*, 12; G., 1, 150-154.
[2] G., 1, 115, 172; Liv., 39, 9; Aul. Gel., 12.
[3] G., 1, 176, 178, 180, 194; Ulp., 11, 16-22.
[4] Cic., *pro Mur.*, 12; G., 1, 190-192.
[5] G., 1, 171, 194; Ulp., 11, 8; 29, 3.—**XXXIII**, 30, 173.
[6] *Pap. Cair.*, 67023.

II. Guardianship of Children under the Age of Puberty

The Law of the Twelve Tables left to the *paterfamilias* the task of appointing guardians by will for children below the age of puberty who were rendered *sui juris* by his decease.[1] He was free to choose any man whom he could have instituted as his heir, although later on, after the creation of the Latin-Junians, members of that class were excepted. The appointment had to be made in imperative form but might be subject to a time-limit or the fulfilment of some condition. These guardians, *tutores dativi*, were permitted to resign their guardianship.[2]

Failing a *tutor dativus*, the Twelve Tables established a statutory guardianship which was conferred upon the nearest agnate or, in his absence, upon the *gentiles*; but its exercise was soon limited by the decision of jurisprudence that any appointment of a testamentary guardian, even if irregular and invalid, rendered statutory guardianship impossible.[3] The guardian of enfranchised children below the age of puberty was their patron, in whose succession *ab intestato* this right of guardianship was included. Although passed over in silence by the Law of the Twelve Tables, it formed a part of the rights of patronage.[4]

Established in the interest of the family, guardianship was a power (*potestas*) over the person and property of the wards, which were intrusted, as it was said, to the faithful supervision of the guardians. Its preservation for the family was a peculiarly sacred duty which took precedence even of those towards guests and clients.[5] But since on the one hand the family interest was confounded in practice with that of the statutory guardians or intrusted to the good faith of the testamentary guardians, who were often the same persons, while on the other hand no distinction had yet been drawn between acts of administration and acts of disposition, the guardian was, as regards the property of his ward, *in loco domini*. He disposed of it as if it were his own, and if anything was stolen, he had the action for theft (*actio furti*)[6].

---

[1] XII T., 5, 3; Liv., 1, 34. [2] G., 1, 149, 155; 2, 231; Ulp., 11, 14, 16, 17.
[3] Cic., *de Nat. Deor.*, 2, 46; G., 1, 155, 164; 3, 17; I. J., 1, 15, 1; D., 26, 2, 1-pr.—**CCXXXVI**, 1, 385.
[4] G., 3, 58; D., 26, 4, 3-4; I. J., 1, 17, 1.
[5] Aul. Gel., 5, 13. [6] D., 26, 7, 27.

THE LAW OF THE FAMILY 141

Moreover the income derived from the property belonged to him. This idea, which was common to all primitive legislations, is here confirmed by the fact that the property was said to be intrusted to the good faith of the guardians, and that the depositary, of whom the same thing was said, became the owner. Hence there was no administrative obligation.

The guardianship ended when the age of puberty was reached. On becoming an adult, the *paterfamilias* immediately assumed the government of his *familia*, and the guardian at whose disposal it had been hitherto was obliged to restore it. If he did not do so with scrupulous exactness, he neither violated his ward's right of ownership nor committed a theft, since until that moment he had himself been the proprietor (*dominus*). It was, however, an act of perfidy on his part, a breach of faith with his ward (*perfide agere, fraudare pupillum*), who may once have been protected by religious sanctions; and the Twelve Tables, regarding this as a delict, provided the ward with an action *rationibus distrahundis*, in which the condemnation was twice the amount embezzled and no inquiry was made whether the guardian's intention had been fraudulent or not.[1] To the Twelve Tables was also attributed the introduction of a criminal prosecution (*crimen suspecti tutoris*), but the origin is doubtful, because this action, which was *popularis* and involved the dismissal and disgrace of the guardian, implies that his rights had lost their force and that guardianship was in course of being transformed into an institution for the protection of the ward.[2]

This new point of view, in accordance with which the word *tutela* was substituted for *vis* and *potestas*,[3] involved (i.) the appearance of honorary guardianships; (ii.) a different theory of the duties and responsibility of guardians; (iii.) a very complex jurisprudence concerning the capacity of wards.

Since the guardian had become a protector, it was just that the State, which took great pains to protect individuals, should provide a guardian for the ward who was without one. Already, in cases where the interests of the ward and his acting guardian conflicted, the prætor had taken it upon himself to appoint a guardian *ad hoc* (*tutor prætorius*).[4] Thus

[1] G., 1, 59, 60; D., 26, 7, 55-1.
[2] D., 26, 10, 1-2; I. J., 1, 26, pr.
[3] XIII, 13, 1-20; CV, 106
[4] G., 1, 184.

guardianship passed out of the sphere of family Law into that of public Law, and *filiifamilias* could be burdened with it as with any other public duty.[1] A *Lex Atilia* of the sixth century assigned the task of appointing guardians to the Prætor Urbanus assisted by the majority of the tribunes of the plebs, which was particularly interested; but it passed under Claudius to the consuls, under Marcus Aurelius to a *prætor tutelaris* at Rome and to *juridici* for the rest of Italy, and, a little later, to the Prefect of the City in cases where sons of the *clarissimi* were concerned.[2] These were the Atilian guardians. The Titian and Julian Laws, which were later than the one just mentioned, intrusted this power in the provinces to the provincial governors, who exercised it on the motion of the local magistrates. Under the Empire these latter themselves appointed guardians for wards of humble position.[3] The appointment could be demanded by anybody and had to be demanded by the mother or the father's freedmen or, later, his heirs presumptive.[4] Jurisprudence and various statutes established a whole series of incapacities and exemptions which varied in the course of the centuries.[5] Then, passing beyond even the statutory requirements, this jurisprudence extended the appointment of honorary guardians to all cases in which the testamentary or statutory guardianships had disappeared or were suspended either *de facto* or *de jure*.[6] Finally, under the Empire, guardians irregularly appointed by will had to be confirmed by decree, either with or without inquiry according to circumstances, whether the appointment had been formally invalid or had been made by someone other than the *paterfamilias*.[7] Guardianship had become a public duty (*onus, munus civile*), a fact which still excluded women therefrom.

Since the ward remained owner of his patrimony, the guardians' duty was transformed into an obligation to render assistance which might take one of two forms: (i.) a voluntary administration of the ward's fortune sanctioned according to some authorities by an *arbitrium tutelæ* at the end of the

[1] D., 1, 6, 9.
[2] G., 1, 185; *Fr. vat.*, 232; Liv., 39, 9; Suet., *Claud.*, 23; D., 27, 1, 45-3.
[3] G., 1, 185; *Fr. sin.*, 20; D., 27, 8, 1-9-10.—**CXI**, 2, 151; **CXCV**, 2, 286. Guardianships were only allotted by the higher magistrates after inquiry.
[4] *Fr. sin.*, 20; D., 26, 6, 2-1-2; C. J., 5, 31, 2.
[5] *Fr. vat.*, 123-127; D., 27, 1; C. J., 5, 62; 10, 48.
[6] **XLIX**, 1, n°. 135.
[7] D., 26, 8.

THE LAW OF THE FAMILY 143

guardianship,[1] according to others by the action for agency (*actio negotiorum gestorum*),[2] and according to others again by a *satisdatio*, a guarantee supported by fidejussors and required of the guardian when he entered upon office,[3] though in any case these were afterwards replaced by a special action for guardianship (*actio tutelæ*) with characteristics of its own, which Cicero already numbered among the actions *bonæ fidei* ;[4] (ii.) an *auctoritas tutoris* by which the personality of the ward acting in his own name was made perfect, and the validity of his act guaranteed. For a long time jurisprudence dared not compel the defaulting guardian to render either kind of assistance; but at last he was obliged to undertake administration by an order (*jussus*) of the magistrate.[5] Marcus Aurelius assumed this order to be given as soon as the guardian was finally appointed.

An *actio tutelæ utilis* was granted when the duty of administration was not discharged.[6] Since the guardian's administration was now compulsory, it was compulsory for him to render an account. The conditions governing his guardianship were reflected in the nature of the *actio tutelæ* which was degrading without being penal and at first sanctioned theft alone, though it was gradually extended to mere negligence on the part of the guardian.[7] Meanwhile an *actio tutelæ contraria* was framed to enable him to recover his outlay and repair any losses incurred through his administration.[8]

Carrying precision still further, the Jurists drew up a programme of this administration: first of all an inventory of the ward's property and of the bequests that he received, failing which, he himself could fix its amount on oath when reaching the age of puberty;[9] then sale of perishable or useless things, recovery of outstanding debts, investment of disengaged moneys within a limited period under pain of paying interest on them, payment of debts owed, cultivation of rural estates, actions at law, if one should arise, education of the ward according to his fortune and his rank,[10] etc. But any act diminishing the ward's fortune was forbidden. No

[1] **CXI**, 1, 566; cf. **XXXIII**, 19, 168.   [2] **CCC**, 24 et seq.
[3] **XIII**, 25, 634; **CCXCVII**; **CLVIII**, 227 et seq.
[4] Cic., *de Off.*, 3, 17.—**XIII**, 22, 255.
[5] Cf. **CXI**, 2, 155, where this obligation is connected with a Lex Claudia.
[6] G., 4, 182; *Fr. vat.*, 155; D., 26, 7, 1-pr.-1.—BGU, 1113.
[7] D., 27, 3, 1-pr.   [8] D., 27, 4.
[9] D., 26, 7, 7-pr.; C. J., 5, 51, 31-2.   [10] D., 26, 7, 11.

144 FORMATION OF CLASSICAL LAW

donation was allowed.[1] Novation, the proffer of an oath, acceptilation or desistance were only valid when they benefited the ward. Under the Empire the doctrine gained in wealth and in subtle distinctions. A great addition was made to it in 195 by the *oratio Severi* which forbade the sale of *bona rustica et suburbana* except on the magistrate's decree pronounced in accordance with the advice of a family council and with the sole object of avoiding *bonorum venditio*.[2] If the sale was void, it was not even covered by usucapion;[3] but necessary alienations were accepted, as well as those ordered by the person of whom the ward held the property.

The absence of representation at law from the Roman system caused the guardian to become creditor and debtor in the contracts which he made with third parties. When rendering account of his guardianship, he had therefore to make over the claims thus acquired to his ward, and the latter had to agree to the transfer of the obligations to his own account. In the second century of the Christian era alienations and purchases could be made on the ward's account by the agency of the guardian as by that of any other mandatary. Under the Severi *cessio actionum* was often taken for granted, at least in the doctrine of Ulpian. *Actiones utiles* could be brought for or against the ward immediately.[4] The obligations and responsibilities of the guardian were extended by fictitious actions to the *protutor* or *falsus tutor*, i.e. the person who had served as guardian *de facto* without having been appointed. Third parties with whom he had transacted business as guardian had recourse against him either in the civil or penal courts according to his good or bad faith.[5]

The obligations of the guardian were guaranteed first of all by a *satisdatio rem pupilli salvam fore*, a security required under threat of *pignoris capio* from statutory and honorary guardians appointed without inquiry, and stipulated on behalf of the *infans* ward by one of his slaves or by a public slave.[6] As we have said, some think that this was earlier than the action for guardianship, but it does not seem to go further back than Claudius.[7] Afterwards they were guaranteed successively by (i.) an *action sbsidaria* framed by a

[1] D., 27, 3, 1-2-5.—I, 10, 84. [2] D., 6, 2, 13-2; 27, 9, 1-pr.-2.
[3] D., 25, 9; C. J., 5, 39, 1. [4] I. J., 2, 9, 5.
[5] D., 27, 2; 27, 6, 11; Ed.-P., 1, 135.
[6] D., 46, 6; I. J., 1, 24, pr.-1-3. [7] **CXI**, 2, 155, 157; **CXII**, 214, 2.

THE LAW OF THE FAMILY 145

senatusconsultum of the time of Trajan against municipal magistrates who had admitted insolvent fidejussors to the preceding *satisdatio*;[1] (ii.) a *privilegium inter chirographarios* giving the ward the right to be paid what was owed him by his guardian before creditors of the latter who had the obligation in his own handwriting.[2]

Auctoritas, a formal act, was the result of a short dialogue between the guardian and the third party contracting with the ward in person: *Auctorne fis? Auctor fio.* That was all. No modality was allowed. It assumed that the ward had emerged from *infantia*, for he was a party to the act and acquired the obligation, either as creditor or debtor. It placed the guardian under no responsibility to the third parties, but he was responsible to the ward if by granting or refusing it he involved him in loss.[3] This procedure could be used in all acts which the guardian was able to perform alone, and had to be used in those which required the direct action of the owner of the right: viz. enfranchisement, mancipation, *aditio hereditatis* and *acceptilatio*. Henceforward it was only allowed when the ward had emerged from *infantia* (*infantia major*); but the guardian could cause acts of acquisition to be performed by one of the ward's slaves who acquired for his master, and could himself appear in the statutory process because he had originally been *in domini loco*, regarded as proprietor.

The personal intervention of the ward in the administration of his patrimony led to the establishment of a doctrine concerning his capacity.[4] A distinction was drawn between the *infans* under 7[5] who was held to be incapable of any legal act except at last, as a special favour, of stipulating the *satisdatio rem pupilli salvam fore* and entering upon an inheritance with *auctoritas tutoris*, and the ward *infantia major* who could perform alone acts that bettered his condition, but only with *auctoritas tutoris* those that made it worse. The former were acquisitions of real or personal rights; the latter gifts or transfers of real rights and entry into personal engagements.[6] The effects

---

[1] D, 27, 8, 1-1; C. J., 5, 75, 1, 5; I. J., 1, 24, 2-4.—**XXXIII**, 24, 418; **XLIV**, 2, 143.
[2] D., 27, 3, 22, 25.   [3] Ulp., 11, 25.
[4] D., 26, 7, 1-2.—**CCLVI**, 131, 1.
[5] But D., 22, 1, 14; 26, 7, 12 appear to be interpolated.—**XXXVIII**, s.v. *Infans*; **XXI**, 89, 252-264.
[6] Ulp., 11, 27; C. J., 6, 31, 5; I. J., 1, 21, pr.-1.

of synallagmatic acts and of certain unilateral acts with complex consequences were dissociated. They were valid in so far as they enriched the ward, but otherwise void: a harsh solution which Antoninus Pius modified by enacting that the ward should be bound up to the amount of his profit and the other contractor furnished with an *exceptio* to that extent.[1] If the nature of the act did not admit of this dissociation, *auctoritas tutoris* was required to give it validity.[2] The ward like every *impubes proximus pubertati* was answerable for his delicts.

Jurisprudence was not diverted by the rescript from a course that was both uneconomic and damaging by its excessive precautions to the credit of wards. During the period of classical Law it arrived at some strange solutions: (i.) in acts performed by the guardian alone the ward was only bound up to the amount of his profit; for the balance the third parties had a recourse against the guardian; (ii.) in those performed by the ward alone the rule was what we have just described; (iii.) in those performed with *auctoritas tutoris* the ward had an *exceptio* beyond the amount of his profit. Moreover classical Law required that all acts during the period of guardianship, whether performed by the guardian or the ward, and in whatever circumstances or under whatever guarantees they had been performed, should be subject to *restitutio in integrum* if the injured ward had no other way of recourse. This was the ruin of his credit.[3]

Guardianship was terminated by the ward on his arrival at the age of puberty, on his death or on his *capitis deminutio ;* by the guardian on his death, on the realization of some condition that could affect testamentary guardianship, on his exemption during the course of the guardianship, on his *capitis deminutio* (except that, in case of capture by the enemy, statutory guardians could avail themselves of the *jus postliminii*), on his resignation, if he was a testamentary guardian (though Hadrian afterwards substituted certain grounds of exemption for this right), and on his condemnation for *crimen suspecti tutoris*.[4]

[1] G., 2, 84; D., 26, 8, 5-pr.   [2] I. J., 4, 21-pr.   [3] D., 44, 27-pr., 49-pr.
[4] D., 26, 4, 2, 5-5; I. J., 1, 22, pr.-5.—**XIII**, 41, 455.

II
CURATORSHIP

I. CURATORSHIPS OF MADMEN AND SPENDTHRIFTS

Ancient custom had established in the interest of the family group another *potestas* over the person and property of lunatics and spendthrifts.[1] We have the text of the Law of the Twelve Tables which, in pursuance of this tradition, handed over the lunatic who had no guardian to the care of his agnates and, failing them, his *gentiles ;* but the text referring to spendthrifts has not survived, so that the field has been left open for conjectures.[2] As adult *patresfamilias* were concerned, statute or jurisprudence had limited their subjection to the period in which their derangement was an obvious danger to the hereditary interests of the group. Every form of mental ailment, every act of extravagance did not require it.

The Twelve Tables only took account of the *furiosus*, the lunatic who is unconscious of his own acts or subject to hallucinations,[3] and the spendthrift who wasted his *bona paterna avitaque*, i.e. property received by intestate succession from his paternal ascendants;[4] and this was in accord with the view taken of lunatics by people at a low stage of civilization, and with their idea of the rights of the group over property that is in any way incorporated in it. In strict law the curatorship of the madman began and ended with his madness and was suspended during his lucid intervals: a logical system, but one that was hard to apply in practice and full of risk for third parties, who found it difficult to ascertain when the period of incapacity began or ended.[5] On the other hand curatorship of the spendthrift was begun by a magisterial decree forbidding commercial dealings in the property concerned, and was ended by another decree of withdrawal.[6] The decemvirs did not concern themselves

---

[1] Ulp., 12; Paul, 3, 4a, 7. Some think that the spendthrift was only forbidden management of his own affairs when he had children.—**CXI**, 1, 314; cf. **LVII**, 1, 121-124.
[2] XII T., 5, 7a ; Ulp., 12, 2; Paul, *l.c.*—**CXI**, 315; **LVII**, 81 et seq.
[3] Cic., *Tusc.*, 3, 5; D., 29, 7, 2, 3.
[4] Paul, 3, 4, 7; cf. **LVII**, 1, 101-120.
[5] C. J., 5, 70, 6.   [6] Ulp., 12, 2; Paul, 3, 4a, 7; I. J., 2, 12, 1.

either with the other varieties of mental incapacity that have since become so numerous, or with the waste of other kinds of property. During their time of office, the property of the lunatic or the *bona paterna avitaque* of the spendthrift were entirely at the curators' disposal: they could administer them or not, as they pleased.[1]

But curatorship, like guardianship, came to be regarded as an institution for the protection of the incapable person, and this transformation gave rise to (i.) honorary curatorships; (ii.) an increase in the classes of persons *in cura ;* (iii.) a more complex theory of the capacity of persons *in cura* and of the duties of curators.

Curators for lunatics and spendthrifts were nominated by the prætor if statutory curators defaulted or if, in any particular case, none was appointed by statute; and this practice made for the substitution of honorary for statutory curators in all cases.[2] At the same time the solicitude of the magistrate was extended to feeble-minded persons of every kind and degree that a closer observation could discover or a more advanced civilization could produce; then, by analogy, to deaf, dumb or infirm persons;[3] and finally to spendthrifts who wasted any kind of property, perhaps assimilating them to lunatics.[4]

The new curators could not be allowed the *potestas* which had been granted to the old ones: it was changed into *cura, curatella*, the mere right to administer another person's fortune,[5] sanctioned only by actions for administration (*actiones negotiorum gestorum directa* and *contraria*) which could be brought after each transaction without waiting for the period of curatorship to come to an end.[6] Jurisprudence made this administration subject to rules modelled on those which applied to guardianship. It covered all acts which did not require the personal intervention of the owner of the right and, as a general rule, suffered the same embarrassments from the principle of non-representation, which were afterwards removed in the same way. The *oratio Severi* was extended to it also. Later on, failing entry on the inheritance, the curator could demand in the name of the incapable that he should

---

[1] G., 2, 64. [2] G., 1, 197; Ulp., 12, 1-3; D., 27, 10, 1.—**XIII**, 15, 310.
[3] D., 3, 1, 3-4; I. J., 1, 23, 4.—**LVII**, 1-60.
[4] D., 26, 5, 12-2.—**LVII**, 142-153; **XVII**, 1891, 236.
[5] **CVIII**, 1, 59 [6] D., 27, 3, 4-3, 13.

THE LAW OF THE FAMILY 149

be put in possession of his hereditary property (*bonorum possessio*).[1] These incapables benefited by the guarantee derived from the *satisdatio rem salvam fore* which was imposed upon honorary curators, from the *actio subsidiaria* against local magistrates, from the *privilegium inter chirographarios* and from the *restitutio in integrum*, with the same consequences for their credit as for that of wards.[2]

The doctrine that was established concerning the capacity of the lunatic or spendthrift certainly seemed logical, for as the former was incapable of giving a valid consent[3] and the latter was deprived of *commercium*, neither could be a party to any legal act.[4] Nevertheless classical Law allowed the spendthrift to perform those which bettered his condition.[5]

The same grounds of disqualification or exemption were recognized in the case of curatorship as of guardianship.[6] It came to an end for the same reasons, except that attainment of puberty was replaced by recovery of reason or good sense, for the honorary curatorship of spendthrifts seems to have ended without any new decree[7]—another danger for third parties.

II. CURATORSHIP OF PERSONS UNDER 25 YEARS OF AGE

The curatorship of persons under 25 years of age was the first institution concerning personal status whose origin cannot be traced back to the solidarity of the family or clan. It appeared when the decay of this solidarity made men realize that attainment of puberty was not sufficient to enable young *patresfamilias* to administer a patrimony which was often large and complex. The first sign of a legislative system fixing *ætas legitima* or *plena ætas* at the twenty-fifth year is to be found in a *Lex Plætoria* of the sixth century A.U.C., to which Plautus alludes. It made the act of defrauding minors (*circumscriptio adolescentium*) liable to a criminal prosecution (*judicium publicum rei privatæ*) which involved a fine as well as the accessory penalties of ignominy and

---

[1] G., 2, 64; D., 27, 10, 7.
[2] D., 27, 3, 25; 9, 1, 2, 11; C. J., 5, 37, 20; I. J., 1, 24-pr.-2-3. On these various points see pp. 143-6.
[3] G., 3, 106; D., 50, 17, 14; I. J., 3, 19, 8.
[4] D., 45, 1, 6; 50, 17, 40.   [5] D., 29, 2, 5-1.
[6] Cic., *de Inv.*, 2, 4.—LVII, 219.   [7] D., 27, 10, 1-pr.—LVII, 300

150 FORMATION OF CLASSICAL LAW

degradation from any public office.[1] The act thus vitiated was not annulled; but owing to its heavy fine this public action was protective as well as penal, and although *minus quam perfecta*, the statute seemed to be a sufficient defence.[2] Some have thought, however, that besides the criminal prosecution the statute organized a civil action for recovery of the *datio* or *obligatio* agreed upon by the injured minor.[3] As such a risk for those who made contracts with them threatened to destroy the minors' credit, either practice or, according to Capitolinus, the statute itself advised minors to request the magistrate to appoint a curator for certain specified transactions,[4] whose help would render third parties less liable to incur the sanctions of the *Lex Plætoria*.[5]

After the *Lex Æbutia* the edict went further still. It added to the preceding legislation (i.) an *exceptio legis Plætoriæ* enabling the minor to repel the action of the *circumscriptor* and available concurrently with the *exceptio doli*, because the manœuvres conceived of as *circumscriptio* did not at that period come within the definition of fraud;[6] (ii.) a *restitutio in integrum* based upon his minority (*ob ætate*), which was granted even in the absence of *circumscriptio* or fraud simply because the minor found himself injured (*captus*) and there was no other means of repairing his loss. Moreover the latter continued to be available for a year.[7]

Under the Empire practice extended the employment of curators. Curatorship could become permanent if the minor demanded it or if the *paterfamilias* had kindly appointed a curator in his will—an appointment which had no validity but was almost always confirmed by the magistrate's decree.[8] Third parties treating with a minor often demanded that he should have assistance, and when the guardianship of women had ceased to have any serious effect, some women in their minority also had curators.[9] But the rule was never absolute. In classical times there were always some minors of

---

[1] Plaut., *Pseud.*, 1, 3, 69-70, 84; Cic., *de Off.*, 3, 13; *L. Jul. mun.*, 1, 111; T. G., 87; D., 4, 4, 16-1.
[2] The action was probably granted for twice or four times the amount embezzled, according to the rule in penal actions: **CLXXXII**, 4, 118; **CCLIV**, 2, 193.
[3] D., 44, 1, 71; 4, 4, 24-3; *For. fabian :* T. G., 457.—**CLVIII**, 239.
[4] **CXII**, 228, 5-6.   [5] Capitolinus, *Vit. Marc. Aur.*, 10.
[6] D., 4, 4, 24-1; cf. D., 4, 3, 7-pr.; 46, 3, 48-2 (interpolated).—**XLIX**, 1, n° 172.   [7] D., 4, 4, 11-4, 13-1.
[8] I. J., 1, 23; D., 26, 3, 1-3, 6.   [9] *Fr. vat.*, 110; C. J., 5, 31, 1-7.

THE LAW OF THE FAMILY

both sexes who had had no curator or, after having had one, recovered the power of administering their property,[1] except in the eastern provinces where the Greek practice was maintained of appointing an official curator compulsorily.[2]

Jurisprudence concerned itself especially with the permanent curators whom it assimilated to guardians, for they could administer the minor's fortune in accordance with the rules governing administration (though it has recently been maintained that only curators of lunatic minors, spendthrifts, soldiers or female minors administered their property, and that the texts on the other side are interpolations),[3] or else cause the minor to act with the support of their *consensus*—an informal act.[4] *Satisdatio rem salvam fore, actio subsidiaria, privilegium exigendi* and the *oratio Severi* were extended to permanent curatorship.[5] It was admitted logically that if minors who had no curators administered their own patrimony, those who had permanent curators could perform no acts alone except those which bettered their condition;[6] but any act performed by any minor, with or without the *consensus* of his curator, was liable to *restitutio in integrum* merely on the proof that he had lost by it.[7] Curatorship became a second and more prolonged sort of guardianship.

There had been a transition from complete liberty to excessive protection, and the benefit of *venia ætatis* was devised in the third century by way of reaction. Men over 20 and women over 18 could at their own request be relieved by rescript of every incapacity, except that they were obliged to respect the prescriptions of the *oratio Severi* and were forbidden to dispose of their property gratuitously.[8]

---

[1] D., 26, 7, 39-18.—**CCLXXXII**, 319 et seq.   [2] **VII**, 888.
[3] **CCLXXXII**, *l.c.* Cf. **XIII**, 41, 459.
[4] D., 27, 4, 1-2; C. J., 21, 23, 3; 3, 6, 2.—**XIII**, 41, 460.
[5] D., 27, 8, 1, 11; C. J., 5, 37, 20; I. J., 1, 24, pr. 3.
[6] D., 45, 1, 101.—**CLVIII**, 241.   [7] C. J., 2, 21, 3.
[8] D., 4, 4, 20-pr.-1; C. J., 2, 45, 1, 3-pr.—**XIII**, 4, 460.

CHAPTER IV
CORPORATIVE LIFE AND ARTIFICIAL PERSONS

I. CORPORATIONS AND ASSOCIATIONS IN THE LAW OF THE REPUBLIC

BEFORE the Twelve Tables there existed some professional corporations and a certain number of *sodalitates*, perhaps religious colleges established to perpetuate the cults of vanished *gentes* or to provide for those of new gods,[1] but more probably, as a general rule, plebeian associations with a religious or philanthropic object, sometimes pleasure meetings, which had their own heads and assemblies and a disciplinary jurisdiction.[2] The Law of the Twelve Tables confirmed this state of affairs and allowed members of societies (*sodales*) to adopt whatever rules they pleased, so long as they did not conflict with any public statute.[3] Whether this applied to the trade-bodies as well as the *sodalitates* is a matter of dispute; some say that the former must have received their regulations from the State,[4] but this is not certain. The *Lex Gabinia* concerning private assemblies, the *Sc. de Bacchanalibus* (568 A.U.C.) and some other enactments merely applied the principle of this liberal and purely restrictive legislation. After Catilina, the political factions, electoral associations and suspicious meetings of oriental and orgiastic cults provoked a reaction. A senatusconsultum and perhaps certain statutes proclaimed the dissolution of many *collegia*,[5] and an attempt was made to establish the rule that there should be no associations, or at least no new ones, without authorization. But in 696 the *Lex Clodia de collegiis* reestablished the suppressed colleges with absolute freedom.[6] Three years afterwards, however, the *Lex Licinia de sodaliciis* forbade the electoral comitia trafficking in votes; and in 707

---
[1] CCXXXV, 8-25.   [2] CCXXXVI, 2, 734
[3] XII T., 8, 27; D., 47, 22, 4.   [4] C, 100 et seq.
[5] Cic., pro Sext., 25; D. Cass., 38-13.—CCXCIII, 1, 98-111.
[6] Cic., ad Att., 1, 16; 3, 15; D. Cass., 39, 37.

CORPORATIVE LIFE

Cæsar suppressed all the colleges except the most ancient, i.e. the professional corporations dating back to the regal period. His statute was extended to the provinces.[1]

II. THE STATUTES AND JURISPRUDENCE OF THE EMPIRE

The imperial era was inaugurated by a *Lex Julia de collegiis*. The old trade-bodies, consecrated by tradition and statute, were maintained; but, apart from them, no association was allowed unless authorized by the Senate on the ground of public utility.[2] This was the classical doctrine which we see applied in Egypt under Tiberius, at Rome under Claudius, in Bithynia under Trajan. Some exceptions were admitted: (i.) by Augustus himself in favour of the Jewish religious associations, according to Philo;[3] (ii.) by a senatusconsultum earlier than 133 for Rome and Italy, by a rescript of Septimius Severus for the provinces, in favour of *collegia tenuiorum*, associations of humble folk who, provided that their meetings did not serve as a cloak for any illegal proceeding, could assemble once a month to pay their subscriptions (*stipes*) or even more often to hold festivals or religious ceremonies. Slaves and aliens were admitted to them,[4] and most of them were burial societies, though neither banquets nor drinking parties were excluded. Following de Rossi, many historians have imagined that the first Christian-communities were disguised as philanthropic and burial societies of this kind. The *Apologeticus* of Tertullian suggests this conjecture, which remains a plausible one in spite of all that has been said since and of the difficulty caused by the late date of the rescript of Septimius Severus for the provinces.[5] Must we really suppose that, in addition to those recognized by statute, administrative practice made a third exception in favour of associations that were not authorized, but merely tolerated because, although their form was illegal, their object was inoffensive ? If they had escaped the penal statutes for this reason, they would have been assimilated *de facto* to the

---

[1] Suet., *J. Cæsar*, 42; Fl. Joseph., *Arch. jud.*, 14, 18.
[2] Suet., *Oct.*, 32; T. G., 887; D., 3, 4, 1-pr. Some think that the statutes of Cæsar and of Augustus were in reality one. On what follows see **CCXII**.
[3] D. Cass., 40, 6; Pliny mi., *Ep.*, 43, 93, 94, 97; D., 47, 22, 1-pr.; 11, 2.
[4] D., 47, 22, 1, 3-2; T. G., 888. It does not seem likely that they had to be exclusively burial societies; but see **CCXCIII**, 1, 313.
[5] **XLIV**, 469-509 gives a summary of the controversy; also **XCIX**.

authorized colleges;[1] but this is very improbable. The truth is that illegal association gave rise either to criminal prosecutions or, out of consideration for the members' good faith, to a mere decree of dissolution.[2] Under this double form of *collegia opificum* and *collegia tenuiorum*, whose activity moreover was by no means confined to the conduct of funerals, associations increased in number. Trajan, Antoninus Pius, Pertinax and Alexander Severus seem to have especially favoured them. As early as the third century some colleges were intrusted with public services which gave their members certain privileges, so that they became adjuncts of the government before they were incorporated in it.[3]

III. Artificial Personality: the "Universitates"

The problem of artificial personality did not confront the Romans in a purely direct and theoretical manner. It was as a body of property which had to be administered, although there was no individual owner living, that they first had a dim presentiment of it; and the empirical methods by which administrations of this kind were provided for led to the establishment of a system that was somewhat awkward and incomplete. Classical Law named this body of property a *universitas*, for which a *corpus*, a fantom proprietor, was provided by a legal fiction.[4] The most ancient *universitates* were the public treasury (*ærarium populi*), as regards which the sovereignty of the State long took the place of the right of ownership which was afterwards dissociated from it, and the inheritance lying in abeyance, which was first given the personality of the heir and afterwards that of the dead man.

We can divine a period of indecision when associations lived solely according to the system of joint ownership or of partnership. Traces of it have remained in the language.[5] Cities, colonies and municipia had an organization identical with that of the State; and the colleges and lawful associations, whose administration so closely resembled that of the cities, imitated them in this also. On any supposition, the artificial

[1] CCXCIII, 1, 132-136.　　　　　　　　[2] D., 47, 22, 2, 3-1.
[3] CCXCIII, 1, 169; CCXII, 229; CXXV, 143.
[4] D., 3, 4, 1-pr.-1; 7, 1-2; 44, 1, 22.—CCLII, I, 254, 289; XIII, 13, 504-506.
[5] Ulp., 22, 5; D., 3, 4, 2-20-21.

CORPORATIVE LIFE 155

personality depended on the State which gave it and could also withdraw it. It seems to have been bound up with the possession of a coffer (*habere arcam*), otherwise called a patrimony;[1] and the existence of this alone explained that the juridic entity had rights analogous to those of physical persons: right of patronage, *potestas dominica*, right of ownership, capacity to place itself and others under obligations and to bring actions, a limited *factio testamenti* in the passive sense, etc.[2] The *jus arcam habendi* was synonymous with civil personality, and under the Empire the *jus coeundi*, permission to form an association, included it in strict law. *Universitates* of the public order were administered by their magistrates, their priests or special officials; those of the private order were at first represented by a slave agent (*servus actor*) and afterwards by a free *actor* or *syndicus*. These administrators were gradually assimilated to guardians. The whole body of regulations concerning guarantees, rendering of accounts, representation in legal acts or before the magistrate, was adapted to them.

There is no evidence that in the time of the earlier Empire the Romans had conceived the idea of endowment, i.e. of a body of goods definitely set apart for some determined purpose, some fixed object. The mortgaged patrimony was unknown to them. What the exegetes sometimes call endowments for maintenance were merely bounties subject to taxation and bestowed on legal personalities already in existence.[3]

[1] D., 3, 4, 1-1; 34, 5, 20-21.—**CXCV**, 2, 68; **CCXCIII**, *l.c.;* **CCXXXV**, 36-39, 117-129; **CCLXIX**, 2, 234.
[2] D., 3, 4, 1-3, 3-2-3, 7, 8; 34, 4, 20; Ulp., 22, 5, 6.—**CXXV**, 75-79; **CCXCV**, 214.
[3] T.-G., 840 et seq.—**XIII**, 13, 506-591.

CHAPTER V

THE LAW OF PROPERTY AND REAL RIGHTS

I

THE PATRIMONY. DISTINCTIONS BETWEEN THINGS. RIGHTS TO THINGS OR ARISING OUT OF THINGS

THE power of the *paterfamilias* extended not only to persons but also to things that constituted the family patrimony. *Res*, in legal language synonymous with *bona*,[1] included all material objects of any value to legal persons, whose seizin of them was described by the word *mancipium*. The lawful advantages that persons derived from things were called rights, *jura* ; and the term *res* was often applied to the rights themselves. Later on, the material objects perceptible to the senses were termed *res corporales*, and the abstract rights inherent in them *res incorporales*.[2]

The nature and form of rights depend upon the social environment. In Rome's earliest days they were adapted to the association of the *gens*, and afterwards to the more restricted and dependent association of the *domus*. Then things, like persons, acquired in course of time a sort of autonomy, an ever more marked individualization; and the rights over them were strictly defined and also distinguished. Considered abstractedly according to their characters and effects, without regard to their beneficiaries, they became more objective and more mobile. They could pass from hand to hand, accumulate about the same thing to the profit of various persons, and form artificial or fortuitous combinations; so that the patrimony which had once been composed of a few elements everywhere the same, became at last an aggregate of very different rights collected together by chance or by the taste or energy of the owner.[3]

In the city, however, all usable things were not absorbed

[1] Cf. D., 50, 16, 49; 1, 8, 1-pr.
[2] G., 2, 12-14; D., 50, 16, 23; Cic., *Top.*, 27
[3] D., 50, 16, 122.

PROPERTY AND REAL RIGHTS 157

by private patrimonies. The ancient Jurists derived from the Pontifical Law a *summa divisio rerum* which was based not upon the nature of the things but upon the use to which they were put, since the same things could be devoted to various objects. Following this method of classification they drew a distinction between *res divini juris* and *res humani juris*, which in course of time were further subdivided and complicated.[1] Thus besides *res divini juris*, i.e. *res sacræ* consecrated or dedicated to the gods above,[2] there were also *res religiosæ*, things given up to the *di manes* or land definitely set apart by its owner as a permanent place of burial,[3] and *res sanctæ* used for purposes of national defence;[4] while *res humani juris* were afterwards subdivided into *res publicæ*, public land owned by the State,[5] *res universitatum*, public land owned by the cities,[6] and *res privatæ* which alone composed the patrimony of individuals and were, within limits prescribed by authority, objects of trade between them. Hence we have such late expressions as the following, which correspond to no juridical distinctions: *res in patrimonio nostro vel extra patrimonium; res in commercio vel extra commercium*.[7] The gods, the State, and the cities also acquired at different periods a private patrimony analogous to that of individuals and distinct from *res divini juris* and *res publicæ*.[8]

Rome's economic history made other classifications necessary.[9] The agricultural and patriarchal system gave rise to a distinction between *res mancipi* and *res nec mancipi*. The first were slaves and beasts of burden or of draught: oxen, horses and asses used for the development of the country estate and thus constituting the necessary foundation of the patrimony of every *domus;* to which were added, when they became objects of trade, landed property both in the country and in the town, and prædial servitudes. The second were at first chiefly flocks (*pecora*), but gradually came to include all the new elements of private moveable property, which were

---

[1] G., 2, 1, 2.   [2] G., 2, 3-5; Cic., *pro dom.*, 20, 45.
[3] G., 2, 4, 6; D., 1, 8, 6-4.   [4] G., 2, 8.
[5] G., 2, 11; D., 50, 16, 15, 17.—XIII, 13, 459 et seq.
[6] G., 2, 11; D., 1, 8, 6-1.   [7] G., 2, 1.   [8] D., 18, 1, 16-pr.; 50, 16, 17.
[9] Later on, a category of *res communes* was introduced, comprising things associated with the idea of *jus naturale* and incapable of being appropriated: e.g., the air, the sea-shore, etc. D., 1, 8, 2-1. For another meaning of the term *communis* see Cic., *de Off.*, 1, 16; 2, 21.

at length described, from the point of view of their value, by the term *pecunia* used in something the same sense as we use the word *wealth* to-day.[1]

Considering still further the economic part played by property, Roman Law distinguished between immoveables and moveables,[2] but without attaching to this distinction the important consequences that were afterwards drawn from it, because at Rome power was never associated with territorial possessions as it was in Western Europe during the Middle Ages.

From the same point of view, the logic of the Jurists opposed *genera*, things considered as belonging to a more or less indeterminate group, to *species*, things regarded individually and therefore liable to disappear or to have only one use. Money was the typical *genus*.[3] The rights to things, real rights, which the beneficiary exercised over the thing directly, without any intermediary, whether it belonged to him (*jus in re sua*) or to someone else (*jus in re aliena*), were opposed to personal rights or rights of claim, which gave one person, the creditor, power to exact some prestation from another, the debtor, and were for this reason called by the Romans *obligationes, nomina*. A real right was available against all the world and persisted even if its object was in the possession of a third party, whereas a personal right only existed as against one or several definite persons and was diminished by the existence of similar rights against the same persons. Real and personal rights together constituted the patrimony.

II

THE RIGHT OF OWNERSHIP

I. ORIGIN AND NATURE OF THE RIGHT OF OWNERSHIP. FAMILY OWNERSHIP

The right of ownership, *dominium, mancipium*, was equivalent to absolute lordship over a thing, subject to certain limitations rendered necessary in an organized State by the coexistence of similar rights and by public interest and

---

[1] G., 2, 14-17, 47; Ulp., 19, 1.—**LXXIX**.
[2] Ulp., 19, 6, 8; D., 50, 16, 93, 211
[3] G. 3, 90; D., 45, 1, 54.

PROPERTY AND REAL RIGHTS

security.[1] Being the right which was recognized and guaranteed to the *gentes*, when the city was founded, over the lands and other things belonging to them, it retained an appearance closely resembling sovereignty, *dominium* from *domare*, because in primitive times ownership was not distinguished from sovereignty, and groups or individuals became lords of a thing when they seized it and had the power to defend it. The spear, *hasta*, continued to symbolize this mode of acquisition.[2]

The origin and fulness of this right, *plena in re potestas*, involved confusion in the later language. Although it was a right and therefore an abstract conception, it was identified with the object itself and reckoned among the *res corporales* : a reminiscence of the time when it was only acquired by force. For the same reason it excluded any other right and was by its very nature perpetual; and it was not until quite a late period that the advantages of ownership were regarded as capable of enjoyment by persons other than the owner. The rights afterwards classified under the title of personal servitudes were a comparatively modern creation in the classical period, and the earliest real rights, at first few in number, were not easily associated with any direct advantage of ownership. Finally, as a result of more advanced analysis, the following classical formula was evolved: *dominium est jus utendi, fruendi, abutendi re sua quatenus juris ratio patitur*;[3] " ownership is the right of using, enjoying, abusing one's property, in so far as the reason of the right allows "—a definition whose success cannot altogether hide its clumsiness.

At first quiritarian ownership, *dominium ex jure Quiritium*, was reserved to members of the city alone, except for the grant of *commercium* to certain allied peoples;[4] but ownership at Rome, with a tendency to become individual, remained to the end a family ownership, i.e. connected with a group of relatives living under the authority of a *paterfamilias*. The patrimony was common to them all.[5] Nevertheless the idea of collective ownership by the *domus* was strangely limited by certain practices. The absolutism of the *paterfamilias* required that this patrimony should be at his exclusive disposal, that all the effects of legal acts in which the property

[1] On the nature of these limitations see **CLVIII**, 267-270.
[2] I. J., 2, 4, 4.
[3] D., 7, 5, 5-1; 8, 1, 2.
[4] Ulp., 19, 4.—**CXI**, 1, 707, 5.
[5] G., 2, 157; D., 28, 2, 11

was concerned, whether performed by himself or by persons placed under his *potestas*, should be concentrated in his own person. So long as he lived, he was sole owner of the patrimonial rights in the eye of the administrative and legal authorities. This concentration was modified by the custom, which was only another way of exercising his arbitrary power, of constituting *peculia* for the persons *alieni juris*, either in order to devolve upon them the task of developing part of the patrimony, or to allow them more independent action.[1] In course of time the prætorian Law devised for these *peculia* and for the capital thus made over with a view to exploitation a sort of fictitious personality, but they did not thereby cease to form a part of the common patrimony, liable to be called in at the sole pleasure of the *paterfamilias*. Then, after the time of the Twelve Tables, the absolute power of the head of the *domus* over the common property was extended beyond his death by the grant of testamentary freedom; and the reaction of statute and jurisprudence against this state of affairs, however serious it may have been, was never more than partial.[2] But when they were left masters of this patrimony, the *heredes sui* did not continue to live communistically except in cases of voluntary association.[3]

Nevertheless the patrimony took the form of an individual fortune in the hands of celibates and of women *sui juris*, whose statutory guardianship became illusory. We know how Augustus created such a fortune for *filiifamilias* in the army by means of the *peculium castrense* ;[4] and on this model Constantine devised the *peculium quasi castrense* for the profit of those who served in the palace or followed one of the liberal or administrative professions.[5] The system of "adventitious goods" (*bona adventitia*) was an analogous venture less perfectly realized in practice. Without ever reaching the goal of its evolution, Roman ownership developed unceasingly in the direction of greater individualization.

[1] *Fr. vat.*, 260; D., 39, 5, 7-pr.   [2] **XIII**, 29, 413.
[3] Liv., 41, 27; Aul. Gel., 1, 9; Festus, s.v. *Sors* ; D., 10, 2, 39-3.--**XXXIII**, 3, 71.
[4] D., 14, 6, 2; 49, 17, 2, 11.   [5] D., 12, 31,1.

PROPERTY AND REAL RIGHTS 161

II. OWNERSHIP OF MOVEABLES AND OWNERSHIP OF LAND

The *dominium* covered every kind of physical object and there is no proof that originally only *res mancipi* were subject to it.[1] When the flocks were the most important moveable property, it is not likely that they would have been excluded from the protection due to ownership, and the Law of the Twelve Tables grants it to them.[2] The truth is that the *res nec mancipi*, a sort of rolling stock, did not require the formal methods of transfer employed in the case of things whose sale deprived the family of its instruments of labour. The content of moveable property rapidly increased and its component parts were infinitely diversified. Monetary wealth was considerable from the time of the Republic. But in order to become objects of quiritarian ownership, moveables had to belong to a Roman, or at least to someone who enjoyed the *jus commercii*. It was only under the Empire that attacks upon an alien's ownership were punished by the edict, by means of fictitious actions in which he was assumed to be a citizen;[3] but there is no trace of a claim for restoration of ownership on behalf of an alien, whether by means of a fiction or an *actio utilis*.

As a result of the dissolution of the *gentes* and the royal *assignationes*, ownership of land was developed unceasingly thereafter at the expense of the State: (i.) by the *assignationes viritanæ*, granted by a magistrate in virtue of a statute to the citizens who claimed them. These were allotments of various size limited by the process of *centuriatio* and sometimes of *scamnatio*;[4] (ii.) by the *assignationes colonicæ*, in virtue of a *lex coloniæ* ordering the drawing up of a *forma colonica* (plan of a colony) and the *deductio colonorum*, i.e. an expedition to establish a colony under the command of a promagistrate. These *assignationes* were divided among the colonists by the promagistrate according to lot,[5] were excluded from *centuriatio* (*subcesiva*, *extraclusa*), and were left in the colony's possession as communal land,[6] being after-

[1] **CXI**, 1, 77; **CLXXXV**, 45; **CCXXXI**, 1, 79; **LXXIX**.
[2] G., 4, 17. [3] G., 4, 87; Ed.-P., 2, 50.
[4] Festus, s.v. *Viritanus ager*; Varro, *de R. r.*, 1, 2; Siculus Flaccus (ed. Lachmann), 154.—**XIII**, 17, 639; **XL**, 1, 100-108; **CCXCIV**, 71.
[5] Festus, s.v. *Adscripti*; Dion. Hal., 7, 13, 28; Cic., *L. agr.*, 2, 7, 11, 13. —**XIII**, 12, 587, 593, 633; **CCXXXVIII**, 2, 715; 9, 152; 10, 118.
[6] *Lex Agraria* (643), ll. 8-9, 19-20: T. G., 48-50; Hygin, Sic. Flac. (ed Lachmann), 117, 162.—**CCXXXVIII**, 9. 173.

wards encroached upon or granted to individuals; (iii.) by the *agri quæstorii*, public land sold by auction by the quæstors at the order of the Senate or of the people.[1] These concessions and sales conferred in principle quiritarian ownership if they involved the *ager romanus*, the original territory of the Roman State, and afterwards if they involved Italian land or what was reputed to be such. Less quickly but perhaps more widely appropriated were the *agri occupatorii* :[2] vast, unfenced regions of waste land, which the State allowed individuals to occupy and fence off. A great deal of capital was required to clear them; and they were occupied on precarious tenure, in consideration of a rent (*vectigal*) paid to the State, by rich capitalists, who sublet them, generally on the same terms, to small tenants. These lands were handed down from generation to generation either in prospect of death or *inter vivos ;* and this, together with the work done upon them, finally gave the occupiers a legal title which was alleged against the tribunes of the people when they claimed surrender of the land in order to make *assignationes* of it to the proletariate. Though constantly attacked and several times restricted, especially by the *Lex Sempronia* (621 A.U.C.) which limited it to 500 acres for each head of a family plus 250 for each male child, the *jus occupandi* triumphed through its own disappearance. Some statutes of the seventh century, that of 643 for instance, confirmed their uncertain tenure in the occupiers' possession and finally changed it into quiritarian ownership.[3] These confirmations and some wholesale grants of the same right of ownership by the emperors produced the great estates or *latifundia*,[4] which were not by any means so widely spread as some have maintained.

To the *ager romanus*, the only land which could originally be the object of quiritarian ownership, all the land of Italy was gradually assimilated, and so finally were those colonies, very few in number, which had been endowed under the Empire with the *jus italicum*, i.e. assimilated to the Italian soil.[5]

[1] Hygin., *l.c.*, 115; Sic. Flac., *l.c.*, 1, 36, 152; Liv., 2, 17.—**XIII**, *l.c.*, 162; **CLXXXIV**, 1, 93 et seq.
[2] Festus, s.v. *Possessiones ;* Hygin., *l.c.*, 115; Sic. Flac., *l.c.*, 138; Agg. Urbicus, ibid., 2.
[3] Cic., *de Off.*, 2, 22; 3, 23; *Lex agraria* (643): T. G., *l.c.*; D., 47, 21, 3, 1.
[4] **I**, 1, 41; **XXXIII**, 4, 260; **XXXIV**, 10, 67; **CCXCIV**, 131.
[5] D., 50, 15, 1, 6-8; Pliny, *N. H.*, 3, 3, 21.—**CCXXXVIII**, 6, 456.

PROPERTY AND REAL RIGHTS

III. PROVINCIAL OWNERSHIP

In the seventh century the land of the provinces was also to a great extent, though less completely, consolidated in the hands of individual owners. By right of conquest it was the property of the Roman people,[1] and it was generally divided into two parts: one, *agri publici*, annexed to the territory of the State, the other, *agri redditi*, abandoned or restored to the original owners for enjoyment in accordance with their own laws and customs at the good pleasure of the Roman people, in whose eyes they were mere occupiers without right of ownership.[2] Let them be allowed to hold it, to possess it, to use it, to enjoy it (*habere possidere uti frui liceto*), said the statutes, thus revealing a *de facto* situation which had no corresponding legal title.[3] The invention of a system of double ownership of land, reserving quiritarian ownership for the Roman people and yet bestowing upon the occupiers of the soil a definite right which, in the second century of the Christian era, was still vaguely called right of occupation (*possessio*) or right of usufruct (*usufructus*), has been attributed to the government of Caius Gracchus and the speculations in landed property which were made in the province of Asia by the leaders of the democratic party.[4] Whatever we may think of this theory concerning the origin of provincial ownership, it is certain that the transition from the earlier situation of precarious tenure to one defined and guaranteed by law, which must assuredly have been accomplished at least in the last century of the Republic, produced a sudden and considerable increase in the value of provincial estates to the profit of those who occupied them at the moment.

This provincial ownership differed from the complete *dominium* over Italian estates, in so far as Public Law was concerned, in that it was subject to a land tax, *stipendium* or *tributum*, which Italy had not paid since 587, and could in theory be more easily expropriated; and, so far as concerned Private Law, in that it could not be the object of any legal acts proper to the Civil Law, but only of those governed by the

---

[1] D., 49, 15, 5-2, 20-1.
[2] Cic., *in Verr.*, 3, 6; *de l. agr.*, 1, 6; 2, 22; Sic. Flac., *l.c.*, 155.
[3] *L. Antonia de Thermessibus; Lex agraria* (643): T. G., 59-69.
[4] G., 2, 7; Frontin., *l.c.*, 430.—**CCXXXVIII**, 6², 366; **XIII**, 18, 114.

164 FORMATION OF CLASSICAL LAW

Law of Nations—a fact which especially affected the modes of transfer and the creation of real rights.[1]

IV. THE SANCTIONS OF THE RIGHT OF OWNERSHIP

The sanction of the right of quiritarian ownership was a real action called *vindicatio*, of the type which we have already described in our account of procedure.

Under the statutory processes it was the *actio sacramenti in rem* of which Gaius has given us a description.[2] Before the *Lex Æbutia* a more simple procedure, *per sponsionem*, substituted for the *sacramenta* a promise of a sum of money made by each litigant to the other in the event of the promisor losing the case: an indirect means of instituting a trial, because the magistrate delivered a formula for each promise thus made. The judge had to decide which should be executed and was thus indirectly constrained to discover who was the owner: but the amount promised was not actually paid; it was merely an artifice of procedure to secure a hearing in court, and was therefore termed præjudicial (*præjudicialis*).[3] It was followed by a personal engagement on the part of the interim owner, guaranteed by fidejussors, to restore the subject of dispute, if he lost the suit, together with its fruits in kind or a sum equivalent to twice their value.[4] This procedure was not double, like that which followed the *sacramenta*, for on each formula the promisor's attitude was purely defensive. It was for the opponent to prove his ownership and his right to the sum which had been promised him on that condition.[5]

Without entirely superseding the foregoing methods, another which was known at least as early as 684 A.U.C. took precedence of them. The suit, *actio per formulam petitoriam vel arbitrariam*, was based upon a formula whose *intentio* directly put the question of ownership,[6] and the judge was empowered to discover what ought to be assigned to the plaintiff.[7] This action was discretionary, and the condemnation was not pronounced unless the defendant failed

[1] G., 2, 21; D., 50, 15, 1, 6-8. [2] XIII, 17, 345.
[3] G., 4, 91-95; Cic., *in Verr.*, 2, 1, 45.
[4] Paul, 1, 13*b*, 8; 5, 9, 1, 2; D., 46, 7, 5-2; Ed.-P., 2, 266.—CXLVI, 191.
[5] Cf. G., 4, 16.—CLXXXII, 4, 491; CLXXXIII, 67; XIII, 18, 13.
[6] G., 4, 91, 92; D., 6, 1, 57, 58; Cic., *in Verr.*, 2, 13, 31.
[7] G., 4, 41; D., 6, 1, 68 (interp.).

PROPERTY AND REAL RIGHTS

to make the restitution which the judge had decided to be due. In that case it was fixed at a sum estimated by the plaintiff, under oath, to represent the value of the object claimed, with or without a preliminary limitation (*taxatio*) according to circumstances.[1] But lest the plaintiff in this purely pecuniary action should have to be content with a mere right of claim against a defendant who might be insolvent, the latter was required by the magistrate at the beginning of the suit to furnish the *satisdatio judicatum solvi*, a promise guaranteed by fidejussors to satisfy the final judgment, to commit no fraud and to keep the object in dispute, unless the plaintiff was armed with an interdict (*interdictum quem fundum*) authorizing him to claim interim possession, if an immoveable was at stake, or was granted interim possession by decree in the case of a moveable.[2]

Granted only to the owner not in possession,[3] the action for ownership could at first be brought only against the possessors; then, in the second century of our era, it was granted against holders and occupiers on behalf of others; and, finally, a person who had fraudulently abandoned possession before the *litis contestatio*, or had feigned possession in order to mislead the plaintiff, was deemed to be the possessor.[4]

Provincial ownership was guaranteed by means of an action whose formula is uncertain; very probably it was an action for ownership granted *utilitatis causa*.[5]

III

POSSESSION AND ITS VARIOUS TYPES

I. POSSESSION : ITS LEGAL VALUE AND ITS CHARACTERISTICS

As soon as the nature and characteristics of ownership have been clearly defined, it is perceived that the management of property and the advantages derived therefrom are often

---

[1] D., 6, 1, 15-3; 50, 17, 63.—**CXLVI**, 194; **CCLII**, 2, 254.
[2] D., 46, 7, 6, 7; 2, 3, 1-1; *Fr. Vien.*, 4: T. G., 492; Ed.-P., 2, 266.—**CCXLIX**, 30; D., 4, 7, 4-1; 50, 17, 131; C. J., 3, 1, 9, 3.
[3] D., 41, 2, 12-1; 43, 17, 12-1.—**XLIX**, 2, n° 805, **CXI**, 2, 253.
[4] D., 6, 1, 25, 26, 27; I. J., 3, 29, 2.
[5] *Fr. vat.*, 315, 316; Ed.-P., 1, 215.—**XXXIII**, 11, 277; cf. **CCXLVII**, 106 et seq.

166 FORMATION OF CLASSICAL LAW

independent of ownership; whereupon legislations supplement their theory of ownership with a theory of possession.[1]

At first possession was regarded as a mere fact, but practice showed that in legal matters this fact could become an abstraction. Troubles arising out of attacks on this *de facto* situation, presumptions that could be derived from it, the uselessness or injustice of disputing it without proving a higher right caused it to be fenced about with a protection which, at Rome, was organized by the prætor by means of interdicts.[2]

Various explanations of the prætor's intervention have been given. Niebuhr derived its origin from the protection granted to possessors of the *agri occupatorii*, from which it would be extended to objects of every kind; Savigny from suppression of the wrong and compensation for the loss suffered by a possessor who had been dispossessed or threatened with dispossession; others from police measures introduced to prevent persons taking the law into their own hands. Ihering, following certain French jurists and showing that ownership and possession, though in reality distinct, are generally united, and that the acts of the possessor are those of the owner, has seen in possession the outwork and advance guard of ownership; protection of the former protecting also the latter which is presumed.[3] But whatever the starting-point of the Romans may have been, they did not as a matter of fact establish either a logical system or a single theory of possession. They merely sought for the exterior elements in the fact of possession and attached consequences to it in accordance with the nature of each case and the requirements of equity: a fact which explains why all the different theories to which we have just referred can be based upon the texts and deduced from the particular solutions contained therein. The Jurists took as the basis of possession two elements which they called the *corpus* and the *animus*.[4] The acquisition of both involved possession, but the loss of either brought it to an end.

The *corpus* was the material element, for if the enjoyment of a right considered objectively has sometimes been termed *possessio*,[5] possession in its strict sense never referred to any-

[1] D., 43, 17, 1-2.   [2] D., 41, 2, 12-1; 43, 17, 53.
[3] **CCLXX**; **CII**; **CLXXXIII**; cf. **CXCV**, 1, 321; **XXXIII**, 17, 199.
[4] G., 4, 153; D., 41, 2, 3-1.   [5] C. J., 7, 22; Ed. of Claudius (41): T. G., 188.

PROPERTY AND REAL RIGHTS

thing but corporeal objects that could be owned.[1] Originally perhaps a physical seizin of the object was essential in order to acquire possession of it, but it was not necessary that this direct contact should be maintained, or even that it should be renewable at will. It sufficed for the object to be " where one would habitually find it in daily life," or, let us say, in the situation where it would normally be if the possessor was its owner.[2] This made it possible to admit possession founded on intermittent usage, e.g. that of summer pastures, which was not lost when the snow in winter made them unusable, and possession *corpore alieno*, first through the medium of persons *alieni juris*, then, in the second century of the Empire, through stewards, guardians or curators,[3] and finally through any mandatary, thus recognizing the agreement by which the possessor undertook to hold his possession for the future as an agent for others.[4]

The *animus* was the element of intention determining the nature of the possession, which could vary in degree (*affectio tenendi, animus possidendi, animus* pure and simple), merely by determining its effects.[5] Some texts without general application, expressing a tendency which became marked in the classical period, identified it with the intention to hold as absolute owner;[6] whence the term *animus domini* of the commentators. As an act of volition it could only proceed from the possessor; but in the second century guardians, curators, administrators of artificial persons, could substitute their own will for that of persons incapable of willing.[7] Moreover, the *animus* had not got to be proved; it was the adversary's task to prove from the facts that it did not exist or differed from what was maintained.[8]

But the *animus* was often closely connected with the cause of possession, i.e. with the way in which it had begun, for no one can deliberately change the original cause of his possession—*nemo causam possessionis sibi mutare potest.*[9] On this depended the good or bad faith of the *possessor*, as well as the principal effects of possession.[10] The result was a hierarchy of different kinds of possession: (i.) *possessio*

[1] D., 41, 2, 3-pr.; 3, 4, 27
[2] D., 41, 2, 3-1, 51.—**CCLXX**, 184; **CLXXXIII**, 174.
[3] G., 2, 89-95; Paul, 5, 2, 1; I. J., 2, 9, 5   [4] D., 41, 2, 18-pr.
[5] D., 41, 2, 1, 3, 20; I. Th., 2, 9, 4.   [6] C. J., 3, 32, 2.
[7] D., 41, 3, 1-20, 44-7.   [8] Paul, 5, 2, 2.—**CLXXXIII**, 24.
[9] D., 41, 2, 9-1.—**CLXXXIII**, 303   [10] D., 41, 2, 3-22.

naturalis, corporalis, mere retention of the object by those who had begun by holding the *corpus* in another's name and continued of necessity in this position;[1] (ii.) possession of a legal kind, protected against third parties by the possessory interdicts, but invalid (and therefore exposed to interdicts in its turn) as against the claim of the person robbed, when the *corpus* had been acquired through theft of the object either secretly or with violence;[2] (iii.) another kind of legal possession involving the right to possessory interdicts not only against third parties but even against the previous possessor, e.g. that of a creditor holding a pledge; (iv.) possession received in good faith as the result of a legal act, providing, besides the interdicts, the opportunity of usucapion.

Possession ceased on the loss of the *corpus* or the *animus* or both.[3] The *corpus* no longer existed when the object ceased to be where it would normally have been if the possessor had been the owner, whatever reason there might be for this displacement. The *animus* was ended by manifestation of the intention not to possess any longer—a thing which could not be done by the lunatic or the child below the age of puberty.[4] Both disappeared together on the death of the possessor, on his voluntary and final abandonment of the object, or on the transfer of possession to a third party; and this held good even when the possessor was acting as agent for others.[5]

II. The Possessory Interdicts

Possession was protected by means of two groups of interdicts, *interdicta retinendæ possessionis causa* and *interdicta recuperandæ possessionis causa,* which were known, or at any rate the first was, as early as the sixth century.

The object of those of the first group, viz. *interdictum uti possidetis* in the case of immoveables, *interdictum utrubi* in the case of moveables, was to protect the existing possession and determine the respective parts of the litigants in the action for ownership, if one should arise. They were introduced at the time when the action ceased to be *duplex,*[6] and

---

[1] D., 6, 1, 9.   [2] D., 43, 17, 2.   [3] D., 41, 2, 8, 44-2; 50, 17, 153.
[4] D., 41, 2, 17-1; 42, 7, 11, 15.   [5] D., 41, 2, 17-1, 19-1.—**XIV**, 2, 4, 355 et seq.
[6] G., 4, 148, 149; D., 41, 2, 35; 43, 17, 13.—**CXCV**, 2, 313; **CCLXX**, n° 120; **XIII**, 18, 22 et seq.

PROPERTY AND REAL RIGHTS

were themselves double in its stead, the successful party in the interdict being the defendant in the action. The interdict *uti possidetis*, accorded to the man whose claim to possession conflicted with a contrary claim, was an order of the prætor to maintain the existing situation, provided that it was not tainted by violence or fraud and had not been brought about by leave of the adversary, to whom possession would otherwise be restored.[1] Violation of this order gave rise to a *judicium duplex* in which the possessor now appeared as claimant. *In jure* the magistrate put up the interim possession to auction, the price paid for it being regarded as a penalty. A *sponsio* or promise to restore the object and its fruits on the judge's *arbitrium* was imposed upon the higher bidder, and then each party bound the other by a stipulation, promising to pay a fixed sum in case he should have violated the interdict. As many formulas were drawn up for the judge to decide upon as there were stipulations. The winner was confirmed in his possession and remained defendant instead of claimant.[2] But if no violation of the interdict was shown to have occurred, the party who, as possessor, was interested in bringing the suit to an end had to obtain from his adversary a show of violence (*vis ex conventu*) in order to secure a ground for the action, and, failing this, was granted a special interdict against him, *interdictum secundarium*, as a result of which the latter seems to have been deprived of all hope of acquiring the position of defendant in place of that of claimant.[3] The interdict *utrubi* contained an order to those who were disputing the possession of a moveable to replace it where it had been for the greater part of the year preceding the interdict. The same double and complicated procedure was followed, and victory went to the party who had been in possession for the greater part of that year (even possession by his principal, whether he succeeds him as universal or singular successor, being reckoned as his own), provided that his possession was not tainted by one of the three flaws mentioned above.[4]

The only interdicts certainly contained in the second group were those *unde vi, de vi cottidiana* and *de vi armata*, which date back almost as far as the foregoing and have regard to

[1] D., 43, 17, 1-pr.-9, 3-pr.   [2] G., 4, 166-170; Ed.-P., 2, 217.
[3] Cic., *pro Cæc.*, 16, 45.—**XIII**, 16, 275 et seq.
[4] G., 4, 150-152, 160, 170; Ed.-P., 2, 234.

the dispossession of immoveables.¹ The interdict *de vi cottidiana*, i.e. for ordinary violence, which was granted to the dispossessed party within one year of his ejection against whosoever had benefited by the act of violence (whether physical or moral is a matter of dispute), so long as the former's possession was not defectively obtained from the latter, resulted in a penal action, which however lost this character after the expiry of one year and was no longer granted except for the value of the fruits which the dispossessor had gathered.² The interdict *de vi armata*, which presupposed ejection by force of arms, was granted without limit of time and even when the possession of the person ejected had been defectively obtained from the defendant.³

With these interdicts was associated that granted to a person who had leased his property on precarious tenure (*interdictum de precario*), enabling him to recover his property at will and obtain damages for fraud if there had been any.⁴

III. "In Bonis Habere": Bonitarian or Prætorian Ownership

Towards the end of the Republic cases of privileged and better guarded possession were distinguished by the term *in bonis habere*. Whether they were the object of one edict only or of two, and whether one of them was merely an extension by jurisprudence, is a matter of dispute; but the two most ancient cases, generally connected with the prætorship of a certain Publicius, were that of the acquirer of a *res mancipi* by mere delivery of the object, which could not transfer the quiritarian ownership to him and only protected him with an *exceptio venditæ et traditæ rei* against the alienator, based on the sale and delivery of the object, and that of the acquirer of any kind of object *a non domino*, i.e. from someone who was not its owner, although he truly believed him to be.⁵ So long as the period of usucapion had not expired, these acquirers could not reclaim the object if they lost possession of it. Now the Publician edict framed for them against third parties in possession of the object a fictitious action,

---

¹ D., 43, 16, 1-29. ² G., 4, 155; Ed.-P., 2, 233.
³ Cic., *pro Cæc.*, 19, 32, 55; D., 48, 7, 51.—**CXII**, 310; **CXIII**, 315.
⁴ D., 43, 26, 1-pr., 21.—**CXII**, 320.
⁵ G., 2, 40-43.—**LIII**, 1, 49; **CXII**, 304; **XIII**, 16, 275, 296.

PROPERTY AND REAL RIGHTS 171

afterwards termed *actio Publiciana*, which was modelled upon the *formula petitoria*,[1] directing the judge to pronounce sentence on the assumption that the period of usucapion had expired. That placed these possessors in the position of quasi-owners. In the second case, however, the Publician action was invalid against the true owner (*verus dominus*), and so too was the *exceptio rei venditæ et traditæ*.[2] If one or the other of these cases of *in bonis habere* applied to two persons simultaneously, so that both were in process of acquiring the object by usucapion, ownership went to the one whose possession had been longer or who held it of the true owner.[3]

In course of time other possessors benefited by the Publician action: the acquirer by way of *adjudicatio* in a *judicium imperio continens*, the plaintiff authorized to carry off the slave if the master did not defend a noxal action, the person given possession of an immoveable by a second decree after the *cautio damni infecti*, the *bonorum emptor* or acquirer by auction of a bankrupt's patrimony, the *bonorum possessores* with a title to rights of succession organized by the prætor's edict. All these were said to have the objects thus acquired *in bonis*, for these modes of acquisition had their origin not in the Civil Law but in the edict which, as opposed to the former, could not give them power to transfer the quiritarian ownership but only provided a provisional copy of it. These privileged possessions finally came to be regarded as a second kind of ownership, an idea which we find already in Gaius; and, later on, this gave rise to the Byzantine expression *bonitarian ownership*, which was unknown to the classical jurists, who therefore had no need to inquire whether it applied to the two most ancient examples of the system—a question which is anxiously debated.[4]

The sphere of this prætorian ownership, as the moderns call it, was thus superimposed upon that of quiritarian ownership —the former being possible only where the latter was too— and it constituted an interim title which could be quickly transformed by usucapion into a permanent one. All that has been written about other applications or extensions of the Publician action is mere conjecture and very improbable.[5]

[1] D., 44, 7, 35-pr.   [2] D., 44, 7, 17. Cf. D., 17, 1, 57.
[3] D. 4, 2, 9-4; 20, 4, 14. Cf. **CXCV**, 1, 320.   [4] G., 2, 40; I. Th., 1, 5, 3.
[5] **LIII**, 1, 81 et seq.; 2, 345, 352; **XIII**, 14, 276; **XVII**, 1891, 317; **XXXIII**, 11, 214; 13, 175.

IV

MODES OF TRANSFER OF REAL RIGHTS

I. THE MODES OF ACQUIRING OWNERSHIP: CONVENTIONAL MODES; ASSIGNATIONS BY STATUTE

In ordered societies ownership is only acquired by juridic acts consecrated by custom or statute and performed by agreement between persons capable of alienating and acquiring property, or, in very rare cases, in virtue of positive assignations by statute.

It was only by right of a legendary reversion that the Romans claimed to hold as peculiarly their own property which had been seized from the enemy. Booty had long been the property of the State.[1] Under the misleading name of *occupatio* they grouped together a small number of particular cases founded on positive Law, which could easily be referred to general principles, such as the discovery of treasure or the finding of an object that had been abandoned. Whether the Jurists connected the methods of acquisition with Natural Law, the Law of Nations or the Civil Law, their thoughts were always recurring to a concrete solution by jurisprudence or statute. At Rome more than elsewhere the modes of transfer were originally involved in a formalism of which I have already mentioned the causes, but they moved unceasingly in the direction of greater freedom and flexibility. This gradual decrease of formalism can be traced from one mode of transfer to another, and constitutes for each one the very woof of its history.

It became the custom to describe as voluntary the conventional modes of acquisition, and as involuntary those in which acquisition was the result of an imperative or interpretative legal assignation; but this had no juridic consequences.

II. "MANCIPATIO." "IN JURE CESSIO." "TRADITIO." "ADJUDICATIO"

Mancipation was closely connected with the use in central Italy of *æs rude*. Every transaction conducted by means of

[1] D., 41, 1, 8-pr., 9-1, 7-3; 48, 13, 1, 13.—CCLII, 1, 350.

PROPERTY AND REAL RIGHTS 173

this coarse bullion involved the use of scales; and the *æs signatum* did not render them unnecessary, because the *signum* prevented neither breaking nor clipping. Every conveyance of ownership in exchange for this money involved public weighing, verification of the amount of metal handed over to the vendor and an actual grasping of the object sold to him by the purchaser.

This sale, which was necessarily a sale for cash, proceeded as follows. In the presence of 5 witnesses, Roman citizens above the age of puberty who had consented to bear witness to the act on the interrogation of one of their number, the *libripens*, provided with a balance and weights, weighed the metal given in payment, while the purchaser seized the object sold and asserted his right to it: "I affirm that the slave is mine according to the quiritarian right, and he is thus acquired by me with this piece of bronze and this balance: *Hunc hominem ex jure Quiritium meum aio isque mihi emptus esto hoc ære æneaque libra.*" Then striking the balance with a piece of bronze in order to fix the attention of those present, he paid over the price; so that payment of the price and appropriation of the object were closely linked together. The nature of this ritual shows that it was created only for the sale of moveables.[1]

When immoveables became objects of commerce, they were allowed to be sold by mancipation without the immediate and physical handing over of the object sold.[2]

When the decemvirs introduced copper money at Rome with the *as liberale* as its unit, weighing also became unnecessary, but the purchaser declared in a loud voice the price that he was paying.[3] The Law of the Twelve Tables made the juridic effects of the transaction depend upon the verbal formulas: "When there is *nexum* or mancipation, let the right be that which the tongue has spoken: *cum nexum faciet mancipiumque uti lingua nuncupassit, ita jus esto.*"[4] Gestures, balance and piece of bronze remained as symbols, revealing to those who were used to them the kind of transaction that was taking place. The sphere of mancipation grew wider, and it tended to become the fictitious sale (*venditio ima-*

---

[1] G., 1, 118-119, 122; 2, 22, 25; Ulp., 19, 3-6; *Fr. vat.*, 50.—**CCLII**, 2, 364 et seq.
[2] G., 1, 121.   [3] **LIII**, 2, 30 et seq.
[4] XII T., 6, 1.—**XXXIII**, 29, 233; **CCLXXXIV**, 48.

174 FORMATION OF CLASSICAL LAW

ginaria) of which Gaius speaks.[1] Hence the possibility of a sale on credit wherein only the symbolic piece of bronze, not the real price, was handed over at the moment when the object was delivered; but the Twelve Tables, dominated by the idea of concomitant effects, delayed the transfer of ownership until the payment was made.[2] Recently, however, this concomitance has been assigned to a much later period.[3] In the same way donations, dowries and noxal surrenders were made by reducing the price to an insignificant sum (*nummo uno*);[4] and finally mancipation enabled the lawyers to organize a system of dispositions in anticipation of death, in which it covered a whole body of goods.[5]

This was the only mode of conveyance of *res mancipi*,[6] but it does not seem to have been void in the case of *res nec mancipi*, since its use was bound up with that of *aes rude*. It should be noted that, even when invalid as mancipation, it had always been a *traditio: traditio alteri nexu*, Cicero says.[7]

Since its object was the transfer of quiritarian ownership, it presupposed the possession of this ownership by the vendor and of the *jus commercii* by both parties. The purchaser definitely stated in the formula the rights which he expected to acquire, and the vendor was obliged to show his agreement thereto by lending him assistance in case of any attempted legal eviction by a third party, as soon as it was brought to his notice. This obligation, which was the immediate effect of the mancipation, lasted until the period of usucapion had expired. If, on the demand of the purchaser, he refused to assist him or did not enable him to win the action for ownership, this defeat or this refusal constituted a delict sanctioned by the *actio auctoritatis* whose condemnation was double the price declared in the mancipation.[8] Until the time of Labeo it could be brought for the whole amount against each person responsible for the delict; but this Jurist admits that, after the first prosecution, the others were set aside by means of

---

[1] G., 1, 119; T. G., 825.—**CCVIII**, 19 et seq.   [2] I. J., 2, 1, 41.
[3] **XVII**, 1920, 255 et seq.; **XIV**, 1923, 647, n. 1.
[4] T. G., 829.—**LXV**, 1, 47.   [5] Paul, 2, 17, 1-3; T. G., 801-805.
[6] Cic., *Top.*, 10, 45; Ulp., 19, 3.
[7] There are examples in the triptychs of Transylvania, and see T. G., 845, 847.
[8] Cic., *de Off.*, 3, 16; *Top.*, 4, 23; Varro, *de r. r.*, 2, 10; Paul, 2, 17, 1-3; Ed.-P., 2, 288.—**CLX**, 2, 5-45, 155-305 (an analysis by Girard of the interpolated and restored texts concerning *auctoritas* and the *actio auctoritatis*).

PROPERTY AND REAL RIGHTS

an exception. In the same way a false statement of the area of a piece of land that had been sold gave rise to the *actio de modo agri* whose condemnation was twice the value of the deficiency.[1]

In jure cessio was a result of the adaptation, at some period unknown, of judicial actions to the conveyance of rights; in particular, of the adaptation of the action for ownership to the transfer of ownership—a process which would naturally occur to men's minds and can be paralleled at other times among other peoples. It could only take place between persons capable of bringing an action.[2] The purchaser laid claim to the object which had been transferred, the vendor either made no defence or admitted the claimant's right, and the magistrate, establishing this right, granted a certificate in confirmation of the parties' wishes, after which the purchaser enjoyed all the advantages of a plaintiff who had won his suit. *In jure cessio* was an act of voluntary jurisdiction.

Traditio, unlike the two preceding modes of transfer which belonged exclusively to the Civil Law, was connected with the Law of Nations, for " nothing is so agreeable to natural equity as to ratify the desire of the owner to transfer his property to others."[3] This means that it produced the same effects between citizens and between aliens, or between citizens and aliens, whether the latter had *jus commercii* or not, and whether the objects concerned were capable of quiritarian ownership or not; except that it remained for a long time inapplicable to *res mancipi*, and never secured more than *in bonis habere* where they were concerned.[4] But this classical definition does not give us a clear idea of its history.

It was indeed of very ancient usage but, however universally practised, it had no validity at first unless performed on Roman territory. It was not borrowed from aliens, but the idea of a Law of Nations extended its sphere of application indefinitely. In its original sense it was the actual handing over of the object by the transferrer to the transferee, so that it could only be used for corporeal things and signified a transfer of ownership; but as time passed and economic questions became more complicated, its purpose and meaning

[1] Paul, 2, 17, 4; Ed.-P., 1, 225.
[2] G., 2, 24, 96; Ulp., 19, 9-11; Festus, s.v. *Addicere*; T. G., 833.—Cf. CLX, 1, 382; CXLII, 256.
[3] D., 41, 1, 9-3; I. J., 2, 1, 40.   [4] G., 2, 19, 41; Ulp., 1, 16; 19, 17.

changed. In order to ascertain whether ownership had been transferred, an intellectual element had to be added to it, viz. the discovery of the parties' intention; and the Jurists then developed a twofold doctrine concerning *traditio* properly so called and this intellectual element of intention.[1]

The former seems at first to have been a real symbolic formality, the transferrer (*tradens*) actually handing over the object to the transferee (*accipiens*). This is proved by the study of comparative Law and even by the classical texts themselves.[2] When immoveables entered the commercial field, it became permissible to take possession by a look or a thought, and transfer of ownership was conceived to be possible without direct and visible conveyance from the hands of the transferrer to those of the transferee. In a word, it was caused by placing the object at the transferee's disposal.[3] Hence these consequences followed more or less quickly: it could be made or received through the medium at first of persons *alieni juris*, then of third parties; a debtor could be legally required to hand over to the transferee the objects, e.g. money, which he owed to the transferrer—a process that has been called *traditio brevi manu ;* the *traditio* was deemed to have been made on handing over the keys of the immoveable which contained the objects to be delivered; it became possible when the parties were absent; if the objects were already in the transferee's hands, it was made by the agreement, and the same was true if they had to remain in the hands of the transferrer (a state of affairs which, in the Middle Ages, will give rise to the *constitutum possessorium*).[4] All these were solutions of particular cases, not systematized or always presented in accordance with the rules of logical progression.[5]

The intention of the parties, which was added to the actual *traditio* in order to give it a meaning, is termed *justa causa* by modern Romanists. It was the " special and reciprocal desire to alienate and to acquire"; and if it had "actually presided over the delivery of the *corpus*, whatever the motive may have been, the alienation was complete."[6] This was no doubt the Roman solution, but the Roman texts do not call this special and reciprocal desire *justa causa*. For them

[1] Ulp., 19, 7, 8; D., 41, 1, 31.   [2] D., 41, 2, 1-21, 18-1.   [3] **XLIX**, 1, n° 225.
[4] Cf. **XIV**, 1925, 355 et seq.   [5] D., 12, 1, 15-1; 18, 1, 74; 41, 2, 1-21; 1, 9-1.
[6] **XLIX**, 1, n° 226; **CCLXXI**, 2, 420.

the *justa causa* was the preliminary act—sale, donation, legacy, etc.—which caused and explained the intention of the parties to the transfer. Whether the *justa causa* existed or not, this intention, even if misguided, sufficed to bring about the transfer;[1] but in its absence the transferrer who had delivered the object was armed against the transferee with a *condictio indebiti* or *sine causa*—a means of procedure leading to recovery of the property which he had abandoned in error and without motive. This doctrine, which was a consequence of the old formalism, had the advantage of making these transactions very secure; but the *condictio*, a personal action against the transferee, could not touch subsequent acquirers either of the object or of the real rights over it.

There were cases, however, in which the transfer of ownership was postponed to a date subsequent to the actual *traditio* and even to the parties' mutual consent. In the case of a sale it did not occur, unless there was a clause to the contrary, until the payment of the price or the acceptance of an equivalent guarantee;[2] and the imposition of a term or a condition could also delay this transfer, even if the *accipiens* was already in possession of the object. It is clear that, during this period of delay, the transferee could not transfer to third parties the rights which he did not possess.[3]

The judge's *adjudicatio* in actions for division of property and determination of bounds also had the effect of transferring ownership, either in order to put an end to a state of indivision or to establish more regular boundaries. The judicial contract by which the parties had agreed to accept the judge was the source of his power, being included in the formula of the action.[4] Ownership thus transferred was quiritarian if the *judicium* was *legitimum*, prætorian if it was a *judicium imperio continens*. In both cases the ownership was transferred with all its burdens.[5]

III. USUCAPION; THE "PRÆSCRIPTIO LONGI TEMPORIS"

Usucapion was the acquisition of corporeal objects through undisturbed use of them for a period prescribed by statute

[1] G., 2, 20; Ulp., 19, 4; I. J., 2, 1, 41.   [2] D., 18, 1, 53; I. J., 2, 1, 41.
[3] D., 41, 2, 38-1; 7, 9, 9-2; T. G., 849.   [4] G , 4, 42; Ulp., 19, 16.
[5] *Fr. vat.*, 47a ; D., 10, 2, 44-1; 3, 6-8.

and under conditions which varied from time to time.[1] Some have seen in it a means invented to complete the *traditio* of a *res mancipi*, or a way of covering the nullity of sales by persons other than the owner. The truth is that all legislations have had to allow prolonged possession to be transformed at last into ownership, in order that fact might not be too long in conflict with right—a state of affairs which had been the cause of uncertainty in commerce and the source of obscure, sometimes insoluble, litigation.[2] But the conditions of primitive legislations are changed when we come to those of more advanced epochs.

In the former the prescribed period is generally very short: at Rome it seems to have been one year for all cases. The Law of the Twelve Tables extended it to two years for landed property, to which jurisprudence afterwards assimilated buildings.[3] In ancient days the actual possession of the object sufficed, without any condition as to its origin or morality: at Rome apparently neither just title nor *bona fides* was at first necessary.

Reminiscences of this primitive conception survived even in classical Law, where the old definitions preserved by Ulpian and Modestinus knew nothing of these conditions.[4] *Usucapio pro herede* caused the ownership of a vacant inheritance to go to the third party, who had seized it, at the end of one year's possession. Later on, this form of acquisition was regarded with disfavour, restricted to corporeal objects included in the inheritance, and forbidden to those who were in possession of it on another title. Then Hadrian established a fictitious claim to the inheritance (*petitio hereditatis*) against the person who had thus acquired it by usucapion, and Marcus Aurelius introduced a criminal prosecution (*crimen expilatæ hereditatis*) in case of *mala fides*.[5] In the three cases termed *usureceptio* the depositor acquired by one year's usucapion the object which he had alienated as a deposit *fiduciæ causa*, if he recovered possession of it; the discharged debtor acquired by usucapion in one year the moveable, in two years the immoveable given in pledge; and this was also true of the debtor to the State who had recovered his pledge

---
[1] Ulp., 19, 8; 41, 3, 1.   [2] G., 2, 44; Cic., *pro Cæc.*, 26; D., 41, 10, 5-pr.
[3] XII T., 6, 4; Cic., *Top.*, 4, 23; Ulp., 19, 6.
[4] Ulp., 19, 8; D., 41, 3, 3.
[5] G., 2, 54-57; 3, 201; D., 41, 2, 3-19; 6, 2-1.

PROPERTY AND REAL RIGHTS 179

from the *prædiator* after it had been sold.[1] Before the *Lex Scribonia* the usucapion of rural servitudes, which were then regarded as corporeal things, was realized without any other condition than that of possession; and even in classical Law the *usurpatio libertatis* of prædial servitudes only required that they should not have been used for two years.[2]

This system was completed by certain exceptions. Usucapion of a thing stolen had been forbidden by the Twelve Tables and by a *Lex Atinia;* that of things possessed by violence, whether moveables or immoveables, by the Lex Plautia of the sixth century.[3] These statutes were aimed at the offenders themselves; but when usucapion was made conditional upon moral right, they were in danger of becoming useless, because the persons they had in view were already excluded by their failure to satisfy this condition, and jurisprudence, seeking some employment for them, made them applicable to all subsequent possessors until the taint had been purged by returning the object stolen or seized to the owner's hands.[4]

The Law of the Twelve Tables also excluded from usucapion the *forum sepulcri*, a space of five feet between the bounds of adjoining lands measured half from the right hand side and half from the left, and the *res mancipi* of a woman *sui juris* which had been delivered without *auctoritas tutoris*, though this rule may not have applied later on to things bought and paid for.[5]

Taking fright at so brutal a doctrine, juridic sensibility presently limited the cases of usucapion by submitting it to certain excessive requirements, the *causæ possessionis*. The *causa possessionis* was the origin of the possession, the manner in which the possessor had acquired it;[6] and three of them, acquisition by violence, fraud and leave, were declared incapable of leading to usucapion. In a word possession must have begun in good faith, a fact which possessors often proved or sought to prove by alleging the juridic title in virtue of which they had entered upon it. After being merely a piece of evidence in support of good faith, the just title (*justa causa*)

[1] G., 2, 59-61.
[2] D., 8, 2, 3-pr., 6, 7, 32-1; 4, 17; 6, 18, 2.—**CXLVI**, 179 et seq.
[3] XII T., 8, 17; Aul. Gel., 17, 7; G., 2, 45.—**CCLII**, 2, 157; **CCLXVI**, 2, 207
[4] G., 2, 49; D., 50, 16, 215.   [5] G., 2, 49.—**CXCV**, 2, 404.
[6] D., 41, 2, 6-pr.; 3, 31-4.—**CXLVI**, 194-215.

180 FORMATION OF CLASSICAL LAW

finally became an independent condition added to the first. A putative title was declared invalid, except by some Jurists who admitted it when the *traditio* alone and not the previous act transferred the ownership, or in cases of very excusable error.[1] As an exception, good faith was required in cases of sale not only at the time of the *traditio* but also at the time of the contract.[2] Finally usucapion could only be the result of possession begun with just title and in good faith and continued for one or for two years, in reckoning which the day of entry upon possession was omitted but the last day was counted as soon as it had begun.[3] The possession must not be materially interrupted;[4] but on the other hand it was facilitated by the *successio possessionis*, which enabled the universal successor to benefit by his principal's time of possession, and by the *accessio possessionis*, which gave the same advantage to the singular successor provided that he had himself entered upon possession in good faith.[5]

In course of time usucapion was forbidden in the case of dotal lands in Italy, things received by a magistrate in violation of the *lex repetundarum*, property of the Fiscus, such property of incapables as was covered by the *oratio Severi*, and finally every kind of property belonging to wards.[6]

Usucapion was only applicable between citizens and, in the sphere of immoveable property, to land in Italy. For provincial land the governors or the Emperor adapted an institution based upon the hellenic principle that one cannot avail oneself of a right too long neglected, viz. the *longi temporis præscriptio*, which the edict extended in the interest of aliens to all corporeal things.[7] This *præscriptio* was a clause inserted in the formula of the action directing the judge to acquit the defendant if he had been in possession for 10 years when plaintiff and defendant lived in the same province (*inter præsentes*), or for 20 years when they lived in different provinces (*inter absentes*), without distinguishing between moveables and immoveables. It required that possession should have been obtained in an honourable way, but the doctrine concerning good faith and just title was soon ex-

---

[1] *Fr. vat.*, 266a, 297; D., 41, 3, 46, 48.
[2] D., 41, 3, 10-pr., 48.
[3] Aul. Gel., 3, 2; D., 41, 3, 6, 7.　　　　[4] D., 41, 3, 2; 4, 74.
[5] D., 41, 3, 11; 44, 3, 5-pr.; I. J., 2, 6, 13.
[6] G., 2, 47, 48; D., 50, 16, 28-pr.　　　　[7] D., 44, 3, 5-1; T. G., 201

PROPERTY AND REAL RIGHTS 181

tended to it.[1] Apart from material interruption, the *præscriptio* was liable to civil interruption due to the bringing of an action for ownership before the expiry of the prescribed period.[2] This means of defence was supplemented later on by an action, and its beneficiary was thus invested with provincial or alien ownership as the case might be.[3] Finally it was made applicable as well as usucapion to land in Italy.

IV. ASSIGNATIONS BY STATUTE

For reasons of order and economy the Law itself in a number of cases declared the ownership of a thing to be vested in such and such a person. Thus, on the strictly logical principle that the fruits and products of a thing belonged to its owner, it established exceptions in favour of certain owners of real rights. It also assigned these fruits and some products to the *bona fide* possessor. The origins of the latter's right are obscure. At first every possessor seems to have been able to acquire the fruits individually by usucapion after their separation from the thing itself, with the exception of those gathered after the *litis contestatio* while the suit was in progress.[4] The part played by the possessor in their production, the fact that he regulated his expenditure in accordance with the income which he expected to receive, the ever greater importance attached to good faith in questions of possession led the Jurists at the beginning of the Empire to assign them to the *bona fide* possessor after their separation from the thing itself, whether this had taken place with his knowledge or not, so long as his good faith still endured.[5] He also benefited by the indirect products, except those obtained at the cost of the thing's integrity.[6] The just title, now serving merely as evidence of good faith, could be putative;[7] but there is every reason to regard those texts of the Digest as interpolations which extend to this possessor the Sc. Juventianum and oblige him to restore the fruits in being to the owner who claimed the thing.[8]

[1] D., 18, 1, 76-1; C. J., 7, 33, 2, 4, 12.—**LIII**, 1, n° 95; **XVII**, 20, 612.
[2] D., 41, 3, 2, 25; C. J., 7, 33, 10; 44, 3, 16.
[3] D., 44, 3, 3-pr., 9; C. J., 7, 36, 2.
[4] **CXLVI**, 190; **CXCV**, 2, 1; **CCLII**, 2¹, 358.
[5] D., 22, 1, 25-1; 41, 1, 23.—**CCXLIX**, 306; **CCLII**, 2¹, 528.
[6] **XLIV**, 1. [7] Cf. **XLIX**, 1, n° 250.
[8] **XLIV**, *l.c.*; **CCLII**, *l.c.*; **CCXLIX**, *l.c.*; **XIV**, 2, 82-117, 187-209.

In another way, under the name of *occupatio*, the Law sanctioned the seizure of wild animals, of things derelict or belonging to no one (either wholly or partially, according to the period), of treasure-trove[1] and of islands in the sea.[2]

After some hesitation, objects made out of raw material belonging to others were regarded as the property of the *bona fide* maker, subject to payment of damages if the raw material could not be restored to its original form.[3] If one owner alone mixed or joined together two moveables in such a way that they were henceforward inseparable, the result was joint ownership if the things were of equal importance; if not, the owner of the more important thing became owner of the whole, subject to payment of the damages due to the other.[4] If a moveable was incorporated with an immoveable by the owner of the former acting in good faith, the case was met by paying him compensation and assigning ownership to the holder of the immoveable, to date from the time of taking root or of germination if plants were concerned,[5] or, in the case of a building, by following the rule *superficies solo cedit*, with payment of compensation varying in amount according to the *bona fides* of the builder.[6] Alluvion, islands in beds of rivers, river beds drained of water were assigned to the owners of the bordering *agri non limitati* in shares measured by lines drawn perpendicularly to the middle of the river from the borders of the estates; but if they lay between *agri limitati*, classical Law left them to the first occupier.[7]

V

SERVITUDES AND OTHER REAL RIGHTS

I. THE "JURA IN RE ALIENA": SERVITUDES AND OTHER REAL RIGHTS

However exclusive the owner's right might be, when things were once caught in the economic stream it was hard to prevent the attachment of different rights to them at one time or another. At first they were thought of as kinds of ownership analogous to that of the *dominus*; then they were

---

[1] G., 2, 66-69.—**XLIV**, 1.   [2] D., 41, 7, 2-1.
[3] G., 2, 79.   [4] G., 2, 78.   [5] G., 2, 73-75; XII T., 5, 7.
[6] **XLIX**, 1, 645; **CCLII**, 2¹, 317.   [7] **XIII**, 29, 461 et seq.

PROPERTY AND REAL RIGHTS

considered in their abstract form apart from the thing to which they were attached (*jura in re aliena*). The most ancient of them, called servitudes (*servitutes*), had been charges burdening one piece of landed property to the advantage of another. Others of more recent origin had the effect of detaching certain advantages from the property for the benefit of a particular person. Some of these, which were created by the Civil Law, came to be regarded as forming a second class of servitudes, viz. personal servitudes;[1] others derived their rules and sanctions from the edict, which gave them birth, and were termed prætorian real rights.

II. THE PRÆDIAL SERVITUDES

As was natural in Rome's primitive circumstances, the most ancient servitudes were suggested by the needs of agricultural development. It was a case of making one farm (*fundus serviens*) help the development of another (*fundus cui servit*)[2] in the two forms of right of way (*iter*) or right of leading water through it (*aquæductus*), which in the Law of the Twelve Tables were already subdivided into *iter*, passage on foot or on horseback, and *actus*, passage with flocks and carriages; *aquæductus*, leading of water through a farm, and *haustus*, power to go and draw water there.[3] Subsequent Law added *via*, the upkeep of a road through the *fundus serviens* ; right of watering cattle; an obligation on the *fundus serviens* to receive water passed on by the superior farm;[4] and then others as well, such as rights of pasturage, of removing sand, lime, etc.[5] Being at first assimilated to property, the rural servitudes were regarded as corporeal things and *res mancipi* until shortly after Cicero's time, when a *Lex Scribonia* declared that they could not be objects of *possessio* or consequently of *usucapio*.[6]

Lack of plan in the rebuilding of Rome after the sack by the Gauls involved the creation of urban servitudes, first those of drainage (*jus cloacæ*) and of rain water dropping from the roof (*jus stillicidii*),[7] and afterwards those of party

---

[1] **XXIV**, 11, 281 et seq.; **CV**, 271.   [2] Cic., *pro Cæc.*, 26; *de Orat.*, 1, 39.
[3] Varro, *de L. l.*, 5, 24-25; Isid. Sev., *Orig.*, 15, 13-16.
[4] Cic., *pro Cæc.*, 19, 26; D., 2, 43, 20, 1-18; 8, 3, 29.
[5] D., 8, 3, 3-1, 6-1.
[6] G , 2, 14; Ulp., 19, 1; cf. Cic., *pro Cæc.*, 26.   [7] Liv., 5, 53-55.

walls, of supporting a building or a beam, of lights and prospect, of increasing or being forbidden to increase the height of one's house, etc.—all rendered necessary in the case of lofty and adjoining buildings by the crowded condition of the city.

But it is uncertain by what criterion the Jurists distinguished rural from urban servitudes. The idea derived from certain texts that it depended upon whether the dominant estate was built over or not is very unsatisfactory, and the same may be said of the theory of continuity based by the commentators on certain solutions of particular cases.[1] As the servitude appears to have been essential to the development of an estate, it has been concluded that it could not be detached by alienation, that it was perpetual like the estate itself and could only be established in this form,[2] that it was indivisible and could not itself be burdened with a servitude.[3] But all these are rash generalizations.

Before the *Lex Scribonia* rural servitudes could be acquired by mancipation or usucapion; all, rural and urban alike, could be established by means of a reservation (*per deductionem*) made by the alienator of an estate in the interest of another or reciprocally; by a similar reservation or directly in an *in jure cessio*; by means of the type of legacy called *legatum per vindicationem*; by the judge authorized in an action for dividing an inheritance to award servitudes on estates placed in one lot to the advantage of those placed in another;[4] and also perhaps, from the classical period, by the assignment of the *paterfamilias*.[5]

From a practice at first allowed in the case of legacies of usufruct and afterwards extended to servitudes sprang the idea of a quasi-possession and a *quasi-traditio* consisting in the *de facto* exercise (*usus*) of the servitude by the acquirer without protest on the part of the alienator. This doctrine, which was at first opposed but was generally accepted at the end of the first and throughout the second century of the Empire, was confirmed by the edict both as regards Italian and provincial land.[6] On the same ground the *præscriptio*

---

[1] **XXX**, 14, 52; **XXI**, 50, 388-402; **XLIX**, 1, no. 268; but cf. D., 8, 5, 6-1, 20.
[2] D., 8, 1, 1; 3, 2-pr.; 6, 2, 11-1.—**XXX**, 4, 165; 3, 23-3; T. G., 834; but cf. D., 8, 6-11.
[3] **XLIX**, 1, 266.   [4] G., 2, 29; *Fr. vat.*, 47-50.—**CXII**, 343.
[5] D., 8, 2, 41; 33, 2, 15-1.—**CV**, 261.
[6] *Fr. vat.*, 45; D., 8, 1, 20; 2, 4-pr.—**XXX**, 23, 2 et seq.

longi temporis was applied to servitudes in consequence of a long and untainted enjoyment of the right.[1]

Rights of servitude were at first guaranteed by real actions (*servitutum vindicationes*) and by special interdicts protecting the four most ancient among them.[2] These actions took successively the three forms already described in connection with the action for ownership. Except for a few details determined by the nature of the servitudes, the action was the same whether it sought to establish a right of way or of *aquæductus* over an estate or to maintain that estate's freedom.[3] In the former case the quiritarian owner of the dominant estate had to prove his ownership and the existence of the servitude; and the action was granted to him against any person who disputed the servitude, whether he actually exercised it or not, for the idea of quasi-possession was never thoroughly developed and did not give rise to the preliminary procedure which we have met with in the case of claims to ownership, where the possessor appeared as defendant. In the second case the action allowed the owner of the estate claimed as servient to deny the existence of the servitude against whosoever affirmed it. Probably these actions were discretionary like all real actions. The promise exacted from the party who had wrongfully disputed a servitude to abstain from doing so henceforward shows that things were restored to their original condition.[4] Servitudes established by the *quasi traditio* were guaranteed by a Publician action *utilitatis causa*.[5] Four interdicts framed at an early date by the Prætorian Edict in favour of the four most ancient rural servitudes, and one other (*interdictum quod vi aut clam*) forbidding the obstruction of urban servitudes, were extended on the same ground to the new servitudes in accordance with their points of resemblance to the old ones.[6]

III. USUFRUCT, USE, HABITATION, SLAVES' LABOUR

A certain number of advantages almost always bequeathed by will to neighbours, friends or servants were also detached at a later period from ownership.

The most important of them was usufruct, the right to use

[1] Paul, 5, 5a, 8; D., 8, 5, 10-pr.
[2] D., 8, 5, 4-2; 22, 1, 19-1.
[3] G., 4, 3; *Fr. vat.*, 92.—**CXII**, 348 et seq
[4] D., 7, 6, 5-6.
[5] D., 6, 2, 11-pr.-4.
[6] **CXII**, 351.

186 FORMATION OF CLASSICAL LAW

and enjoy for life what belongs to another without impairing its substance.[1] In Cicero's time it was hardly used except on behalf of widows in their husbands' wills, no doubt in imitation of Greek Law.[2] The usufructuary and the bare owner, each holding his rights directly from the testator, had no personal relations with each other. They have been compared to two neighbours. Only corporeal things which were not consumed by the very fact of use were at first the object of usufruct;[3] but under the Empire a senatusconsultum declared it applicable to all things included in the patrimony. The quasi-usufructuary then became owner of things consumed by the very fact of use and of arrears of interest which he could consume or spend, provided that he guaranteed restitution on the expiry of the usufruct of things equivalent in quality and quantity or of the capital invested.[4] Usufruct itself and perhaps also prædial servitudes were covered by the senatusconsultum, the quasi-usufructuary benefiting thereby so long as the owner's right lasted.[5] In principle the usufructuary was intitled to use the thing and its accessories for the needs of everyday life and to gather its fruits, this last word being taken to mean all that can be derived from a thing at regular intervals without impairing its substance and in accordance with its natural and accepted use.[6] Products that lacked one of these characteristics remained the property of the bare owner; but in the second century of the Empire[7] appropriation of the fruits required actual collection of them by the usufructuary or by another person acting in his name.[8] Hence only the bare owner could claim fruits stolen while on the tree or on the ground, and those left ungathered on the expiry of the usufruct reverted to him.[9] As an exception, the rents of houses and some slaves' services seem to have belonged to the usufructuary, even if he had not collected them, in proportion to the duration of his right.[10] Under the Empire the usufructuary of a slave acquired in virtue of the slave's juridic acts, but this did not entirely withdraw the same right from the bare owner, who continued to acquire gifts *inter vivos* or legacies received by the slave on his account

---

[1] Ulp., 24, 26; I. J., 2, 4-pr.
[2] Cic., *Top.*, 3, 14, 17.
[3] Cic., *ad Fam.*, 7, 29; G., 2, 30.
[4] D., 7, 5, 1, 2-1, 3; I. J., 2, 4, 2.
[5] Paul, 3, 6, 27*b* et seq.
[6] **XLIX**, 1, n° 275; D., 33, 2, 1.
[7] Cf. D., 7, 1, 12-5 and 20, 1, 2, 8-pr.
[8] I. J., 2, 1, 36.—**XIII**, 622 et seq.
[9] D., 7, 1, 26.
[10] D., 45, 3, 31, 39.

PROPERTY AND REAL RIGHTS 187

and to benefit by the acts which the slave performed on his order.[1] Being established *intuitu personæ*, usufruct was at first untransferable: only its exercise could be transferred or let for the duration of the usufructuary's right. But a day came when the edict sanctioned its transference and even its mortgage.[2]

Use was the right to avail oneself of a thing in order to satisfy one's personal needs in everyday life, without gathering its fruits or causing it to produce any. Nevertheless the usuary of a herd was intitled to the milk, and the usuary of a house might let one part of it if he and his family lived in the other.[3]

Habitation (*jus habitationis*) was the right bequeathed to someone to inhabit a house in person and perhaps, in the classical period, to let it.[4] The *operæ servorum* were practically the same as a legacy authorizing the legatee to benefit by a slave's personal services, and were enjoyed on the same conditions.[5]

Originally the owners of these rights were only required to refrain from violating the right of the bare owner under penalty of losing their own, and to let him recover the property on the expiry of their right; but economic considerations caused the prætor to provide a better guarantee for the preservation of the property. He imposed on them as a condition of their entry upon possession a personal undertaking (*cautio usufructuaria*, etc.) to use it and enjoy it like good *patresfamilias* and to surrender it on the expiry of their rights: an undertaking which obliged them to keep the property in a state of repair, to replace dead trees, to supply deficiencies in seedbeds and herds, to exercise the servitudes and to interrupt usucapion.[6] There was no longer any need for the bare owner to make a claim when their rights expired, because they were obliged to surrender the property to him of their own accord. Later on this obligatory guarantee was taken for granted.

Although it originated in the practice of testators, usufruct could in course of time be established *inter vivos* in the ways already described for the establishment of servitudes, and even by pacts and stipulations;[7] but there is no instance of

[1] G., 2, 30.
[2] I. J., 2, 5, 1.
[3] D., 4, 5, 10; 7, 8, 10-pr.
[4] D., 7, 7, 5; 33, 2, 2.
[5] Paul, 3, 6, 27; I. J., 2, 5, pr.; Ed.-P., 2, 98, 283.
[6] D., 7, 1, 7-2, 9-pr.
[7] G., 2, 30-33; Paul, 3, 6, 32; Ulp., 19, 11; D., 7, 1, 6-1.

this in the case of the other three rights. Being regarded as irreconcilable with sound economy, they were all subjected to many kinds of extinction: renunciation by the holder, reversion on expiry of a prescribed term or realization of a prescribed condition, *capitis deminutio minima* (unless there was a clause to the contrary), non-usage for one or two years according as moveables or immoveables were concerned, and loss by the property of any essential characteristic.[1]

These rights were sanctioned by a real action (*vindicatio*), and another (*vindicatio negativa*) could be opposed by the owner to an unjustified claim to any one of them, both actions being discretionary and governed by the same conditions as those already noted in the case of prædial servitudes.[2] They could only be brought against the possessor, for the prætorian edict had extended the possessory interdicts (*utrubi, uti possidetis*) to the usufructuary and the usuary *utilitatis causa*, taking its stand on their quasi-possession.[3] The quasi-possessor appeared as defendant when making his claim, in a procedure analogous to that of the action for ownership.[4]

IV. THE OTHER REAL RIGHTS

The edict introduced and confirmed certain real rights which also appeared to be scraps or, if the term is preferred, dismemberings of ownership. The most ancient was certainly mortgage, which will be discussed elsewhere. The others appeared at various dates; and there is scarcely one of them which did not in subsequent history play a part of some importance under the Lower Empire and through the Middle Ages.

Superficies was the right of a person who rented land, either on a perpetual lease or for a long term or on any other title, to immoveables built by him upon the leased land.[5] Setting aside in this case the principle *superficies solo cedit*, the edict granted him an interdict (*interdictum de superficie*) against anyone who disturbed his possession, provided that it had not been obtained from the adversary by violence, stealth or leave, and that he established his title to it (*lex locationis*).

---

[1] Paul, 3, 6, 28-33; I. J., 2, 4, 3, 4; *Fr. vat.*, 61-64.   [2] G., 4, 3.
[3] *Fr. vat.*, 90-91; Ed.-P., 2, 215, 221.
[4] *Fr. vat.*, 91-93.—**CXII**, 248; **XXXII**, 2, 118, 126.
[5] D., 6, 1, 74; 2, 12-3; 23, 3, 82.—**I**, 6, 1585; **XXXIII**, 11, 121; **CV**, 275.

PROPERTY AND REAL RIGHTS

Moreover, it offered to the renter for a long term, after examination by the magistrate, an action modelled upon that of the Civil Law for recovering ownership, which could be brought even against the owner of the land, whose own claim was set aside by an *exceptio*.[1] Then the right of the lessee or *superficiarius* was assimilated to ownership, recognized as conveyable in prospect of death or *inter vivos*, capable of being mortgaged, and provided *utilitatis causa* with all the means of procedure necessary to preserve full use of it or to secure its possession.[2] It was terminated by loss of the property, expiry of the lease or concession, and non-payment of rent (*pensio*, *solarium*) for a certain period of time.

Cities, temples, sometimes the State itself allowed perpetual or long leases on their domains.[3] In the case of farmers thus established for several generations the edict recognized a sort of real right, granting them *utilitatis causa* full use of the methods of procedure which have just been mentioned. Jurisprudence allowed them to acquire the fruits by the mere fact of separating them from the property.[4] The farm could not be taken from them unless they failed to pay the tax.[5]

Some inscriptions dug up in the ancient province of Africa have revealed certain types of tenure which were unknown before their discovery. These are the *usus proprius* or *jus colendi* of the inscription of Henchir-Mettich, whose nature is very much disputed, and the *jus possidendifruendi heredique suo relinquendi* of the inscription of Aïn-Ouassel, which is evidently a right of hereditary possession. They were granted to the colonists who cleared uncultivated districts or restored to cultivation fields in the imperial domains within the province which had been left derelict for ten years. They have been compared with *emphyteusis* which, in the third century, was still a purely oriental institution. But disturbance of possession and enjoyment only gave a recourse to the owner, i.e. the Emperor, who was the source of all rules and regulations governing the imperial domains. Alienation seems to have been impossible, since the right passed only to the *heres suus* and survived only two years unclaimed.[6]

[1] D., 6, 1, 73-1, 75.—**CXCV**, 2, 1263.   [2] D., 39, 2, 39-2.
[3] G., 3, 145; Hygin. (ed. Lachman), 116-117.—**XXXIII**, 23, 42; **CIX**, 1, 129.
[4] D., 6, 3, 1-1; 2, 12-7; 8, 1, 16; Éd.-P., 1, 213.
[5] D., 6, 3, 1-pr.   [6] **LXIV**, 265 et seq.

CHAPTER VI

OBLIGATIONS OR PERSONAL RIGHTS

I

THE CHARACTERISTICS OF PERSONAL RIGHTS

I. PERSONAL RIGHTS. "DEBITUM" AND "OBLIGATIO" DEFINED

To the real right the Romans opposed, under the name of *obligatio*, the personal right defined as a legal bond constraining one person to do something or leave something undone in the interests of another;[1] and as they generally attributed to this prestation, whether positive or negative, a pecuniary value, the personal right also constituted an element in the patrimony.

But neither this opposition nor this assimilation had anything absolute about them.[2] We need only see in them the conclusions of a jurisprudence which tended to reduce the whole mass of legal relations between human beings to the economic plane. In the classical period personal rights were not confined to so limited a sphere; some of them never became part of the patrimony except through innovations due to accidents of procedure. In the past still fewer had been included in it. The principal idea expressed by the word *obligatio* is that of "dominion over a stranger by reason of certain determined acts," and it is regarded above all as "a restriction of his liberty and a subjection to our will,"[3] more or less complete at various periods of history and exercised in different ways at those various periods, originally going so far as the power to dispose unreservedly of the debtor's person.[4] The addition to the patrimony which could be derived therefrom often appeared accidental and sometimes did not occur at all. That is why in our own time

[1] D., 44, 7, 3-pr.; I. J., 3, 13-pr.   [2] D., 40, 7, 9-1-7; 50, 16, 10, 12-pr.
[3] CCLXXI, 1, 16.   [4] XXXVIII, s.v. *Obligatio* ; CLXIII, 9 et seq.

some have thought that *obligatio* in the strict sense, regarded merely as an aspect of the right of persons, and *debitum*, a prestation of value to the patrimony to be rendered by the debtor, originally had a separate existence and were not artificially joined together until classical times or even until the time of Justinian.[1] They were certainly joined at a much earlier period. In historical Law the *obligatio* is only a means of obtaining the *debitum*,[2] and if it is conceived without too much difficulty as existing independently of a concrete *debitum* that can be valued in money, e.g. in certain delicts, the *debitum* without the *obligatio*, i.e. without a sanction, would be deprived of all juridic utility. The *debitum* is the counterpart of a wrong done to somebody or of an unjust alteration, whether real or fictitious, in the relative value of two patrimonies, whence arises the necessity of restoring the normal condition. The *obligatio* is the means of compelling this to be done. There is an essential legal connexion between the two.[3]

The truth is that the formal act announcing together with the injustice or alteration the desire of the creditor to put an end to it—an act which in primitive Law could alone render the prosecution legal—was often subsequent to the act of fraud or the alteration which justified it. The *debitum* could not remain isolated indefinitely. In an organized society a right only exists if it is sanctioned by positive legislation. The action is the true foundation of the right, and there can be no right within the city bounds unless it is sanctioned by a civil or a prætorian action.[4] It is not until the second century of our era that we find under the name of natural obligations various *de facto* situations to which were attached in default of an action, especially after Julian and Gaius, certain legal effects determined by criteria which were never made clear.[5]

II. THE GENESIS AND SOURCES OF OBLIGATION

Failing speculative research concerning the nature of obligation, some attempts to define its characteristics or classify its species were made, at Rome, only at the end of a long historical process. This was the case with the famous

[1] **LXXXVII**, 2, 306; **XXXVI**, 60, 371; **XLIX**, 2, n° 488. [2] **CIX**, 1, 135-139.
[3] Cf. **CLXXXI**, 6 et seq., 30 et seq. [4] I. J., 3, 13,8.
[5] **CCLXXI**, 1, 35 et seq.; **CLXV**; **CCXIV**, 3 et seq.

classification of obligations according to their sources—delicts and contracts, to which another composite group, *ex variis figuris*, had to be added.[1]

At first the number of facts giving rise to obligations was limited. They were described in detail, and it was not a matter of classification but of enumeration. Then the list grew longer, but the method remained the same; not only in consequence of the Roman's lack of taste for abstract speculation, but also of the genesis of the idea of *obligatio*.

The human will is naturally free. Force alone can bring it into subjection and creates slavery. But Paul takes care to distinguish the latter from the legal bond (*vinculum juris*) which is obligation. *Obligatio*, which assumes the existence between two persons of a relation explained by this metaphor, was conceived only at a late date and not without difficulty. By sanctioning it with an action, the State gave it the desired stability; but where there is no State, men are confronted only with physical facts which they interpret according to their own sensibility. Each man estimates how and to what extent his claims, i.e. his rights, have been violated by the actions of others, measuring the extent of the violation by the resentment which he feels. The violent reaction which he makes against his opponent is the origin of the legal sanction. It is exercised almost always without restriction on the person and property of the offender and his kin. In those days the violation of the right was identified with the offence. From his power of feeling offended man derived the consciousness of his right, which was then purely subjective since it was commensurate with the irritability of the individual. Any unlucky action which excited this irritability roused a desire for vengeance which did not stop to consider whether the act was intentional or not, or whether the opponent had or had not exceeded his own right. It was also unnecessary to know whether the offensive action conflicted with a claim of the victim's own making or with one that was based upon convention. In either case there had been the same irritating restriction of his movements or of his desire, and therefore the same violation of his personality. The feeling of resentment, the reaction, and the form of vengeance taken were alike in both cases: it seemed just to inflict an injury

[1] G., 3, 88; I. J., 3, 13, 2.

OBLIGATIONS OR PERSONAL RIGHTS

equivalent to the one received and disgraceful not to do so.[1]

After the organization of public authority, custom or statute restricted to a more limited sphere the disputes in which they judged it fitting to allow freedom of action, making the annoyance of the community instead of that of the individual the criterion of punishable acts. Thus Law became objective, dependent upon custom or statute. In an organized society there is no such thing as natural delict: it is the statute that creates the delict by attaching a penalty to an act, and nothing could be more contingent upon time and place. Thus the jurisconsults Servius Sulpicius and Massurius Sabinus counted four sorts of theft because in their time there were four actions which could be brought against thieves.[2] Henceforward a distinction was drawn between the legal and the illegal act, even an injurious and ill-intentioned act being exempt from vengeance if the Law did not grant an action in respect of it. But for offences resented by the whole community, although an amicable settlement was not forbidden,[3] the Law allowed a disciplined form of vengeance in accordance with a procedure which transformed the violent deeds of the past into symbolic gestures and made the penalty (*pœna*) proportionate to the gravity of the offence.[4]

Thus *obligatio* first became apparent in the form of delict (*maleficium*): the misdeed, whether intentional or not, obliged the misdoer to submit to a vengeance regulated by public authority, i.e. to pay the *pœna*. This origin left its traces in classical Law: in the archaic character of certain delictual actions, in civil actions caused by or consequent upon delictual actions that were out of due form, in the system of *leges imperfectæ* that punished acts without annulling their effects, etc.

The ancient statutes were based upon these data; but after a time juridical practice was led in two ways to form a less one-sided conception and a wiser system of Law. On the one hand a new element appeared in the description of certain delicts, viz. the intention to injure, and the penalty was attached to this.[5] But as the injury or the illegal acquisition could be unintentional and the latter might even profit other

[1] CXXIV, 9, 11, 99-115; CLXXXVIII, 29, 48; CLXXXI, 9.
[2] G., 3, 183. [3] Cic., *pro Rosc.*, 11, 12; Paul, 1, 19, 2; D., 2, 14, 17-1.
[4] XIV, 1, 442. [5] D., 9, 2, 5-1; I. J., 4, 3, 2.

persons than the offender, jurisprudence anticipated numbers of special cases in which a good—some advantage due to one person—actually went to the profit of another without any culpable action on his part or even any action whatever. Hence came the recognition of a civil *obligatio* contrasted with delictual *obligatio*; and as this arose, in the doctrinal works, from examination of the formulas, these latter were classified as penal, recuperative or mixed, though the analysis was not pressed to its logical conclusion.[1] The new obligations were based upon unjustified or ungrounded enrichment.

On the other hand the practitioners had at length discovered certain technical means of pledging one man's will to that of another. Contracts as they were then conceived were realized by means of a very simple act whose meaning could not be doubted because it was quite definite. The rights arising therefrom were provided by public authority with actions which could be executed in accordance with certain strictly defined rules, but the plaintiff was bound to confine himself to the actual content of the act. Though the sanctions had long been harsh enough, the city regarded them simply as means of coercion for the recovery of what was due; and as the amount due was determined by the extent to which the plaintiff's patrimony had been impaired, it was no longer regarded as a penalty. Thus classical Law drew a sharp distinction between delictual and contractual *obligatio*, the former based upon an injury done to one of the parties, the latter upon an agreement between them.[2] But the obligations to repair loss due to an injury and loss caused in the execution of a contract remained very closely akin. Modern doctrine tends to assimilate them anew.[3]

II

DELICTS

I. DELICTUAL OBLIGATION. PUBLIC AND PRIVATE DELICTS

Delicts, *maleficia*, were acts involving what dominant opinion regarded as a wrong, and as the Law punished them or allowed them to be punished on this ground, they varied in number and in kind according to the degree of civilization

[1] G., 4, 6-9; I. J., 4, 6, 16-19.   [2] D., 44, 7, 1-pr.   [3] **CCLXVII**, 1, 12, 368.

attained and the complexity of legal relations. The old statutes gave without further definition a list and description of the acts which they condemned,[1] as did the Twelve Tables, our most ancient document on this subject.

It is true that the spurious *leges regiœ* allude to certain delicts, prohibitions derived from ecclesiastical[2] or family discipline;[3] and some very vague information is also supplied by certain legendary stories. From this it has been deduced that the State must already have had the benefit of criminal jurisdiction and that a rudimentary distinction had already been drawn between public delicts threatening the order and safety of the political community, which punished them by the religious or secular means which it had at its disposal,[4] and private delicts apparently affecting only the interests of individuals, who were left to secure their punishment on their own initiative under the authority of the Law. In these days the delictual act is followed by public action; but then, when the State was no more than an aggregate of individuals, a number of acts were injurious only to such and such individual members of the community, who had not abdicated the right to take action when their persons or interests were at stake. The State merely imposed forms and restrictions upon their action. This system was maintained in the case of a small group of delicts during the whole history of Roman Law, although after all it had no other basis than tradition. Public vengeance, at first aroused by the needs of defence or by the sin involved in the delict, which obliged the judicial authority to appease the gods by punishing the offender, and afterwards by the disorder which any injustice introduced into the city, constantly extended its domain, allowing free scope to private vengeance in the cases where it did not take its place.

The Law of the Twelve Tables, like all Law in which primitive customs are absorbed, included a list of delicts. In this uncertain list, which has not reached us complete, it is hard to distinguish between the delicts which already have an exclusively public character and those which are still private. The competent jurisdictions (which would decide

[1] G., 3, 181; I. J., 4, 1-pr. [2] T. G., 5 et seq.—**CLX**, 1, 106; 2, 116-118.
[3] T. G., *l.c.;* XII T., 9, 6; 8, 12-13.
[4] *Consecratio capitis, interdictio aquœ et ignis*, death or fines.—**CLIX**, 1, 27-37; **CLXXXII**, 2, 127 et seq.

the question) are as a rule not indicated. The sanctions granted to the injured party's feeling of resentment are sometimes of the same kind and severity as the penalties imposed in order to appease the gods and maintain the social order.

No doubt after the distinction of *jus* from *judicium* this procedure was only applicable in suits where the sentence could be executed by the personal action of the successful party; but that left a very large field still open to it, for if almost all the delicts punished by death or by corporal penalties in the Law of the Twelve Tables were assigned to the jurisdiction of the *quæstores parricidii*, there is doubt about some of them. The judge's sentence could only affirm the existence of the facts on account of which the Law authorized the injured party to kill or inflict corporal punishment upon the offender, as in the case of the bankrupt debtor; and this can be paralleled in other legislations. In the decemviral legislation this was certainly the solution as regards the penalties (death or flogging) imposed upon thieves taken in the fact, the retaliation allowed when a limb was broken, and probably the death by cudgelling on account of *occentatio* or magical incantation, which seems to have been allowed in certain cases of execration (*consecratio capitis*).[1]

II. Private Delicts and their Sanctions in the Law of the Twelve Tables and in the Civil Law

Henceforward we are concerned only with private delicts, for Rome had reached the stage at which Law has become paramount, private justice has been set aside, except that limited and easily controllable form of it which involves the killing of a thief caught by night and armed,[2] and the State, without forbidding amicable settlements,[3] has imposed its own scale of penalties instead: scourging and slavery for the thief taken in the fact (death if he is a slave) and for the receiver assimilated to him in consequence of formal search for the stolen object (*quæstio lance licioque*);[4] retaliation in kind upon the breaker of a limb; a fine fixed at 300 or 150 asses for the assailant who had fractured a bone; 25 asses for any

---

[1] XII T., 8, 1-2, 14, 25; cf. 9, 6; Cato, *Orig.*, 4, 5.—**CLX**, 1, 106; 2, 302; **XIV**, 2, 449 et seq. [2] XII T., 8, 1, 2, 13; 9, 6.
[3] XII T., 6, 7; 8, 2; G., 4, 37; D., 2, 14, 7, 14.
[4] G., 3, 192; Festus, s.v. *Lance et Licio*; Aul. Gel., 11, 18; 16, 10.

other personal injury or for the cutting down of a tree;[1] double the value of the wrong in the case of a thief not taken in the fact, a usurer, a depositary who did not repay the deposit, a vendor who did not prevent the distress of the thing sold or misrepresented the area of the land sold, a guardian guilty of maladministration; three times the value in the case of an ordinary receiver; an expiatory sacrifice (*piaculum*) for accidental homicide, etc. From that time forward a delict is merely an act against which the Law authorizes reaction in accordance with a formal ritual and in pursuit of a penalty prescribed by itself. Formerly the injured party avenged himself as far as he could; now the Law established the principle of equivalence, *pœna noxiœ par esto*.[2] By describing the illegal act, which always had to be positive and due to direct contact between the offender and the *corpus delicti*, it left no room for any doctrinal interpretation and bound the judge to its text.

This manner of regarding the delict in its material aspect caused, in some cases, closely analogous acts to be made the object of different dispositions (e.g. the breaking of a limb and the fracture of a bone), in others, acts clearly distinguished by more developed legislations to be blended together in a single species, e.g. theft (*furtum*), which then included any fraudulent handling (*contrectatio*) of the property of others, whether moveable or immoveable. Even intent to enrich oneself (*animus lucrandi*) was not necessary and was not made part of the essence of theft before Justinian.[3] This was because the moral intention of the agent still counted for nothing in estimating the delict. In primitive societies man instinctively reacted with all his might against whatsoever injured him, making a direct attack upon the visible cause of the injury or loss and looking for nothing behind it. Law which moderated his violence and provided a channel for it, nevertheless followed its lead as soon as resentment was shown. The punishment which was made commensurate with the injured party's anger and resentment or with the degree of facility with which he could have avenged himself— a fact which explains its intensification in cases of flagrant delict—was not affected in the opposite direction by the

[1] Cic., *de Leg.*, 3, 11. [2] XII T., 2, 5, 10; 18, 14, 15, 16-20, 24.
[3] CLVIII, 322; CXII, 563; XIII, 42, 73-101.

intention of the offender, or by his irresponsibility if he was a child under the age of puberty, a lunatic, an animal, or even an inanimate object.[1] The question of imputability was the only question raised. Now the individualistic character derived by this legislation from the political revolution which led up to it and agreeing perhaps with some earlier ideas would have all purely personal. There is no longer any trace in it of the solidarity of clan or family, whether passive or active. The injured party alone had a right to vengeance, which lapsed at his death or if he forgave the wrong; the offender alone incurred the penalty, which his death rendered impossible but not his change of condition, *capitis deminutio*, enfranchisement, etc., so long as the city's legal authorities kept possession of his physical person.[2]

Nevertheless this individualistic Law still conflicted in several points with the organization of the *domus*. As the latter did not admit the interference of the State in its internal administration, there could first of all be no question of illegal acts as between its members; everything there depended exclusively upon the domestic magistracy of its head.[3] In the second place, since persons *alieni juris* were incapable of taking legal proceedings, delictual actions could only be brought by the head of the family when he felt himself personally affronted on their behalf. Finally, the right of vengeance belonging to the victim of a delict caused by a person *in potestate* or an animal conflicted with the paternal or dominical power or with the right of ownership, whence arose the system of noxal actions and action *de pauperie*.[4] Formerly, in order to avoid private warfare, the head of the group handed over the offender to the victim or paid a composition. Henceforward, provided that he had not had him under his own *potestas* at the moment of the delict or since, the victim was legally intitled to claim possession of the guilty party, whether living or dead, from the person who had him *in potestate* or *in dominio*, in order to take vengeance on his body; and this was finally understood to apply both to legal *potestas* and to actual possession on the day of the prosecution or, more accurately, at the *litis contestatio*:

[1] XII T., 8, 6; D., 9, 1, 1-pr.; Festus, s.v. *Noxia, Pauperies*.
[2] G., 4, 112.   [3] D., 47, 2, 17-pr.
[4] D., 9, 4, 2-1.—**CLX**, 2, 309-382; **CXI**, 112-114. To the action *de pauperie* should be added the action *de pastu*: D., 19, 5, 14, 3; Paul, 1, 15-1.

noxa caput sequitur.[1] If the punishment was a corporal one, the offender had to be given up and vengeance took its course, failing an amicable settlement. If it was a fine, the *paterfamilias* had the choice given him either by statute or, more often, by the edict, and finally made general and extended to all delictual actions, between this surrender, which was achieved by a mode of transfer of *potestas* or ownership (*mancipatio, traditio*), and payment of the fine: *aut noxiam sarcire aut in noxam dedere*.[2] After he had become *sui juris* the offender alone was prosecuted.[3]

As a reminiscence of the practices of private justice, the delictual action preserved the characteristic of satisfying alone and entirely the victim's feeling of resentment, without distinguishing from the penalty, which was incurred in its entirety by each of the offenders or their accomplices,[4] an adequate reparation of the wrong.[5]

In the same analytic and fragmentary form other statutes had added to the list of delicts[6] when the *Lex Aquilia*, a plebiscite caused perhaps by certain popular movements,[7] e.g. the third secession of the plebs in 468, and in any case earlier than the seventh century, sketched out the beginnings of a synthesis. In three chapters, it tried to repress wrongful damage (*damnum injuria datum*) to anything included in the patrimony[8] by means of a *damnatio* authorizing against the offender, for recovery of the penalty, the *manus injectio* which was then the means of taking a legalized vengeance, although later on it was changed by the formular procedure into an action whose condemnation was doubled in the event of fraudulent defence (*infitiatio*).[9] Its penalty was: for the killing of a slave or of an animal reckoned among the cattle, the highest estimated value that this property attained in the course of the preceding year; for the fraudulent extinction of a debt (*acceptilatio*) agreed to by the *adstipulator* without the creditor's consent, the amount of this debt; for any other damage to a corporeal object, its highest estimated value

---

[1] G., 4, 75-78; *Fr. Aut.*, 82-86: T. G., 366. As an exception, in delicts under the Lex Aquilia the noxal action is always granted against the owner and is granted in all circumstances, whether he is in possession or not: D., 9, 2, 27-32; **CLX**, 2, 333 et seq.
[2] XII T., 8, 6-7; 12, 2a; G., 4, 76; Paul, 1, 15, 1.   [3] D., 44, 7, 14.
[4] D., 50, 16, 53-2.—**XXI**, 1891, 438.   [5] **CLXIII**, 408.
[6] D., 9, 2, 1-pr.; cf. **CXI**, 1, 206, 1.   [7] **CXII**, 568; I. J., 4, 3, 15.
[8] G., 3, 214-219; I. J., 4, 3, 2.   [9] D., 9, 2, 2-pr., 11-6, 27-5.

during the 30 days before the delict.¹ The advance made here lay in the fact that the formulas of the plebiscite seemed to cover everything included in the patrimony; but the old requirement of a positive act, shown in this case by the necessity for direct damage (*corpori corpore datum*), left acts of omission unpunished as well as those by which damage was caused only indirectly. To kill a slave was a delict; to cause him to die of hunger was not one. Perhaps, failing delictual intention, the Law required some fault on the part of the author of the delict; but it is equally possible that certain indications pointing in this direction may belong to a very much later jurisprudence.²

III. THE PRÆTORIAN REFORMS TOUCHING THE ANCIENT DELICTS

After the *Lex Æbutia* the prætor recast this legislation. Indeed the additions to the ancient data which he made or suggested in collaboration with the Jurists were no less than genuine creations, and in consequence of them the abstract conception of delict took a more prominent place. Previously the chief object in view had been vengeance on the delinquents; henceforward it was repression of the injurious act.

One of the first tendencies of the edict was to make financial penalties general and sometimes to graduate them according to scale, which involved an enlargement of the sphere of noxal actions. Thus against certain kinds of theft—*furtum manifestum, non exhibitum, prohibitum*—and against highway robbery there were actions for four times the value of the object stolen;³ and against all kinds of personal injury there was an action involving ignominy, *in æquum et bonum concepta*, which could not be brought except by the victim in person,⁴ the fine being estimated by the plaintiff within limits imposed by the judge, except in cases where the injury was regarded as *atrox*⁵ either on account of its seriousness or of the place where it had been committed or of the high rank of the victim, for then the magistrate fixed the amount of the con-

---

¹ G., *l.c.;* I. J., 4, 3, p-3.
² D., 9, 2, 5-1: *contra jus, id est si culpa quis occideret.*
³ G., 3, 189, 192; I. J., 41, 4; Aul. Gel., 20, 1, 7; Quint., *Inst. orat.*, 7, 6. —**XIII**, 21, 263.
⁴ G., 3, 224; Paul, 5, 4, 12.—**XLIII**, 256 et seq.; **CLXXII**, 83.
⁵ Ulp., 7, 2, 2; G., 3, 225; Paul, 5, 4, 10.

demnation and the judge made no change in it.¹ This action, called estimatory (*æstimatoria*), was inspired by the δίκη αἰκίας of Hellenic Law and had already, before the Lex Æbutia, been adopted by the Prætor Peregrinus for injuries resulting from the acts of violence contemplated by the Twelve Tables.²

Under the influence of economic changes and of a more acute moral susceptibility successive edicts sought to condemn an increasing number of acts in which the injury was caused by gestures or words: *convicium* or public insult, *ademptata pudicitia*, any *factum infamandi causa*, *convicium* in a wider sense including blows and all kinds of insolence, an injury to the master in the person of his slave,³ a noxal action granted against the person who had the author of the injury *in potestate*. Finally, after the *Lex Cornelia de injuriis* had distinguished the various ways in which they might be committed, the edict tended towards a synthetic definition of injury and could be called in so far as that was concerned an *edictum generale*. Then the Jurists explained how by reacting on several persons at once apart from the immediate victim an injury might constitute several delicts and give rise to an equivalent number of actions.⁴ A *judicium injuriæ contrarium*, a sort of action for slander, was inscribed in the edict in order to secure the condemnation of plaintiffs in an action for *injuria* whose charge was proved to be unfounded. In another direction, the edict extended the action of the *Lex Aquilia utilitatis causa* to all damages that had not been produced either *corpori* or *corpore*, and to those inflicted on the physical person of a free man.⁵

All this labour was condensed and systematized in the official work of Julian. But to the teachers was due the extension of the idea of theft to the fraudulent gain acquired by selling other people's property, to fraudulent enjoyment of use and possession, to the abuse of confidence, to the withdrawal of his own person by the runaway slave, etc.⁶ The definition of theft (*furtum*) became more precise and omitted immoveables,⁷ whose protection, like that of the property as

¹ G., 4, 184. ² **XLIII, 256; CLXXII**, 183.
³ Aul. Gel., 20, 1, 12.—**CLX**, 2, 385 et seq.
⁴ G., 3, 222; Paul, 5, 4, 3.—**XLII**, 469 et seq.; **XLIII**, 257.
⁵ D., 9, 2, 9-pr., 13-pr.; G., 3, 219; Ed.-P., 2, 132.
⁶ G., 3, 156, 200; D., 47, 2, 15-1, 2; 46, 3, 38-1; C. J., 9, 1, 1; Aul. Gel., 6, 12.
—**XLIX**, 2, n°. 667. ⁷ G., 3, 195; Paul, 2, 31-1; D., 41, 3, 38.

a whole, was secured by the edicts concerning pillage and highway robbery (678 A.U.C.) or delicts committed during riots and accidental misfortunes, which were punished by actions available for one year with fines amounting to four times or twice the value of the loss incurred.[1]

It was also necessary to protect the largest possible number of persons from the consequences of the delict. We have just spoken of the many actions arising out of an injury aimed at one person alone but reacting through him on a father, husband or master. There is also the wrong done to the memory of a dead man, which injures his heirs, and we know of an action for *injuria* which was granted to a *filius-familias* in person under certain conditions. The actions for theft and those of the *Lex Aquilia*, which at first were only available for the quiritarian owner, were extended to aliens by means of fictitious actions in whose formula the condition of citizen was assumed, and then, somewhat riskily, to anyone who had a direct interest in the case and had been at the moment of the delict in immediate contact with the object stolen or injured.[2] The action for theft, *utilitatis causa*, that of the *Lex Aquilia*, either on this ground or by means of a fiction, were granted, concurrently with the owner, to those who did not hold their right to the object of him, and, if he were excluded, to those who held it of him, were responsible to him for it and were not insolvent:[3] e.g. the usufructuary and usuary in the former case, the *bona fide* possessor, the trustee, the lessee, and sometimes the *commodatarius* in the latter.[4]

IV. THE PRÆTORIAN DELICTS. DISSOCIATION OF THE PENAL AND RECUPERATORY ELEMENTS

A more original and advanced work of the prætor was the repression of new delicts of a kind less simple than the deeds considered hitherto. The artifices here concerned were sometimes connected with consent given to certain juridical acts or to certain consequences arising out of those acts: e.g. intimidation (*metus*), fraud (*dolus malus*), deceit (*fraus*);[5]

[1] G., 4, 182; Ed. -P., 2, 123.
[2] G., 3, 203; 4, 37; D., 9, 2, 11-8-10, 12, 17.
[3] D., 9, 2, 17, 30; I. J., 4, 1, 13-17.
[4] D., 9, 2, 11-9.—**XIII**, 17, 5 et seq.; **XXXIII**, 32, 28.
[5] Cic., *ad Att.*, 1, 1, 3; T. G., 457.

sometimes with the more or less complete discharge of various obligations: e.g. obligations arising out of deposit, loan, *fiducia*, pledge, commission, etc. Until Rome's seventh century—for these creations belong especially to the last quarter of that century—the infliction of a punishment had been the method of repressing artifices of this kind and repairing their unjust consequences: a fact which proves the at any rate formal persistence of the ancient idea that every action at law took the form of a legalized act of vengeance. It is further remarkable that under this guise began the movement away from the old paths towards more modern points of view.

Of course the guilty acts of the first group—violence, fraud, deceit—had not been absent hitherto from the juridical relations of mankind, but for two reasons Law had taken no account of them. On the one hand these relations, originally rarer and more clearly defined, could only be established by means of formal, material processes, to which the plain and unchangeable meaning of a straightforward act was attached, so that fraud and violence were assumed to be excluded. On the other hand, if they were not always excluded, the accommodating conscience of the lawyers found no fault with methods of procedure whose daring or subtlety did more to establish the reputation of their authors than to injure it. Craft, concealment, snares were guarded against by similar means or by abstention; sometimes by clauses expressly forbidding certain dreaded practices, traces of which may be found in the classical formularies.[1] But moral sensibility in legal matters gradually became more refined, and the very discovery of the misdoings that shocked it rendered it more exacting. The successive attempts of magistrates and Jurists to define these delicts, especially fraud, are the proof of this.

Violence causing intimidation (*metus*), whose repression dates back as far as the edict of the prætor L. Octavius in about 677 A.U.C.,[2] was, according to the classical conception of it, actual physical or moral constraint produced by acts of a third party that were condemned by statute or morality—acts that indangered the victim or his kin, and were of such a nature that the strongest of men would be influenced by

[1] Cic., *de Off.*, 3, 17; D., 45, 1, 53, 119, 121-pr.
[2] CXII, 585, 2.

them.¹ Fraud (*dolus malus*), which was restricted by the prætor Aquilius Gallus in his edict of 688 to simulative acts, embraced later on every stratagem, trick or artifice calculated to defraud others, and became at last, with Paul, a question of fact for the judge to decide upon.² Deception of creditors (*fraus creditorum*), made actionable from the time of Cicero, covered the acts by which a debtor knowingly made himself insolvent or increased his insolvency.³ A later edict made actionable in the same way a freedman's donations *inter vivos* to the injury of his patron's right of inheritance.⁴ Our modern legislations would annul the acts tainted by these vices; the edict punished their authors by means of penal actions *in factum conceptæ* which varied in character according to the turn of mind of the magistrate who created them.

All were at first strictly penal, non-transmissible against the offender's heirs, and occasionally noxal;⁵ but whereas the action *quod metus causa* was granted for fourfold damages, the condemnation in all the others was for simple damages only. The action *de dolo* involved ignominy. While the action *quod metus causa* was always granted against the author of the violence and the action *de fraude creditorum*, which Justinian's compilers were to term *pauliana*,⁶ against the disseized debtor and the conscious beneficiaries by his fraudulent acts, the action *de dolo* was only granted against the author of the fraud subsidiarily, when there was no other juridical means of obtaining redress, and if the defendant was neither ascendant nor patron of the victim.⁷ The texts show that the first was originally combined with the means of recuperation and that it was granted for the whole amount against each joint author or accomplice, but there is no trace in them of any solution of this kind for the two others.⁸

It was perhaps in connexion with these delicts that the idea was first conceived of connecting the punishment (*pœna*) with the guilty intention. Violence, fraud, deceit presupposed it; but it is remarkable that these actions, which are explained by this intention, differed sharply from the normal type of penal actions. The action *quod metus causa*

---

¹ D., 4, 3, 1-pr., 4-6, 9-pr.
² Cic., *de Off.*, 3, 14; *de Nat. Deor.*, 3, 30; D., 4, 3, 1-2 (Serv. Sulpicius, Labio); 44, 4, 1-2 (Paul). ³ D., 42, 8, 1-pr.=P.-L., 1450; 8, 3, 4, 6, 17-1.
⁴ D., 38, 5. ⁵ D., 4, 2, 16-12; C. J., 2, 9, 4.
⁶ D., 4, 3, 1-4.—**XIII**, 43, 186-208. ⁷ D., 4, 3, 1-4, 7-pr. ⁸ **LXXV**, 44.

OBLIGATIONS OR PERSONAL RIGHTS

was only granted in default of spontaneous restitution, the action *de dolo malo* only when there was no other means of repairing the loss; the action *de fraude creditorum* was discretionary.[1] By restitution or reparation (which produced a result analogous to the cancellation of the tainted act) the penal condemnation was avoided. Further, jurisprudence extended the action *quod metus causa* to all the beneficiaries, even if they were unaware of the act of violence, and the action *de fraude* to all who benefited gratuitously by the debtor's acts, even if they were ignorant of his insolvency, thus apparently going back to the primitive conception of a breach of law as something non-moral. At the same time however it refused to allow, even in the action *quod metus causa*, combination of the penal action with the means of recuperation and a number of separate sentences against the joint-authors and accomplices.[2] Finally, declaring these actions available for one year, the edict itself substituted for them on the expiry of that year actions *in factum* for simple damages or recovery of the amount lost. Under the Empire an action was granted even in the course of that year against the heirs of the deceased offender for an amount commensurate with their enrichment.[3]

Thus, in these creations of the edict or in connexion with them, the ideas of vengeance, of which the legal *pœna* was only a milder form, and of reparation of the loss caused to the patrimony began to be dissociated from one another, though not without trouble and confusion. The tendency to separate this reparation from the system of penalties was clearly marked in the following series of facts.

(i.) Each of these actions was matched with a corresponding exception[4] and, sooner or later, with a *restitutio in integrum*, for there is no longer any serious doubt about this chronological order of appearance.[5] The exceptions *quod metus causa* and *de dolo*, which are the best known and could be alleged against charges that an act was tainted with violence or fraud, were at first purely civil acts combined with the penal action; but later on this was no longer allowed, the action having been associated with the *negotium perfectum*,

[1] D., 4, 2, 14-1, 14-11 (interp.)=P.-L., 2, 464; 3, 1-4.
[2] D., 4, 2, 14-15 (interp.).—CXII, 583.
[3] D., 4, 2, 16-2, 20. [4] D., 4, 2, 14-9; 4, 4. Cf. 42, 5, 25.
[5] CXII, 581, 583, 589; CCLXIX, 7, 115-120; XIII, 21, 266.

where execution had taken place, the exception with the contrary hypothesis, though we are not very sure how widely this doctrine was applied or at what date it was fixed for *metus*.[1] The *restitutiones in integrum*, which were of ancient introduction *ob metum*, known only from the second century of the Empire and in the sphere of judicial acts *ob dolum*,[2] obscure *ob fraudem creditorum* and regarded, on the authority of texts that have been tampered with, as an action *de fraude in rem*,[3] annulled by a decree of the prætor the juridical effects of the tainted act and restored, if the act had already been executed, the means of procedure necessary to re-establish the *status quo ante*, both morally and materially. The power to avoid an action by making restitution or reparation, the *exceptio* and the *restitutio in integrum* thus led by three different ways to a result very similar to that of the action for cancellation and the theory of relative nullity in modern Law.

(ii.) At an uncertain date towards the end of the Republic the recuperatory procedure in the matter of theft, which had hitherto been limited to an action for ownership, was completed by granting the robbed owner, regarded out of hatred for thieves as creditor of his own property, a personal action, *condictio furtiva*, which was especially valuable when one of the conditions necessary for an action for ownership was lacking.[4] It was granted even if the object was accidentally lost and for the greatest amount that it had been worth since the theft.[5] Here, clearly, the punishment with the *actio furti* was separated from the reparation with the claim and its accessories (*actio ad exhibendum, interdictum utrubi*) plus the *condictio*.

(iii.) In certain cases governed by old customs and included under the head of delicts the edict and jurisprudence, which reorganized them at the beginning of the Empire, seem to have had in view the mere recovery of the loss. Thus the offence of keeping an immoveable or one of its parts in a state of possible danger to one's neighbour gave, under the statutory processes, the right to anticipatory guarantees obtained by the action *damni infecti*.[6] Under the Empire the edict allowed any person interested to make an application to the prætor in order to oblige the owner or any other possessor of

---

[1] Cic., *pro Flacc.*, 21; D., 4, 2, 9-3, 14-9; but cf. D., 13, 7, 22-1 = P.-L., 1902.
[2] D., 4, 1, 7-pr.; 42, 1, 33; E.-P., 1, 130.
[3] D., 42, 8, 1; I. J., 4, 6, 6; C. J., 5, 75, 1-1. [4] G., 4, 4.—**CCLII**, 1, 312.
[5] D., 13, 1-1, 20, 31-2; C. J., 6, 2, 12-1.
[6] G., 4, 31; D., 39, 2, 6, 7-1, 9-pr.—**CXCV**, 2, 481; **LXVII**, 46; **CCCII**, 1, 269.

the dangerous immoveable to give the *cautio damni infecti*, a guarantee against the possible damage, under the threat, if he refused to do so, of giving the applicant an entry on the immoveable in order that he might carry out the necessary repairs.[1] If the order of the magistrate was not obeyed, he granted, after the damage had been done, a fictitious action on the assumption that the guarantee had been given.[2] The interdict against changing the natural course of rain-water between rural estates, which seems to have been very ancient, only gave rise during the classical period to an action *aquæ pluviæ arcendæ*, which was personal, discretionary and, if circumstances allowed, noxal, but merely resulted in reparation of the damage estimated by an arbitrator.[3] The edict, resorting for this purpose to the old *operis novi nuntiatio*, framed to the transgressor's cost a perpetual and restitutory interdict, to which the latter could make no defence unless he furnished a *cautio* or guarantee, in case he lost the suit, to restore the land to its original condition; but the plaintiff had the right to choose between this restoration and payment of damages equivalent to the injury.[4] The interdict *quod vi aut clam*, a restitutory interdict, also granted *noxaliter*, which was issued by the prætor to check any interference with the property of others, whoever the person might be who had to suffer by it, and the *judicium secutorium* which was granted in case of violation of the interdict up to the amount of the damage done, both pointed steadily in the same direction.[5] In these procedures the idea of punishment was altogether eliminated.

(iv.) In the seventh and eighth centuries A.U.C. almost all the penal actions by which the ancient Law and even the edicts had sanctioned the observance of agreements were replaced or duplicated by actions *in jus conceptæ* or *in factum* which no longer had any penal character: e.g. the actions for *fiducia*, mandate, or guardianship, which had become actions *bonæ fidei* before the time of Quintus Scævola;[6] those for deposit, loan, or pledge, which became such at the end of the Republic;[7] the prætorian action *de pecunia constituta*, etc.

[1] D., 46, 8, 18.   [2] D., 39, 2, 7-pr., 17-pr.   [3] D., 40, 7, 21-pr.
[4] D., 39, 1, 1-4, 2, 3-12, 20-pr., 21-4-7.   Cf. D., 43-25, 1-pr.; Ed.-P., 2, 297, 465.
[5] D., 43, 24, 1-15, 7-5-7, 11-14, 13-3, 20.
[6] Cic., *de Off.*, 3, 17; *ad Heren.*, 3, 13, 9.
[7] *L. Julia mun.*, l. 111: T. G., 87; G., 4, 471.—Cf. **CXCV**, 2, 605.

V. THE PART PLAYED BY "INTERPRETATIO." PRIVATE LAW AND PENAL LAW

Besides dissociating the penal and recuperatory elements, jurisprudence became more concerned than the edicts had been with the delictual intention, tending to make it the very essence of the delict. It introduced it retrospectively into the ancient conceptions of injury, theft and *damnum injuria datum*,[1] and more or less expressly into the other delicts. This doctrine raised the problem of responsibility. It admitted the necessity of deciding who was responsible and who was irresponsible, the madman, the *infans*, the victim of malign influences or even of a mistake, being regarded as irresponsible.[2] As a result of these ideas, which were never carried to their logical extreme, the distinction between penal Law and private Law became ever more marked and the two had to be separated from each other.

But this more important severance was not to be completely achieved, and the Law of the Lower Empire inherited, as we shall see, a number of private delicts. Nevertheless a movement in that direction can be traced from the end of the Republic. The *Lex Cornelia de injuriis* (673 A.U.C.) had already placed within the competence of a *quæstio perpetua* and sanctioned with public penalties the delicts of physical violence (*pulsatio*, *verberatio*) and violation of domicile, thus separating them from the private delicts; but they were connected with them again by Caracalla. Theft, highway robbery, slander and some other injuries were the object of *judicia publica*, at least if proceeded against by means of a *persecutio extraordinaria*; and the same was true of the murder of a slave.[3] Title iv of the fifth book of Paul's *Sententiæ* bears witness throughout to the triumph of this tendency in the sphere of *injuria*, and other texts show that when there was a choice between the traditional private prosecution and public prosecution, the latter was almost always used.[4]

[1] G., 3, 197, 198, 211; D., 47, 2, 46-6; 48, 19, 15-pr.=Paul, 5, 4, 2; D., 9, 2, 5-2; I. J., 1, 7; 3, 7. [2] See the texts quoted in the last note.
[3] D., 47, 10, 7-1-6.—CLX, 2, 407. [4] I. J., 4, 4, 8.

III

CONTRACTS

I. AGREEMENTS IN THE TIME OF PRIVATE JUSTICE

Primitive Roman Law did not provide even the outline of a general theory of contract, which was not sketched out until after the creation of a long series of concrete acts. The clear conception of contract, i.e. of "agreement between several persons in a common expression of will in order that an obligation may be caused thereby,"[1] does not occur quite simply to men's minds. An interchange of vague proposals seemed an insufficient basis for any regulations concerning the fulfilment of the agreement which had been made.

It is true that the breach of a promise given could be resented as a personal injury and followed by vengeance; but it is supposed that the chief original purpose of contract was to stop or prevent private warfare, and it would have been useless if its observance had only been secured by reopening hostilities. Presently occasions arose, however rarely, in which, by act and consent of the parties interested, a transfer of property was made between two men or two families who had neither the wish nor the power to betake themselves to the hazard of arms. In such cases legend shows us that the parties had recourse to solemn vows; but still it was necessary that the debtor should have an immediate interest in swearing, and moreover the vow only armed the gods against him, not the adverse party.[2] Now the most important thing in the agreement was its sanction, the means of compelling its execution; and it is by his manifest intention (which could be expressed in many ways) to have recourse to this means that the creditor really becomes a party to the juridical act.

Since ancient customs show that the situation was guaranteed by sureties who were even substituted immediately for the debtor, it has been supposed that there was a system of giving a hostage who, in the earliest times, would have been a third party and, later on, the debtor himself, placed in a state of subjection to the creditor and answerable in his own person for the execution of the agreement—a system which would have left its traces in Roman Law on the one hand

[1] CCLXXI, 1, 142;   [2] CXXIV, 12-17, 118-121.

in the *vades*, *prædes* and *sponsores*, and on the other in the *nexi*.¹ Since these customs show that objects of varying value were handed over at the moment of making the agreement, it has been supposed that there was a system of giving something in pledge which, if it was a thing of consequence, provided the creditor with a means of compensating himself,² or if, as often happened, it was something trivial that the debtor surrendered, served as a means of bringing magic influences to bear against him.³ But even in the societies where they could be employed neither of these systems was used exclusively. No stone was left unturned; neither force nor craft was neglected; and there were some classical artifices, if we may use the word, recommended by the practitioners and even by the codes.⁴ Still more important was the part played by magic or religious sanctions, some within reach of the parties themselves, others placed at their disposal by the priests. There was a judicial and juridical magic of which philology finds echoes in the primitive meaning of certain words: *obligatio, nomen, damnatio*, etc.⁵

These obscure but terrible sanctions had the advantage of operating automatically when once they were set in motion by performance of the ritual, or at any rate of insuring divine assistance, satisfying the conscience of the man who took action and finally, in a slightly more advanced state of society, emboldening him to reveal his intentions beforehand, since they were thus placed under the control of the gods and of public opinion. Here we have that publicity which was often required in primitive Law, both civil and penal, with a view to establishing the legitimacy of the act; and later on this will be the sole reason for the lawsuit and the judge's sentence— an important development because it introduces an element of order. Juridical acts were at first contrived to meet this problem: by what external signs can it be recognized that a situation has been created in which the sanction can be legitimately exercised ? Hence the few acts involving some ritual performance: stereotyped gestures and words with a strictly defined meaning and application, which alone can open the way for recourse to human justice and authorize

---

[1] **CLX**, 4; **CCLXXI**, 1, 47; **XXXIII**, 1904, 253, Mitteis, *Mél. Bekker*, 117.
[2] **CLXXXI**, 16. [3] Huvelin, *Magie et droit individuel*, 30.
[4] **CXXIV**, 17, 83-91, 110-112. [5] **CLXXXI**, 13-54.

the interested party to avail himself of legal constraints. The desire to limit and organize sanctions led to a strict definition and regulation of the acts which gave birth to rights. The contract was this external act, and the intention of the parties was presumed to be in conformity with the meaning which custom or statute attached to these particular gestures and words. The Law was not concerned with the conditions or grounds of consent, or even with its existence; for the causes of the obligation produced this automatically, and their importance was in inverse ratio to that of the consent.

II. THE MOST ANCIENT CONTRACTS OF ROMAN LAW. FORMAL CONTRACTS

These origins explain the first contracts practised at Rome. The *nexum*, confirmed by the Twelve Tables: *cum nexum faciet . . . uti lingua nuncupassit, ita jus esto*,[1] was perhaps the most ancient. In our days it has given rise to the most magnificent display of private judgment in the interpretation of the texts. Some have seen in this act, regarded as an element in a contract or as altogether distinct from any contract, the pledging of the debtor, of his *alieni juris* or of their services; some have regarded it as a conditional sale by the debtor of himself in case of failure to repay the debt, or again as the giving of a hostage or a pledge for a pre-existing debt. Moreover, its contractual nature has been alternately maintained and denied.[2] But we must continue to regard it as a very old contract of loan for consumption realized by a twofold operation. First the money lent was transferred by means of the bronze and balance (*per œs et libram*), with the assistance of the *libripens,* and weighed in the presence of 5 witnesses who must be Roman citizens above the age of puberty—the weighing being actual in the time of *œs rude*, but symbolical after the introduction of money.[3] Secondly, in order to oblige the borrower to make restitution, a *damnatio* was pronounced by the lender and justified by the enrichment of the borrower's patrimony at his expense. Originally no doubt it placed the former, in case of failure to repay, under the doom of a magic punishment; later on it authorized *manus*

[1] XII T., 5, 1, 1; Festus, s.v. *Nexum*.
[2] **CLVIII**, 500; **XIII**, 29, 49 et seq.; **XXXIII**, 22, 92 et seq.; **XXXVIII**, s.v. *Nexum*. [3] G., 3, 173-175.

injectio against him.¹ Whether subsequent practice, in accordance with a development observed in other legislations, used the formalities of this act as the general mode of contracting when the object of the obligation was a sum of money, is a doubtful and disputed question.²

The effect of the *damnatio* is also disputed, some denying that *manus injectio* was originally the sanction of anything except a judgment;³ but the texts prove the contrary.⁴ It was the *Lex Pœtelia* of the fifth century A.U.C. that, by depriving the *damnatio* of executory force, set free all the *nexi* except those bound by a delictual debt, and thus in fact destroyed the utility of the *nexum*.⁵ The truth is that the position of the *nexi*, which gave rise to so much trouble, was not directly the result of the *manus injectio* which, in the absence of a *vindex*, involved after a respite of 60 days the *addictio* of the debtor, e.g. his death or his enslavement in a foreign country, but of a compromise often made during this period of respite by which, in order to save his life or liberty, the debtor placed himself under the control of his creditor in such a manner that the latter benefited by his work and his acquisitions and could keep him chained up in private confinement. The name *nexus* was derived from the fact that it was most often the *nexum* that had brought the debtor to this pass. This compromise, which involved more or less serious consequences according to the importance of the debt, might sometimes be no more than an undertaking to work for the creditor's profit (*stipulatio operarum*).⁶

The oath, *jusjurandum*, another method of confirming agreements which was allowed by the Twelve Tables,⁷ doubtless varied in form according to the deity invoked, the most simple being the joining of the parties' right hands (*junctio dexterarum*).⁸ It involved the utterance by the future creditor of an exact formula (*concepta verba*) which was repeated by the debtor in an *execratio* against himself in case he broke the agreement.⁹ By so doing the latter submitted himself to the judgment of the god to whom he gave a pledge, a piece of

---

[1] Cic., *Top.*, 5, 28; *pro Mur.*, 2, 3; Festus, s.v. *Nuncupata*.
[2] **XXXIII**, 23, 429; 25, 105; 26, 84.
[3] **XXXIII**, 2, 5, 94 et seq.; 26, 84 et seq. [4] **XIII**, 29, 73-84.
[5] Cic., *de Rep.*, 2, 34; Liv., 8, 18; cf. Varro, *de L. l.*, 7, 105.—**CXII**, 842.
[6] **XIII**, 29, 91. [7] Dion. Hal., 1, 40; Cic., *de Off.*, 8, 31.
[8] Liv., 1, 21; Pliny, *N. H.*, 11, 45; Festus, s.v. *Feretrius*.
[9] Liv., 22, 38; Aul. Gel., 2, 24; 16, 4.

OBLIGATIONS OR PERSONAL RIGHTS 213

money or any other object. As a religious act the oath was not subject to the ordinary conditions of the Law and could be used both by aliens and by slaves for whom it survived in the warped form of the *juramentum liberti*, constant preoccupation with the juridical capacity of the debtor having caused the slave's oath to be supported by that of a freedman, although there was still doubt as to which of the two incurred the obligation.[1]

For some reason unknown the sacramental formula containing the word *spondere* could only be used in agreements between Roman citizens.[2] We do not know what legal sanction was attached to it, or even whether it had one. It has been supposed that this kind of agreement served at first to guarantee the payment of a composition (the ransom of private vengeance) by sureties, whence the terms *sponsores, consponsores*, used to describe the most ancient sureties;[3] but, whatever may have been said to the contrary, it does not seem to have been derived from the engagements either of the *vas* or of the *præs*, which were perhaps only species of it.[4] Secularized in the course of the fourth century A.U.C., the *sponsio* degenerated into a dialogue between the contractors in person, in which, now that the oath was excluded, the creditor asked: *Spondesne mihi* . . . *dare?* and the debtor replied, using the same word: *Spondeo*. Use of the dialogue and of the sacrosanct word, exact repetition of the declaration of the object—a sum of money (*certa pecunia*), these were the formalities of the new act which sanctioned first the *actio sacramenti in personam* and afterwards, in virtue of the *Lex Silia*, the *legis actio per condictionem*.[5]

Another form of oath, used throughout central Italy, was open to aliens as well as to citizens, secularization in this case involving first of all delivery of the pledge (*stips, stipula*) to the creditor himself, and afterwards its abolition. This also took the form of a dialogue, but was more flexible: *Promittisne? promitto;—Fidejubesne* . . . *? jubeo; Dabisne* . . . *? dabo*, etc. Finally, in classical times, this contract tolerated the use of a foreign language and of any terms whatever, provided that question and answer were clear and in accordance with each

---
[1] D., 46, 12, 44-pr.; 58, 1, 72.   [2] G., 3, 92; Fest., s.v. *Spondere*.
[3] XLIII, 76-86.   [4] CLVIII, 509; XXXIII, 22, 97.
[5] G., 3, 92, 93; 4, 18-20.

other.¹ Under the name of *stipulatio* this less rigid form became, like *sponsio*, a kind of mould in which the most diverse agreements could be cast and shaped, and it was sanctioned in the same way as *sponsio*. These institutions drew closer to one another, and their application was extended first by the *Lex Calpurnia* to any definite object (*de omni certa re*), and then by the jurisprudence of the sixth century to every kind of prestation. Before long it became possible to include in one stipulation all the objects stated in a previous agreement, whether written or not.² The prætor Aquilius Gallus made a remarkable use of this process in a formula that bears his name (*stipulatio aquiliana*).³ The use of writing as an accompaniment of important stipulations became general, with the result that classical Law held the utterance of the words to be genuine, in the absence of proof to the contrary, when it was thus certified by the parties in person.⁴

After the *Lex Æbutia* the verbal contracts were sanctioned by one or other of three actions of strict law according to the nature of their object. If it was a sum of money (*certa pecunia*), the sanction was a *condictio certæ pecuniæ* (an action *certæ pecuniæ creditæ*), with *sponsio* and *restipulatio tertiæ partis* against the loser, with *intentio* and *condemnatio certæ* ; if it was a definite object (*certa res*), the sanction was a *condictio triticaria* (an action *certæ rei*) with *intentio certa* and *condemnatio incerta* ; while the sanction for any other prestation (*incertum*) was an action *ex stipulatu* with a *demonstratio* declaring the terms of the *stipulatio*, both *intentio* and *condemnatio* being *incerta*.⁵ Thus Roman practice was provided with a very handy instrument which it knew how to use in very different ways, all that was necessary being to adapt the *verba* to the object of the contract. The following are some typical cases in common use.

The verbal contract, which had been framed to establish the obligation to pay a composition, deviated to some extent from its original purpose in the stipulation of a penalty (*stipulatio pœnæ*), by which the parties fixed what *pœna* they liked by agreement, provided that they did not seek thereby to circumvent the public statutes, those concerning the rate

¹ G., 3, 92, 93; D., 45, 1, 1-2, 6, 5-1.
² G., 4, 19; Cato, *de R. r.*, 144, 2; D., 45, 1, 140-pr., 134-1.
³ D., 46, 4, 18-1.   ⁴ Paul., 5, 7, 1, 2; D., 45, 1, 134-2.
⁵ G., 4, 13, 41-50, 131, 136, 171; Ed.-P., 1, 171, 274.

OBLIGATIONS OR PERSONAL RIGHTS

of interest for example.[1] This stipulation was necessary so long as the repression of fraud and violence was left to the parties concerned, or there was no other means of rendering agreements obligatory when their object was something else than money; and later on it was used for other purposes, e.g. to transform an obligation for something *incertum* into the more strictly sanctioned obligation for a sum of money (*certæ pecuniæ*), to guarantee a promise made by others, to estimate the damages by agreement in advance, etc.[2] It took several forms, especially those of a stipulation conditioned by the occurrence which it sanctioned and an accessory stipulation guaranteeing the execution of a principal one.[3] Doubts have been raised about its nature,[4] but not about the fact that the *pœna* was incurred in its entirety as soon as the condition was fulfilled.[5] The *clausula doli*, a clause precluding fraud on the part of one or both parties in the execution of contracts, had not served as a substitute for it in case of fraud, since it left the power of fixing the damages to the judge. Nevertheless, in spite of this disadvantage, it continued to be of use even after the creation of the action *de dolo* mentioned above, since it gave rise to a perpetual civil action which was transmissible for the whole amount against the heirs of the delinquent and always led to recovery of the loss incurred.

The verbal contract also served to introduce by *adstipulatio* an accessory creditor—a third party who, by making the same stipulation as the principal creditor by a separate contract after him, acquired the right to proceed against the debtor when the debt fell due, to receive the payment and to cancel the debt. The *adstipulator* became a sort of attorney and served as a substitute for the representative at law whose employment was forbidden. Business men made a profession of it which was ruined by the use of judicial mandataries (*cognitores* and *procuratores*).[6] The *adstipulator* was distinguished from the *adjectus solutionis gratia*, who was merely named in the creditor's stipulation as authorized to receive payment.[7]

This contract also served to create multiple creditors or

[1] D., 4, 8, 32-pr.; 21, 2, 56-pr.; 45, 1, 69.
[2] D., 45, 1, 38-2, 45-17; I. J., 3, 15, 7, 19, 21. Cf. G., 4, 176.
[3] D., 45, 1, 71, 115-2, 137-7.
[4] **XLIX**, 2, nos 539-41; **CLVIII**, 697; **CCXLIV**, 3, 808-814.
[5] D., 45, 1, 85-6; 47, 7, 23. [6] Cic., *ad Oct.*, 9; G., 3, 110-117.
[7] D., 45, 11, 16-pr.; 56, 2, 131-1.

216 FORMATION OF CLASSICAL LAW

debtors, or in other words to establish solidarities and personal guarantees which we shall consider when dealing with the organization of credit.

One of the most original applications of the *stipulatio* was the process of novation which jurisprudence derived from it.[1] Novation (*novatio*), transfer of the content of one obligation to another, involves the disappearance of the first and is therefore reckoned among the methods of extinguishing obligations. But it was not created for this purpose. It was doubtless a result of the ancient formalism which, if one contract had already been made and a second was made with the same object, forbade their coexistence, whether the contracting parties were the same in each case or one of them had been changed.[2] The use of this artifice for purposes of novation is therefore ancient, but its doctrinal development given in the texts is evidently classical. The operation required (i.) a prior obligation of any kind or origin followed by a new obligation created by *stipulatio*;[3] (ii.) a common object (*idem debitum*) for these two obligations: it was not until towards the end of the classical period that the estimated value of the object could be substituted for it and the two regarded as equivalent; (iii.) a new element (*aliquid novi*) which explained the necessity for the operation and could be an addition or an alteration but not a diminution.[4] It is difficult to define this process *a priori*. Gaius proceeds by giving examples of it: change of creditor with the consent of the original creditor (*jussu antiqui creditoris*);[5] change of debtor;[6] addition, alteration or suppression of a term or condition, although at first it was probably impossible to novate a conditional obligation, since there was no *debitum*, no object of such an obligation, until the condition was realized; addition of a surety; change of the cause of the obligation when the first had not arisen out of a verbal contract.[7] For a long time the effect of novation was attached to the *verba*: perhaps there were as many different formulas as there were kinds of novation possible.[8] The intention to novate (*animus novandi*) seems to have played no part until the

---

[1] G., 3, 176 et seq.
[2] D., 45, 1, 18, 25; 46, 9-2. Cf. D., 19, 1, 10; 44, 2, 14.
[3] **CLV**, 216.   [4] G., 3, 177-179; D., 45, 1, 83-7, 91-6.
[5] One of the operations termed *delegatio*: **CLVIII**, 740.
[6] Cf. D., 46, 2, 8-5.   [7] D., 45, 1, 126-2.   [8] D., 46, 2, 2.—**CLV**, 120 et seq.

OBLIGATIONS OR PERSONAL RIGHTS

time of Ulpian.[1] By extinguishing the first obligation, *novatio* completed its term and caused its accessories to disappear.[2] It is uncertain how far the exceptions at law which could be alleged against the first obligation remained available for the new one.[3]

The great flexibility of the verbal contract was only limited by the necessity of a dialogue between the parties interested: hence the uselessness of any promise or stipulation made on behalf of others.[4] At first this act had been found too complicated, involving interpretation by the judge and search for a consideration. When the principle was admitted, it was transferred to other juridical acts, but in their case it soon had to be abandoned.[5] The stipulation itself could be sanctioned, in this case, by means of a penalty (*pœna*) stipulated for the benefit of the contractor if the prestation to be rendered to the third party was not executed. In the same way a promise on behalf of others was sanctioned by the stipulation of a penalty on the part of the promisor or his representative in order to secure its execution: what we call *la clause de porte-fort*. Then classical jurisprudence made valid any stipulation whose terms revealed either some advantage to the stipulator in the performance of something by the promisor on behalf of others, or even an act, however indirect, to be performed by the promisor. Ulpian admits the validity of the stipulation even when this advantage or this act only became apparent to the judge as a result of interpretation or inquiry.[6]

Two other verbal contracts, the *juramentum liberti*, which seems to have been an undeveloped form of engagement by oath, and the *dictio dotis* have already been explained.

An obligation arising out of any one of the contracts of which we have just spoken was perpetual. Even payment was insufficient to cancel it unless accompanied by the necessary formalities. It only disappeared if the parties were agreed either to substitute another one for it—which, in the case of an obligation arising out of *nexum*, could only be done when prosecution of the suit was restricted to the *vindex*,

---

[1] D., 45, 2, 3, 6-pr.
[2] D., 13, 1, 17; D., 46, 2, 18; **CXIX**, 64 et seq.; **XL**, 1899, 49-57.
[3] **CLV**, 251 et seq.; **CCXCIX**, 2, 355.
[4] D., 45, 1, 17, 38-pr.   [5] D., 44, 5, 21; 7, 11; 50, 17, 73-4.
[6] D., 45, 1, 38-20, 25, 81; I. J., 3, 19, 3; 4, 11-pr.-3.

and in the case of an obligation arising *verbis*, when the matter had been carried as far as a novation or the *litis contestatio* ; or else to extinguish it by a formal act (*actus contrarius*) subject to no condition or reservation which, in the case of *nexum*, was a restitution *per æs et libram* of the things lent,[1] in the case of verbal contract, a dialogue: "Have you received what I promised you ? I have" (*Quod ego tibi promisi, habesne acceptum ? Habeo*), which was the counterpart of the stipulation and was called *acceptilatio*.[2] These acts which had once served only to complete actual payments could be mere imaginary performances of the obligation (*solutiones imaginariæ*), realizing donations or executing testamentary or judicial obligations.[3]

III. The Contract "Litteris." The "Mutuum" and the "Pactum Fiduciæ"

Between the Law of the Twelve Tables and the *Lex Æbutia* two other contracts were introduced into legal practice: the contract *litteris* and the *mutuum*. Some regard them as simplifications of or substitutes for the *nexum*, because their obligations were the result of a transfer of property and involved, as in the *nexum*, restoration of the normal position.

Our information about the first is scanty and vague. This contract was brought about by an entry in an account-book which, according to a tradition already ancient in Cicero's time,[4] had to be kept with scrupulous care by the *paterfamilias* ; but it is not certain that this *codex* served from its origin as a means of realizing contracts. It has even been maintained—wrongly, in my opinion—that the register used for this purpose under the name of *codex accepti et expensi* was distinct from the general *codex rationum* of the *paterfamilias* which was similar to our ancient books of accounts.[5] We are altogether ignorant of the composition of this register and of the way in which it was kept. Operations affecting the family patrimony which were entered daily in the *adversaria*[6]—a sort of day-book also called *ephemeris*—were

---

[1] Liv., 6, 14; G., 3, 174-175. [2] G., 3, 169, 170.
[3] G., 3, 173; D., 34, 7, 1; 46, 4, 5, 19-1.
[4] Cic., *de Orat.*, 47; *pro Cœl.*, 7; *pro Cluen.*, 30.
[5] **CCXCII**, 107; **CXVII**, 83; **CCLXXX**, 277. Cf. **XXXIII**, 1890, 345. Even the expression " codex accepti et expensi " is rare.
[6] Cic., *in Verr.*, 2, 33, 2, 4, 6; D., 32, 29, 2.

OBLIGATIONS OR PERSONAL RIGHTS 219

periodically transferred to it, generally each month, but we no longer know in what order or in what manner the entries were made.[1] Gaius, our principal authority, states that two kinds of *nomina*, i.e. debts, were entered in it: the *nomina arcaria* representing actual counting out of cash, whatever the cause might be, and the *nomina transcriptitia*, comprising the two possible forms of contract *litteris*. Both assumed that a pre-existing debt already entered in the *codex* was, no doubt with the debtor's consent, cancelled and replaced by another based upon a fictitious loan of money.[2] In the *transcriptio a re in personam* the creditor entered that what had been owing hitherto as a result of some previous operation—selling, letting, etc.—had been lent (*expensum*) by him to the debtor; in the *transcriptio a persona in personam*, that what was previously owed him by a third party had been lent (*expensum*) by him to another person. In both cases it was necessary, in order to make the entries regular, that before being entered as *expensum* the amount of the original debt should have been entered as *acceptum*, so that this debt might be cancelled.[3] In accordance with the Roman point of view, which derived every juridical situation from the activity of the person who benefited by it, the juridical force of the act was due to the entry of the amount owing under the name of the debtor.[4] Some mysterious power has been ascribed to the use of the word *nomen*, but it had probably ceased to have such power when it began to be used in this contract.[5] The transfer of something valuable, the *expensum*, from the creditor's patrimony to that of the debtor gave the initiative to the former. It does not appear that the *litteræ* allowed any condition to be imposed except the limit of time within which the loan had to be repaid.[6] In the silence of Gaius we must reject, notwithstanding opinions to the contrary, the possibility of creating a first obligation directly by means of an entry,[7] of substituting another creditor by *transcriptio*,[8] and finally of attaching to the operation all the effects proper to novation.[9] Considering the presumed date of the intro-

[1] Cic., *pro Rosc.*, 2; C. Nep., *T. Pomp.*, 13. Cf. **CCXCII**, *l.c.*; **CXCV**, 2², 752; **XXXIII**, *l.c.* [2] G., 3, 128-133.—I. Th., 3, 22 gives no exact information.
[3] **CLVIII**, 522-523. [4] **CLVIII**, 522-523.
[5] **CLXXXI**, 27-29; **CXCV**, 2¹, 753. [6] Cic., *ad fam.*, 7, 23.
[7] But see **CLVIII**, 522, 5. [8] **CXCV**, 2, 755.
[9] G., 3, 180 regards the " t. a. p. in p." as a mere " delegatio ": **CLV**, 213; **CXCV**, 2, 760.

duction of this contract, its original sanction must have been the *legis actio per condictionem*, which was succeeded by the action *certæ pecuniæ creditæ*.[1] Comparatively modern, this contract though formal had no peculiar *actus contrarius* or mode of extinguishing the obligation.[2] Under the Empire the Sabinians declared the *transcriptio a re in personam* to be available for aliens. But owing to the decay of family customs, registers kept by the heads of *domus* went out of fashion and the *nomina transcriptitia* ceased to be used.

Neither ancient Law nor classical Law knew of any other writing that gave rise to obligations. Roman practice was either unwilling or unable to take over in the form of the *syngrapha* or *chirographum* the written and abstract contract, which also bore the semblance of a loan of money and was so widely used among the Greeks.[3] Although very general, at least from the last century of the Republic, the συγγραφή δάνειου did not get beyond the provincial edict in so far as it governed the relations between aliens or between aliens and Roman citizens.[4]

The *mutuum*, also a contract of loan for consumption, was the most ancient and the only contract of strict law among those which the Romans described as being formed *re*, i.e. by transfer of property. It is defined as a transfer by one person, *tradens*, to another, *accipiens*, of the ownership of a certain number of things capable of being measured, weighed or counted, in consequence of which the recipient was bound to restore an equivalent quantity of things of the same nature.[5] Its line of development was parallel to that of *nexum* when the **Lex Poetelia Papiria** and the use of money rendered the operation *per æs et libram* doubly useless. It is undoubtedly ancient, for the Jurists named the obligations formed *re* before any of the others.[6] This was because the transfer of property from one patrimony to another was regarded by Law as giving rise to obligations long before any spontaneous undertaking with no apparent consideration. It serves to explain the *damnatio* of the *nexum* and the *litteræ* of the *nomina transcriptitia*, and the *sponsio* was at first no more than a solemn recognition of debt! One passage

---

[1] Cic., *pro Rosc.*, c. 5.   [2] But see **CXCV**, 2, 799.
[3] G., 3, 134.—**CCXXX**, 460 et seq.; **XXXVI**, 17, 551-581.
[4] Cic., *ad Att.*, 6, 1, 15; in *Verr.*, 2, 1, 52.—**CCXXX**, 484.
[5] G., 3, 90; D., 44, 7, 1-2; I. J., 3, 14-pr.   [6] G., 3, 90; D., 44, 1, 1.

in Gaius bears traces of a time when no care had yet been taken to distinguish obligations in which the transfer of property was the result of an agreement between the parties from those in which it was caused in any other way.[1]

The act which gave its objects the name of *mutuum* (this adjective is not found alone in the literary language, where the terms *mutuæ pecuniæ, mutuum argentum* are used) began then with a *datio*. This latter, which was a mode of transferring ownership, could not have two effects in Law and also create an obligation; but it led to a change (*mutatio*) in the relative value of two patrimonies, and if the borrower did not make restitution when his debt came due, he enriched himself unjustly at the expense of the lender. In the *nexum* this had justified *manus injectio* and here it justified the less violent *legis actio per condictionem* which was framed to repair the consequences of unjust occurrences other than delictual, and was succeeded after the *Lex Æbutia* by the *actio certæ pecuniæ creditæ* and the *condictio certæ rei*. The amount of their condemnations was strictly measured by the enrichment, i.e. by what the borrower had received; but on the other hand he bore the risks, because the debt was a general one.[2] Later on, although the action was of strict law, the admission within the Law of other contracts formed *re* gave the judge the further power of ascertaining the parties' intention—a real innovation, due to the fact that a *datio* could now lead to some other result besides a *mutuum*, and that the actual handing over of a thing to someone else could be something other than a *datio*, e.g. a transfer of possession or of mere detention.[3]

Thus the *datio* became the very centre of the *mutuum*, and it was so regarded in the work of jurisprudence until classical times, both as regards the conditions determining the existence of the contract and the amount of the obligation. Moreover it was in connexion with the *datio mutui* that the Jurists generally sought to discover what constituted the material element in the *traditio*.[4] Other problems were concerned with the effects of the operation if the lender had no right of ownership over the things lent (*res mutuæ*) or if there was no capacity to alienate.[5] The solutions were easy, but the Jurists were sometimes guilty of awkwardness

[1] G., 3, 90, 91.   [2] D., 45, 1, 1-4.   [3] See p. 231 et seq.
[4] See p. 175, and on D., 12, 1, 11-pr., 15, 20; 17, 1, 34-pr.—CLVIII, 309; CCLII, 3[1], 227 et seq.   [5] D., 12, 1, 19-1.

and vagueness therein and the commentators made them still more obscure.¹ They can be reduced to two alternatives: either the things lent by the lender without right of ownership or capacity to alienate were still in existence, in which case the owner (*verus dominus*) could claim them or the *tradens* could recover them by means of a *condictio possessionis* (*sine causa*);² or else the things had been consumed, in which case the texts allow a *condictio* whose exact nature they leave unexplained.³

Under the name of *pactum fiduciæ* the Law of the end of the Republic admitted another contract of the same type as the *mutuum*, which was also founded on a *datio* or transfer of ownership of any kind of property with the most diverse objects in view: security (*fiducia cum creditore*), deposit, loan for use, gift by means of an intermediary (*fiducia cum amico*), etc.—every operation in fact where it was necessary for a third party to have the property temporarily at his disposal.⁴ When the object was attained, the third party had to retransfer the ownership; otherwise he would have enriched himself unjustly. It has been said that a *condictio* was granted to the *tradens* to enable him to compel this restitution;⁵ but we have no certain trace of anything except an action *in factum* involving ignominy, an action of the same type as those *in bonum et æquum conceptæ*, which was very soon succeeded by an action *fiduciæ directa* with its parallel action *fiduciæ contraria*, both already included in Q. Mucius Scævola's list of actions *bonæ fidei*.⁶ The system was completed by a *usureceptio fiduciæ* which must have existed much earlier.⁷ In the legal acts of which we have record the fiduciary agreement (*pactum fiduciæ*) is no longer met with except in combination with *mancipatio* and *in jure cessio*.⁸

IV. THE CONSENSUAL CONTRACTS: SALE, HIRE, PARTNERSHIP, COMMISSION

In the seventh century A.U.C. four actions *bonæ fidei* noted by Q. Mucius Scævola reveal to us four agreements founded on the bare consent of the parties and confirmed not long

---
[1] On the *reconciliatio mutui* see **CLVIII**, 536; **CXII**, 432.
[2] D., 12, 1, 19-1; 6, 15-1.   [3] D., 12, 11, 2, 12, 13-pr.
[4] **CLXXXIX; CXLIV**, 3, 129-146.   [5] **CLXXXIX**, 215, on D., 22, 1, 4-1.
[6] G., 2, 220; 4, 182; Cic., *Top.*, 17; *de Off.*, 3, 15; 17, 70; Ed.-P., 2, 3-10; **XIII**, 21, 254.   [7] G., 2, 59-60.   [8] **CLVIII**, 547.

afterwards by the Civil Law: viz. the consensual contracts of sale, hire, partnership and commission.[1] Nothing of the kind existed before them, and afterwards Roman Law admitted no others. This spontaneous generation is explained by the frequency and economic importance of these agreements, and it has been asked how their place had been filled hitherto. Some say that it had been filled by two stipulations which, as a matter of fact, dissociated the obligations and the combined effects of the operation, only connecting them after a fashion if each was subject to the condition of the other's execution, so that only the party who had already executed was able to prosecute.[2] Others say that as good a result was obtained without recourse to stipulation by founding the second obligation on the fact of the unilateral execution of the first,[3] on the idea of enrichment. But is not this equivalent to constructing for these juridical operations a theory which, as we know, did not appear until long afterwards ?[4] Moreover there is no clear transition from these practices to the consensual type of contract. For sale and hire an origin has been sought in the administrative jurisprudence concerning the *venditiones* and *locationes* which the State allowed in the form of auctions (*auctiones*) of public property, and which were imitated by private individuals. The absence of formality, the interpretation in good faith of the detailed conditions resulting from a specification, the tacit renewal of the lease, the fact that money is the object of one of the obligations would point in this direction;[5] but what of partnership and commission ?

Sale, *emptio-venditio*, was the contract by which one party, *venditor*, undertook to secure to the other, *emptor*, the peaceful possession of a thing in exchange for a sum of money.[6] This perfect, synallagmatic contract had therefore two objects: (i.) a thing, *merx*, which could be any object of commercial dealings, whether corporeal or incorporeal, present or to come,[7] belonging to the vendor or to a third party,[8] but

[1] G., 3, 135; Cic., *de Off.*, 3, 17.—**LXVII**, 1, 311; **LXV**, 1, 505; **CVIII**, 366.
[2] **CLXXXII**, 3, 232; 4, 195; **XIII**, 7, 539.
[3] **CCLII**, 1, 456; **XXXIII**, 9, 22; **XXXVIII**, s.v. *Obligatio*.
[4] This idea could hardly admit an obligation on the party prosecuting to offer to make execution himself, on which a supposed *exceptio non adempleti contractus* has been grafted.—Cf. **CLXIII**, 532, 4.
[5] **XXXIII**, 1886, 260; **CXII**, 451.
[6] G., 3, 141; D., 18, 1, 1-1; T G., 848 et seq.
[7] D., 18, 1, 8, pr.; 20, 4-7; 11, 17.
[8] D., 18, 1, 28.

probably a determinate thing;[1] (ii.) a sum of money, *pretium*, which the Jurists required to be *certum*, i.e. dependent neither on the caprice of one of the parties nor on chance,[2] and *verum*, i.e. real. Failing this the operation would not have been a sale.[3] The bare consent of the parties who were agreed upon the two objects of the contract sufficed to complete it. The addition in classical Law of a written memorandum or of earnest-money had merely a probative effect.[4] But the formation of the contract could be delayed by inserting a condition in the vendor's interest (*in diem addictio*) or in that of the vendee.[5] This contract then gave rise to a double series of obligations.

The obligations of the vendor, sanctioned by the *actio empti*, were (i.) to take as much care (*custodia*) of the thing sold as a good *paterfamilias* would; i.e. the vendor was responsible for even slight negligence, but accidents (in the absence of a clause to the contrary) and loss of the thing after he had made delay (*mora*) were at the cost of the vendee, who was no longer intitled to anything but the material and juridical ruins, whereas on the other hand, though the fact has been disputed, he remained liable for the whole of the price;[6] (ii.) to deliver the thing sold, i.e. to give the vendee vacant possession of it (*vacua possessio*), not always or necessarily ownership, for there were many things involved in commerce whose legitimate alienators lacked quiritarian ownership, but each vendor was obliged to transfer all the serviceable rights which he himself possessed, consequently, if he was owner, to effect the mancipation of the *res mancipi* and the *traditio* of the others;[7] (iii.) to give a guarantee against eviction or flaws in the thing sold. The guarantee against eviction was at first only consequent upon mancipation and was then sanctioned by the *actio auctoritatis* ; later, in the case of mere *traditio* of *res mancipi*, use was made, at any rate from the seventh century A.U.C., either of a *satisdatio secundum mancipium* in which vendors and fidejussors promised under penalty of double the price to act as *auctores*, i.e. guarantors or protectors of the threatened vendee, or, preferably and more simply, of a *stipulatio duplæ* or *dupli pretii* by which

---

[1] **CXCV**, 2, 616; **LXV**, 2, 332.   [2] G., 3, 140.   [3] D., 18, 1, 35-1, 36.
[4] G., 3, 139. It was otherwise in provincial Law: **VI**, 1, 68-72; **LXV**, 1, 520.
[5] D., 18, 2, 1.   [6] Cf. D., 18, 6, 3; 19, 1, 54; I. J., 3, 23, 3, 3a.
[7] G., 4, 131a ; Paul, 1, 13a, 4.

OBLIGATIONS OR PERSONAL RIGHTS 225

the vendor promised in sales of this kind, and afterwards in sales of any valuable things, to pay a similar penalty in case of eviction. Special clauses extended this benefit to the vendee's assigns and took account of cases of partial eviction. The edict of the curule ædiles imposed this stipulation as a police measure on the sellers of slaves in the public markets. It assumed a judicial eviction depriving the vendee of the thing sold or of its value after it had been delivered to him and he had paid the price for it.[1] In sales of *res nec mancipi* a stipulation contained the vendor's promise to the vendee to see that he " had the thing sold " (*ut habere liceat*), and thus guaranteed reparation of the loss caused by any disturbance of the latter's possession, whoever the author of the disturbance might be.[2] In the second century of the Christian era the *actio empti* itself became a means of guarantee, in as much as it compelled the vendor to furnish the usual stipulations.[3] It could even serve as a substitute for them, if the eviction took place before they were made, by means of a condemnation equivalent to that which the stipulations would have secured if they had preceded the eviction.[4] Finally, in their absence, the obligation *rem habere licere* became an intrinsic part of the sale and a consequence of *bona fides*.[5] Though it was comprised in the *actio empti*, it could be invoked even by means of an exception.[6] There were also ancient stipulations against flaws in the thing sold which, as we can see from the examples given by Varro and the recorded legal acts, came to be combined or blended with those concerning eviction.[7] Against vendors of slaves or animals in the public markets the ædiles framed two successive actions which at first had a repressive character. The original object of the first seems to have been to compel the vendor within the two months following the sale to furnish either the usual stipulations as regards eviction, or those employed in these same markets as a guarantee against flaws

---

[1] Cic., *ad Att.*, 5, 1; Paul, 2, 17.—**I**, 2, 5042; **LXV**, 1, 104 et seq.; **CLX**, 2, 1-65, 78-100.
[2] Varro, *de R. r.*, 2, 5, 10; Paul, 2, 17, 1; D., 10, 2, 49; 46, 7, 3-pr.; 21, 2, 6; 37, 1, 56-pr., 61, 62; T. G., 849.—**CXII**, 462-465; **CLX**, 2, 65-78.
[3] D., 12, 2, 13-1; 19, 1-11, 8, 13.—**CLX**, 2, 128-141, but cf. Ed.-P., 2, 294.
[4] Paul, 2, 17, 2; *Fr. vat.*, 6.
[5] G., 4, 131*a*.—**CLX**, 2, 244 et seq.
[6] D., 21, 2, 17; 3, 1-2.
[7] Varro, *de R. r.*, 2, 2, 5; D., 21, 2, 2, 60; 19, 1, 11-9, 37, 2, 21-2.

in the things sold.¹ Later on, the system is revealed to us as follows: the *actio redhibitoria* enabled the vendee to obtain within 6 months, on the ground of flaws in the thing sold, the cancellation of the contract on the judge's *arbitratus*, plus a condemnation equivalent to its bare price or, if the vendor did not make restitution, a condemnation for double the price and the accessories; while the *actio quanti minoris* or *œstimatoria* enabled him to secure within one year a reduction in the price, which was arbitrated by the judge according to the gravity of the flaws. This latter action could be brought again if new flaws appeared;² moreover both were available against the vendor who refused to make the *stipulatio duplæ*, the first for two months, the second for six months after the sale, with perhaps some special characteristics in the latter case.³ At the beginning of the Empire jurisprudence allowed recourse against the vendor even for flaws unknown to him, and extended this responsibility to all sales.⁴

The obligations of the vendee, sanctioned by the *actio venditi*, were in principle summed up in the payment of the price, which was the condition of the transfer of ownership in sales for cash.⁵ To this must be added the payment of interest, if there has been delay or acceptance of delivery of the thing sold;⁶ but when the interest fell due, the vendee had the right to refuse payment if delivery had been refused to him, or if it did not allow at least the *vacua possessio*, or if he was already threatened with eviction.⁷ This was the counterpart of the vendor's right to retain the thing if he had not received payment for it.

The contract of hire, *locatio-conductio*, included three different operations under the same title: (i.) *locatio rei*, hire of things, by which one person (*locator*) bound himself to provide another (*conductor*), in consideration of a sum of money (*merces*), with the enjoyment or use of this thing; (ii.) *locatio operarum*, by which the *locator* undertook to furnish certain services for the benefit of the *conductor* in consideration of a *merces*; (iii.) *locatio operis faciendi*, in which the *conductor* pledged himself to work upon a thing intrusted to him

---

[1] Cic., *de Off.*, 3, 17; Aul. Gel., 4, 2; D., 21, 1, 1-1, 38-pr.—**CLIX**, 1, 221; **CLX**, 2, 118; **CCLII**, 2², 51. [2] D., 21, 1, 19-6, 45; Ed.-P., 2, 306, 307, 397.
[3] D., 21, 1; 23, 4; 28.—**CLX**, 2, 124-127.
[4] D., 19, 1, 11-13; 21, 1-pr.—**LXV**, 1, 653; **CCLII**, 2¹, 179-182.
[5] I. J., 2, 1, 41. [6] Paul, 2, 17, 9; *Fr. vat.*, 2. [7] D., 19, 1, 30-6, 11-3.

by the *locator*, again in consideration of a *merces*.¹ In all three cases a prestation in kind was furnished in exchange for a sum of money which had to be fixed by the contract and real (*certa* and *vera*);² although, in leases of rural property, the rent could also be paid with part of the fruits (*colonia partiaria*).³ In all three cases the thing or the services placed with others (*locare*, to place) were only placed temporarily, so that even as late as the second century the Jurists hesitated whether to describe as hire or sale the perpetual leases and the transaction which exposed the thing to destruction as a result of the use which the *conductor* was authorized to make of it.⁴ There was the same hesitation, though for the opposite reason, when the artisan supplied the raw material of his work.⁵ The antiquity and the part played in Roman economic life by these contracts which, with the exception of *colonia partiaria*, clearly imply the use of money, is now a matter of dispute. Leases for rent were widely used at an early date. Let us also restore to the *locatio operarum* the place which it is too often the custom to deny to free labour, a more important factor in ancient societies than is usually admitted. In all three cases the obligations of the *locatores* were sanctioned by an *actio conducti* and those of the *conductores* by an *actio locati*, both actions having similar *demonstrationes*, both having *intentiones* and *condemnationes incertæ*, and both available against slight negligence.⁶

The *locator rei* had to provide undisturbed enjoyment of the thing hired, and was therefore obliged to keep it in repair and to guarantee its possession and use against eviction and against flaws rendering it unusable or dangerous. The *locator operarum* had to do the work agreed upon.⁷ The corresponding *conductores* had to pay the rent (*merces*) at prescribed intervals so long as the enjoyment or the services lasted, their obligations beginning when they began to benefit by these and ceasing with them. Losses resulting from accident were borne by the *locatores*.⁸ But every *conductor* had the care of

---

¹ Not all services could be the object of hire; a distinction was drawn between salaries and fees: G. T., 856 et seq.; **XXXIII**, 8, 242; 9, 245; the latter were the object of a *cognitio extra ordinem*. ² G., 3, 142-144.
³ D., 19, 2, 25-6.—**XXXIII**, 3, 57; **CXV**. ⁴ G., 3, 145-146.—**XXXIII**, 6, 264.
⁵ G., 3, 147. ⁶ Ed.-P., 2, 15; I. J., 324-5.
⁷ D., 19, 2, 30-1, 25-6; but cf. 19-10, 38-pr., T. G., 860.—**XXXIII**, 19-95.
⁸ In the two other kinds of hire it is the *conductor* who pays the *merces*. On this inversion see **XXXIII**, 6, 264; **CCXXXVIII**, 4, 129, 136.

the thing hired, which he was bound to restore on expiry of the contract. The *conductor operis faciendi*, on the contrary, bore the losses resulting from accident,[1] except (i.) those incurred at sea, for which the *Lex Rhodia de jactu*, adapted to Roman Law, divided the loss proportionately between the owners of the things saved, and (ii.) those incurred in the construction of immoveables.[2]

The effects of hire ended on expiry of the agreed period. The length of rural leases was presumed to be 5 years. All leases of immoveables were continued from year to year by tacit renewal.[3]

They were terminated by the action for cancellation which was founded either on abuse of possession or failure to pay the rent for two years, or on the need of the lessor to dwell in his house, or on failure to carry out repairs, or on any other negligence in the execution of the contract.[4]

Societas, the contract of partnership organized at about the same period, assumed that two or more persons undertook, for a legitimate purpose,[5] to share certain properties in common with a view to deriving some advantage therefrom. Four kinds of partnership were known at Rome. Two of them were for all purposes: viz. the *societas totorum bonorum*, a partnership involving all the property of the partners both present and to come, which in fact was originally caused by the agreement of co-heirs to live a life in common, a *consortium* that imperilled the rule of the Twelve Tables that no inheritance can remain undivided;[6] and the *societas quæstuum*, which is believed to be less ancient but was at first used especially between freedmen (*colliberti*) and involved property acquired after the contract.[7] Classical Law deemed it equivalent to universal partnership.[8] Originally they were rarely contractual, and perhaps this was still the case in the classical period. The *judicis postulatio* and, later, the *actiones familiæ erciscundæ* or *communi dividundo* served at first to put an end to the joint ownership which economic theory condemned.[9]

---

[1] D., 19, 2, 62; but cf. D., 19, 2, 59.
[2] D., 14, 2, 1-3; 19, 2, 22-2.—**XXXIII**, 19, 84.
[3] D., 19, 2, 13-11.—**CXLVI**, 224; cf. **XXXIII**, 19, 92.
[4] D., 19, 2, 4, 25-2, 54-1, 56; C. J., 4, 65, 3. For types of *locationes* see T. G., 855-861. [5] D., 17, 2, 57.
[6] Aul. Gel., 1, 9; Fest., s.v. *Sors* ; Varro, *de R. r.*, 6, 65; G., 3, 148.
[7] D., 17, 2, 71-1; T. G., 862. [8] D., 17, 2, 7-13.
[9] Cic., *pro Rosc. Com.*, 1, 3, 7; D., 17, 2, 5-pr., 58-pr.

The judge was given power to divide up the property and award a separate portion to each copartner for his own individual possession.[1] The other two partnerships were for particular purposes: viz. the *societas unius rei*, which involved only one or more determinate objects, and the *societas alicujus negotiationis*, whose object, like that of our commercial partnerships, was a series of operations of the same kind conducted with a view to profit, e.g. partnerships of bankers, slave-merchants, agricultural workers, tax-gatherers, etc.[2] These last partnerships, formed at first by *datio*, i.e. by contributions to a common fund or by stipulations promising to contribute to it, were the most influential in promoting the development of consensual contract, but its character was also influenced by the old universal *societas* which caused it to retain the form of a *jus fraternitatis*, and attached as consequences to the action *pro socio*—the sanction of the rights and obligations of each partner in relation to the rest— both ignominy and at the same time the *beneficium competentiæ*.[3] The intention of the parties, here termed *affectus societatis*, distinguished the new contract from the other kinds of copartnership and served as foundation for this action.[4] The partners had to agree upon (i.) the fixing of a contribution which might differ in kind and value (capital, credit, ability, etc.) with the different partners, the risks of a contribution of capital being borne by the whole company, of a contribution of interest by the contributor;[5] (ii.) a common interest, i.e. an equal share in the profits for each partner, unless there was an agreement to the contrary (though this could never go so far as to exclude some partners from sharing at all, which would have involved a leonine partnership unrecognized by law), and also a share in the possible losses, failing, in classical times, a clause to the contrary;[6] (iii.) the administration of the common property which in principle devolved upon each partner with responsibility for slight negligence (*in concreto*), but could be intrusted to one or more of them by subsequent contract or regulation.[7] Since the administrators bound themselves alone in their dealings with third parties, accounts

[1] G., 4, 42.
[2] Cato, *de R. r.*, 144; Cic., *ad Heren.*, 2, 13; Liv., 23, 48, 49; D., 17, 2, 52-2; T. G., 862.—**XXXIII** 7, 97. [3] G., 4, 182.
[4] D., 17, 2, 31, 33. [5] D., 17, 2, 58-pr.-1; C. J., 4, 37-1.
[6] G., 3, 149; D., 17, 2, 19-2, 29-pr.-2. [7] D., 17, 2, 63-pr., 72; 10, 2, 25-16.

had to be rendered and the other partners had to be informed of the profits and expenses.[1] The partnership was dissolved voluntarily on fulfilment of the term or condition agreed upon, or by the unanimous consent of the parties;[2] accidentally by the death, *capitis deminutio*, bankruptcy or honourable retirement of a partner,[3] or by loss of the common capital. Its liquidation was effected either by friendly agreement or judicially by means of the action *pro socio* which fixed the gain or loss of each partner and, if there was a possibility of making division in kind, was combined with the action *communi dividundo*.[4]

Mandatum, commission, which was regarded for a long time as a mere friendly service (whence its persistently gratuitous nature) and may have been sanctioned at one time by penal actions *in factum*, appears in Q. Mucius Scævola's list as a consensual contract, imperfectly synallagmatic,[5] and could be defined thenceforward as that by which the discharge of one or more duties, whether of a juridical character or not, on his own premises and at his own risk, is intrusted to someone who pledges himself to render an account of them.[6] The object of the mandate, which might vary in importance, had to be a lawful one and to possess an interest for the mandator in order to justify an action—an interest which was finally taken for granted.[7] Soon the action *mandati directa*, which involved ignominy and required the mandatary to account for his total or partial failure to discharge the duty, was balanced by an action *mandati contraria*[8] calculated to recompense the mandatary for expenses incurred in the discharge of the mandate, and also, on occasion, to compel the mandator to allow the transference to his own account of obligations contracted by the mandatary on account of the mandate. But Papinian authorized third parties to take action against the mandator immediately (*ad exemplum actionis institoriæ*) and Ulpian authorized the mandator, *utilitatis causa*, to proceed immediately against third parties.[9] The mandate was

[1] D., 3, 41-pr.; 17, 2, 38-1.   [2] D., 17, 2, 1-pr.-2.
[3] D., 17, 2, 59-pr., 65-9.   [4] On the combination see D., 17, 2, 36-1, 43.
[5] Cic., *pro Rosc. Am.*, 38, 39; D., 17, 1, 1-4; Ed.-P., 2, 11. In the end the claim of *honoraria* was allowed in some cases: D., 50, 13, 1; cf. C. J., 4, 35, 1.   [6] Cic., *de Off.*, 3, 2.—XIII, 1, 271.
[7] G., 3, 155, 156; D., 17, 8, 6; I. J., 3, 26, 7.
[8] G., 4, 182; Ed.-P., 2, 10, 11. At first they were only held responsible for gross negligence but afterwards for slight negligence as well: D., 19, 5, 5-4; 17, 1, 11, 13, 21.   [9] D., 17, 1, 10-7; 19, 1, 13-25.

terminated by the desire of both parties, by the desire or the death of one of them, and by fulfilment of the term or condition prescribed beforehand.[1]

V. CONTRACTS " RE " OF THE SECOND PERIOD: LOAN, DEPOSIT, PLEDGE

After these contracts had been organized, the Law's creative activity based itself once more on a transfer of property, though only to the extent of possession or retention, in the three usual cases wherein a thing was temporarily surrendered to someone else for a definite purpose: viz. loan (*commodatum*), the lending of a determinate thing to a person who pledged himself to restore it after making use of it; deposit (*depositum*), by which a thing was committed to the care of a third party who was bound to return it at the depositor's request; and pledge (*pignus*), the surrender of a thing to a creditor as security for his debt on condition that he restored it as soon as he had been paid.[2] For a long time the good faith of the *accipiens* was relied on, subject only to the guarantee of actions based upon the ownership of the *tradens*, if he was the owner; except that deposit was provided by the Law of the Twelve Tables with a penal action for double damages.[3] After the *Lex Æbutia* these operations could be effected by a transfer of ownership and a fiduciary agreement—an unfortunate combination soon rendered useless by actions *in factum* which were framed by the edict with a condemnation, in the case of deposits made from compulsion, of twice the amount involved.[4] In the last days of the Republic[5] these three operations became contracts *bonæ fidei*, imperfectly synallagmatic and considered to be formed *re*, in which the obligations of the *accipiens*, who was held responsible either for slight negligence or only for fraud, according as the contract was made in his interest or not,[6] were sanctioned respectively by the actions *commodati*, *depositi* (which involved ignominy) and *pignoratitia*,[7] while the contingent obligations of the *tradens*, arising out of expenses incurred in taking care of the thing or losses caused by its flaws, etc., were sanctioned

[1] G., 3, 159-160. [2] D., 13, 2, 8, 9. [3] *Col. Leg. mos.*, 10, 7-11.
[4] G., 2, 60; 4, 47; Ed.-P., 1, 293. [5] CLVIII, 555, 5; CXCV, 2², 603.
[6] D., 13, 6, 5-2; 44, 7, 1-9. [7] G., 4, 47.

232 FORMATION OF CLASSICAL LAW

by corresponding actions *contrariæ*, to which was sometimes added a right of retention.[1]

From time to time jurisprudence elaborated certain details. First, in the case of deposit, it distinguished three exceptional kinds: deposit made from compulsion, which was governed by the edict;[2] sequestration or deposit of goods under dispute, which were intrusted to the care of an administrator against whom the winning party had an action *sequestraria*;[3] and irregular deposit with bankers, who could make use of the things intrusted to them on condition that they returned things equivalent in value. Secondly, in the case of pledge, it distinguished those whose possession was guaranteed to the creditor by interdicts not only against third parties, but also against the debtor, who was nevertheless allowed to regard his possession as uninterrupted for the purpose of usucapion;[4] those whose fruits, in the absence of a condition of reciprocal usage, had to be deducted from the interest and, later, from the capital of the debt;[5] and finally those which the creditor was authorized to sell if he was not paid when the debt fell due, in order to pay himself out of their price.

VI. THE OTHER SYNALLAGMATIC AGREEMENTS AND THE ATTEMPTS OF JURISPRUDENCE TO SANCTION THEM

Apart from the formal, consensual or real contracts which have just been described and were given a name, all other agreements remained without legal value or juridical effect.

At first the strict declaration of the content of contracts left uncertain the classification of those operations which escaped any kind of sanction because it was unknown whether their object was a sale or a hire and, if the latter, what kind of hire, etc.[6] A wholesaler intrusted goods to a retailer on condition that he sold them for a predetermined price or returned them to him. Was this sale, hire or commission? In such cases the Sabinians adapted to the operation the action for the contract which it most nearly resembled; but it might be doubtful which contract that was. On the other hand Labeo proposed an action whose *intentio incerta*, modelled

---

[1] D., 13, 7, 8-pr.; 47, 2, 15-2. [2] D,. 16, 3, 1-1.
[3] D., 16, 3, 17-pr.-1; Ed.-P., 2, 3. [4] D., 45, 3, 16.
[5] D., 20, 1, 11-1; C. J., 4, 24, 1. [6] D., 10, 3, 23; 19, 3, 1-pr.; G., 3, 141.

on that of the actions *bonæ fidei*, should be preceded by a *demonstratio* describing the agreement (*præscripta verba*), i.e. what the texts call an *actio civilis incerta*[1] or, later and less commonly, an *actio præscriptis verbis*;[2] but this was only used by the edict for the kind of operation which I have just described, to which the name of *æstimatum* was given.[3]

Agreements by which the parties bound themselves reciprocally to furnish different prestations, having a content other than that recognized in contracts, remained mere pacts. If one of the parties executed spontaneously and not the other, the result was an unjustified enrichment which could be retrieved by a *condictio ob rem dati* or *causa data, causa non secuta*, etc.[4] As restitution was not always possible, e.g. when the service rendered took the form of a deed, the Jurists advised the magistrates to make use of actions *in factum* which were probably based upon the unseemliness of having received something without giving anything in return.[5] These methods, of which traces can still be found in the texts and for which the action *doli mali* was sometimes substituted,[6] served until the time of the Lower Empire, although after the publication of the Edict of Julian some Jurists, cleaving herein to the idea of synallagmatic agreement, had on the strength of their own personal inspiration extended the *actio civilis incerta* to a few situations of this kind, e.g., barter.[7] These parallel currents continued to flow side by side; but under the earlier Empire the *condictio ob rem dati* or *sine causa* was not combined with the action for execution. Their combination and the system that has been deduced from it were a later result of interpolated texts.[8]

VII. THE PACTS ACCESSORY TO A CONTRACT AND THE PRÆTORIAN PACTS

This arsenal of contracts did not meet all the needs of practice. The retouchings of jurisprudence and the prætorian interventions which this latter brought about were manifested in two forms: they developed from the last years of the seventh

[1] D., 2, 14, 7-2; 10, 3, 23.   [2] Cf. **XXVII**, 22, 76 et seq.; **CLXII**, 123 et seq.
[3] Ed.-L., 2, 16-8.—**XLVI**, 1, 37-58.   [4] D., 12, 6, 26-12; 19, 5, 25.
[5] D., 2, 14, 7-2; 19, 5, 1-pr., 13-pr.-10.   [6] D., 19, 5, 5-3.
[7] D., 2, 14, 7-3.—**CLXII**, 132, 155-169; **CCLII**, 3¹, 221, 304; **XXXIII**, 14, 122
[8] D., 12, 6, 25, 26-12.—**XXVII**, 22, 86; **XIII**, 30, 77 et seq.

234 FORMATION OF CLASSICAL LAW

century A.U.C. a theory of what the commentators have called *pacta adjecta*, i.e. accessory to a contract; and the edict established sanctions for the independent pacts which were not provided with any by Civil Law.

Formalism restricted the content of even the most flexible contracts. Nothing could be added to them which depended upon the mere caprice of the parties. Moreover nothing could be changed in a contract when once it had been made. In ancient times the first inconvenience was met by a separate contract whose object was the clause which had been omitted from the principal contract, and the second by making the contract anew after cancelling the obligation already created. A distinction was drawn therefore between pacts *in continenti* and pacts *ex intervallo*, and the innovations made for each group differed according as these pacts tended to increase or to diminish the obligation (*ad augendam* or *ad minuendam obligationem*).

First the prætor framed an *exceptio pacti* for the man who proved that a pact had extinguished or diminished his obligation.[1] Then jurisprudence incorporated the pacts *in continenti* with contracts *bonæ fidei*, of which from the eighth century they were merely clauses,[2] and further, though perhaps only after a long interval, with those of strict law.[3] The *exceptio pacti* then became useless, and the pact was alleged by means of the action belonging to the contract; but these dispositions did not apply to agreements to pay usury.[4] In the case of pacts *ex intervallo* the *exceptio pacti* was taken for granted in the formula of contracts *bonæ fidei*, and its insertion could be demanded in that of actions of strict law provided that the pact diminished the obligation.[5] Pacts increasing the obligation continued to be without effect, and in their case the *exceptio pacti* was not available.[6]

On the other hand the prætor had long repressed certain unseemly acts by means of penal actions *in factum*. Now this penal character gradually became less marked and sometimes disappeared altogether, and some of these actions, which had been framed to punish misdoings concerned with the execution of pacts, came at last to be regarded as their sanctions, in as much as they had a corresponding *exceptio* which

---

[1] Cic., *ad Heren.*, 2, 13; G., 4, 119, 122. [2] D., 2, 14, 7-5; 19, 1, 13-30.
[3] D., 2, 14, 4-3; 12, 1, 11-1-7, 40. [4] Paul, 2, 14-1; D., 19, 5, 24.
[5] D., 2, 14, 27-2. [6] D., 18, 1, 72-pr.

OBLIGATIONS OR PERSONAL RIGHTS 235

could not be in any sense penal. We have seen that the *actio* and *exceptio doli mali* were put to this use.

The pact of oath (*pactum de jurejurando*), by which two litigants agreed to refer their dispute for settlement to the oath of one of them, was also thus regarded. If the voluntary oath had to be taken by the creditor, this pact gave rise to an action *in factum*, wherein the judge had only to say whether the oath had been taken or not; if by the debtor, to an *exceptio jusjurandi* against the creditor's suit.[1] The same was the case with the *receptum argentarii*,[2] an operation in which a banker pledged himself, perhaps in error, to pay someone else's debt;[3] and with the *receptum nautarum, cauponum*, by which sailors, tavern-keepers, innkeepers were made responsible, except in cases of *force majeure*, for the destruction or deterioration of the property intrusted to them by travellers.[4] It was the same too with the *pactum de pecunia constituta*, an undertaking by a debtor in return for a period of grace to pay on a fixed date a sum of money or a certain quantity of goods.[5] The action, which was at first a penal one available in some cases for a year, was finally modelled on the *actio certæ pecuniæ creditæ*, but with an increase in the amount of the *sponsio* annexed to it to half the value of the object in dispute.[6] In the classical period the scope of this action *de pecunia constituta* was extended. The nature and origin of the original obligation on which the pact supervened being indifferent, it was used to sanction obligations which had no actions or less stringent actions to protect them; a *delegatio* was effected by binding the debtor to a new creditor, or a surety was annexed to the debt.[7] In the silence of the texts, the novatory character of this pact is a matter of dispute.

[1] D., 4, 13, 4; 12, 2, 9-pr.-1, 2, 7.
[2] On account of C. J., 4, 18, 2-pr.-1, it has also been regarded as an ancient formal contract: **CXCV**, 2, 67; **LXVII**, 2, 234; **XXXIII**, 2, 62; 3, 1 et seq.; **XXI**, 45, 555. [3] D., 13, 5, 28.
[4] D., 4, 9, 1-pr., 3-1.—**XXXIII**, 13, 403; 19, 132.
[5] G., 4, 171; D., 13, 5, 2-1, 14-3.—**CXCV**, 1, 186.
[6] D., 13, 5, 18-2; Ed.-P., 1, 185 et seq.   [7] D., 13, 5, 1-7, 2.

IV

AN ATTEMPT TO CONSTRUCT A GENERAL THEORY OF CONTRACT

I. OUTLINE OF A GENERAL THEORY OF CONTRACT

Each contract, each pact had therefore a history of its own; but the Jurists extracted from them certain rules common to all alike and thus prepared the way for a general theory of contract which was destined to be brought to perfection long afterwards by our ancient jurists.

This work was begun in connexion with the stipulation, the most common juridical act, whose very flexible form could be assumed by any agreement. Study of the cases in which stipulations were useless, i.e. void, led to a clear conception of the essential elements of contract and of its possible modalities; but it was not until late in the classical period that these principles, formulated *pari passu* with the advance of juridical psychology, were plainly declared to be applicable to every contractual act.

Doctrine has since grouped the Jurists' solutions, in so far as the essential elements of contract are concerned, about the three ideas of consent, object and consideration; and, so far as concerns the possible modalities, about those of term and condition and a few others.

II. THE CAPACITY AND CONSENT OF THE CONTRACTING PARTIES. FLAWS IN THE CONSENT

The question of consent includes another: viz. that of the capacity to consent, which at first was comparatively simple but became more delicate when, with the development of their juridical personality, a certain field of legal activity was opened to the *alieni juris,* and still more so when incapable persons *sui juris* had the actual control of their patrimony and it became necessary to set limits to their power of disposal and administration. These extensions of juridical capacity in one case and restrictions of it in the other have already been studied and defined, and it will suffice to refer back to the previous discussion.

It is known that the part played by consent was only considered by the old practitioners in the case of verbal contracts. The other contracts, whether more ancient or of the same date, caused an actual transfer of wealth, and the obligation was then explained by this enrichment which became unjust at a given moment. But in the verbal contract the obligation was deemed to arise exclusively from the intention of the parties expressed in the form of an accordant question and answer. It was based upon the mutual consent of the contracting parties who were agreed upon the constituent elements of the convention. A question left unanswered or followed by an answer involving something more or less than or different from its content remained without effect;[1] for it was not until very late that this intention of the parties was interpreted in such a way that in case of disagreement as to quantity the contract could be valid for the lesser amount. A promise not preceded by a question (*pollicitatio*) was invalid; though here also at a very late date an exception was made by the emperors in favour of cities, if the promise had been made to them in exchange for some legitimate profit or if its execution had begun.[2] Originally then it was only the exterior apparatus of the contract that was taken into account: had the words been spoken or not, or at most had they been spoken seriously or in jest ?[3] But a day came when there was anxiety to know whether they had been prompted or extracted by intimidation, fraud or deceit. In that case the contract was not annulled, but there was ground for the actions *quod metus causa, de dolo*, and afterwards for the corresponding *exceptiones* and even, though less commonly, for the *restitutio in integrum*. But in the contracts *bonæ fidei* the judge's powers allowed him to take account of these blemishes and pronounce sentence accordingly.[4] No doubt the whole body of doctrine was influenced by the appearance of the consensual contracts.

Finally it was discovered that the intention of the parties or of one of them might be influenced by a mistaken belief either as regards the nature of the contract (which in formal contracts was impossible), or the person of the other contractor, or the thing or prestation which constituted its

---

[1] G., 3, 102; D., 45, 1, 1-4. [2] D., 50, 12, 1-pr.-2, 3-pr.
[3] Varro, *de L. l.*, 6, 72; D., 44, 7, 3-2. [4] See p. 223 et seq.

object.¹ The two first kinds of mistake annulled any contract; the third had the same result when it concerned the thing's identity,² but only affected contracts *bonæ fidei* when it concerned its substance, and finally was dependent on interpretation of the parties' intention when only quantity was involved.³

III. THE OBJECT AND GROUND OF OBLIGATIONS

The doctrine of the object of a contract was at first closely bound up with the development of the stipulation; first of all a *datio*, i.e. a stipulation *certæ pecuniæ* or *certæ rei*; then an act or an abstention: *stipulatio incerti*. Study of the *bonæ fidei* contracts has shown what might be the object of the reciprocal obligations in each one of them. When it was desired to consider the object independently of the nature of the contract, a distinction was drawn for practical reasons between individualized determinate things (*species*) liable to perish, and universals (*genera*) or things determined solely in kind and quantity, capable of being replaced, so to speak, indefinitely. *Genera non pereunt*; universals do not perish.⁴ *Species* and *genera* were *res certæ*; any other prestation was *incerta*. Finally Paul had recourse to the terminology of the formulas of actions to describe the object of obligations and said that it consisted in *dare, facere, præstare*, i.e. in the transfer of a real right, in a personal act or in any other prestation.⁵ Obligations were further distinguished according to their object as divisible or indivisible. From particular solutions furnished by the Jurists, who were specially concerned with the question whether an obligation could or could not be discharged at various times and by various fellow-debtors, the Romanists of the Middle Ages have derived, and those of modern times have developed, a learned and obscure theory.⁶

Thus little by little this analysis was extended over the whole sphere of contracts and came to include every kind of obligation. It required certain qualities in the object of all alike, without which they disappeared. First of all the object

---

¹ D., 12, 1, 18-1, 32; I. J., 3, 19, 23. ² D., 18, 1, 9-pr.
³ D., 18, 1, 9-2; 45, 1, 22. ⁴ D., 45, 1, 54-pr., 106.
⁵ D., 45, 1, 74, 75-pr.-7.
⁶ D., 44, 7, 3-pr.—CCLXIX, 5, 584 et seq.; CCXCIX, 2, 252.

OBLIGATIONS OR PERSONAL RIGHTS 239

must be possible both naturally, i.e. it must exist or be capable of existing, and juridically, i.e. it must be such that the law allows the contract in view to be made in respect of it;[1] but the difficulty of executing an obligation, however great it might be, was never assimilated to the impossibility which annulled it.[2] Secondly the object must be lawful, for it was clear that Law could not make a thing obligatory if it was incompatible with statute and morality.[3] Finally it must have an appreciable interest for the creditor, for this interest alone could at all times serve as a basis on which to estimate the condemnation. If it was lacking, the debtor was discharged. In synallagmatic contracts its inexistence or excessive vagueness rendered even the other party's obligation *sine causa*.[4] Some texts seemed to require that it should be appreciable in money, but that was certainly no absolute condition.[5]

The idea of consideration was foreign to the ancient formal contracts. By consideration is meant the immediate end for which a man places himself under an obligation. Now the external formalities of the formal contract were sufficient in themselves, and that is why Roman Law did not recognize the word *causa* in that connexion; but all contracts that were not formal had to have an honest and lawful consideration which, in perfect synallagmatic contracts, was for each party the other's obligation, but in imperfect synallagmatic contracts varied for each party. A false or unlawful consideration rendered the contract null. The unjustified results of a contract of strict law made without consideration or for an unlawful consideration were finally redressed by means of *condictiones* or *exceptiones*, provided that the consideration of both parties was not unlawful or immoral.[6]

IV. MODALITIES AFFECTING OBLIGATIONS

Modalities were in principle not authorized in the formal contracts with their unchangeable formalities prescribed once for all; but since the term has a very wide meaning, it could be applied to such conditions in the oral declaration

[1] D., 18, 1, 8-pr.; 50, 17, 185. [2] D., 45, 1, 34, 137-4.
[3] D., 45, 1, 26, 27, 123. [4] D., 18, 1, 61; 50, 17, 45-pr.
[5] D., 40, 7, 9-1.—CCLII, 3[1], 172 et seq.
[6] G., 4, 116a and b; D., 12, 7, 2, 3, 8; 45, 4, 2, 3

(*nuncupatio*) as were involved in the contract of *nexum* after the Law of the Twelve Tables.¹ Moreover the character of "mould of contracts" which the stipulation acquired, allowed the insertion of the most diverse conditions in it, to the extent of affecting the operation so profoundly that it appeared to be a special contract: e.g. contractual solidarity, securities, *adstipulatio*, alternative² or optional³ obligation, etc.

The Jurists concerned themselves especially with the most common modalities: term, condition, *modus*.⁴ Term and condition are suspensive, extinctive or resolutory; and under these last forms their application in Roman Law met with very strenuous opposition.

The suspensive term had the effect of postponing the date on which a right became due. The obligation created at the moment of making the contract must not be executed until a particular moment in the future which, if known, was the *dies certus*, if unknown, the *dies incertus*, but which could not be the day before the death of one of the parties or subsequent to his death.⁵ It was allowed to be either express or tacit, and the party in whose favour it existed was at liberty to renounce it. Claim of payment before the term consumed the right.⁶

The suspensive condition, an uncertain future event, prevented the right from coming into existence until the day on which it was fulfilled; and if it was never fulfilled, no right could exist.⁷ In the classical period it could, like the term, be inserted in *bonæ fidei* contracts and in stipulations. Whether express or tacit, it rendered the contract null if it was physically or juridically impossible, unlawful or immoral.⁸ The Jurists classified conditions as positive and negative, casual, potestative or mixed, and attached different effects to each category. The question is sometimes raised whether the

¹ XII T., 6, 1.
² An obligation having two things for its object either of which the debtor can give so long as both exist, though he must give the survivor if one perishes: **CXII**, 373.
³ An obligation having one thing for its object but from which the debtor can free himself by giving another. Loss of the first extinguishes the obligation: **CXII**, 373, 1.
⁴ D., 44, 7, 44, which is also the *adjectio solutionis gratia*; see p. 215.
⁵ G., 3, 100-101; D., 33, 2, 5; 45, 1, 46, 73-pr.
⁶ D., 46, 3, 70; I. J., 3, 15, 2; 4, 6, 33-36; but the debtor who paid before the term did not pay what was not due: D., 12, 6, 10.
⁷ G., 3, 146; C. J., 4, 37, 6.—**CXII**, 395.
⁸ G., 3, 97-98; D., 45, 1, 61, 137-6.

OBLIGATIONS OR PERSONAL RIGHTS

fulfilment of the condition had a confirmatory or creative effect; the texts appear to be contradictory.[1] The Romans seem to have distinguished between the contract deciding the modes of existence of the right, which was immediately valid and created for the profit of the creditor the right to benefit by the fulfilment of the condition,[2] and the right dependent on this event, which only came into existence when it occurred.[3] If then the condition was not fulfilled, it must not be said that there had never been a contract, but that one of the occurrences anticipated in the contract had taken place: viz. the non-realization of the right in prescribed circumstances.[4] Notwithstanding later interpretations this was the Roman doctrine.[5]

The extinctive term was for a long time useless. So long as the Law admitted only formal modes of extinguishing obligations, they could not be created for a definite period of time. The promise to pay up to such and such a period remained unconditional and perpetual, as also did that of arrears or of life-rent, which Pomponius terms *una, incerta et perpetua*.[6] The action for securing payment of this rent could only be brought once, without restriction as to time, and it brought the whole right before the *judex* in a single suit. But in other than formal contracts this term was at first received as an integral condition of the contract, and later on the prætor allowed it to be used by means of an *exceptio* if it was included in a stipulation, e.g. in the stipulation of life-rent, where moreover a *præscriptio* entered at the head of the formula of the action excluded from its scope the annual instalments yet to come.[7]

The extinctive condition must not be confused with the resolutory condition. Fulfilment of the former causes the cessation of the right for the future without touching its existence or its effects in the past, while that of the latter extinguishes the right retroactively and cancels all that has been already accomplished. In both alike the right arises immediately out of the contract, but fulfilment of the condition affects it in different ways in the future. In formal contracts, where it was at first without effect, the extinctive

---

[1] **CLVIII**, 496-499; **CXII**, 396.
[2] D., 45, 1, 78; 50, 17, 161.
[3] D., 12, 6, 16-pr.; 41, 4, 2-2.
[4] D., 20, 4, 11-1, 18, 6-8-pr.
[5] **CCXCIX**, 1, 91, 1.
[6] D., 45, 1, 16-1; I. J., 3, 15, 3.
[7] G., 4, 131; I. Th., 3, 15, 3.

condition was subsequently alleged by means of an *exceptio*, but there is no trace in the texts of the resolutory condition.¹ In the others the first was an integral condition of the contract, and the same is true to a certain extent of the second, but only if it was expressly stated therein, even in the case of synallagmatic contracts (cf. C. Civ., art. 1184). Its effects were determined by the Jurists especially in the matter of sale, where in practice it took various forms.² The sale, regarded as unconditional, had to be executed; but on fulfilment of the condition the *status quo ante* had to be re-established, the thing sold (*merx*) restored and the prize repaid. For this purpose the Sabinians granted the action belonging to the contract, the Proculians the action *præscriptis verbis*. Alexander Severus enacted that the vendor should choose between them;³ but classical Law seems never to have had an action for claim founded on the return of ownership to the vendor in strict law.⁴

V

OBLIGATIONS ARISING NEITHER FROM DELICT NOR FROM CONTRACT

The mass of obligations arising neither from a delict nor from a contract were grouped together by the Jurists under the title *variæ causarum figuræ*, which did not commit them in any way. The division, borrowed from Gaius, into quasi-contractual (*quasi ex contractu*) and quasi-delictual (*quasi ex delicto*) obligations is very ill suited to the mass of these juridical situations which are produced neither by man's misdoing nor by any intention, whether expressed or not.⁵ Some of the obligations thus artificially grouped together owed their extinction to a restoration of equilibrium between the patrimonies by means of those ancient actions called *condictiones*, whose object was to abolish unjust enrichments,

---

¹ D., 44, 7, 44-2, where one has been found, contains a negative suspensive condition.
² *Lex commissoria*, reserving to the vendor the right to cancel the contract failing payment of the price: D., 18, 3; *addictio in diem*, the same right if he gets the offer of a better price within a prescribed period: D., 18, 2; *pactum de retrovendendo*, reserving to the vendee the right to cancel: D., 14, 5, 12; *pactum displicentiæ*, the same right within a set time: D., 18, 5, 6.
³ D., 18, 1, 61; Ed.-P., 2, 314.
⁴ Cf. **CLVIII**, 760-766; **CXII**, 398; **CCXLIX**, 274-285; **LXV**, 2, 480; **CXLI**, 2, 95, 5-6.   ⁵ D., 45, 1, 1-pr.; 44, 7, 5-4.

OBLIGATIONS OR PERSONAL RIGHTS

while others were executed under the constraint of actions *bonæ fidei*. On these grounds they were considered akin to contracts. But others again gave rise to prætorian actions *in factum*, analogous to those which had served the prætor for the repression of acts of fraud, and that is why the Jurists regarded them as quasi-delictual.

It was an old juridical conception, as well as the command of morality, that any unjust enrichment, however acquired, ought to be restored. We know that in such cases the Jurists held a man to be bound *re*, by the fact itself; and the means granted by procedure to restore the original situation were the already familiar *condictiones certæ pecuniæ* and *triticaria*.[1] Classical Law added to them a *condictio incerti* for the cases where the amount of the enrichment had to be assessed by the judge.[2] Then doctrine attempted to analyze the causes which stamped the character of injustice upon the transfer of wealth, and thence arose the various titles given to the *condictio*. The *condictio indebiti* was for the recovery of a sum not due and paid by mistake in circumstances when, if the obligation had existed, the condemnation would not have been doubled in consequence of *infitiatio*.[3] The *accipiens* in good faith had to restore his enrichment at the moment of the *litis contestatio*, while the *accipiens* in bad faith had to make good all loss incurred by the *tradens*.[4] The *condictio ob rem dati* or *causa data, causa non secuta* was for the recovery of anything surrendered to another in consideration of an advantage which had not been obtained.[5] The *condictio sine causa*, a vague term, covered any possibilities that had not been foreseen. The *condictio ob turpem* or *ob injustam causam* applied to enrichments obtained by unlawful or immoral acts or processes. If the act involved immorality on the part of the *tradens*, the *condictio* was refused, for it was said that *nemo auditur turpitudinem suam allegans*, no one can allege his own disgrace.[6]

The *variæ figuræ* sanctioned by actions *bonæ fidei* were many in number. As representation was not allowed in juridical acts, guardianship, curatorship, *negotiorum gestio*, joint-ownership enriched or impoverished the administrator of

[1] D., 12, 4, 8; 5, 6; 6, 52.
[2] D., 12, 6, 22-1.—**XXXIII**, 21, 422; **CXII**, 536 et seq.
[3] G., 3, 91; D., 12, 6, 26-3, 65-9; 50, 17, 53.
[4] D., 12, 2, 15-pr.   [5] D., 12, 4.   [6] D., 12, 5, 1, 4-pr.-3.

another's fortune to the latter's cost or profit, but the complexity of these relations made an abstract action impossible in practice. This group was increased by the addition of other obligations resulting from common ownership, vicinity, physical detention of a thing, or arising out of kinship and patronage.

Negotiorum gestio, administration of another's business without mandate, whether voluntarily or in error, with the intention of profiting by its development, gave rise in the classical period to two actions:[1] the action *negotiorum gestorum directa*, sanctioning the obligation of the *gestor* not to cease administration to his principal's loss and to render an account of his administration—acts which, in principle, involved his responsibility for slight negligence;[2] and the action *negotiorum gestorum contraria*, by which the *gestor* obtained repayment of expenses advantageously incurred, though the principal could dispute their advantage so long as he had not ratified them.[3]

The state of indivision which arises when a thing is held in common by several persons not in partnership was early regarded as incompatible with sound economy. No one was obliged to remain in that position.[4] If division was not made by friendly agreement it could be claimed by each joint-owner, first *per arbitri postulationem*, then by the action *communi dividundo*, an action for partition which was personal but said to be *in rem scripta* because it was available against third parties who had acquired any share before the property was divided,[5] and because its formula contained an *adjudicatio*, authority for the judge to decide and allot the portions. Each joint-owner had the right to administer the common property, acting then in the interest of all, but he could do nothing that affected the property materially without at least the tacit consent of the others. The opposition of one alone could prevent even urgent repairs, for it was allowed that *in pari causa potior est causa prohibentis*. This administration, to which each must devote the same care as he gave to his private affairs,[6] involved *communicatio lucri et damni*, a settlement of accounts obtained by an action *bonæ fidei* which could be brought even while the property was undivided.[7]

---

[1] Cic., *Top.*, 10, 42; D., 3, 5, 3-pr.; 17, 1, 40.
[2] D., 3, 5, 2, 10, 21-pr.; 17, 22, 10.
[3] D., 3, 5, 6-9, 9, 10-1.   [4] D., 8, 2, 26; 31, 20, 77.
[5] D., 10, 3, 14-2-3; I. J., 4, 6, 20.   [6] D., 10, 2, 25-16.
[7] Ed.-P., 1, 236.—**XLII**, 1, 1 et seq.; **XIII**, 28, 273; **XXXIII**, 25, 446.

OBLIGATIONS OR PERSONAL RIGHTS

These two actions which were fused together in the time of the Severi became at last a mixed and double formula in which each party was plaintiff and defendant simultaneously.[1]

The obligation concerning the boundary of lands not built over, viz. to allow the interval of 5 feet which according to the Law of the Twelve Tables must separate them from one another, had also given rise to a double action with an *adjudicatio* in its formula enabling judge or arbitrators to regulate the bounds (*fines*): viz. the action *finium regundorum*, which differed slightly according as the lands concerned had been assigned in specified quantities or not (*agri limitati* or *arcifinales*).[2]

The obligation to produce a person or thing in dispute, in order to ascertain against whom the principal action should be directed, was sanctioned at any rate at the end of the Republic by the *actio ad exhibendum*, a discretionary action tending to secure reparation for the prejudice caused.[3] In other cases the necessity or desirability of producing a thing or person gave rise to actions *in factum* or to interdicts.

The cases of *variæ figuræ*, also very numerous, which were artificially assimilated to delicts especially on account of the nature of their actions, cannot be enumerated here. These actions of prætorian origin, sometimes of the kind *in bonum et æquum conceptæ*, as when the judge has made the process his own or damage has been caused by throwing something out of doors, sometimes *populares*, as in the case of an immoveable where something is in danger of falling, are of very diverse character.[4]

VI

EFFECTS OF OBLIGATIONS

I. EFFECTS OF OBLIGATIONS BETWEEN CREDITOR AND DEBTOR: VOLUNTARY AND FORCED EXECUTION. PAYMENT. FAILURE TO EXECUTE AND FAULTS COMMITTED IN THE EXECUTION

The end of an obligation, an abstract term, is to procure by its execution a concrete advantage. This execution is

---

[1] D., 10, 2, 2, 7, 52; 2, 1, 11-2.—**XIII**, 28, 403.
[2] D., 10, 1.—**CCLXVI**, 2, 422; **CXCV**, 2, 459-465.
[3] D., 10, 4.—**CXCV**, 2, 442, 454; **CLXXXV**, 45.
[4] D., 44, 7, 5-4; Ed.-P., 1, 190-198.—**CXII**, 589-592.

246 FORMATION OF CLASSICAL LAW

either voluntary or forced. If voluntary, it was at Rome the payment (*solutio*), the prestation owed to the creditor by the debtor; and the payment was valid in all cases of civil or natural debt. If forced, it was obtained by judicial coercion in consequence of an action in which the creditor had been successful. Natural obligations escaped this kind of execution because they were not provided with actions.

In voluntary execution the object of the payment was that of the obligation itself: *datio*, act, abstention.[1] For a long time it could not be anything else; but at the beginning of the Empire the giving in payment (*datio in solutum*), liberation by means of anything other than what was due, was admitted by way of *exceptio* according to the Proculians, in strict law (*ipso jure*) according to the doctrine of the Sabinians which finally prevailed.[2]

From the seventh century mere proof of payment seems to have sufficed to liberate the debtor. Modes of extinction corresponding to the formal acts by which the contracts had been created were no longer necessary.[3] This payment had to embrace the object in its entirety: no one was required to accept a partial payment.[4] If it was a *datio*, payment by anyone capable of alienating freed the debtor; but this was not the case if it involved an act or abstention whose effects, if it was discharged by someone else, would not be the same as they would be if it was discharged by the debtor.[5] On the other hand it could only be validly received by a capable or qualified creditor, or by his representative: *adjectus solutionis gratia*, mandatary, slave, guardian or curator.[6] When specific things (*species*) were owing, loss of the thing did not exempt from payment unless it happened accidentally; if it was imputable to the debtor, it made his obligation perpetual. If *genera* were owing, the debtor remained always bound since *genera non pereunt*.

Forced execution did not always procure for the creditor the object of the obligation. Obligations to act and many obligations to abstain from acting could hardly ever be executed in kind against the debtor's will. Almost the only obligations that can be executed directly are obligations to give, if the thing has not deteriorated or perished; but even in

[1] D., 50, 16, 176; D., 46, 3, 54. [2] G., 3, 168; D., 46, 3, 46.-pr.—**CLV**, 131.
[3] **XXV**, 17, 19; **XXXIII**, 20, 191. [4] D., 12, 1, 21; C. J., 8, 42, 1.
[5] D., 3, 5, 68; I. J., 3, 29-pr. [6] G., 2, 84; D., 46, 3, 12.

OBLIGATIONS OR PERSONAL RIGHTS 247

these cases the formular procedure ceased to enforce payment in kind when it made the system of pecuniary condemnations general and substituted damages assessed in money. Sometimes the parties forestalled them by having a valuation made in anticipation by means of a stipulation of penalty. The debtor who allowed matters to proceed as far as the condemnation saw his debt commuted therein to a sum of money: viz. the *judicatum,* which was fixed by various processes according to the nature of the action and assessed as from the moment of the *litis contestatio* in actions of strict law, as from that of the sentence in actions *bonæ fidei.*[1]

For a long time only the real loss incurred by the plaintiff, the diminution of his patrimony (*damnum emergens*), was taken into consideration, but presently jurisprudence began to take account of all other kinds of damage as well, in particular of the gain left unrealized in consequence of inexecution (*lucrum cessans*).[2]

It often happened that there was not absolute inexecution but only delay or some fault committed in the course of execution. Delay constituted arrearage (*mora*), a fault that differed in kind according as it was committed by the debtor or by the creditor. The debtor's arrearage in contract was a culpable delay, i.e. one caused neither by force majeure, nor by the creditor's artifices, nor by a pardonable error,[3] and established by an informal summons, the *interpellatio* addressed to the debtor in person.[4] In delict the debtor was considered to be always in arrears.[5] Arrearage made the debtor responsible for the loss of the thing,[6] caused the interest to run on in respect of sums of money owed in virtue of a contract *bonæ fidei,*[7] and involved reparation of the loss caused by the delay. It was ended by payment, by real composition tendered to the creditor, or by his renunciation.[8] The creditor's arrearage consisted in his refusal to accept real composition, or in the fact that he had by his own fault made execution by the debtor impossible. Thenceforward he bore

[1] D., 13, 6, 3-2.
[2] D., 19, 1, 13-pr., 21-3; 50, 16, 179, 193.—**XLIX**, 2, n° 763; **CXXX**, 2, section 44.   [3] D., 50, 17, 63; 45, 1, 91-3.
[4] D., 22, 1, 24-pr., 32-pr.,; 45, 41-1. On the maxim *dies interpellat pro homine* see **CCLXVII**, 23; **CCXCIX**, 2, section 278.
[5] D., 13, 1, 18-1.
[6] D., 45, 1, 82-1, 91-6; cf. **CCLII**, 2^1, 323, 2^2, 102.
[7] D., 19, 1, 42-1; 22, 1, 32-3.   [8] D., 45, 1, 93-1

the risks and was bound, on occasion, to pay damages for the prolonged custody of the thing.[1]

The other acts of the debtor in the execution of obligations produced, towards the end of the Republic, a first outline of the theory of contractual negligence, which has been constantly revised until our own time, when it has given place to some extent to that of risk. In the formal contracts the responsibility of the debtor was commensurate with the words used (*verba*).[2] Even abstention from fraud had to be the object of an express clause. The new theory was based upon the freedom of agreements, and the rules admitted were interpretative of the parties' intention, except that no one could obtain exoneration for fraud that he might commit in the future.[3]

As regards the obligations of strict law, it was first laid down that the fact of knowingly putting oneself in such a position that execution was impossible made the obligation perpetual;[4] and, later on, jurisprudence prompted the judge, who was invested with wider powers when an *incertum* was involved, to take account in the condemnation of bad administration by the debtor.[5] In the obligations *bonæ fidei*, the Jurists opposed good faith (*bona fides*) to fraud (*dolus malus*), diligence (*diligentia*) to negligence (*culpa*), and required of all debtors *bona fides* and *diligentia*, though they interpreted the latter more or less widely according to circumstances.[6] At the end of the second century of our era gross negligence (*culpa lata*) which its very grossness made unpardonable was assimilated to fraud: the debtor was always responsible for it.[7] Then in a somewhat doubtful fashion obligations were classified in three groups: those requiring *bona fides*, i.e. generally those arising out of operations in the interest of the creditor alone—deposit and, originally, commission, guardianship, curatorship, etc.;[8] those requiring *diligentia* measured strictly by the administration of a good *paterfamilias*,[9] i.e. generally those where the debtor was personally interested—*commodatum* and *precarium*, to which were after-

[1] D., 18, 6, 1-3, 18; 19, 1, 38-1.   [2] D., 4, 3, 7-3; 45, 1, 91-pr.
[3] D., 50, 17, 23.   [4] D., 22, 1, 35-5; cf. D., 36, 1, 26-2.—**XXI**, 78, 321.
[5] D., 45, 1, 137-3.   [6] D., 18, 1, 68.
[7] D., 16, 3, 32; 50, 16, 213-2, 223-pr.
[8] *Col. leg. mos.*, 10, 2, 1-5; D., 13, 6, 5-2; 50, 17, 232.—**XLIX**, 2, n° 663; **CCLII**, 2², 332.
[9] D., 13, 6, 18-pr.: the *culpa levis in abstracto* of the commentators.

wards added guardianship, curatorship, commission, *negotiorum gestio*; and those where the *diligentia* was leniently measured by the care which each debtor gave to his own affairs, e.g. those incurred by partners, joint-owners, husbands.[1] On the other hand, under the name of *custodia*, special care was required of carriers, ferry-men, inn-keepers and cornchandlers for the things committed to their charge.[2] The whole of this doctrine seems to have been organized by Julian and his contemporaries.[3]

II. EFFECTS OF OBLIGATIONS AS REGARDS THIRD PARTIES. ABSENCE OF JURIDICAL REPRESENTATION: RELAXATIONS OF THIS PRINCIPLE

As a result of the ways in which Roman Law conceived persons to come under obligations, the legal bond only existed between the persons whose contract had engendered the obligation. Whether they had acted spontaneously or at the order of others, in their own interest or not, regard was only had to what appeared on the surface. Hence an obligation had to be executed by the debtor only, to the profit of the creditor only. This involved the following consequences which classical Law strove to mitigate: (i.) it was impossible to represent others in juridical acts, to become either creditor or debtor by the agency of others; (ii.) the effects of a juridical act could not be transferred: debts were inalienable.

The idea of juridical representation postulates some measure of refinement and does not occur immediately to the mind. The obligation attached to certain words or rites appertained to the persons who had spoken or performed them. Contrary to what has sometimes been said, there was no exception to this principle when the *paterfamilias* acquired debts through persons under his power (*per personas in potestate manu mancipioque*). The persons *alieni juris* did not represent the *paterfamilias*: acquisitions by the *filiifamilias* went to him on account of the unity of the patrimony, and acquisitions by slaves on account of his power over them and all that depended on it.

[1] D., 17, 2, 72; 23, 3, 17-pr.: their *culpa levis in concreto*.
[2] **XXXIII**, 12, 66; 13, 403; **CCLII**, 2², 345; cf. **XXI**, 5, 45-95.
[3] **CCLII**, 2², 149.

And yet the principle was limited in some points by the Civil Law itself. Conservatory acts soon escaped from it, and classical Law admitted the validity of payment made by a third party even without the debtor's knowledge. So too the edict provided with an *exceptio* the agreement not to sue that had been obtained by a third party. The most serious modifications, due to the prætors of the end of the seventh century, were suggested by the necessity of giving persons *alieni juris* a share in the administration of the family patrimony and in the conduct of business, and then of making it possible for them to pledge this patrimony. The reforms were based upon two facts deemed sufficient to justify placing the head of the *domus* under an obligation to third parties.

The first was a declaration (*jussus*), tacit or expressed, that he assumed responsibility for the acts. He was held responsible when the *alieni juris* contracted *jussu patris* or *domini*.[1] According to the present doctrine of representation he alone would be responsible, but the Romans allowed this obligation to be combined with the civil obligation of the *filiusfamilias* or the natural obligation of the slave.[2] In the second century of the Empire these are even the principal obligations, that of the *paterfamilias* or of the *dominus* being merely accessory to them (*adjicitur*). When once this was admitted, the *jussus* could cover a series of acts of the same kind: the ship's captain (*magister navis*) *alieni juris*, so far as his commission extended (*lex præpositionis*), the manager *alieni juris* of some business on land (*institor tabernæ, negotio*) were successively empowered to pledge the head of the *domus* by their professional operations.[3] The actions *quod jussu, exercitoria, institoria*, of whose formula we have no certain knowledge (whether they were actions for transformation[4] or *in factum*,[5] they were in any case perpetual and transmissible), were granted for the whole sum against the principal who made the appointment.

In the second place, when a share was given to the *alieni juris* in the administration or exploitation of the patrimony, it followed that this patrimony was pledged in so far as it

---

[1] G., 4, 70; D., 15, 4, 1-19.—**XIII**, 24, 27 et seq.; cf. **CLV**, 388, 450-475.
[2] D., 14, 1, 5-11; 3, 5-1; 15, 1, 44.   [3] G., 4, 71.
[4] Ed.-P., 1, 300-314, 330-334.—**CLVIII**, 703 et seq.; **XXXIII**, 4, 108; **CXII**, 406.   [5] **LXXXVII**, 2, 103.

OBLIGATIONS OR PERSONAL RIGHTS

benefited by their transactions (*in rem versum*).[1] But if the head of the *domus* handed over a fixed portion of the family patrimony to the management of a *filiusfamilias* or of a slave, they could pledge the whole of this *peculium*. The constitution of a *peculium* intended to take rank for the time being as a distinct patrimony showed that the *paterfamilias* gave the person in charge of it open credit to that extent only. His position was that of a sleeping partner. Therefore, on the liquidation of the *peculium*, if there had been any profits, he deducted them before the payment of any other debt, in order that his intention not to be pledged beyond the original sum might be respected.[2] The other debtors had against him the action *de peculio* or the action *de in rem verso* by which to obtain payment in the order in which they made their claim until the assets of the *peculium* or of the principal's enrichment had been exhausted;[3] but these actions were only available for the judicial year following liquidation of the *peculium*.[4] When however the *peculium* was transformed, with the knowledge of the *paterfamilias*, into commercial stock (*merx peculiaris*), the interest of the creditors led the prætor, in case of bankruptcy, to return to the ordinary rules of liquidation, i.e. to pay a dividend to the creditors without any privilege for the *paterfamilias*. To secure this result the other creditors had the *actio tributoria* against the latter, a perpetual, transmissible action based on the fraud or mistake that had been committed in the distribution (*tributio*).[5]

There was nothing to forbid these solutions when the agent was a third party, and very soon the actions *exercitoria*, *institoria*, *tributoria* and even *de in rem verso* were granted on the same conditions against the *paterfamilias* who had appointed a stranger to his *domus* (*extraneus*) as agent to manage a part of his patrimony. Thus third parties dealing with the latter had two debtors.[6]

This reform, however, which was achieved at the beginning of the Empire so far as commercial mandate was concerned, does not appear to have been extended to ordinary mandate until the time of Papinian, who granted to third parties an *actio utilis* (*ad exemplum institoriæ actionis*) against the

[1] G., 4, 73; D., 15, 3, 1-1.
[2] D., 15, 1, 5-4, 10, 52-pr.
[3] Ed.-P., 1, 326.—**CXCV**, 2, 1143.
[4] D., 15, 3, 1-1; 2, 1.
[5] D., 14, 4, 1-pr.; 5, 15-19.
[6] G., 4, 71; D., 14, 3, 19-1; I. J., 4, 7, 2a.

252 FORMATION OF CLASSICAL LAW

mandator as well as the *actio mandati* against the mandatary.[1] If this latter action had been abolished, true juridical representation would at last have been attained. Perhaps Papinian desired this, but he had no followers,[2] and that goal was only reached in favour of the legal administrators of other people's fortunes, who were protected (*exceptionis ope*) against prosecution by third parties.[3]

A question was raised concerning the mandataries who were *extranei*: they were capable of pledging the mandator, but could they acquire claims for him immediately ? At the end of the second century it was admitted that on expiry of guardianship or curatorship claims passed (*jure prætorio*) exclusively to the former incapable.[4] Was this principle carried still further ? Some maintain that this solution was made general in the third century, under Ulpian's influence, by means of a tacit *cessio actionis*; but the texts—even some of Ulpian's own inserted in the Digest—bear witness to the contrary until Justinian's reign.[5]

III. INALIENABILITY OF CLAIMS: HOW THE PRINCIPLE WAS ELUDED

The creditor may wish to realize the value of the obligation before it has produced its effects, or to transfer it to others with various ends in view. Modern legislations have therefore organized modes of transferring claims, but for a long time Roman Law knew nothing analogous to them.[6]

When economic necessity prompted traffic in values of this kind, certain indirect methods of procedure were adopted. The first was delegation, in which the creditor gave order (*jussus*) to the debtor to promise what was due to him to a third party by means of a verbal contract.[7] But for this the consent of the debtor was necessary and, further, the qualities and guarantees of the original claim disappeared. The second was the *procuratio in rem suam*, a judicial mandate realized by means of a formula which directed the judge to condemn the debtor in favour of the grantee (*mandatarius*), if the claim

---

[1] D., 14, 3, 19-pr.; 19, 1, 13-25.　　[2] *Fr. vat.*, 328.
[3] C. J., 5, 39, 1.　　[4] D., 12, 1, 26; 13, 5, 5-9.
[5] D., 41, 2, 49-2; 45, 1, 126-2; C. J., 4, 27, 1.—**XIII**, 24, 33 et seq.
[6] D., 7, 1, 25-2.　　[7] G., 2, 38.—**CLV**, 231-276.

of the grantor (*mandator*) shown in the *intentio* was justified.[1] The sentence made the *judicatum* payable to the mandatary, and the original right was extinguished by the *litis contestatio*. Here nothing was changed at first in the nature of the right; but the cession did not become operative until the debt fell due, so that its value depreciated; and further, if the grantor changed his mind, he could revoke the grant. The operation was only permissible for those who could plead for or through others.[2]

The imperial Law, however, came very near to our modern cession. First, in case of voluntary cession, the actions of the grantor, which could no longer take effect, were retained for the grantee *utilitatis causa*;[3] while in case of obligatory cession, the latter was invested with them in strict law.[4] Then it was admitted that the cession became irrevocable when it had been intimated to the debtor, or if the latter had recognized it by making a partial payment;[5] and these facts, whose value was merely probative, were supplemented by others of the same kind. Thus the third century saw the establishment of a system of transfer which, though less perfect than those of existing legislations, was nevertheless the origin of them.[6]

VII
EXTINCTION OF OBLIGATIONS

I. EXTINCTION OF OBLIGATIONS: PRINCIPAL MODES OF THE " JUS CIVILE "

Execution or payment caused the disappearance of the obligation which had thus attained its end; but there were other modes of extinction.

We know that for a long time the payment did not suffice to break the legal bond created by a formal act, which could only be broken by a corresponding act in the opposite sense (*solutio per œs et libram, acceptilatio*). A mere pact had always sufficed to extinguish delictual obligations. Even when the payment had this effect *ipso jure*, other causes of

[1] G., 2, 39.—CLV, 313-318. [2] Paul, 1, 2, 2; D., 3, 3, 8-2, 25.
[3] D., 3, 3, 55.—CXLV, 24. [4] D., 2, 14, 16; C. J., 4, 10, 2.
[5] C. J., 8, 41, 3. [6] D., 2, 15, 17; cf. CLVIII, 776 et seq., 1.

ancient or recent origin led to the disappearance of the obligation before its normal effect had been produced, some of them connected with the Civil Law, others with the Law of the Prætors.¹

Among the causes of ancient origin, the *novatio* and *litis contestatio*, whose consequences we have already described, only suppressed the obligation in order to substitute a new one in its place.² Others were the result of events which made the execution actually impossible. Hence arose the confusion or combination in the same juridical person of the two qualities of creditor and debtor. Obligation assumes the subjection of one person to another; if there is no more than one, he is deemed to have paid himself.³ Nevertheless the distinction between the two qualities was maintained in so far as anyone had an interest in maintaining it, which was often the case either when the qualities of creditor and principal debtor were combined or above all when the quality of principal debtor was combined with that of accessory debtor.⁴ Another cause was loss of the thing owed, whether material or juridical loss, which however could only occur in the case of specific things,⁵ not of *genera*: at least this was true in principle, but in practice the reverse might happen, because the decision as to what constituted a *genus* was sometimes left to the parties.⁶ But when a thing was lost or destroyed fragments of it, whether material or juridical (e.g. actions), often survived, and these had to be surrendered by the debtor if the obligation was *bonæ fidei*.

Other causes of extinction had to do with the application of higher principles to the agreement of the parties. Such first of all was the death of one of them. Without inquiring whether, in the most ancient Law, every obligation was extinguished by the death of one of the parties, we can say that in classical Law (i.) delictual obligations were extinguished by the death of the delinquent, and those termed *vindictam spirantes* by the death of the victim also; (ii.) the claim of an *adstipulator* and that of a wife for restitution of dowry did not pass to their heirs; (iii.) the debts of sureties (*sponsores* and *fidepromissores*) died with them. Another cause was change

---

[1] G., 3, 169, 173; D., 50, 17, 35, 100.
[2] G., 3, 176, 180; 4, 103-106.   [3] D., 21, 2, 41-2; 46, 1, 50.
[4] D., 35, 2, 1-18, 87-8; 46, 3, 95-3.—**XLIX**, 2, nº 712; **CLVIII**, 766.
[5] D., 46, 3, 107; 50, 17, 23.   [6] D., 35, 2, 80-5.

OBLIGATIONS OR PERSONAL RIGHTS

of condition which, like *capitis deminutio*, involved the extinction of claims in certain cases and of debts other than those arising out of a delict, whether their juridical titular had disappeared or his patrimony had been absorbed by another. Another cause was the expiry of a certain period after which it was no longer possible to plead the obligation at law. Normally obligations and the actions which sanctioned them were perpetual; but the prætor framed a number of actions which could only be brought within one year (*intra annum*), and the ædilician actions in the sphere of private Law were also temporary. The prescribed period began to run from the first day on which the creditor could have taken action.[1] When it had expired, the action lost its penal character but often continued to be available to the extent of the creditor's enrichment or that of his heirs. Within the sphere of Civil Law, the obligation of *sponsores* and *fidepromissores* was extinguished, in Italy, at the end of two years in accordance with the provisions of the *Lex Furia;* the *querela inofficiosi testamenti* could not be lodged after 5 years.

II. SET-OFF

Finally set-off, which in Roman Law had peculiar characteristics and was not a direct mode of extinguishing obligations,[2] assumed the existence of two persons indebted to one another in such a way that their claims balanced.[3] For a long time this balance could only be made use of by the agreement of the parties and by the modes of extinction of debt which they had at their disposal; but at an uncertain date it was established that bankers (*argentarii*) who had a current account with their clients could no longer sue them, when debts of the same kind were owing on both sides, except for the balance of the account, under pain of *plus petitio* involving loss of the suit;[4] and this notwithstanding the fact that the clients were not bound in the same way.[5] Later on, the *bonorum emptor* suing for recovery of debts due to a bankrupt was compelled, if the debtor was at the same time a creditor of the latter, to have the amount of the claim deducted even if it was not yet due, without however incurring

---

[1] G., 4, 110-111; D., 44, 3, 1-pr.; 7, 35.—**XXXIII**, 13, 184.
[2] **LIV ; CXXXI ; CCLII**, 2¹, 261-290. [3] D., 16, 2, 1. [4] G., 4, 64-68.
[5] But see D., 22, 3, 19-3; Ed.-L., 2, 252.—**LIV**, 108-122.

the risk of *plus petitio*, since this deduction was made in the condemnation, not in the *intentio*.¹ Finally, in synallagmatic contracts *bonæ fidei*, it seemed natural that the defendant should ask the judge to take account of the debts owing on each side and, if possible, to regard the one as set-off against the other—a thing which could easily be done since the condemnations were assessed in money.²

The set-off then appeared to be judicial, i.e. to depend on the judge's assessment invoked by the interested parties; and that was the true character of the Roman set-off as organized by a rescript of Marcus Aurelius which allowed the defendant in actions of strict law to allege against the plaintiff a debt which had come due, even if it originated *ex dispari causa*, for to claim what would have to be immediately restored constituted fraud.³ It remained optional for the defendant and for the judge, and was claimed by means of the *exceptio doli* which in some cases allowed the condemnation to be reduced by the difference between the two debts and in others involved acquittal, thus impelling the plaintiff to limit his claim voluntarily.⁴ In course of time the set-off *ex dispari causa* was extended to all the *bonæ fidei* actions. Ulpian shows us that it operated even in penal actions.⁵

III. PRÆTORIAN MODES OF EXTINCTION

The Law of the Prætors also provided its share. The *exceptio* practically extinguished the right in many cases: the *litis contestatio* in the *judicia imperio continentia*, the set-off *ex dispari causa*, etc., were used *exceptionis ope*. But the edict created a direct and voluntary mode, the agreement not to sue, *pactum de non petendo*, a pendant to the *contrarius consensus* of synallagmatic contracts and to the pact extinguishing delictual obligations. An informal agreement by the creditor, whether tacit or express, to forgo the whole or part of the debt, it was subject to all the permissible modalities,⁶ and was made either *in rem*, for the advantage of all the debtors, or *in personam*, for the advantage of one of them alone, in which case it only extinguished the debt in so

---

¹ G., 4, 65.   ² G., 4, 61-63.—**LIV**, 60-81; **XXXIII**, 21, 362.
³ D., 16, 2, 3; 50, 17, 173-3.   ⁴ **LIV**, 318-400.
⁵ D., 16, 2, 10-2; cf. **LIV**, 89 et seq.   ⁶ D., 14, 2, 2-pr.-2, 10-2, 28-2.

far as its payment would injure the beneficiary.[1] It provided the debtor with a plea of agreement (*exceptio pacti*),[2] and should be compared with the pact of oath (*pactum de jurejurando*) in virtue of which the debtor swore that he owed nothing, though this always operated *in rem* out of respect for the oath.[3]

[1] D., 14, 2, 7-8, 22, 25-pr.-1-5.   [2] G., 4, 126; D., 14, 2, 27-2.
[3] D., 12, 2, 28-pr

CHAPTER VII

THE ORGANIZATION OF CREDIT

I

THE IDEA AND THE PRINCIPAL FORMS OF CREDIT

I. THE IDEA OF CREDIT: ITS PRINCIPAL FORMS

THE economic development of a nation shows itself juridically in an organization of credit. Primitive barter allowed of none; it proceeded on a system of give and take. Now credit implies reliance on the word and the solvency of others, supported by a more or less adequate system of guarantees, for it is "the exchange of present wealth for future wealth," the abandonment of what one has in order to obtain something of greater value. Of the two principal operations which it suggests, sale on credit and loan, the first which was unknown to primitive Law never had the importance at Rome which it has in our time. Classical Law said truly that in such cases the vendor was dependent on the good faith of the vendee and assimilated him to one who had received satisfaction, but the guarantees which it offered him against the vendee's insolvency—precarious tenure or provisional hire, *lex commissoria, pactum reservatæ hypothecæ*—were either too inconvenient to handle or too uncertain for the operation to become an essential element in credit. As a matter of fact loan at interest was the usual and fundamental form of credit in this society, and its history is closely bound up with that of all the revolutions of ancient Rome.

II. THE LOAN FOR CONSUMPTION; LOAN AT INTEREST AND ITS LEGISLATION

Loan for consumption in its various forms was rather a means of helping and exploiting a certain social class than a means of production. As the things lent were not

THE ORGANIZATION OF CREDIT 259

consumed with a view to acquiring a new form of wealth but to satisfy the immediate needs of the borrower, they diminished his patrimony to that extent and their restitution was uncertain. Hence they were severely sanctioned and an excessive rate of interest was exacted to compensate for the risks,[1] so that the operation was discredited and led to popular disturbances in critical times and to restrictive or prohibitive statutes. Rome lived under the threat of troubles caused by the debtors, especially after the introduction of money, which made this traffic easier and more regular. This was the chief cause or pretext for the secessions of the plebs, for the revolutionary movements in the time of the Gracchi, Catilina, Cæsar and even Tiberius. The juridical construction of the *nexum* and afterwards of the *mutuum*, where the borrower's obligation was calculated in strict accordance with the value of his loan, followed the ancient conception of loan as a philanthropic contract whose nature it was wrong to change by seeking to make profit out of it. It was not until the end of the Republic that the Romans conceived the idea of regarding loan at interest as a form of hire (*conducti nummi, pecunia conducta*) in which the *usura* was the *merces*.[2] But the juridical mechanism was in no wise modified by this theoretical conception. The agreement to pay interest, which was excluded from the *mutuum*, a contract of strict law in which no pact increasing the obligation could be inserted, had always to be a stipulation of interest (*stipulatio usurarum*), giving rise when the interest fell due, i.e. on the kalends of each month, to an *actio kalendarii*.[3] Often a *stipulatio sortis et usurarum*, including at the same time return[4] of the capital and payment of the interest, served as a cloak for a usurious rate.

Loan at interest was almost the only means of turning capital to account, and the fundholders kept the entries in their bill-book, *kalendarium*, with meticulous care; but the number of borrowers prevented any depreciation in the value of money and compelled the voting of statutes in their defence. At an early date the maximum rate of interest was fixed at

[1] XIII, 42, 467-544; cf. **XXXVIII** and **XXXIX**, s.v. *Fœnus;* **CLXXIX**.
[2] Horace, *Sat.*, 1, 2, 9; 3, 88; Juv., *Sat.*, 11, 46. Cf. Cic., *de Sen.*, 15; Pliny, *H. N.*, 2, 63; Tac., *Ann.*, 6, 16-17.
[3] Paul, 2, 14, 1; D., 19, 5, 24; 45, 1, 79-9; 26, 7, 39-14.
[4] Cic., *ad Att.*, 6, 1, 3; D., 45, 1, 135-pr.; T. G., 845.

the *unciarum fœnus* by the Law of the Twelve Tables and the *Lex Diulia Mœnia* (397 A.U.C.). According to an opinion that has been generally adopted since Niebuhr, the *unciarum fœnus* would be an interest of one twelfth per *as* per annum, which would be equivalent to $8\frac{1}{3}$ per cent.; but according to another, more ancient view, that of the commentary and of our ancient scholars, which has just been brilliantly restated, this rate would not have been calculated per annum but by the normal duration of the loan, i.e. one month, and would therefore have been equivalent to 100 per cent. However excessive this may appear, it seems to be nearer the truth; for the rate of $8\frac{1}{3}$ per cent. would have been, in the circumstances, comparatively low and would not explain why the question of debt and of the *nexi* should have been the most distressing problem of Roman society.[1]

A *Lex Genucia* forbidding loan at interest was not long enforced (412 A.U.C.). After many changes the legal rate was fixed at the end of the Republic at 12 per cent. (*centesima usura*), and the usual rate until the time of the Lower Empire must have varied between 4 and 8 per cent.[2]

The usurer, *fœnerator*, who had been punished from very early times by a fine of fourfold damages, was subject after the *Lex Marcia* to nothing worse than a *manus injectio pura*.[3] A stipulation of a very high penalty, sanctioning delay in repayment after the Greek fashion, was forbidden by imperial jurisprudence as being a means of exceeding the legal rates of interest.[4] The difficulty of paying when the interest fell due had spread the practice, also borrowed from the Greeks, of compound interest, which was forbidden by a senatus-consultum of Cicero's time, at least in the case of interest that had not come due.[5] At length it was enacted by certain constitutions that unpaid interest should cease to multiply when it had reached a sum equivalent to the capital.[6] The *Sc. Macedonianum* of Vespasian's reign completed this restrictive legislation by authorizing the prætor to allow a *paterfamilias* and even the *filiusfamilias* himself an *exceptio* against a claim for repayment of loan brought against the

---

[1] **XIII**, 42, 467 et seq.
[2] Liv., 6, 19; 7, 16, 42; ic., *ad Att.*, 1, 12; 4, 15; 5, 21. Paul, 2, 14, 2; D., 26, 7, 39-14.—**LXXIV**, 320; **XXXIII**, 5, 130.
[3] XII T., 8, 18; G., 4, 23.
[4] Aul. Gel., 18, 14.
[5] Cic., *ad Att.*, 5, 21; D., 12, 6, 26-1; 42, 1, 27.
[6] C. J., 4, 32, 10.

THE ORGANIZATION OF CREDIT 261

latter,[1] except when the borrower was *sui juris*, when the loan was contracted by the father's *jussus* or for the benefit of the father's estate, and in some other cases.[2]

A constitution of Caracalla framed a very remarkable system for the protection of debtors under the name of *querela non numeratæ pecuniæ*.[3] Loans were generally acknowledged by a note of hand which had only a probative value but was sent to the lender before the money was paid over. The common Law required that when this written acknowledgment was produced in court, it should be opposed by contrary evidence; but Caracalla laid the burden of proof of payment on the holder of the note of hand. At first perhaps only in money loans but afterwards in any loan of fungible things, the debtor could deny the validity of the note of hand either by an *exceptio*, which might put a stop to the creditor's prosecution, or by a *contestatio*, by which he took the initiative and disavowed the note of hand held by his opponent or by the judge, or perhaps by a *condictio* aiming at the recovery of this note.[4] The period of one year for which this extravagant privilege was at first available was extended to 5 by Diocletian. After that time the note of hand could no longer be disputed.[5]

This distrust of loan at interest yielded certain points for the sake of commerce and even of equity. Classical jurisprudence attached to the mere informal agreement to pay interest a natural obligation which prevented its recovery even if it had been paid in error.[6] In loans or advances of commodities, the agreement obliging the borrower to return more than he had received was justified by the unstable value of these wares, the value being indeed the object of the contract.[7] But the best known and most ancient exception was the *nauticum fœnus*, a contract *sui generis* concerning the *pecunia trajectitia* or money lent for commerce by sea. If this money or the merchandise representing it was lost through sea risks, the loss was borne by the lender; while on the other hand, so long as the voyage lasted, interest claimable in virtue of an informal agreement could be charged at more than the legal rates.[8]

[1] Suet., *Vesp.*, 11; D., 14, 6, 1-pr.   [2] D., 14, 7, 12, 19; C. J., 4, 28, 2.
[3] C. J., 4, 30-3 (a 215); 8, 1, (228).—**CCXXXIX**, 2, 78 et seq.; **XXXIII**, 13, 273; 18, 267.   [4] C. J., 4, 30, 3, 7, 8-1, 9.
[5] C. Herm., 1, 1; C. J., 4, 3, 8.   [6] C. J., 4, 32, 3.
[7] C. J., 4, 32, 11, 23.   [8] D., 22, 2, 1-7.

III. IRREGULAR DEPOSIT AND THE "RECEPTUM ARGENTARII"

Apart from loan at interest, credit had only imperfect instruments. Irregular deposit, conceived on the model of the oriental παρακαταθήκη, was an agreement by which the depositary was authorized to make use of the deposited funds in return for payment of interest on them, for any pact inserted in a contract *bonæ fidei* was sanctioned by the action belonging to the contract; but it never played so important a part as our *comptes de dépôt*. There is some difficulty in identifying it in the texts of Scævola and of Papinian,[1] while Paul and above all Ulpian regarded it as equivalent to a loan.[2]

The little understood *receptum argentarii*, where it seems probable that the banker undertook to pay a client's debt by some arrangement that involved no security, may not have had the importance which the abstract character of the operation and its practical advantages ought to have given it. Things of any kind were admitted as its object—a fact explained by the very diverse operations undertaken by bankers in those days—but it may have been especially used in connexion with the sales by auction over which they presided.[3]

The practices akin to bills of exchange or bills to order which some think they have discovered in certain literary texts are doubtful and probably illusory.

II

PERSONAL GUARANTEES

I. PERSONAL GUARANTEES: THEIR ANTIQUITY

The system of giving guarantees in support of credit involved originally personal guarantees which were used from a very early period in the forms of solidarity and security. Both had their origin in the primitive conception of the family and in the relations between members of the same clan; they were born of the social organization of those days but they survived it. They were incorporated in the Law of the

---

[1] CCLI, 61-72; **XXIV**, 19, 197; **CI**, 1, 114-123   [2] D., 19, 2, 7-2, 9-9, 26-1.
[3] E-P. 1, 148.—**CXCV**, 1 section 67; **CLXXXII**, 3, 214; **XXXV**, 1, 85.

city, which modified and regulated them in order to adapt them to the purely individual relations for which it provided within the bounds of the State.

The delicate mechanism of real securities did not attain a sufficient degree of facility and perfection until the late period when pledge and mortgage were introduced; but these new creations did not limit to any appreciable extent the vast and well-stocked domain of personal securities.

II. SOLIDARITY

The texts reveal to us an active and a passive solidarity, *duo rei stipulandi vel promittendi*.[1] A solidary obligation was that in which a single thing was owed, simultaneously and in its entirety, in the first case by one debtor to several creditors, in the second by several debtors to one creditor, in such a way that payment to one of these creditors or by one of these debtors extinguished the obligation of the others.[2]

The origin of this juridical solidarity was the solidarity of the family in which it doubtless had its birth. The members of the same family, of the same group, stipulated or promised all together what they must receive or pay as a substitute for private vengeance, and this practice was afterwards used as a security and convenience in the pursuit of a right;[3] but the usage of passive solidarity was especially prominent, almost relegating active solidarity to the position of an academical hypothesis.

Although cases are cited of several debtors bound *in solidum* for the same debt without preliminary agreement,[4] the Roman principle was that no solidarity existed without agreement by means of a stipulation in which each debtor replied individually to a single question put by the creditor, whence they were termed *correi*.[5] Nevertheless classical Law allowed it in other contracts: *mutuum*, sale, hire, etc., where it was established by a pact inserted in the contract and alleged by

---

[1] D., 45, 2, 9-pr.; I. J., 3, 16.—**XIII**, 7, 237-266; 8, 137-154, 305-404.
[2] D., 45, 2, 3-1, 9-1, 15-pr.; 2, 14, 9-pr.—**CXLI**, 2, 72.
[3] **CCLXXI**, 1, 160, 246.
[4] The solidary obligation must be distinguished from the obligation *in solidum* binding the joint-authors of an injury, which is extinguished as soon as one of them has repaired the wrong. In this case there are rather as many obligations as debtors, but when the wrong has been repaired, the obligations disappear for lack of an object. D., 16, 3, 1-13; 27, 3, 1, 2.—**XIII**, 8, 404 et seq.
[5] I. J., 3, 16-pr. Cf. D., 45, 2, 3-pr.

means of the action belonging to that contract; and even in wills, when it was imposed by the testator on heirs responsible for payment of the same legacy.[1]

Sometimes the solidary debtors all had an interest in the operation, in which case they were called partners, *socii*; sometimes all the others were merely guarantors of one of their number. In either case the creditor was provided with a security and with the convenience of being able to sue which of them he pleased for the whole amount. They were all responsible for each other's faults, excepting the fault of delay (*mora*), and if one of them rendered execution impossible, the obligation was made perpetual for them all.[2] On the other hand payment, *acceptilatio, novatio, litis contestatio* or an oath furnished by one of them cancelled the debt of all alike.[3] The same was true of the agreement not to sue *in rem*; but when this agreement had been made with one alone, it did not procure an *exceptio* for the fellow-debtors, unless they were *socii*, and even then only to the extent of the freed debtor's part.[4]

The distinction between *socii* and *non socii* was not primitive. The abstract nature of the stipulation was incompatible with the idea of any rule governing the relations of the debtors with one another. But when solidarity came to be used more extensively, equity gave the debtor who had paid a recourse against the others by means of the *actio pro socio*, if they were *socii*, and if they were not *socii*, by means of the *actio mandati* against the interested party alone.[5] Moreover the sued debtor could require the creditor whom he indemnified to cede his actions against the other debtors, and was armed for this purpose with the *exceptio doli mali*.[6]

III. Security and its Various Forms: "Sponsio, Fidepromissio, Fidejussio, Mandatum Pecuniæ Credendæ"

In primitive times there was no conception of a debt owed by several persons who did not all belong to a common social group with a common patrimony: hence the solidarity among

[1] D., 13, 5, 16-pr.; 45, 2, 9-pr.
[2] D., 45, 2, 18; 50, 17, 173-2.
[3] D., 12, 2, 28-3; I. J., 3, 16, 1.
[4] D., 45, 1, 21-5, 25-pr.
[5] D., 35, 2, 62-pr.
[6] D., 19, 2, 47.—**XIII**, *l.c.*, 262; but see **XLIX**, 2, n° 551.

the debtors and the refusal to admit as surety anyone unrelated to the principal debtor—a phenomenon which seems to appear again in Roman Law in the cases of *præs* and *vas*.¹ Later it was admitted that, as the debtor's liability persisted, the surety was only a sort of advance-guard; and finally a *chassé-croisé* re-established the logic of the position, which may have been recognized as a result of the debtor offering himself as his own guarantor along with the others.²

The Roman Law that is known to us shows security already realized above all by verbal engagements which were introduced one after the other, each more completely dissociated than its predecessor from the ancient ideas.³

The first, *sponsio*, obviously developed out of solidarity with which it shares the terms *sponsio*, *spondere*, the verbal form, the assignment as guarantee for a debt itself contracted *verbis* by the promise of an identical thing (*idem*). But thanks to a mechanism involving between creditor and debtors (originally all present)⁴ as many questions and answers as there were debtors, in order to show, while maintaining them all on the same level, that the engagements concerned did not all affect the same patrimony, it no longer substituted the guarantor for the principal debtor, though this did not mean that the accessory obligation could be extinguished independently of the principal one or could not arise if the latter was void.⁵ A *Lex Publilia* marking the exclusive interest of the principal debtor, armed the surety who had paid with an *actio depensi* against him under the form of *manus injectio*, which was left intact by the *Lex Vallia* but changed by the formular procedure into an action involving double damages in case of *infitiatio*.⁶ *Sponsio* was only possible between citizens: hence the introduction later on of a second type of security, *fidepromissio*, which was also available for aliens.

Resembling each other in juridical form and effects, they underwent some amendments at a time when the State was endeavouring to limit the number of debts. It was enacted that *sponsores* and *fidepromissores* should pledge themselves alone, and that their obligation should not be transmissible to their heirs—regulations which have been found elsewhere.

¹ **CLIX**, 1, 73; **CXCV**, 2, 47; **XXXIII**, 23, 96.   ² T. G., 64, ll. 5-10; 860.
³ **XIII**, 1, 541.   ⁴ **CLVIII**, 793, 3.
⁵ G., 3, 116-119.   ⁶ G., 3, 127; 4, 22.

266 FORMATION OF CLASSICAL LAW

Then a *Lex Appuleia* made some sort of partnership between the guarantors of a common debt and divided the burden among them so as to make it less heavy in case of the debtor's insolvency. Finally a *Lex Furia de sponsu* of the sixth century enacted that in Italy *sponsores* and *fidepromissores* should no longer be liable for more than two years after the debt fell due and that, since the liability was divided between them *ipso jure*, each one could no longer be sued for more than his share under threat of recovery from the creditor by means of *manus injectio pro judicato*, which could only be opposed by a *vindex*. In order to make the application of this principle complete, the *Lex Cicereia* obliged the creditor to declare, before engaging the sureties, their number and the amount of the debt, and created a *præjudicium* to insure that failure to fulfil these requirements should be established within the 20 days following, with consequent lapse of the engagement.[1]

It was then, in the course of the seventh century, that practice devised the *fidejussio*.[2] The mechanism was the same, but the formula was different: *id fide mea esse jubeo*,[3] an obscure expression which some identify with the *idem*, though this is doubtful. *Fidejussio* was a wider form of security than its predecessors. Its obligation was transmissible to heirs, it could guarantee any sort of debt, even a natural one, it could precede or follow the principal debt, be equal or inferior to it in value, and be subject to different modalities.[4] This time the accessory followed the principal; the nullity or extinction of the debtor's obligation destroyed those of the *fidejussores*. The *Lex Furia* was not applicable here;[5] but a rescript of Hadrian, which however could be set aside by a contrary clause, authorized the *fidejussor* sued for the whole amount to claim the benefit of division of liability among those who were still solvent. A *Lex Cornelia*, perhaps of the Dictator Sylla, had forbidden a surety to pledge himself for more than 20,000 sesterces, and jurisprudence adapted the *Lex Cicereia* to this new form.[6] Moreover it devised the formula *Quanto minus a reo consequi poteris, fide-*

[1] G., 3, 120-123; 4, 22; Ed.-P., 1, 271.—**XXXIII**, 25, 379.
[2] **XIII**, 1, 548. [3] G., 3, 116, 118; D., 16, 1, 28-1; 45, 1, 75-1.
[4] G., 3, 119-120; D., 46, 2, 8-7; I. J., 3, 28, 5. [5] G., 3, 120.
[6] G., 3, 120, 123, 125; C. J., 5, 57, 1; I. J., 3, 26, 4; cf. Ed.-P , 1, 248; D., 46, 6, 12.

THE ORGANIZATION OF CREDIT 267

jubeo, pledging the surety to pay as much as the debtor was unable to pay, and the *fidejussio indemnitatis*, both of which in fact made it compulsory to distress the debtor's property before prosecuting the surety.[1] As the action regarding this security was less strict in character, the judge gave much consideration to the parties' intention. The clauses requiring distraint upon the debtor's goods often involved an inquiry; the *fidejussor indemnitatis* could allege against the creditor that he had by his own fault allowed the debtor to become insolvent. *Bona fides* came into consideration; the *fidejussor* who had paid had against the debtor not the *actio depensi* but the action for mandate (*actio mandati contraria*).[2] A friendly service from the point of view of the debtor, the security was regarded in the same light from the creditor's point of view whom it enabled to make a transaction without risk; it was just that the *fidejussor's* own risk should be reduced to the minimum and that the creditor on receiving payment should cede all his actions to him. For that reason it was held that by indemnifying the creditor the *fidejussor* did not pay him, which would have consumed the actions, but bought them from him for the amount of the debt; and if the creditor still had them, he could not refuse them without fraud.[3] However, jurisprudence limited the right of recourse which the *fidejussor* thus acquired against his fellow guarantors to the share of each one of them in the debt.[4]

Classical Law adapted the *mandatum* and the *pactum de constituto* to serve as securities. In order to stay proceedings, the debtor offered a third party who undertook to pay on a fixed date if he did not pay himself, thus giving the creditor the action *de pecunia constituta* against the third party; or else the surety played the part of *mandator* and gave the creditor a mandate to advance a sum of money to the debtor, this being the *mandatum pecuniæ credendæ* which gave the creditor a *condictio ex mutuo* against the debtor and an *actio mandati contraria* against the surety, actions which were not mutually exclusive because the two debtors did not owe the same thing, *eadem res*.[5] But the *mandator* and the new

[1] D., 12, 1, 42-pr.; 45, 1, 116; cf. CLV, 150.   [2] Cf. D., 17, 1, 6-2, 40.
[3] D., 21, 2, 65; 46, 1, 17, 36; 3, 76 (7); D., 46, 1, 10-pr.; 50, 15, 5-pr.
[4] G., 3, 171; D., 13, 5, 1-5. The original action was thereby consumed: D., 13, 5, 16-3.
[5] G., 3, 156; Paul, 2, 17, 16; D., 17, 1, 32; C. J., 8, 41, 19.

debtor by *pactum de constituto* had an absolute right, on making payment, to the cession of actions; and further, the *mandator* considered as principal had a right that the mandatary should not only cede to him, but should preserve for him the actions and sureties to which he was intitled on this ground. The rescript of Hadrian was extended to them.[1]

III

REAL SURETIES

I. THE REAL SURETIES EARLIER THAN MORTGAGE

Real guarantees were introduced later and used less freely. At first only two very imperfect forms were available: (i.) fiduciary sale of a thing to the creditor, who had to re-transfer the ownership of it to the discharged debtor under the sanction, only established at a late period, of the *actio fiduciæ directa*, and with possibility, from an earlier date, of *usureceptio*; (ii.) pledge, *pignus*, whose character was not clearly defined until after the definition of *possessio*, which was all that it transferred to the creditor, leaving the ownership and the right of claim to the debtor. At first a mere right of detention, it was very soon made more serious by a clause authorizing sale by the unpaid creditor in order that he might compensate himself with the price. This clause became a regular formality so that the right of sale was naturally inherent in the pledge.[2]

The thing thus sold or pledged ceased to be an instrument of credit for the debtor; he lost the enjoyment of it, unless the creditor allowed him to keep it on precarious tenure or on hire, in which case the latter had to deduct the fruits from the interest and afterwards from the capital of the debt.[3]

II. MORTGAGE

Mortgage was derived from the simplified form of pledge in cases of letting houses or leasing land. There was no need to deprive the lessees of the moveables required in daily life or for trade purposes; they were merely forbidden to remove them

[1] D., 46, 2, 17-pr.; 3, 55-20, 95-11; C. J., 4, 18, 3. [2] See p. 231.
[3] T. G., 823-826.

THE ORGANIZATION OF CREDIT 269

from the leased property before the lessor had been paid or otherwise satisfied.[1] The latter was provided with an *interdictum salvianum*, a possessory interdict to give him possession of these things, when the debt fell due, in case of non-payment.[2] The edict added an action *in factum* called the *actio serviana* from the name of the prætor who had devised it; a real action, i.e. one that authorized recovery of the thing from third parties as well as from the debtor.[3]

At the beginning of the Empire this arrangement, which left the ownership and enjoyment of the pledge to the debtor while arming the creditor with a right of pursuit and of priority, was extended to all things offered as guarantees for any sort of debt.[4] Under the title of *utilis* or *quasi serviana* an action was framed for these cases and the new institution borrowed the name of ὑποθήκη, mortgage, from a parallel Greek system, from which however it was distinguished by the absence of publicity, and by the possibility of being general and of pledging the thing to successive creditors without the first creditor's consent.[5] Moreover it was at once more flexible and more precise than the Greek system, which was hardly distinguishable from antichresis.[6]

The effect of mortgage was to set apart one or more of the debtor's possessions for the payment of a particular debt in preference to others. Whether special or general, it was originally a mere private agreement; but afterwards, in a sequence whose chronological order is uncertain, implied legal mortgages were allowed to the Treasury on the property of its debtors, to lessors of urban property on the moveable furniture of the leased houses, to lessors of rural property on its crops, to lessors of capital on the immoveables which this capital had served to construct, to incapables on the property of their guardians or curators, to legatees on the inherited property, etc.[7] But Roman Law knew nothing of judicial mortgage.

The mortgage could be established on goods capable of being sold, and could effect a real right[8] over those goods or

---

[1] D., 20, 1, 5-1.—**CLXX**, 105 et seq.; **CXCIII**, 142 et seq.
[2] G., 4, 147; Ed.-P., 2, 238; cf. **XIII**, 18, 50.
[3] I. J., 4, 6, 7.   [4] Cf. D., 13, 7, 3, and 9-2, 18-3.
[5] D., 13, 7, 1-pr.; 20, 4, 9-3, 12-7.   [6] D., 20, 1, 15-1.
[7] *Fr. de jur. fisci*, 5; D., 20, 2, 1, 4-pr., 7; C. J., 4, 53, 1.
[8] D., 13, 7, 16-2; 20, 1, 9, 1; Ed.-P., 242.—**CCXCIX**, 1, n° 239.

a right of claim,[1] whether present or to come, whatever condition it might be subject to.[2] It was even extended to the accessories of debts, e.g. interest.[3]

It produced effects both before and after the guaranteed debt fell due. Before that date the thing mortgaged remained in the hands of the debtor, who might neither impair it nor change its nature, additions and accessories going to the profit of the mortgage. After that date the unpaid creditor could secure possession of the thing, sell it and pay himself with the proceeds.

The first of these rights, right of pursuit, was exercised by means of the *actio quasi serviana*, a discretionary action *in factum concepta* and granted against the debtor or any other holder of the thing mortgaged, the *jussus* of the judge being to pay or relinquish possession.[4] A rescript of the year 205 A.D. directed the creditor of both a general and a special mortgage to exhaust the effects of the latter before having recourse to the former.[5] Third parties holding the thing mortgaged could claim the benefit of cession of action in exchange for payment of the amount of the debt, or could allege an *exceptio* based upon a mortgage prior to that of the plaintiff.[6] The second right, right of sale, assumed preliminary settlement of the right of priority among the mortgagees, for sale by the first of them alone cleared the mortgage.[7] Now mortgages ranked as follows: if made by agreement, from the date of their establishment; if legal, from the date on which the debt began; if privileged, from the day fixed by the statute.[8] When making the mortgage, the debtor had to declare under penalty of stellionate whether the thing was already burdened and, if so, to what extent.[9] Until the end of the second century the right of sale (*jus distrahendi*) could only follow from an express clause which was sometimes replaced by a *lex commissoria* authorizing the appropriation of the thing mortgaged as a means of payment;[10] but the Jurists preferred to incorporate the *jus distrahendi* with the mortgage, failing a clause to the contrary.[11] When the debt came due,

[1] D., 13, 7, 18-pr.; C. J., 3, 39, 7.
[2] D., 20, 1, 1-pr., 5-pr.
[3] D., 13, 7, 8-5; C. J., 8, 26, 1.
[4] D., 20, 1, 13-4, 16-4, 21-3; Ed.-P., 2, 242.
[5] C. J., 8, 3, 2.
[6] D., 20, 4, 7, 12-pr., 19.
[7] D., 20, 5, 1; C. J., 8, 20, 1.
[8] D., 20, 4, 5, 6; C. J., 4, 46, 1; 8, 18, 2-4. Cf. **CXXX**, n° 274; **CLVIII**, 771; **CCXCIX**, 1, n° 225.
[9] D., 20, 15, 2; C. J., 8, 20, 1.
[10] G., 2, 64; D., 20, 1, 16-9, 35; 3, 3.
[11] Paul, 2, 5, 1; D., 13, 7, 4.

the creditor first in order could sell, after demanding payment, in what manner he pleased or, in the absence of a purchaser, could have the thing assigned to him on estimate by an imperial decree.[1] The effects of this sale were the same as if it had been carried out by the debtor himself; he was responsible for the guarantee.[2] This creditor paid himself out of the proceeds and then paid the others in order of priority,[3] the balance being returned to the debtor. But the creditor last in order who feared that the proceeds would not be sufficient to indemnify him had the right, after indemnifying the first creditor, to take his place (*jus offerendæ pecuniæ*).[4] By so doing he gave priority to his own mortgage and thus acquired the right to sell for his own profit. This was the *successio in locum creditoris*.[5]

The mortgage was extinguished with the debt that it guaranteed, but persisted in its entirety so long as any fraction of that debt remained unpaid.[6] It was also extinguished by exercise of the *jus distrahendi*, by renunciation, by merging the qualities of creditor and owner of the thing mortgaged, and by the *præscriptio longi temporis*.[7]

[1] D., 20, 5, 1; 41, 1, 63-4; C. J., 8, 17, 8; 33, 1, 3.
[2] D., 20, 5, 12-1; 21, 2, 38, 71-1.   [3] D., 20, 4, 12.
[4] D., 13, 7, 42.   [5] D., 8, 14, 22; 18, 5.—**XLIII**, 299.
[6] D., 8, 31, 2; 46, 3, 43.   [7] D., 20, 6, 4-1; 8, 6; C. J., 8, 17, 6.

CHAPTER VIII
THE LAW OF INHERITANCE AND GIFTS

SECTION I

THE LAW OF INHERITANCE

I

PRIMITIVE LAW AND THE LAW OF THE TWELVE TABLES

I. THE LAW OF INHERITANCE AND THE SOCIAL AND POLITICAL CONDITIONS

THE relations between a people's political and social constitution and its Law of inheritance, which influence one another reciprocally, make the transmission of property in prospect of death a delicate legislative problem. The former often suggests the latter, and the latter may be either conservative or destructive of the former. Sometimes the conflict is between a society that desires life and statutes that prevent it from living and hasten its destruction; while at other times the statutes are means of salvation for a decadent society. This accounts for those actions and reactions which are revealed to us in Roman history: a rather confused revelation, but one that some attention will make clear.

It is often said that in primitive societies only intestate succession is to be found, but this is not always entirely correct. At Rome the clan or family group was proprietor; at its head was a chief who succeeded a former chief. It has therefore been thought that the primitive form of inheritance was the transmission of sovereignty over the agnatic group; but the idea is open to criticism, and in any case does not hold good of Roman society during the historical period.[1] There can be no true succession, however limited in scope, until some conception of individual ownership has been formed and the authority of the *paterfamilias* has acquired that appearance

[1] Cf. **LXXVII**, 435; **CCXXX**, 99; **CXLVII**.

of autonomous supremacy which it derived from the break up of the clan system and of agrarian collectivism, in other words from the establishment of independent *domus*. The *patresfamilias* then secured the power to dispose freely of all the family patrimony; and since aristocratic societies tend, while keeping individual initiative within just bounds, to relegate the Law of inheritance to a secondary position, making it merely supplementary, in order to substitute for it a contingent system more conformable to the greatness and perpetuity of each house, the head of the *domus*, who was its master and a member of the State, continued, within limits prescribed by custom, to rule it by his will after his death as he had governed it during his lifetime.

But with the decay of tradition, when the rulers doubt or no longer remember their duty, and use the instrument given them by custom at their own caprice instead of in the interest of their houses, the social sense will give place to anarchy which is the fruit of unregulated individualism. Then the legislator will bring back the Law of inheritance, if it already exists, from its obscure position, invest it with wider authority, and extend or enforce its application by restricting freedom of disposal in prospect of death or even *inter vivos*. This was what happened at a particular moment in the history of Rome when the statutes or the edict imposed stricter conditions on testators both as regards form and matter, created incapacities of giving or taking, multiplied the grounds for invalidating testamentary dispositions, and reserved an important part of the property to the family.

II. THE LAW OF THE TWELVE TABLES: THE "HEREDES SUI"; WILLS; INTESTATE SUCCESSION

The Law of the Twelve Tables only authorized intestate succession in the absence of a *heres suus* and of a will.[1]

The right of the *heredes sui*, i.e. persons directly subject to the paternal power or the *manus* of the *paterfamilias* on the day of his death, followed from their pre-existing joint-ownership: *morte patris continuatur dominium*.[2] They were called self-successors (*sui*) because they were already masters

[1] XII T., 5, 4; Ulp., 11, 14.
[2] G., 3, 7; Festus, s.v. *Heres* (=*herus*); I. J., 2, 19, 17; D., 38, 16, 14.

(*heri*) of the patrimony, and necessary (*necessarii*) because they had neither to accept nor to refuse property which was already their own and whose charges they could not repudiate.¹ The Sabinians maintained further that they could not cede their title and quality.² The Jurists discussed the right of the *heredes sui* not in that division of their works which was devoted to inheritance, but in that which dealt with ownership (*dominium*). The death which rendered these *heredes sui juris* had no other effect than to give them the choice between continuing the family *consortium* and claiming distribution of the property either *per capita* among descendants of the first degree, or *per stirpes* (by stocks) to the furthest degree.³

Failing *heredes sui* the *domus* disappeared and the patrimony escheated to the *gens*. But the head of the expiring *domus* avoided at any rate this second consequence by means of his will. So long as the *gens* was strongly organized, events of this kind do not seem to have called for intervention by the political authorities of the city. All that concerned the *domus* of a common group depended exclusively upon the authorities of the *gens*, those of the city only having to intervene if some occurrence caused the interests of two groups to conflict, e.g. if a testator made his will in favour of a member of another *gens*. But this was no longer the case when the *gens* was broken up and the various *domus* became autonomous within the State: then a bequest in favour of another *domus* was enough to move the intervention of the city authorities.

Nevertheless wills were at first rare. They were prompted by the lack of a *heres suus* and the wish to keep the whole of the patrimony in the hands of a near relative, or by the very improbable desire to choose someone other than a relative to continue the family line and cult, or by the need of prolonging the effect of such and such acts of domestic magistracy as regards either persons or property after the testator's death. Before the Law of the Twelve Tables there were two ways of making a will: (i.) *calatis comitiis*, by a solemn declaration of the testator before the comitia calata which were assembled for this purpose twice a year by the pontifex maximus; (ii.) *in procinctu*, on the battlefield, by a declaration made in the

[1] G., 2, 157; D., 38, 2, 11; 9, 12.   [2] G., 3, 87.
[3] G., 3, 7, 8; Ulp., 26, 2

LAW OF INHERITANCE AND GIFTS 275

presence of his fellow soldiers between the taking of the auspices and the order to fight.[1] The latter method was of later introduction and became available for plebeians after the Servian constitution. It is generally supposed that the comitia played the part of legislators;[2] but it should be noted that the powers assigned to the comitia calata were exclusively religious, and their intervention may perhaps be explained by the fact that the private cults were at stake. It is clear that, *in procinctu,* only the combatants could be the witnesses.

Then the decemvirs made the following enigmatical decree: *uti legassit super pecunia tutelave suæ rei, ita jus esto,* or *uti legassit super familia pecuniave sua, ita jus esto.*[3] This has been regarded sometimes as the origin of the testament *calatis comitiis,* which was obviously much earlier, sometimes as that of the testament *per æs et libram,* which was clearly the creation of later practice, sometimes as a distinct method of appointing guardians and disposing separately of *res nec mancipi* which are thought to be specially referred to by the term *pecunia.* The word *legare* used in a technical sense would point to the existence of an ancient freedom of bequest independent on any appointment of an heir.[4] Finally, Roman tradition saw in it a confirmation by statute of freedom of testation under the previous forms (though these were now reduced to certain instrumental formalities)—a freedom of which neither the pontiff's advice to the contrary nor the vote of the comitia (if there had been one hitherto) could deprive the testator. This explanation would agree well enough with the tendency to make Law secular and with the increasing power of the *patresfamilias,* and as the Jurists made freedom of bequest and of other accessory dispositions dependent on this statute, we may believe that it was the first to authorize this freedom, and that the old forms of testation admitted only the institution of heirs, since they had been inspired by the sole motive of perpetuating the family line and the domestic cults.[5]

If, as has been said, the institution of an heir originally involved the transmission of all the rights, family, patrimonial,

---

[1] G., 2, 101; Aul. Gel., 15-17; Vell. Pater., 2, 5.—**CCXXXVIII,** 3, 307.
[2] **CCXXXVIII,** 6¹, 293; **CLVIII,** 826; **CLXXXII,** 1, 147; 3, 145; cf. **CXCV,** 2², 649.   [3] XII T., 5, 3; Cic., *de Inv.,* 2; Ulp., 11, 14.
[4] **CXI,** 1, 129; **XIII,** 11, 540.
[5] G., 2, 224; I. J., 2, 22-pr.; D., 50, 16, 120.

276 FORMATION OF CLASSICAL LAW

political and religious, which would explain the intervention of the comitia, it now involved no more than the patrimony in its entirety, both active and passive, and the *sacra*.¹ But as society became more complex and more variegated, it found a scope for many diverse institutions and contrivances, such as legacy, enfranchisement, guardianship, all secondary, as the classical texts say, to the appointment of an heir.

Finally, the circumstances in which it was possible to make a will were few. It was still necessary to have the right of entry to the comitia calata or the *jus militiæ*, and moreover to be neither *intestabilis*, nor a declared spendthrift, nor in a state of mental alienation, nor physically incapable of the required formalities, if the Law of intestate succession was not to take effect.² At this period it only regulated the succession of women *sui juris* and of freedmen.³

At first it gave the inheritance to the nearest agnate or agnates, an innovation affording the plebeian *domus*, which had no part in the clan system, a chance to keep their patrimony in the hands of their own kindred, and benefiting those of the *populus* which, at the time when the *gens* was breaking up, had come to regard the *gentiles* as an association of little interest whose members were becoming more and more strange to one another; but very soon custom excluded female agnates unless they were consanguineous.⁴ Failing these, the decemvirs recognized no devolution to the agnates next in degree (*in legitimis hereditatibus successio non est*), but allowed the patrimony to escheat to the *gentiles*.⁵

It has been maintained that the nearest agnate was invested with the hereditary property by a sort of right of reversion, unburdened by debts or *sacra* or by the obligation to make *aditio*, i.e. to declare his acceptance of the inheritance; but the jurisprudence known to us regards him as heir and requires him to accept the inheritance explicitly by *aditio*, though it authorizes him to cede it previously to a third party. After the *aditio* he could only cede the constituents of the property one by one.⁶ As for the *gentiles*, so long as the *gens* survived they recovered the property and disposed of it with sovereign authority; in particular they could assign it in its

---

¹ **CV**, 468; **CLVIII**, 899; cf. **CXXX**, 2, n° 143; **CXLVII**, 2, 875.
² XII T., 5, 9.   ³ XII T., 8, 22; Ulp., 20, 8, 12-13.
⁴ Paul, 4, 8, 30.   ⁵ G., 3, 11; *Col. l. mos.*, 16, 3, 3.
⁶ XII T., 5, 9; Ulp., 26, 1; G., 3, 9, 12; D., 38, 10, 10-pr.—**CXI**, 1, 191

entirety to one of their number who acquired the hereditary title by prescription at the end of one year, and that could benefit the agnates of subsequent degrees when the next of kin did not appear. An argument from analogy derived from Greek Law allowed justification thereby of *usucapio pro herede*.[1] On the few occasions at the end of the republican period when the right of the *gens* was still appealed to, the known *gentiles* seem to have shared the inheritance.[2] In the case of a freedman dying without *heres suus* the patron, the patroness and their descendants took the place both of agnates and of *gentiles*. The division was made *per capita* among the next of kin.[3]

Heredes non necessarii acquired the inheritance either by means of a formal declaration called *cretio*, made in the presence of witnesses within 100 days of the owner's death and requiring capacity to acquire property and to incur obligations, or else by *usucapio pro herede*.[4]

II

TESTAMENTARY PRACTICE

I. IMPORTANCE OF THE WILL. THE CREATIONS OF CUSTOM: WILL "PER ÆS ET LIBRAM"; EXTENSION OF THE "FACTIO TESTAMENTI"

Consciousness of their responsibility to their line and to those who on various grounds lived under their power, the necessity of rectifying an obsolete statute, and the spirit of independence caused heads of families to regard it as a misfortune, almost a disgrace, to die intestate. During his lifetime the *paterfamilias* assigned to each one his place in the *domus*. Failing descendants, he had to choose his heir; if there were descendants, he had to endow them with a sort of posthumous charter, e.g. to exclude the *sui* who were unworthy or doubtful, to release some of them from the disadvantages of appointment in order to compensate them

---

[1] G., 2, 35-37; 3, 85-87.
[2] Cic., *in Verr.*, 1, 45; Suet., *J. Cæs.*, 1; G., 3, 17.—**CXCV**, 2, 884.
[3] Ulp., 27, 1-4.
[4] Varro, *l. c.*, 6, 81; *Fr. Aut.*, 42; T.-G., 360; G., 2, 166; Ulp., 22, 28.—**CXCV** 2, 897.

in other ways. Disinherison served this double purpose, either punitive or beneficent.

The wills in common use did not always serve these ends, so a system was devised to supply their place when they could not be resorted to. The *paterfamilias* mancipated his patrimony for a fictitious price to a friend (*familiæ emptor*) and charged him to transmit the property on his decease to whomsoever he might indicate.[1] Gaius describes this confidant as *in loco heredis*, which means, in spite of the current view, that the mancipation invested him with rights analogous to those of the legal heir. Deprived of its concrete utility, mancipation was adapted to very diverse ends. The *familiæ emptor* who received the property merely to restore it in the long run to those indicated to him by the disposer's desire was in fact a sort of testamentary executor. The mancipation deprived the statutory heirs of the patrimony, and made it possible for the friend chosen to execute the deceased owner's wishes. The fiduciary character of the transfer was revealed by the very formula of this mancipation,[2] which could not have been either forged or adapted to the time when the *familiæ emptor* was no more than a supernumerary or a sixth witness. The danger of the system lay in trusting the operation to the latter's *bona fides* without any guarantee or sanction; but similar situations are found almost everywhere at a certain stage in the history of testation.[3] At Rome this stage of development persisted for some time, but in the sixth century legal practice changed this expedient into a genuine form of testation.

The mancipation became a mere means of insuring publicity, and the *familiæ emptor*, notwithstanding the formula pronounced, became a mere witness. The disposer's declaration, whether oral or written, invested the heir immediately.[4] If written, it could remain secret. The witnesses affixed their seals and their names to the sealed tablets which were then deposited in a temple. After the introduction of this new form of testament the old forms fell into disuse.

Factio testamenti in the active sense, capacity to make a will, was henceforward dependent on the capacity to

---

[1] G., 2, 102, 105.   [2] G., 2, 104.—**XXXVII**, 17, 2.
[3] **CCII**, 46 et seq.; **XVII**, 15, 107 et seq.; **CXI**, 1, 298, 250.
[4] G., 2, 104-105; Ulp., 20, 2, 9; D., 28, 1, 21-pr.—**CCII**, 95; **CXCV**, 2, 885.

LAW OF INHERITANCE AND GIFTS 279

mancipate,[1] although, by way of exception, neither women *sui juris* remaining in their agnate family nor Latin-Junians benefited by it.[2] *Factio testamenti* in the passive sense, capacity to benefit by testamentary dispositions, which was required both on the day when the will was made and at the opening of the succession, was not determined in the same way, because it was the *familiæ emptor* not the beneficiaries who took part in the mancipation.[3] Institution as heirs was not confined to those who could be appointed in the ancient forms of will, but was extended to all who could make valid acquisitions according to the Civil Law: *alieni juris* or *sui juris*, citizens or Latins, aliens possessing *commercium*.[4] The *dedititii* were excluded. Institution of another person's slave was allowed for the benefit of the master, or for his own benefit if he became free before the opening of the succession; and especially institution of a slave to whom the testator, his master, bequeathed freedom (*heres necessarius*) in order that he might bear the disgrace of an insolvent inheritance.[5] All this was dictated by practical considerations;[6] but the Jurists excluded *personæ incertæ*, i.e. those to come in the future, of whom no clear idea could be formed.[7] Posthumous children were at first considered to belong to this class, but in the end they came to be regarded as *heredes sui*.[8] Artificial persons, who had also been considered *incertæ*, were similarly given under the Empire a partial capacity to acquire property in prospect of death.[9]

II. The Institution of an Heir: Contents of the Will

By the institution of one or more heirs, by legacies, testamentary trusts, enfranchisements, nominations of guardians, etc., the will provided for the future not only of descendants and kinsmen, but of a whole clientèle: freedmen, confidants, servants, *alumni*, loyal or aged slaves. It bestowed gifts on favourite friends, and later heaped bounties on the city or village in which the testator had been born or had resided. The record of epigraphy and the special cases cited by the

---

[1] Cic., *in Verr.*, 2, 1, 45; Paul, 5, 25, 6. [2] D., 28, 1, 1; I. J., 2, 19, 4.
[3] G., 1, 115a; Ulp., 20, 14. [4] Ulp., 22, 1, 3, 14, 20.
[5] G., 2, 188-189; Ulp., 22, 7, 1; I. J., 2, 14, 1.
[6] **XLIX**, 1, 328 et seq.; **CLVIII**, 869 et seq [7] G., 2, 238, 242; Ulp., 22-4.
[8] G., 2, 241.—**CLXI**, 371. [9] Ulp., 22, 5-6; C. J., 6, 24, 8.

280 FORMATION OF CLASSICAL LAW

Jurists bear witness to the extreme degree of sociability and the affectionate relations existing between the most widely separated classes.[1] Was it not excess of sentimentality that produced the reaction of the *Lex Voconia* forbidding the institution of women by citizens of the first class ?[2]

But the first object of doctrinal development was the appointment of an heir. Transferring to the new will the conditions and essential effects of the will made before the comitia and most of the rules governing statutory inheritance, the Jurists made these the very foundation of the will.[3] Hence the absolute necessity of an appointment in formal terms: *Titius heres esto*, followed by a similarly formal disinherison of the *sui* who were not appointed.[4] Hence the necessity of assigning the heir the whole of the inheritance (*nemo partim testatus, partim intestatus decedere potest*), and the impossibility of cancelling effects already produced, if the appointment could be affected by a condition (*semel heres, semper heres*).[5] This condition together with the *incertus dies* which was assimilated to it delayed until its fulfilment or failure the effect of the appointment, or the devolution to substitutes, or the opening of the succession to heirs *ab intestato*.[6] A doctrine still undetermined in Cicero's time, but afterwards established in the case of wills by the Sabinians, regarded impossible, immoral or unlawful conditions as if they had not been written, but the judge could in fact annul them on the ground of insanity.[7] Also Q. Mucius Scævola authorized the heir appointed under a negative potestative condition to enter on the inheritance while providing surety;[8] and further, a positive potestative condition was held to have been fulfilled when the appointed heir had done all he could to fulfil it[9]—these being means of carrying out the supposed intention of the deceased.

The appointment of several heirs was common, for far from robbing the *sui* or the statutory heirs, the will was generally a bond between them; moreover, this diminished the risk of dying intestate. Whether the shares were equal or not, each

---
[1] Ulp., 27, 5; T. G., 801-808.—**I**, 13, 5708; **CLX**, 1, 379.
[2] G., 2, 279; Aul. Gel., 17-6; Cic., *de sen.*, 5.
[3] G., 2, 229, 248.—**XXXVIII**, 17, 3 et seq.
[4] G., 2, 116, 117, 229; Ulp., 21, 1.   [5] D., 28, 5, 1-4, 88.
[6] D., 25, 1, 75.—**XLIX**, 1, n° 324; **CCXV**, 542 et seq.
[7] G., 3, 98; D., 35, 1, 3; I. J., 2, 14, 10.—**CIX**, 1, 224 et seq.
[8] D., 35, 1, 101-pr.   [9] D., 38, 7, 4-1, 23.

LAW OF INHERITANCE AND GIFTS

heir appointed had a call to the whole inheritance, and this gave rise to a twofold problem: the division of the inheritance, and the right of increasing shares if one of the heirs appointed made no claim.

The inheritance was regarded as a unity (*as*) divisible by 12 or a multiple of 12 (*dupondius, tripondius,* etc.), and each fraction was called an *uncia*.[1] There was no difficulty if the total of the *unciæ* equalled it; but if not, each share had to be proportionally diminished or increased.[2] When the heirs were appointed without any parts assigned, the *as* was divided equally among them, those appointed in the same phrase being counted as one only. If parts were assigned to some and not to others, the latter shared the residue between them.[3] Even incorrect appointment as heir to a specific thing (*ex certa re*) involved a call to the whole inheritance, according to the rule; and if, in the case of multiple appointments, all were made in this way, the remainder of the inheritance was equally divided, those who thus obtained more than their share retaining this surplus as a legacy *per præceptionem*.[4]

The right of increase (*jus accrescendi*) involved the addition of the defaulter's share, in strict law and proportionally, to those of the heirs who entered on the inheritance.[5] As an exception, it only benefited heirs *conjuncti*, i.e. appointed in the same phrase, or in two different phrases, to the same object.[6] It was both an advantage and a burden, for it involved a proportional liability for the debts. At first the beneficiary was held responsible for nothing more; even the Jurists of the time of the Severi described him as then without burden (*sine onere*); but this was opposed to their own doctrine which burdened him further with the legacies and testamentary trusts with which the testator had burdened the defaulting heir, and thus rendered him *cum onere*.[7]

The desire to multiply bequests and above all the fear of dying intestate suggested the idea of common substitutions, subsidiary appointments, in case the appointed heir should not come to inherit: *si Titius heres non erit, Gaius heres esto*.[8] Subject to the same rules as the appointment of heirs and to no limitation in number, they were dependent for their form

[1] D., 28, 5, 51-2; T., G., 805.
[2] D., 28, 5, 1-4.
[3] D., 28, 5, 11, 35.
[4] C. J., 6, 24, 13.—**XXXV**, 7, 313 et seq.
[5] D., 29, 2, 53-1; 31, 29, 2.
[6] D., 28, 5, 20-2.
[7] Cf. D., 31, 61-1; C. J., 6, 51, 1-3-10.
[8] G., 2, 174-178.

and nature upon the testator: substitutions of several persons for one only, or the reverse; substitutions of heirs or of substitutes reciprocally one to another,[1] in which case acceptance of the substitution was obligatory on those who had already made *aditio*.[2] Often the last person substituted was a slave who, being *ipso facto* enfranchised, guaranteed as *heres necessarius* the fulfilment of the will.[3] Some rectification of details under the Empire completed this jurisprudence: in particular, Severus and Caracalla imposed on the substitutes the charges, legacies or testamentary trusts with which the appointed heir was burdened.[4]

A very widespread practice of the sixth and seventh centuries, to which some formulas quoted by Gaius bear witness,[5] allowed a father appointing his infant children to postpone the effects of the appointment until they reached the age of puberty by naming a substitute in case of a child dying *impubes*. The substitute then received the inheritance directly on the fulfilment of the condition. But from the time of Cicero the *patria potestas* was made to include power of testation on behalf of children under puberty.[6] Under the name of pupillary substitution (*substitutio pupillaris*) the *paterfamilias* was allowed to name an heir to the child even when the latter had not been instituted, and thus to assign two distinct inheritances.[7] Some saw in this two wills joined together;[8] but the father could never make a will on behalf of the child without making his own, and the pupillary substitution always lapsed if the institutions lapsed, though it could be made on separate tablets.[9] The person simultaneously instituted and substituted had to accept or refuse both calls together,[10] and a slave was *heres necessarius* in respect of both inheritances.[11] The child's death or attainment of the age of puberty clearly cancelled the pupillary substitution.

About the same time jurisprudence attempted to make a methodical classification of the grounds of invalidity of wills.

[1] T. G., 802. [2] D., 29, 2, 35-pr.
[3] I. J., 2, 15-pr. For a case in which the substitute shared with the heir first appointed see **CLVIII**, 876, 4. [4] I. J., 2, 15, 2-4.
[5] G., 2, 179; Cic., *de Orat.*, 1, 39; 2, 32; *Brut.*, 52; Quint., *Inst. or.*, 7, 6, 4.
[6] Cic., *de Inv.*, 2, 21.—**CIX**, 1, 222.
[7] G., 2, 182; D., 28, 4, 2-2.—**CXCV**, 2, 875. [8] G., 2, 180; D., 28, 6, 2-4.
[9] G., 2, 181; D., 28, 6, 1-3. [10] But see D., 28, 6, 12.
[11] D., 28, 6, 10-3; cf. C. J., 6, 30-20.—But see **XLIX**, 1, n° 368.

LAW OF INHERITANCE AND GIFTS

They were either *justa*, conformable to Law, or *injusta*, i.e. void through formal defect or lack of capacity in the testator or the appointed heirs. But a will that was *justum* when made might become *irritum*, null, through the testator's change of status, subject to his reinstatement by the *jus postliminii*, though his death in captivity opened the succession retrospectively from the day of his capture.[1] Or it might be *ruptum*, revoked by the making of another will;[2] for it was impossible after making a will to become intestate again, and the material destruction of the first will did not annul it.[3] It might also be *ruptum* by the unexpected appearance of a *suus heres* which shattered the whole arrangement, and the chances of annulment on this ground were increased when posthumous children began to be reckoned among the *heredes sui*, but jurisprudence allowed them to be appointed or disinherited in advance.[4] One after another, between the time of Cicero and Hadrian, all the *heredes sui* who might subsequently appear were placed on the same footing (under the titles of *postumi legitimi, aquiliani, velleiani, quasi velleiani, juliani*) by the edicts and the *Lex Junia Velleia* (780 A.U.C.).[5] Finally, a will was said to be *destitutum* when none of the appointed heirs took the inheritance; failure of the appointment to produce its effects cancelled the will.

III. Nature of the Inheritance: Acceptance, Repudiation, Sanction

Formal acceptance of inheritance by *cretio* was not compulsory unless the testator required it. He decided whether it should be *perfecta*, i.e. required within a prescribed period on pain of disinherison; *imperfecta*, subject to no prescribed period; *continua*, obligatory within 100 days from the opening of the succession; or *vulgaris*, to be made as soon as the heir can make it.[6] If persons *alieni juris* were appointed heirs they made it on the *jussus* of the *paterfamilias* or master.[7] The *cretio* gave the heir his title and constrained him by its rigorous terms not to leave the inheritance long in abeyance or the

---

[1] G., 2, 145.   [2] G., 2, 144, 155; I. J., 2, 17, 7.
[3] G., 2, 151.—**XXXIII**, 7, 91; 8, 109.   [4] See p. 115.
[5] Ulp., 22, 19; I. J., 2, 13, 2.—**CXLVII**, 1, 630.
[6] G., 2, 165-167, 171-173, 177-178; Ulp., 22, 27-34.—**CXCV**, 2, 896; **CLXXIV** 1, 396.   [7] Paul, 3, 4*b*, 13.

various testamentary dispositions unfulfilled. For the sake of these latter, the prætors invited the persons interested to request him to fix a period of deliberation (*spatium deliberandi*) on the expiry of which he would hold the appointed heirs to be *sine cretione* and the statutory heirs to be renunciants.[1] In the absence of *cretio*, acceptance was signified by acting as heir (*gestio pro herede*). Notwithstanding the unsupported opinion of Gaius, mere declaration (*nuda voluntas*) does not seem to have been considered valid until much later, probably under the Lower Empire.[2]

Until the end of the Republic *factio testamenti* in the passive sense involved, together with the right of being inscribed in the will, that of taking under it; but the *Lex Julia Norbana* then made the latter a separate right under the name of *jus capiendi*. Latin-Junians could not take unless they became citizens within 100 days of the devolution in their interest;[3] while the *Lex Julia* and the *Lex Papia Poppœa* (736-762 A.U.C.) forbade unmarried persons to take anything and childless married persons to take more than half, unless they satisfied the requirement of these statutes within the same period.[4]

Death or voluntary renunciation, loss of *factio testamenti*, expiry of the *spatium deliberandi*, or of the period allowed for making *cretio* or acquiring the *jus capiendi* extinguished the heir's appointment and opened the way, in the following order, for common substitution, for intestate succession, perhaps for *usucapio pro herede*, certainly for the claim of the Exchequer after the statutes of escheat had been introduced.[5] Then a rescript of Marcus Aurelius allowed a freedman or a third party to acquire the inheritance, failing heirs, in exchange for an undertaking (*cautio*) to pay the debts and make the enfranchisements, an arrangement which was called *addictio bonorum libertatum servandarum causa*.[6]

Acquisition of the inheritance, *ipso jure* in the case of necessary heirs, by means of *aditio* in the case of voluntary heirs, had the effect of making the heir successor to the deceased's personality and, when there was more than one heir, involved division among them.

The heir was deemed to succeed to the personality of the deceased from the day of his death, and was held responsible

[1] G., 2, 167; D., 29, 2, 69. [2] G., 2, 167, 176; Ulp., 22, 25; Paul, 3, 4b, 11.
[3] G., 2, 2, 52-56, 166, 178. [4] G., 2, 33; Ulp., 17, 4.
[5] G., 2, 150, 286, 286a; Ulp., 15, 6; 28, 7. [6] I. J., 3, 11.

LAW OF INHERITANCE AND GIFTS

for any juridical acts affecting the property which had been performed in the interval; but this theory was afterwards overthrown by Julian, who caused the deceased's personality to survive by a fiction until the acceptance of the inheritance.[1] The result was that the heir acquired the claims simultaneously with the corporeal objects of the inheritance, becoming responsible for the civil debts and for the *sacra*, which were henceforward attached to the patrimony or even to the largest part of it (*major pars*),[2] and paying the legacies, etc. By the merging of the patrimonies he was burdened with all the charges *ultra vires*, i.e. at the expense even of his own estate;[3] but at the end of the Republican period the edict modified the rigour of these logical conclusions by creating three benefits. The first was the right to refuse the inheritance (*jus abstinendi*), granted in favour of *heredes sui* who were below the age of puberty or had not yet taken action as heirs, whereby they avoided liquidation of the inheritance in their name and payment of its creditors out of their own estate, although they kept the *sacra* and the residue left after sale in the deceased's name. The prætor could fix a period within which they must claim this privilege.[4] The second was a separation of estates (*bonorum separatio decretalis*), granted in favour of the enfranchised slave, the *heres necessarius*, which exempted his person and the property acquired by him since enfranchisement from the claims of creditors of the deceased. The third was another separation of estates (*bonorum separatio*), granted in favour of creditors of the deceased against the creditors of an heir suspected of insolvency, a privilege which they could claim within five years provided that they had not recognized the heir as their debtor and that the two patrimonies were physically separate. This amounted to a right of prior claim on the inherited estate; but on the other hand, if we reject the view of Papinian, it deprived them of all recourse against the personal estate of the heir.[5]

The Twelve Tables had enacted: (i.) that debts due or owing should be shared *ipso jure*; (ii.) that, as regards the rest of the inheritance, no one should be bound to remain without his allotted share.[6] They had framed an action for

[1] D., 29, 2, 5-4.—CCLII, 1, 358.
[2] XII T., 5, 9; Cic., *de Leg.*, 2, 8.
[3] D., 29, 2, 8-pr.
[4] Cic., *Philip.*, 2, 16; G., 2, 158-160; Ulp., 22, 24; D., 19, 2, 57-pr.
[5] G., 2, 153-155; D., 42, 6, 1-pr.-18, 11, 55.
[6] XII T., 5, 9.

division (*actio familiæ erciscundæ*) in the form of the *judicis postulatio*, a double or mixed action where all the parties appeared in the same rôle, since its object was to assign to each his share in the inheritance.¹ In the formular system the formula contained an *adjudicatio* giving power to the judge to transfer ownership, and a *condemnatio* giving him power, if necessary, to deprive any heir of property held in excess of his due portion.² Then this formula was combined with that of another action concerning the personal relations between co-heirs while an inheritance remained undivided, viz. the action for the administration of common property; and thus was framed an action *bonæ fidei* which was included in the edict, always under this same title, from the end of the Republican period.³

The rights of the heir were sanctioned by the procedure for claim of inheritance (*petitio hereditatis*), which kept the form of an *actio sacramenti in rem* before the centumvirs until their disappearance but could also be brought, after the sixth century, *per sponsionem*, and later *per formulam petitoriam*, though it is not clear how this concurrence worked in practice.⁴ By means of a *sponsio præjudicialis* the first of these methods of procedure was changed under the Empire into an *actio sacramenti in personam*.⁵ From an early date its object was the actual title of the heir and all that depended on it. At first it was available against all persons denying this title⁶ (what classical Law termed the *possessio juris*), but successive refinements limited its use to two cases: against the possessor (*pro herede*) who claimed to be heir, and against the possessor (*pro possessore*) who relied on no title and was therefore a *mala fide* possessor; these situations being established by means of an *interrogatio in jure*.⁷ With the advent of the formulas it became a discretionary action. Originally the seeming heir was responsible for his acts of administration, and the restitutions which followed were guaranteed by the *prædes litis et vindiciarum* in the *sacramentum* and by the *cautio judicatum solvi* in the formular system.⁸ Under Hadrian a

[1] XII T., 5, 10.—**CLIX**, 1, 78; **CXI**, 2, 511; **XLII**, 2, 7.
[2] G., 4, 42.—**XLII**, 2, 18.
[3] D., 10, 3, 26; Ed.-P., 2, 237.—**XIII**, 28, 273, 401, 649.
[4] Ed.-P., 1, 199.—**XIII**, 29, 9 et seq.
[5] G., 4, 95; Ed.-P., 1, 198.—**CCCII**, 1, 135; **XIII**, 29, 27; **CXI**, 756 et seq.
[6] Cic., *Top.*, 29; D., 5, 3, 18-2.
[7] G., 4, 144; D., 5, 3, 11-pr., 12.—**CXI**, 757. [8] *Fr. vat.*, 92; D., 5, 3, 18-pr

senatusconsultum suppressed *usucapio pro herede*.[1] The *Sc. Juventianum* (A.D. 129) assimilated to possessors those who had fraudulently given up possession, and jurisprudence those who pretended to be possessors. Then this senatusconsultum distinguished between *bona fide* and *mala fide* possessors, and compelled the former to restore their gains, the fruits in being, whereas the latter were further responsible for all that they had spent or neglected to acquire, and were only intitled to the amount by which, on the day of the action, their beneficial or necessary expenditure exceeded these liabilities.[2] The *petitio hereditatis* was finally classed among the actions *bonæ fidei*.[3]

III

THE PRÆTORIAN LAW OF INHERITANCE

I. THE PRÆTORIAN REFORMS

In Rome's seventh century the activity of the prætors was shown in two ways: (i.) in facilitating and confirming the execution of the testators' intention; (ii.) in establishing a new and more extended order of devolution *ab intestato*. A whole new system was created, suitable to the society of the time but at first closely connected with the old one. The explanations of this which have been given from time to time seem unconvincing[4] in view of the obvious necessity of amending the earlier system. Given his means of action, the prætor could hardly have acted otherwise.

As he had no power to abrogate or modify the Civil Law, he conferred possession of inheritances, in specified cases, either by general dispositions of the edict (*bonorum possessiones edictales*) or by decree (*bonorum possessiones decretales*).[5] From this the beneficiary derived three advantages: the position of defendant in the *petitio hereditatis*, the possibility of acquiring by *usucapio pro herede*, and *bona fide* enjoyment, since his possession was founded on a juridical title, with consequent permission to make the fruits his own. But the rights of the heir according to Civil Law were reserved.

[1] G., 2, 57. [2] D., 5, 3, 20-6, 40-1; cf. 4, 7, 1-pr. [3] D., 5, 3, 38, 58.
[4] CCLVI, 622 et seq.; XXXIII, 17, 324; CLVIII, 841, 2. [5] CLVIII, 921, 2.

II. The Prætorian Will and "Bonorum Possessio Secundum Tabulas"

The prætor collaborated with the lawyers in their effort to secure the execution of wills from a more individualistic point of view and with special regard for the intention of the testators: hence the introduction of a simpler form of will, a series of *bonorum possessiones secundum tabulas*. When without either *mancipatio* or *nuncupatio* the testator had merely placed the sealed tablets containing his last wishes before seven witnesses in order that they might attach their seals and signatures, the prætor gave the heir appointed by this act, which was void in Civil Law, a *bonorum possessio* which Antoninus Pius afterwards made available against the statutory heir.[1]

There were also other reforms. If a previous will existed, it became valid again after the erasure or destruction of its successor;[2] and the same was the case with a will that had been *ruptum*, if its maker recovered his previous capacity.[3] The posthumous children neglected by the Civil Law, e.g. the *postumi alieni*,[4] the heir appointed by the wife without *auctoritas tutoris*,[5] the conditional heir until the fulfilment of the condition (provided that he gave a surety)[6] were authorized to claim *bonorum possessio secundum tabulas*.

III. "Bonorum Possessiones ab Intestato"

It was in the sphere of intestate succession that the prætorian system of devolution was developed, confirming, supplementing or even conflicting with the Civil Law.[7] It was not all established at once. Among its various orders Cicero seems to regard only that of the *legitimi* as edictal.[8] But it was completed by the beginning of the Empire and comprised the following orders. First came the *liberi*, i.e. the *heredes sui*, the emancipated children or their descendants by right of succession, and the children given in adoption or their sons since emancipated by the adopter. If all were of the same degree of proximity, division was made *per capita*; if not,

---

[1] G., 2, 120.   [2] G., 2, 151a; D., 28, 6, 1-8.
[3] G., 2, 147-149; Ulp., 23, 6.   [4] D., 37, 11, 3.
[5] G., 2, 118-122.   [6] D., 37, 11, 6.   [7] D., 37, 6, 1-pr.
[8] Cic., *in Verr.*, 2, 1, 44; cf. *pro Cluent.*, 60 (cognates).

LAW OF INHERITANCE AND GIFTS

it was made *per stirpes*. Later on, the perpetual edict of Julian divided the share of their *stirps* in equal portions between the emancipated son and his children still under the power of their grandfather.[1] But in order to guard against the inequitable result of competition between emancipated children who had been able to acquire a patrimony of their own and *heredes sui* who had never acquired anything except for the family patrimony, the edict imposed upon the former the *collatio bonorum*, i.e. the return to the common stock of the property which they would have acquired for the *paterfamilias* if they had remained *alieni juris*.[2] They had to promise the *heredes sui*, under surety, that they would share this property with them whenever their recall to succession by the prætor diminished the others' portion.[3] By analogy another edict required daughters married *sine manu* to return their dowry, for, since they were *heredes suæ*, their dotal property would have been part of the inheritance if they had remained unmarried.[4] The second class was the *legitimi*, i.e. the heirs according to Civil Law in the order in which it called them.[5] Third came the *cognati*, relatives by the female as well as by the male line, without regard for civil relationship. This was a great innovation which substituted natural relatives for the *gentiles* to the sixth and even to the seventh degree in the case of children of second-cousins. The succession devolved upon them according to their degree, the nearest in blood obtaining it unless he was ousted by an heir according to Civil Law. When all were of the same degree division was made *per capita*.[6] Fourth in order was the surviving wife, when both spouses were freeborn; but this *bonorum possessio* concerned only marriages *sine manu*, since in the others the wife was counted among the *liberi*.[7] It was not introduced until after the codification of the edict.

The system presented some peculiarities as regards the succession to freedmen, where it distinguished seven orders: (i.) *bonorum possessio unde liberi*, the patron taking half the inheritance if the children were adopted or the wife was *in manu*; (ii.) *b.p. unde legitimi*, who in this case were the patron, the patroness or their descendants; (iii.) *b.p. unde cognati*; (iv.) *b.p. unde patronus et patrona liberique parentes*

[1] G., 2, 137; Ulp., 28, 8.
[2] Ulp., 28, 4; D., 37, 8, 1, 13.
[3] D., 37, 6, 1-9.
[4] D., 32, 7, 1-pr.; C. J., 6, 20, 4.
[5] D., 38, 7-1, 2-pr.-4.
[6] D., 38, 8, 1-3, 2.
[7] D., 38, 11.

eorum, i.e. the patron's patron and his line; (v.) *b.p. tum que ex familia;* (vi.) *b.p. unde vir et uxor;* (vii.) *b.p. unde cognati patroni,* the patron's cognates.[1]

Besides the double series of *bonorum possessiones*, testamentary and intestate, there was a whole group of others generally common to both kinds of succession and remaining for the most part *decretales*, i.e. granted by decree after investigation: such were that given by the Carbonian Edict to an *impubes* until he attained his majority, if his civil status was disputed; that given to the curator of a lunatic, to the mother of an unborn child, etc.[2]

Bonorum possessio had to be claimed in formal terms from the superior magistrate within 100 days or, in the case of descendants, within one year of the date on which the person called became aware of his right. If it was edictal, it was granted without investigation, subject only to a claim in accordance with the conditions laid down in the edict. The claim could be made by a mandatary, and thus it became possible for the father of an *infans*, the guardian or the curator to make it.[3] After expiry of the prescribed period or on refusal, there was accretion to the benefit of the other claimants or devolution to the next degree.[4]

Originally invalid against *petitio hereditatis*, it was said to be *sine re*.[5] Its only sanction was an interdict *quorum bonorum* (*adipiscendæ possessionis causa*) concerning merely the corporeal objects in the inheritance and granted only against possessors *pro herede* or *pro possessore*. Later, from the time of Hadrian, it was granted against the former even if they had acquired ownership by usucapion, and against both alike when they had fraudulently ceased to possess the property.[6] An interdict *quod legatorum* was added against those who claimed possession as legatees.[7]

At the beginning of the Empire the *bonorum possessor* was deemed to be placed *in loco heredis*, and by means of a fiction all outstanding actions for or against the heir according to Civil Law were granted to him against the deceased's debtors and to the deceased's creditors against him.[8] Similarly,

---

[1] Ulp., 28, 7; *Col. leg. mos.*, 16, 9, 1-2; D., 38, 8, 1-2.
[2] D., 37, 3, 1; 9, 1; 10, 1-pr.
[3] D., 37, 1, 3-8.
[4] D., 37, 1, 3-9, 4, 5.
[5] Ulp., 38, 13.
[6] Cic., *ad Fam.*, 7, 21; G., 4, 144; D., 43, 2, 1-pr.
[7] *Fr. vat.*, 90; Ed.-P., 2, 196.
[8] G., 3, 81; 4, 34; D., 37, 1, 3-1

the effects of certain *bonorum possessiones* were extended, and the prætor provided them with an *exceptio* against the *petitio hereditatis*. They were then said to be *cum re,* and their titular was assimilated to the prætorian owner. A *petitio hereditatis possessoria* in their favour confirmed this evolution at about the end of the first century of our era,[1] and there was a tendency to restrict the cases of *bonorum possessio sine re* to *possessiones decretales*.

IV

THE RESTRICTIONS ON FREEDOM OF TESTATION

I. CHANGED MORAL STANDARDS AND RESTRICTIONS ON FREEDOM OF TESTATION: NEW JURISPRUDENCE TOUCHING DISINHERISON; "BONORUM POSSESSIO CONTRA TABULAS"

With the decline of the Republic, the invasion of cosmopolitanism and the great advances of democracy, moral standards were lowered and the solidarity of the family, in which Cicero saw the very foundation of the State, became gradually relaxed. Each man tended to regard his property as subject to his own caprice and disposed of it despotically. The ancient right of the *heredes sui* and the new right of the *liberi* were both threatened, and the will became an expression of purely personal whims and sentimentalities. Certain conservative institutions marked the reaction against these symptoms of dissolution. Jurisprudence supported by the prestige of the centumvirs, the edict, the Law itself, if they did not save all the old customs, strove by means of various devices to preserve something of their spirit and effects.

About the time when the *Lex Voconia* limited the capacity of women to be appointed heiresses, the centumvirs required that every disinherison of a *filiusfamilias* should be made *nominatim*.[2] The omission of one only, even if he benefited in some other way under the will, even if he died before the opening of the succession, rendered the will essentially void.[3] On the other hand, the omission of a daughter or a grandson

---

[1] D., 5, 5, 1, 2; Ed.-P., 1, 204.
[2] Cic., *de Orat.*, 1, 38, 52; C. J., 6, 28, 4-2.—**CLXXIV**, 88 et seq.
[3] G., 2, 123, 127, 128.

did not invalidate it, but the person omitted came in for a share (*jus accrescendi*) along with the heirs appointed; if the latter were strangers, for a moiety, if they were *heredes sui*, for an aliquot part.¹ Besides this there was the rule that any unexpected appearance of a *heres suus* broke the will already made: a constant menace to the system of testamentary dispositions, though custom, edict or statute gradually diminished its risks. An edict later than Cicero's time² required appointment or disinherison of all the *liberi*, disinherison of male descendants to be made *nominatim*.³ Failing this, provided that the will was otherwise valid and that the person omitted was alive at the testator's death, *bonorum possessio contra tabulas* was offered for one year to all the *liberi* not regularly disinherited,⁴ even the appointed heirs having an interest therein in some cases.⁵ It involved partial cancellation of the will by the exclusion of any strangers appointed heirs and by division among the *liberi*, whether appointed or omitted, according to the rules of *bonorum possessio unde liberi*; but bequests made to the descendants or wife of the testator were maintained, as well as some other dispositions.⁶ The edict made no distinction between *liberi* of different sex, but Antoninus Pius restricted daughters to the *jus accrescendi* granted to *heredes suæ* by the Civil Law.⁷

But the imposition of these more rigid conditions, though troublesome enough for some over-cautious persons, did little to check the errors of individualism. While submitting to them, the *paterfamilias* disposed of his property as he liked. Even when they were appointed heirs, the members of the *domus* found themselves despoiled by the number or size of the legacies. The *Lex Furia* and the *Lex Voconia* gave them very inadequate support;⁸ but more flexible, comprehensive and effective was the idea of the undutiful will, which affected the theory of disinherison and included it within its sphere.

II. The "Querela Inofficiosi Testamenti"; the "Quarta Legitimæ Partis"

The idea of the undutiful will which appears for the first time in the writings of Cicero⁹ rested upon the idea of a pious

¹ G., 2, 124.—**CXCV**, 2, 890. ² D., 28, 2, 8-11.
³ G., 2, 135; I. J., 2, 13, 3. ⁴ G., 2, 135; D., 37, 11, 2-pr., 13-11.
⁵ D., 37, 4, 8-14, 10-1. ⁶ D., 37, 4, 10-5; 5, 1-pr. ⁷ G., 2, 126.
⁸ G., 2, 225, 226; 4, 23; Dion Cass., 48, 33. ⁹ Cic., *in Verr.*, 2, 1, 42.

LAW OF INHERITANCE AND GIFTS

duty towards relatives, whether they were legal relatives or not. What was conventionally called the Law of Nature commanded that they should be given a share in a man's estate, especially at his death when he had no more need of it himself;[1] and this was prompted by a philosophical theory which had already made an impression on Hellenic Law and gave support to the partly reactionary, partly revolutionary schemes of Augustus.

With these ideas were associated more flexible juridical forms. The new jurisprudence applied no longer to *patresfamilias* alone, but to all testators, men and women alike, who violated the *officium pietatis*. The absolutism and prestige of the domestic magistracy were especially affected, since the public magistracy revised its acts and judged whether its decisions were well-founded. We can perceive what unforeseen, what unheard of innovations were comprised in this institution which modern legislators have not taken over, though they have appropriated more or less its complement, the portion natural.

This innovation which was obscure in origin and realized by stages[2] had the following results. At the beginning of the Empire, in consequence of a complaint made in the form of a petition sent to the magistrate or a *denuntiatio* sent to the adversary, the tribunal of centumvirs authorized the statutory heirs to bring a *petitio hereditatis* against the heirs appointed by a formally valid will on the presumption that the testator's violation of natural duty towards his kin could only be explained by insanity.[3] There was no distinction, moreover, between persons omitted and persons formally disinherited. By analogy with this, prætorian successors obtained from the prætors in the second century of our era a *bonorum possessio litis ordinandæ gratia* and, in the procedure thus organized, met the allegation of the will by that of its undutifulness.[4] But the centumvirs, who were presided over by a magistrate, were in a better position to develop so involved a practice, and it was certainly not excluded from the edict of the *prætor hastarius*.[5] The final system of *querela inofficiosi testamenti* is more easily explained by their jurisprudence, followed step by step by the other competent

[1] D., 48, 2, 7-pr.
[2] For the various systems adopted see **XIII**, 3, 755; **XXXV**, 15, 368; **LXVII**, 1, 272.   [3] D., 5, 2, 2.   [4] **XLIII**, 369.   [5] Pliny mi., *Ep.*, 5, 9-5

judicial authorities, than by the creation which has sometimes been conjectured of a doubtful and extraordinary procedure confined to provincials and to prætorian successors;[1] though this does not mean that, when once created, the *querela inofficiosi testamenti* may not have been brought sometimes before a magistrate in the form of a *cognitio extraordinaria*.[2]

After some hesitation, the statutory heirs were classified as follows: descendants, ascendants and, if the heir appointed by will was a *persona turpis*, consanguineous brothers and sisters. The *querela* was open to that one among them who would have been called by Civil Law or by the edict to the intestate succession; if he did not take action, to the one who would have been called next after him.[3] At first the judges decided with sovereign authority whether the omission or disinherison was justifiable or not, and whether the bequests, the *debita portio*, left by the testator to the *querelans* were or were not sufficient; afterwards it was required that the statutory heir should not have received by will in any form whatever one quarter of the amount which he would have received *ab intestato*—the *quarta legitimæ partis*, after the analogy of the *Lex Falcidia*—and that he should not have any means, whether civil or prætorian, of obtaining the equivalent.[4] The death of the statutory heir, his renunciation, or a prescription of 2 years (afterwards of 5) extinguished the right to take action.[5]

In the enthusiasm aroused by its introduction, a *querela* recognized as well-founded was allowed to annul the will and open the intestate succession; but later on partial annulments were often considered sufficient, although they conflicted with the rule *nemo partim testatus, partim intestatus decedere potest*. For example, the *querelans* won his suit against one of the appointed heirs but lost it against another; a brother was faced by two appointed heirs of whom one only was a *persona turpis*.[6] As the *querela* cast a slur on the memory of the deceased, the unsuccessful claimant was deprived on the ground of unworthiness of all bequests made to him under the will.[7]

[1] **XXXIII**, 15, 256.
[2] **XIV**, 2, 105.
[3] Val. Max., 7, 8; D., 5, 2, 1, 5, 15-pr., 24.
[4] Plin. mi., *l.c.*; Paul, 4, 5-5; I. J., 2, 18-6; 3, 1, 14.
[5] Plin. mi., 5, 1-10; D., 5, 2, 6-2, 7, 32.
[6] D., 5, 2 15-2, 24-pr.
[7] D., 5, 2, 8-14

LAW OF INHERITANCE AND GIFTS

V

THE IMPERIAL INNOVATIONS

I. THE REFORMS OF AUGUSTUS AND THE LAWS OF ESCHEAT. THE " JUS LIBERORUM "

The reforms of Augustus in favour of marriage revolutionized the right of testation. Celibacy and childless marriages, which had long been combated by morality and religion or condemned by the censors, had become a menace to the genuine Roman society. The Emperor's preoccupation with this subject led to the *Lex Julia* (736) and the *Lex Papia Poppœa* (762), known by the name of *Leges novœ*, which imposed penalties on celibacy and *orbitas* and rewarded with various privileges those to whom they assigned the *jus patrum* and the *jus liberorum*.[1]

Celibates (*cœlibes*) according to the *Lex Julia*: viz. men of 25 to 60 and women of 20 to 50, unmarried and without children of a previous marriage, were deprived of the *jus capiendi* in respect of all testamentary dispositions in their favour, unless their disqualification ceased within 100 days from the opening of the succession. The *orbi* according to the *Lex Papia*: viz. married persons without a child living or conceived, were deprived of one half of anything bequeathed to them.[2] This legislation did not extend its rigours to the ascendants and descendants who, as far as the third degree, remained subject to the earlier Law (*jus antiquum*),[3] to the cognates, the spouse, the widows of less than two years' and the divorced wives of less than eighteen months' standing, or to persons who had obtained the *jus liberorum* from the Emperor: these latter retaining their normal capacity and receiving the whole of their share in the inheritance.[4] On the other hand the *Sc. Pernicianum* under Tiberius extended these penalties to men and women over 60 and 50 respectively who had not chosen to obey the statutes while there was yet time, and Nero enacted that adopted children should no longer provide exemption.[5]

[1] **XXXV**, 5, 219; **CXCV**, 1, 617; **CXII**, 729 et seq. [2] G., 2, 286, 286a.
[3] Ulp., 18, 1. [4] Ulp., 14, 1; 16, 1; *Fr. vat.*, 216-219.
[5] Tac., *An.*, 15-19; Ulp., 16, 3, 4. For amendments to these statutes under the Empire see Ulp., 13-18.

By *patres* these statutes meant men married or exempted from marriage who had at least one legitimate child living or conceived, or another descendant in the male line.[1] To them were assigned as bonuses (*præmia patrum*): (i.) the *caduca*, objects of dispositions which failed to take effect either for want of the *jus capiendi* withdrawn by the *Leges Novæ* and the *Lex Junia Norbana*, or in consequence of the *Lex Papia Poppæa* which, in the form of the *Lex Julia de vicesima* (760) and with the hope of increasing their number, postponed the right of making *aditio* and the *dies cedens* of legacies until the opening of the will;[2] (ii.) the bequests *in causa caduci*, i.e. those rendered null according to the ancient Law after the making of the will. The *præmia* went to the *patres* without their charges and were acquired *ipso jure* proportionately to their shares in the inheritance, but with the following reservations: heirs who were *patres* had priority even in the case of *caduca* resulting from legacies, while absolute priority was given to him who had a call to inherit by right of accrual.[3] These *præmia* could be declined, and if the *patres* did not accept them they went to the Exchequer. Failure of all the appointed heirs opened the intestate succession.[4]

Under the name of *jus liberorum*, the *Lex Papia Poppæa* and some other statutes organized certain privileges for freeborn persons of either sex who had three children, and for freedmen who had four. For freeborn men the privilege was generally some advancement in public life; for freedmen possessing more than 100,000 HS it was the suppression of all their patron's rights to succeed to them.[5] Freeborn women could make valid wills without *auctoritas tutoris*, escaped the incidence of the *Lex Voconia*, and inherited from their freedmen like male patrons;[6] freedwomen could make wills provided that they appointed their patrons heirs to an aliquot part or, if they had more than 100,000 HS, to a moiety; they had the same right as freeborn women as regards succession to their own freedmen.[7] An imperial rescript often conferred the *jus liberorum* where there were no children, even upon artificial persons.[8]

---

[1] *Fr. vat.*, 195. [2] Ulp., 17, 1; 24, 31; Paul, 4, 6, 1.
[3] Ulp., 18, 3; *Fr. de jure fisci*, 3: T. G., 499. [4] G., 2, 144.
[5] G., 3, 42; I. J., 3, 7, 2.
[6] D. Cass., 56, 10; G., 1, 194; 3, 45-50; Ulp., 29, 6-7.
[7] G., 3, 44, 45, 50, 51.
[8] Suet., *Claud.*, 14; D. Cass., 55, 2; 56, 10; Paul, 4, 9, 9.

II. THE SC. TERTULLIANUM AND ORPHITIANUM

A new premium on fertility was the *Sc. Tertullianum* under Hadrian which called the mother with the *jus liberorum* to the statutory succession to her children after the *liberi*, the patron and the consanguineous brother, and concurrently with the consanguineous sister.[1] By way of reciprocity, the *Sc. Orphitianum* (A.D. 178) called the children to the succession to the mother before anyone else. These senatusconsulta took account only of natural relationship and were prompted by statistical considerations.[2]

There was already an anticipation of the merging of the two parallel rights. Successive rescripts transformed the *bonorum possessiones sine re* into *bonorum possessiones cum re*,[3] and statutes like the *Lex Papia Poppœa* appropriated or made use of the systems framed by the prætor.[4]

The *Leges novæ* did not produce the results that were expected of them. There was no increase in the number of marriages or in the number of children that were brought up. Thanks to the informers, some families were destroyed, and various devices had to be resorted to in the reign of Tiberius to mitigate this evil.[5] The statutes were misapplied, and in order to maintain the old moral standards they adopted the surest means of destroying them.

III. THE "PECULIUM CASTRENSE" AND THE LAW OF INHERITANCE FOR SOLDIERS

If a great part of the Empire's legislation concerning inheritance seemed to be dominated by the *cura morum* of Augustus, another part of it was governed by the emperors' concessions to the army.

The *filiusfamilias*, who was regarded as *paterfamilias* during his lifetime in respect of property acquired through military service, obtained by a concession that was constantly renewed and made permanent under Trajan the right to dispose of such property by will while on service and also, from Hadrian's time, after an honourable discharge (*honesta missio*).[6]

[1] Ulp., 26, 8.   [2] Ulp., 26, 8; I. J., 3, 4.   [3] G., 2, 118-122.
[4] On a *b.p. uti ex legibus* see G., 3, 46-47; I. J., 3, 9, 8.
[5] Tac., *An.*, 3, 25, 28.   [6] Ulp., 20, 10; D., 29, 1, 1-pr.; I. J., 2, 12-pr

As a general rule all soldiers, to the extent of their *factio testamenti* in the active sense, received from Cæsar and the emperors the temporary privilege, made permanent by Trajan,[1] of making wills without observing any rule of civil or prætorian Law. It was only necessary that their last wishes should be proved in some way or other,[2] and they had the same liberty to revoke these dispositions. Similarly most of the fundamental principles were abrogated in their favour, e.g. *nemo partim testatus, partim intestatus decedere potest* and *semel heres, semper heres*. The unexpected appearance of a *heres suus* did not cancel their previous will. Almost all the rules concerning capacity were suspended in their behalf, since their status as soldiers supplied any deficiency. The *querela inofficiosi testamenti* could not be alleged against their wills, nor could any claim be made for the Falcidian portion, the Pegasian portion, or the portion natural.[3] And this act of theirs remained valid even after they had obtained their discharge.[4]

VI

LEGACIES

I. LEGACIES, BURDENS ON THE INHERITANCE. ORIGIN AND UTILITY OF LEGACIES

Legacies or specific bequests took several forms, and the number and diversity of the people that a Roman was bound to remember in his will explain the abundance of the texts. Thus seven books of fragments in the Digest bring us into contact with the most intimate details of Roman life.[5]

At least from the time of Cicero, every legacy had to be inscribed in a will after the appointment of an heir, or in a codicil which might be earlier or later than the will but must be confirmed by it.[6] It is even thought by most people that a legacy was always thus an appendage to or burden on the appointment;[7] but a theory has been propounded that the text of the Twelve Tables: *uti legassit super pecunia tutelave suœ rei, ita jus esto,* should be taken as referring to a legacy

---

[1] D., 29, 1, 1-2.   [2] C. J., 6, 21, 15, 35.   [3] **XLIX**, 1, n° 415.
[4] D., 29, 1, 15-2, 25, 38-1.   [5] D., 30 to 36.
[6] Cic., *de Or.*, 1, 53; Ulp., 24, 1-3, 15; D., 30, 116-pr.; 31, 36.
[7] **CLVIII**, 849 et seq., 936.—**LV**, 58, 1.

made in due form without the appointment of any heir and transferring directly to the legatee the property comprised in the *pecunia*.[1] In support of this theory reference has been made to the passage of Ulpian connecting the legacy *per vindicationem* with the Twelve Tables (though this would be hard to reconcile with the heir's call to the whole inheritance), to the technical meaning of the word *legare*, and to some other texts which, however, are far from conclusive.[2]

II. THE FORMS AND MODALITY OF LEGACIES. THE SC. NERONIANUM

Classical Law recognized four forms of legacy, each with its exclusive and sacrosanct formula: a composite system, obscure in origin, which men sought to reduce to some kind of unity.[3]

The first was the legacy *per damnationem* in which the testator imposed a prestation on the heir: *Heres meus Stichum Titio dari damnas esto,* by means of a *damnatio* whose effects we have described elsewhere, or, in course of time, by means of certain less rigorous formulas. It was the counterpart of the heir's call to the whole inheritance and was regarded as the ideal type of legacy (*jus optimum legati*).[4] Some have sought its origin in the will made before the Comitia, others in a clause of the will *per æs et libram*. Its object might be any thing or group of things, corporeal or incorporeal, even things not yet in being or not belonging to the testator, and any lawful act such as enfranchisement, liberation from debt, etc.[5] The heir was bound to perform the acts required to invest the legatee with the right bequeathed to him. At first the sanction was *manus injectio damnati*, but this was afterwards replaced by an action *ex testamento*, a personal action of strict law with condemnation in double the debt in case of *infitiatio*.[6] The legatees further obtained the benefit of a separation of patrimonies (*bonorum separatio*) analogous to that of the deceased's creditors; a guarantee from the heir to hand over the legacy (*cautio legatorum*), if it was dependent on the fulfilment of some con-

[1] **CXI**, 1, 129; **CXII**, 765. [2] Ulp., 24, 1; D., 33, 4, 9-1; 50, 16, 28-pr.
[3] G., 2, 192; Ulp., 24, 2. [4] G., 2, 201; Ulp., 24, 4, 11
[5] G., 2, 202-204; Paul, 3, 6, 17; Ulp., 24, 25.—**XIII**, 709 et seq.
[6] G., 2, 213, 280; 4, 9.

dition or the expiry of some term; and, later on, an entry on the property (*missio in possessionem antoniana*), if the legacy was not handed over within six months of their claim.[1]

The legacy *per vindicationem : Titio hominem Stichum do, lego*, invested the legatee immediately with the real right bequeathed to him, thereby authorizing him to claim it and contradicting the heir's call to the whole inheritance.[2] Thus the Proculians said that it was acquired merely by declared acceptance; but the Sabinian doctrine which made its acquisition dependent on *aditio* or on the fulfilment of the condition, failing repudiation, carried the day.[3] Its object had to be something owned by the testator both at the moment when he made his will and at his death.[4] The sanction was the action corresponding to the real right bequeathed.[5]

The legacy *sinendi modo*, a variant of the first, imposed an abstention upon the heir: viz. to allow the legatee to take possession of a thing of which the testator or the heir was quiritarian or prætorian owner. Its sanction was an *actio ex testamento* for the bare amount. Interest was payable from the moment when the heir became guilty of *mora*.[6]

The legacy *per præceptionem* or, as we might say, by preception: *Lucius Titius hominem Stichum præcipito*, was at first in reality a *prælegatum*, a legacy charged on the whole inheritance for the benefit of one of the appointed heirs.[7] The object, which must be something included in the inheritance, was assigned to the legatee by means of the *adjudicatio* in the action for division of the estate. But *prælegata* came to be made in other forms, and the Proculians, followed by Hadrian, allowed these legacies to be made to persons other than appointed heirs. Then the bequest, of which the testator was quiritarian or prætorian owner, was claimed from the heir by means of the corresponding real action.[8]

All these legacies were indirectly subject to the same modalities as the appointment of an heir, on which they were dependent, and could be directly affected as follows: (i.) by a

---

[1] Ed.-P., 2, 284; D., 36, 3, 1-15; C. J., 6, 54, 6.
[2] G., 2, 193-194; Ulp., 24, 3; D., 30, 116-pr.   [3] G., 2, 196.
[4] G., 2, 195; D., 7, 1, 12-5.   [5] G., 2, 194; Paul, 3, 6, 17
[6] G., 2, 209, 213, 280; Ulp., 24, 5.
[7] G., 2, 216; Ulp., 24, 6.—**XXXIII**, 15, 26-144.
[8] G., 2, 219 et seq.; C. J., 6, 37, 12.

suspensive condition which, if impossible, unlawful or immoral, was regarded as if it had never been written;[1] if contradictory or *captatoria*, as annulling the legacy;[2] (ii.) by an indefinite suspensive term, which was assimilated to the condition, and even by a definite term, provided that it was not placed after the death of the heir or of the legatee—a very illogical restriction;[3] (iii.) by a *modus*, a condition which did not suspend the vesting of the legacy until after it had been executed.[4] Classical Law annulled the legacy left by way of penalty (*pœnœ nomine*), which was a means of compelling the heir to do something or leave something undone.[5]

Owing to the different effects of the legacies it was essential that the formula belonging to each one should be used exactly; but in order as far as possible to maintain the wishes of the deceased and at the same time to make a move in the direction of unification, the *Sc. Neronianum* (A.D. 64) enacted that any legacy void by reason of a mistake in its formula should be reinstated as if it were a legacy *per damnationem*: e.g. a bequest *per vindicationem* of someone else's property, or a bequest *sinendi modo* of something which belonged neither to the testator nor to the heir. Consequently it came about that the titular of a legacy formally void found himself in a better position than the titular of a valid legacy because of the heavy sanction of the legacy *per damnationem*. Moreover jurisprudence, continuing to advance in the same direction, allowed any legatee who found it advantageous to do so to transform his legacy into a legacy *per damnationem*,[6] and thus the normal type of legacy was made predominant.

The testator was at liberty to revoke the legacy or transfer it. Revocation (*ademptio*) was originally made in formal terms in a new will, but afterwards could be made by codicil,[7] and finally by erasure from the tablets, by subsequent development of a strong antipathy, or by pleading in an *exceptio* the alienation of the thing bequeathed.[8] Transfer (*translatio*) of the same thing to another legatee by will or by

---

[1] D., 25, 7, 13; 33, 1, 4; 35, 1, 7-pr., 67.   [2] D., 30, 64
[3] G., 2, 232; D., 35, 1, 1-2, 79-pr.-1.
[4] D., 30, 54-2; 35, 1, 45.—CCLII, 3¹, 32 et seq.
[5] Ulp., 24, 17; cf. I. J., 2, 20.
[6] G., 2, 197, 212, 220; D., 30, 84-13, 85, 108-2; 31, 76-8.
[7] Ulp., 24, 29.   [8] G., 2, 198; D., 34, 4, 3-11, 5, 22.

a codicil confirmed by the will cancelled the first legacy even if the second was void.¹ Loss of the thing bequeathed, civil or natural death of the legatee, or his acquisition of the thing gratuitously annulled the legacy.²

III. Capacity to Acquire Legacies. Modes of Acquisition

Power to receive legacies was combined in principle with *factio testamenti* in the passive sense, yet it was granted to associations before they were favoured with the latter. Nerva and Hadrian bestowed it on cities, municipalities, boroughs and villages, and Marcus Aurelius gave it to legally authorized *collegia*.³ Moreover, it was possible to make a bequest to a slave without enfranchising him, provided that he was himself bequeathed to a third party *per vindicationem*; otherwise the legacy would be rendered void by confusion of the qualities of heir and legatee at the moment when it produced its effect (*heredi a semetipso legari non potest*).⁴ The body of property distributed among the legatees and that inherited by the heirs were not two distinct bodies in Roman Law as they were in reality.⁵

Legacies were acquired when they were handed over by the heir. In order to guard them against the risks of too late an *aditio* or too long an abstention on the part of the heir, the *dies cedens*, i.e. the day on which the right to the legacy vested in the patrimony of the legatee, was fixed, in all cases where it seemed advantageous, at the death of the testator: e.g. in the case of unconditional legacies or legacies subject to a definite suspensive term.⁶ On the other hand it was postponed until the fulfilment of a suspensive condition or the expiry of an indefinite term.⁷ In the case of the legacy of usufruct, a life-interest whose grounds of forfeiture were multiplied by jurisprudence, and of the bequest made to a slave belonging to the inheritance, in order to allow him to acquire, the *dies cedens* was postponed until the *aditio*. The name of *dies veniens* was given to the day on which the delivery of the legacy came due.

---

[1] D., 44, 7, 17; I. J., 2, 30, 16, 17. [2] Ulp., 24, 30; D., 32, 2, 5-pr.
[3] Ulp., 24, 28; D., 34, 5, 20. [4] Ulp., 24, 22.
[5] D., 30, 17-2, 18, 89 [6] D., 36, 2, 5-2 [7] *Fr. vat.*, 60, 62

LAW OF INHERITANCE AND GIFTS

Failure to take the legacy did not always benefit the heir. When several legatees had the same call to the same object, one acquired in default of another by way of accrual (*jus accrescendi*).[1] In order that this might happen, it was necessary: (i.) that the legacy should be *per vindicationem* or *per præceptionem*, for the rights to debts owing to the deceased were shared *ipso jure* ; (ii.) that the testator should have made no assignation of shares; (iii.) that the bequest of the common object should have been made (*conjunctim*) in a single disposition: *do, lego hominem Stichum Titio et Seio*, not (*disjunctim*) in two: *do, lego hominem Stichum Titio ; do, lego hominem Stichum Seio*.

IV. RESTRICTIONS ON FREEDOM OF BEQUEST. THE " QUARTA FALCIDIA "; THE " LEGES NOVÆ "

The abuse of legacies, which impoverished the appointed heirs at a time when they were generally *heredes sui* or near relations, ruined the families and, by leaving hardly any profit to the heir, multiplied the number of estates fallen into disinherison and the non-fulfilment of testamentary dispositions.

Both jurisprudence and legislation reacted against this state of affairs. The *Lex Furia* (571 A.U.C.) forbade any except cognates to the sixth and seventh degree to receive legacies of more than 1000 asses, under penalty of fourfold damages exacted by *manus injectio pura*.[2] The *Lex Voconia* (585 A.U.C.) prohibited any bequest exceeding in value the amount that would be left to the heir.[3] But this was wasted labour: small legacies increased in number, and the partiary legacy (*partitio legata*) was invented, the bequest of an aliquot part of the inheritance, especially to women.[4] Then jurisprudence imposed upon the legatee the burden of the debts of the inheritance in proportion to the amount of the deceased's patrimony which he had received, and the obligation to make for this purpose stipulations *partis et pro parte* with the heir.[5]

---

[1] G., 2, 199-205, 223; Ulp., 24, 12. In bequests of usufruct accrual took place on the death of one usufructuary for the benefit of the rest: *Fr. vat.*, 77; D., 32, 80. [2] G., 2, 225; 4, 23; *Fr. vat.*, 301. [3] G., 2, 226.
[4] Cic., *pro Cæc.*, 4, 12; *pro Cluent.*, 21; Ulp., 24, 15, 25; D., 30, 26-2; 36, 1, 23-5. [5] D., 34, 7, 1-pr.—**CXI**, 1, 155; **CCXV**, 494.

This reaction against legacies gave rise to the regulation called Catonian because one of the Catos was responsible for its introduction in the seventh century. It was formulated as follows: " Any legacy which would be void if the testator died at the moment of making his will, shall be void at whatever time he may die." It was not left to chance to rectify an act which its author could not legally perform. But the regulation only applied to legacies where the *dies cedens* was identified with the day of the testator's death.[1]

In 714 A.U.C. the *Lex Falcidia* reserved to the heir who accepted succession at least a quarter of the inheritance (*quarta Falcidia*), calculated according to the net assets of the testator at his decease.[2] Legacies whose total exceeded three-quarters of these assets were reduced *ipso jure* to a composition in proportion to their value, excepting the bequest of the dowry made to the wife.[3] The statute belonged to the sphere of Public Law. If he did not renounce it voluntarily, each appointed heir had a right to his quarter and to a surety (*cautio*) furnished by the legatees to guarantee satisfaction of his claim, if there should be ground for it after the delivery of the legacies.[4]

The *Leges novæ* added their grounds of forfeiture: refusal of the *jus capiendi* for the whole amount bequeathed in the case of *cœlibes*, for half of it in the case of *orbi*. Then the *Lex Papia Poppæa* allowed accrual only to co-legatees who were *patres* and only on condition that they were *conjuncti*; but it gave this word a new meaning. The heirs who were *patres* took precedence of the *conjuncti re tantum* (the old *disjuncti*), but themselves yielded place to the legatees *conjuncti re et verbis* (the old *conjuncti*) if the latter were *patres*. Jurisprudence assimilated to them the *conjuncti verbis tantum*, i.e. those called by a single disposition with assignment of shares, who formerly received nothing. In order to multiply the *caduca*, the same statute postponed the *dies cedens* until the opening of the will.[5]

---

[1] D., 34, 7, 3; 30, 41-2, 91-2; I. J., 2, 20, 10, 32.
[2] G., 2, 127; D., 35, 2, 27; I. J., 2, 22, 2, 3.
[3] D., 43, 3, 1-5, 80-1, 81-1-3. For the basis of calculation in bequests of usufruct and of arrearage see D., 43, 3, 68.
[4] D., 35, 2, 46; cf. 1, 4, 78.   [5] Ulp., 17, 1.

LAW OF INHERITANCE AND GIFTS

VII

TESTAMENTARY TRUSTS

I. TESTAMENTARY TRUSTS; THEIR CAUSES; REFORM BY AUGUSTUS. THEIR PROGRESSIVE ASSIMILATION TO LEGACIES

Juridical persons are impelled to transgress the bounds of Law by sentiments that are often worthy of respect or by forming social relations in advance of the statutes or in opposition to them. Testamentary trusts provided a means of advance that was at first unchecked. Cicero shows how they were employed to evade the prohibitions of the *Lex Voconia* concerning women,[1] and that was not their only use.

Lacking the forms of positive Law, the testamentary trust was a request made to an heir, whether statutory or appointed by will, to a legatee, or to a former *fideicommissarius* (all termed fiduciaries) to surrender all or part of the testator's property that is in their possession to a third party, the *fideicommissarius*. It could be made in any terms in a will, in a codicil, by word of mouth, or even by a sufficiently intelligible sign.[2] If only specific items of property were to be surrendered, it was a particular trust, but if it covered the whole inheritance or an aliquot part of it, it was a *fideicommissaria hereditas*.[3] Being mere expressions of individual desire, the trusts had no other guarantee than the *bona fides* of those on whom they were laid. In fact they were dispositions made through intermediate persons on behalf of third parties lacking *factio testamenti*: e.g. aliens, *incertœ personœ*, associations, etc., or of persons deprived by the statutes of the *jus capiendi*, or of others to whom the benefit of the disposition was assured without its burdens or its formalities: e.g. children under the age of puberty, women, lunatics, or mutes who could not make *aditio*.[4]

But Augustus annexed this new domain to the empire of the Law. As moral reformer he charged the consuls to examine whether there was good cause or not for the execution of trusts, and their jurisprudence became constantly more

[1] CIX, 1, 216.   [2] G., 2, 249, 270, 273; Paul, 4, 1, 5; Ulp., 25, 1-4.
[3] I. J., 2, 23, 2; 24, 1.
[4] G., 2, 271, 272, 274-277, 285-289; cf. I. J., 2, 23-pr., 1

306 FORMATION OF CLASSICAL LAW

biassed in favour of execution, so much so that Claudius created two *prætores fideicommissarii*, afterwards reduced to one by Titus. Soon a distinction was drawn between trusts inspired by honourable sentiments and those whose purpose was obviously to evade the statutes in force. The former suggested additional legislation, the latter a system of repression, which subsequent legislation sought to introduce.[1] Thereupon trusts became subject to regulation by Law. They were assimilated to legacies, and although no special form was imposed upon them, they were subjected to most of the rules admitted for the latter as regards modalities, when these had not grown too antiquated,[2] revocation, extinction,[3] acquisition and the *dies cedens*.[4] The *Sc. Pegasianum* applied to them not only the forfeitures of the *cælibes* and the *orbi* imposed by the *Leges novæ*,[5] but also the system of the *Lex Falcidia*, so that we have the Pegasian fourth reserving one-quarter of the inheritance to the trustee, a benefit extended by Antoninus Pius to intestate successors.[6] Some senatusconsulta of Hadrian's reign annulled the trusts assigned to aliens and *personæ incertæ*, so that they lost almost all their original utility. Moreover the Catonian rule was applied to them.[7]

The trust never gave the fideicommissary more than a right of claim against the trustee which he enforced by means of a *cognitio extraordinaria*, first before the consuls and afterwards before the *prætores fideicommissarii*.

In the case of a *fideicommissaria hereditas*, the following dispositions had to be carried out in order to secure the transfer of the hereditary rights from the trustee to the fideicommissary. At first the surrender ordered by the magistrate was accomplished by a sale of the inheritance *nummo uno*, involving transfer of the corporeal objects and stipulations *venditæ hereditatis* which bound both parties to share the debts and claims in common. If the trust was only an aliquot part of the inheritance, stipulations *partis et pro parte* divided liability for the debts between them in proportion to the amount which each received.[8] But this involved the risk of their mutual insolvency, and in order to

---
[1] G., 2, 278; Ulp., 25, 12; I. J., 2, 23, 1; Suet., *Claud.*, 23; Quint., *Inst. or.*, 3, 6.   [2] But see G., 2, 277.
[3] D., 25, 4, 17; 34, 4, 3-11.   [4] D., 36, 2.
[5] G., 2, 285-287; but not the withdrawal of the *jus capiendi* from Latin-Junians: G., 2, 275.   [6] G., 2, 254 et seq.; D., 35, 2, 18-pr
[7] G., 2 285; C. J., 6, 37, 13.   [8] G., 2, 252-254.

LAW OF INHERITANCE AND GIFTS

guard against it the *Sc. Trebellianum* (A.D. 56) placed the fideicommissary, after surrender of the inheritance accomplished by a mere declaration of will, *in loco heredis*, certain actions *utilitatis causa* placing him in immediate contact with the creditors and debtors of the deceased, while the old actions were checked by the *exceptio restitutæ hereditatis* granted to the trustee. Against third parties the fideicommissary was provided with a *fideicommissaria hereditatis petitio*.[1] All this was well enough; but when the trust included the whole of the inheritance, the trustee who had nothing to gain, since he only acquired to surrender to someone else, declined to make *aditio*. That was where the *Sc. Pegasianum* came in, though its operation was not successfully combined with that of the *Sc. Trebellianum*. If the trustee made *aditio* and claimed his fourth, the *stipulationes partis et pro parte* of earlier practice were maintained; if he did not claim it, the sale *nummo uno* was once more resorted to, though some applied the *Sc. Trebellianum* in this case.[2] If the heir did not make *aditio*, the prætor compelled him to do so; but in that case he had to surrender the whole, even if the trust was only partial, and the fideicommissary could not decline to accept the surrender; the *Sc. Trebellianum* once more came into force.

II. "RESTITUTIONES POST MORTEM" AND FAMILY TRUSTS

Under these regulations trusts lost their practical value until, in the second century, new uses of great social importance were discovered for them.[3] Most of the texts have reference to these latter. The *restitutiones post mortem*, trusts whose surrender was postponed until the death of the trustee, who was authorized to enjoy during his life-time the property to which they applied, might involve several trustees in succession, though this was a rare occurrence. Antoninus Pius made this surrender, when a descendant was responsible for it, conditional upon his dying without issue.[4]

Trusts in the interest of the family or the line were prohibitions even *in infinitum* to alienate certain property or allow it to pass out of the family or line. Made in favour of relatives or freedmen, they served as means of maintaining

---

[1] G., 2, 253; D., 4, 5, 5-1; 26, 1, 63-pr., 127-7.
[2] Cf. G., 2, 257; Ulp., 25, 4; Paul, 4, 2, 2; D., 26, 1, 45.
[3] G., 2, 258.—**CXXVII**, 1-5.   [4] G., 2, 277; D., 36, 1, 57-2.

by the perpetuation of common interests either a certain degree of family solidarity or a sort of clientèle.¹

They were prototypes, especially the former, of our fideicommissary substitutions, though less well suited for their purpose, and they exposed subsequent beneficiaries to the risk of the insolvency or caprice of the trustees, against whom lay a simple personal action, though it is true that this was strengthened by a *cautio* or guarantee of surrender imposed by the magistrate and, if that was not given, by an entry on the property (*missio in possessionem rei*) against those who had acquired from the trustee *inter vivos* and *mala fide*.²

SECTION II

GIFTS

I. NATURE AND CHARACTER OF GIFTS

In ancient and classical Law we find no juridical act specially designed to realize a gift: the latter followed from any legal process by which one person with charitable intent enriched another at his own expense. This redistribution of wealth, whether it was due to the transfer of a real right, or to a promise, or to abstention from exercising a right or pressing a legitimate claim, depended on the wishes of the *paterfamilias* alone and had consequences both for society and for the family that were closely akin to those of testamentary dispositions. The gifts might be beneficial where they were made in the interest of members of the family group or of the solidarity which maintained it, and also most harmful when the giver yielded to the promptings of individualism and ceased to have any regard for the order and sound domestic economy on which the prosperity both of the State and of the Roman *domus* depended.

Thus there came a day when the legislator imposed conditions upon them. They were of two kinds: gifts *inter vivos* and gifts in prospect of death, and different conditions were imposed on each kind, since the object of the legislator differed according to the kind of gift with which he had to deal.

[1] D., 80, 114-15; 31, 77-13, 88-6.
[2] D., 31, 24, 67-6, 69-3; 34, 4, 3-4.—**CXXVII**, 11 et seq.

LAW OF INHERITANCE AND GIFTS

II. GIFTS " INTER VIVOS "

As is often the case in primitive rural communities, the suspicious temper of the Romans was inclined to attribute gifts of the first kind to interested motives, to abuse of the father's *potestas* or of the reverence due to him. It was slow to admit that anyone would voluntarily surrender his property gratis. We see tribunes intervening to prevent the organization of *judicia* to take cognizance of gifts, and various statutes imposed restrictions upon them.[1]

The first of these, the *Lex Cincia* (550 A.U.C.), forbade (i.) patrons to receive gifts from their clients, apart from the customary presents, and advocates to take fees;[2] (ii.) all persons except a group of *personæ exceptæ* (cognates, spouses, fiancés, relatives by marriage, wards, etc.) to receive donations exceeding a certain amount which is unknown to us.[3] It was however a *lex imperfecta*, i.e. without direct sanction. Probably it was supplemented by a *condictio* based upon the illegal enrichment of the donee. After the *Lex Æbutia*, the edict granted, so long as the donor was alive and had not made execution, both to him and to any interested person the *exceptio legis Cinciæ* where citizens were concerned and an *exceptio in factum* for Latins and aliens, of whom the statute took no account.[4] These *exceptiones* made the gift altogether void;[5] but there is some doubt whether the *condictio* remained available in all cases after execution.[6]

Augustus vainly sanctioned with a penalty of fourfold damages the prohibitions contained in the first clause of the *Lex Cincia*. Indeed the advocates' fees became the object of a *cognitio extra ordinem*.[7]

When valid, the gift *inter vivos* was irrevocable except on the ground of failure to execute the conditions which might be annexed to it, and excepting also the gift of a patron to his freedman. The donor enjoyed the *beneficium competentiæ*.[8]

The vacillating legislation concerning gifts between husband and wife has been described elsewhere: at first they were

---

[1] **CXI**, 1, 560.   [2] Tac., *An.*, 11, 5; 15, 20.—**CXCV**, 2, 256.
[3] Cic., *de Orat.*, 2, 71; Paul, 5, 11, 6; Ulp., *proem.*, 1; *Fr. vat.*, 298-309.
[4] **CXCV**, 2^2, 587; **CCX**, 42; cf. **CCLVI**, 424.
[5] *Fr. vat.*, 259, 266, 310; Ed.-P., 2, 262; cf. **CXCV**, 2^2, 587; **CLVIII**, 991.
[6] **CLVIII**, 992 et seq.; **CCLVI**, 426.
[7] Tac., *An.*, 13, 42; D., 50, 13, 1, 12-13.—**XL**, 1, 120.
[8] D., 24, 1, 5-8; 39, 5, 1-pr

absolutely unrestricted, even by provision of the *Lex Cincia;* then they were forbidden, with a few unimportant exceptions; finally they were allowed in a form which assimilated them to gifts in prospect of death.

III. GIFTS IN PROSPECT OF DEATH

The gift in prospect of death was conditional upon the survivorship of the donee or of his descendants, and sometimes upon the death of the donor in such and such prescribed circumstances. It was therefore always postponed until the latter's death and revocable in the absence of a clause to the contrary.[1] Ignored by the *Lex Cincia* and always permissible between husband and wife, they were assimilated to legacies under the name of *capiones mortis causa* both as regards the capacity of the beneficiaries and the restrictions of the Voconian and Falcidian Laws and the *Leges novæ*, although they were not made by will and had an autonomous scope and existence.[2] They were accomplished either by means of an immediate transfer of ownership, which was revocable if the condition remained unfulfilled: a mancipation with which was combined a fiduciary agreement, *in jure cessio*, or *traditio ;* or else by means of a stipulation in prospect of death.[3] The survivorship of the donor cancelled them and consequently annulled the acts under suspensive condition,[4] giving rise, after the disappearance of the fiduciary agreement, to a *condictio sine causa* against the donee, which was called by the compilers of the Digest *condictio ex pœnitentia*, if the transfer of ownership had already been made.[5]

[1] D., 39, 6, 13-1, 32.
[2] G., 2, 224-227; D., 39, 6, 35-pr., 37-pr.; C. J., 8, 56, 2-2.
[3] D., 39, 6, 2; 42-pr.   [4] D., 39, 6, 2, 14, 35-4.
[5] D., 39, 6, 18-1.—**XXXIII**, 12, 171; 13, 219; **XIII**, 37, 169-192.

BOOK II

THE LAW OF THE LOWER EMPIRE AND
THE REFORMS OF JUSTINIAN

CHAPTER I
THE STATE AND THE INDIVIDUAL

I. Nationality and the Status of Persons

THE rules concerning the acquisition and loss of Roman nationality were never systematically modified. The ancient jurisprudence was maintained in combination with the constitution of 212.¹ The suppression of the Comitia and the progressive assimilation of the cities of the Empire as regards their political rights and municipal administrations had abolished all inequality between their members.

Moreover, *civis* becoming synonymous with *municeps* henceforward served more often to indicate the relations of an individual with his *origo* than with the State, which had become an absolute unity inclined to treat all its subjects on the same footing.²

A distinction was always maintained between citizens, Latins and aliens,³ but these old categories lost their practical importance. From the aliens—newcomers or soldiers in the service of the Empire or disreputable freedmen condemned to loss of citizenship—the citizens, being subject to the same burdens, were no longer distinguished by the exercise of rights or prerogatives that had now disappeared. Insensibly the old point of view was changed, and the distinction was now drawn between the barbarians, whether subject or hostile, on the one hand and the Roman world, identified with the whole body of civilized peoples, on the other.⁴ The only Latins who still survived were the Latin-Junians, and they seem to have been very few in number, for when Justinian abolished them at the same time as the *dedititii*, he noted that for a long time none of the latter had existed and even the name of the former had been rarely used. The title of *civis* was of so little value apart from its meaning of free man that this Emperor bestowed

---

¹ See p. 52 et seq.   ² **CXXV**, 164-170.
³ **XXV**, 16, 474.   ⁴ **CCXXVIII**, 6², 224, 331.

it upon all freedmen, whatever might be their moral worth or the carelessness with which they had been enfranchised. Not only did he abrogate almost all the statutes restricting the freedom to enfranchise or the political effects of enfranchisement but, under the influence of the new doctrines, he gave additional facilities for obtaining it, and this was the only important innovation concerning the modes of acquiring Roman citizenship, a subject to which, apart from these dispositions, the *Institutes* did not devote a single title.[1]

Classical Law had conceived the rights of a citizen to be derived from three sources in the following order of importance: freedom, citizenship and family. This theory survived, and the juridical personality of the Roman remained liable to three corresponding forfeitures; but in practice, if some penalties imposed by the Law of Nations or the Civil Law still involved loss of liberty, loss of citizenship (*capitis deminutio media*) was less often incurred. Roman nationality had finally been extended to all the peoples with whom it was possible to have recognized legal relations. There was no longer any State with which Rome could deal on equal terms, and to go over to the barbarians was not considered equivalent to a change of nationality. *Deminutio capitis media* hardly ever occurred except as a result of sentences which made their victims *peregrini sine certa civitate*, a penal forfeiture which left the sentenced person still a Roman subject. The *minima* became more unreal every day.

Relations between the State and the individual became ever more direct. The various situations in which the juridical person found himself affected him alone, and there was no more need to break or form any bond with a jealous and exclusive family group. Being no longer the foundation of the Republic, the families ceased to interpose between the individual and the State; but while enfranchising him from these bonds, the State made him its own slave instead, disposing of him without intermediary and assigning him the place best suited to its own ends.

On the other hand the effects of individual disgrace, called generically *infamia*, had been made more severe and their grounds had been multiplied: criminal condemnations, violations of statutes touching the regulation of morals,

[1] I. J., 1, 5, 3; C. J., 7, 5, 1-pr.; 6, 1-pr.

heresy and apostasy were added to the old grounds or took their place.¹ The *turpes personæ* were always penalized with some civil incapacities.²

II. THE STATE AND THE SOCIAL ORDERS. THE " COLLEGIA " AND THE " COLONATUS "

Under the Lower Empire society was in fact arranged in a hierarchy of orders determined by the sovereign authority of the State to suit its own purposes.

After Augustus the nobility (*nobilitas*), men who had held public office, tended to become a sort of caste. They were recruited by *adlectio* to the Senate and by birth as far as the third generation; they were required to possess a high property qualification and to maintain a certain standard of exclusiveness in marriage and in society, and they were given certain privileges of jurisdiction and in the choice of penalties. Being alone admitted to the high senatorial offices, they formed the Senatorial Order (*ordo senatorius*), to whose members Marcus Aurelius reserved the title of *clarissimi*, and they were distinguished both from the Equestrian Order, which formed a lower class in the same scheme, and from the plebs.³ But in the fourth century the system was changed. The Senatorial Order with its hierarchy of *illustres*, *spectabiles* and *clarissimi* was recruited in three ways: by birth without restriction as to degree, by the tenure of public offices giving a title to nobility, and by *adlectio* or grant of *codicilli clarissimatus*, which were lavishly bestowed first on the Equestrian Order (which ceased to exist) and then, under various pretexts, on the high provincial bourgeoisie who were at first generally exempted from, and finally excluded from, the actual discharge of senatorial duties.⁴ There was no longer a property qualification for senators. After the disappearance of the quæstorship, the expensive prætorship was the only magistracy imposed upon them. Excluded *de jure*, afterwards *de facto*, from the army, with little taste for administrative offices that were brought into discredit by the vast number of parvenus, burdened by taxes and by the *munera* of their

---

¹ *Col. leg. mos.*, 9, 2-2; C. Th., 16, 10, 21; D., 3, 1, 1-5; 2, 11-3; 37, 15, 5-1; C. J., 1, 1-1; 7, 3.   ² D., 22, 5, 3-5; 26, 2, 17-1.
³ **CCXXXVIII**, 6², 56, 63, 88; **CCXCVIII**, 459.
⁴ **CCXCVIII**, 575; **CXXV**, 125-133; **XII**, 52, 24, 37, 41-70

rank—though they were often very rich—sharing interests in common for which they sometimes had an authorized representative, the *defensor senatus*, this nobility of the Empire, while lacking any civil privileges, formed a class of their own, inadequately defined, it is true, and still more inadequately utilized, but yet clearly distinguished within the State and destined to be given by events both in their interest and opposed to it a quasi-seigneurial position as protectors of all who were oppressed by the official socialism.[1]

In the class immediately below them this officialism played the tyrant in various ways in the provinces, in the cities and in the country: in the cities by mastering and making use of a syndicalism that was harshly forced into conformity with the State system; in the country by scientifically regulating and gradually extending throughout the provinces a very old oriental institution to which the system of *coloni* was henceforward assimilated.

When the State began, in the fourth century, to lose its military and financial power and to act irregularly and despotically, individuals sought to find in more closely knit societies a protection which it no longer gave them or a means of defence against its caprices. Hence a considerable number of associations had been formed. But the power of the State, though inadequate in so many respects, was in others excessive. It conceived itself to be an absolute Providence, responsible for the present and future welfare of all the Empire's subjects. Desiring to do everything and able to do so little, it conceived the idea of setting apart for each public service, each economic need, a special staff of tax-payers devoted to this *functio* alone and exempted from all others; and it was enabled to do this in the towns by means of the guild system which had been established there under the guarantee of the Law.

In the fourth century the population of almost every town, with the exception of the *ima plebs*, was divided into various *collegia*, each devoted to a special duty (*munus*), to a municipal, provincial or general *functio*, either administrative or economic.[2] The Law of the period required that every man who was not a proletary should be attached to a *collegium*, and this

[1] Cf. **XLVII**, 2.
[2] C. Th., 13, 5, 33, 34; 14, 15, 2; C. J., 10, 52, 1 to 7, 11; 64, 1.—**CXXV**, 145-158.

THE STATE AND THE INDIVIDUAL 317

subordination was termed *obsequium, obnoxietas*.[1] Those who had at first escaped it (*otiosi, vacantes*) very soon became few in number. These administrative or economic guilds, *collegia* of old or recent establishment, whose activities were determined by some need of the time, became the slaves of the State, working henceforward under its control and generally for its immediate advantage.[2]

There were also associations which had taken a similar form after the organization of the urban populations in guilds, and the statutes which compelled all their members to perform a common duty and submit to a common rule had united them in *corpora, cœtus* or *consortia*. Such for example was the *consortium curialium* comprising those of the old *municipes* who had not been absorbed in the *collegia* and constituting the guild responsible for municipal burdens and honours, within which the decurions (*ordo decurionum*) formed a kind of separate nucleus.[3] According to such a conception of society, the existence of the State depended entirely on the continuous discharge of their duties by these secondary associations. Therefore it took care to secure their perpetuity and maintain their organization, perfecting and strengthening it when necessary, or compelling fugitive members to return to their servitude. Restrictions on personal freedom and on freedom to dispose of property were imposed successively on the *collegiati* and the *curiales*: a veritable code of regulations which, in addition to the college code (*lex collegii*) and the Common Law, affected their civil capacity and finally devoted their persons and property to the discharge of the duty for which each member individually and the association as a whole were jointly responsible.[4] Their personal freedom was restricted by the obligation to reside in the same place under penalty of being brought back by force and having their property confiscated, by the duty of devoting themselves personally to the *munus*, and by the prohibition against adopting any profession that could divert them from the *obsequium collegii* or *patriæ*, e.g. that of military or civil service, of religion or philosophy, of any rural pursuit, etc.— very serious, often insurmountable, obstacles to joining the

---

[1] C. Th., 7, 21, 3; 15, 7, 4.
[2] C. Th., 12, 1, 37, 81, 149, 162; 15, 5, 3; 7, 4. *Nov. Valent.* iii, 15.
[3] C. Th., 12, 1 (the whole); C. J., 10, 34, 1.—**CXXV**, 178; 185.
[4] **CXXV**, 196-198.

ranks of the imperial nobility, the priesthood or the Emperor's household.[1] Their freedom to dispose of property was restricted by imposing pecuniary or collegial burdens on property given to or inherited from *collegiati* or *curiales* outside the guild, by forbidding or at least restricting, under conditions which varied from time to time, the alienation of immoveables or slaves, by assigning to the *collegium* or *consortium* the vacant inheritances of its members and, later, the fourth part of any patrimony passing out of their possession in any way whatever, etc.[2] More or less rapidly the right of inheritance was established or accepted for all *collegia* after the first half of the fourth century,[3] so that not only the men but their property as well was devoted to the function of the guild (*obnoxia collegio, functioni*) under the direction of and for the safety of the State.

In the country districts the State Socialism took as its foundation not the guild but the estate, the *villa*, regarded as an economic unity. But the estate, which was often very large, was represented juridically by its owner (*dominus, possessor*). Certain *functiones* were annexed to it for which the owner, like the *collegium* in the towns, was held responsible. On his lands a numerous population (*plebs, populus plebeius*) of farmers, artisans and tradesmen had long been established.[4] The first of these had to pay the land tax and the *annona* on the holdings which they cultivated by agreement or usage, and all had to pay the poll-tax (*capitatio plebeia*) which was levied upon everyone who did not possess immoveables. Little by little the owner came to be regarded by the Exchequer as debtor for the whole, not only of the land tax but also of the *capitatio plebeia* ; and this involved giving him a relative measure of authority over all the dwellers on his lands.[5] The element of public right which the State thus introduced into the existing agricultural system produced in the country districts a quasi-manorial system parallel to that of the city guilds, which continued to develop until it conflicted with and limited the rights of the central authority.

[1] C. Th., 12, 1, 10, 11, 13, 40, 44, 87, 113; C. J., 10, 31, 51.—**CXXV**, 180-185.
[2] C. Th., 12, 1, 108, 123; 3, 1; 4, 1; 13, 5, 3, 20; *Nov.* 38, 2; 86, 1.—**CXXV**, 198-204.
[3] C. Th., 13, 5, 1, 14, 19, 35; 14, 2, 39; 3, 8; C. J., 11, 2, 1.—**CXXV**, 184-189.
[4] *Santa Melania Giuniore senatrix romana*, Rome, 1905: *Vita*, 21.
[5] **CXXV**, 380.

THE STATE AND THE INDIVIDUAL

The normal exploitation of a somewhat extensive estate involved a division of the arable land into two parts: a smaller part worked by the owner by means of slave-labour, and a larger part divided into holdings on which peasant families of various conditions had been settled.[1] Egypt and the other Hellenistic kingdoms had recognized free farmers who were nevertheless attached in perpetuity to the royal domains and whose condition was not changed when these lands were alienated to towns or individuals.[2] Under the Empire many sub-tenants were in fact bound to the soil: slave families attached to the holding by the wishes of their master and inscribed in the census among the instruments of exploitation; freedmen bound by the *obsequium* due to their patron and the obligation of performing *operæ*; barbarians assigned to the *possessores* by the government in the interest of cultivation and made subject to them in the interest of public order; free families established on their holdings by agreement or tacit acceptance of the rules of the estate, *lex fundi*, *consuetudo prædii*, but little disposed to break away from a sure means of livelihood to seek a doubtful fortune elsewhere.[3] The bond between the man and the soil, though varying in nature—sometimes juridical, sometimes moral—was a very strong one, but it was never permanent. In the fourth century it became so; first in particular districts, then by a gradual extension in all alike.[4] The tax was collected with difficulty and the provinces were largely given up to uncultivated land, *ager desertus*. In order to guarantee the income of the Exchequer and a sufficient production to meet the needs of the Empire, the cultivators (*coloni*) were hereditarily pledged to the service of the soil (*functionibus ruralibus*) and, just as the *collegiati* were called *membra civitatis, subjecti collegio*, they were described as *membra* or *servi terræ, subjecti functioni tributariæ!*[5] This attachment to the soil was officially signified by inscribing the free *colonus*, like the servile *colonus*, upon the registers of the census among the list of taxable items belonging to the estate;[6] and this explains the terms *censitus, censibus adscriptus* or *insertus, adscripticius* by which

---

[1] **CLIV**, 1-145. [2] **XXIII**, 1, 295-300, 424; **XIX**, 1901, 8-39.
[3] C. J., 11, 48, 5; 23, 2.—**CLIV**; **CXLVI**, 293 et seq.; cf. **CLXIX**.
[4] C. J., 11, 48, 23; 50, 2; 53, 1; C. Th., 10, 20, 100.
[5] C. Th., 11, 1, 26; C. J., 11, 47, 4.
[6] C. J., 9, 49, 7; *Nov.*, 123, 17.

he was described.[1] At first his civil capacity did not seem to be otherwise changed;[2] but an ever more perfect adaptation of the man to the *functio* gave him at last a special status, the condition called *colonatus*, which was devised in the interest of the State and bound the *colonus* to the *possessor* as firmly as the *collegiatus* was bound to the *collegium*.[3]

The consequences were the same in both cases. A constitution of 332 shows us the system established and already old in some provinces.[4] No statute created it; it followed from the adaptation of earlier systems to the needs of the time; but various statutes gave it precision and gradually extended it. A man might be a *colonus* by birth (*originalis*), and successive dispositions were made to prevent marriage with a woman outside the estate from diminishing the number of recruits;[5] or he might become a *colonus*, either as a result of the allotment of *vacantes* or captives by the State to owners (*possessores*) who were unprovided,[6] or by agreements of various kinds, for which Justinian required a written instrument and a public declaration inserted *apud acta*,[7] or finally by the prescription of 30 years.[8] The *colonus* could not leave his holding: wherever he went, the owner could bring him back by force;[9] he could not follow any profession which diverted him from his *functio*, except a small local trade and the development of his own land, which was only another aspect of the same thing;[10] he could alienate nothing without the owner's authority, neither the fruits nor anything else with which his holding was stocked.[11] His vacant succession escheated to the owner, as that of the *collegiatus* did to the *collegium*.[12] On the other hand no disposition made by the owner *inter vivos* or in prospect of death could deprive him of his holding. He and his direct descendants possessed it and were possessed by it in perpetuity, and the rent payable by them could never be reduced or increased.[13] However,

---

[1] C. Th., 7, 13, 6; C. J., 11, 48, 18, 21, 22; 52, 2.
[2] C. Th., 5, 4, 3; C. J., 11, 48, 23; 52, 1; *Nov. Val.* iii, 30, 5.—Salvianus, *de Gub. Dei*, 5, 9, 45.
[3] C. Th., 5, 10, 1; 11, 1; C. J., 11, 48, 12-2.   [4] C. Th., 5, 9, 1-pr.
[5] C. Th., 5, 10, 3; C. J., 3, 36, 11; 7, 24, 1; *Nov.* 23, 17; 54, pr.-1; 162, 3.
[6] C. Th., 5, 4, 3; 14, 18, 1.   [7] C. J., 11, 47, 23-1.
[8] C. J., 11, 48, 19, 22, 23-1.
[9] C. J., 11, 48, 7, 15; 50, 2; 51, 1; 53, 1; C. Th., 5, 9, 1, 2.
[10] C. Th., 12, 1, 33; 16, 5, 54; C. J., 11, 48, 8, 1; *Nov.* 128, 14.
[11] C. Th., 5, 11, 1; C. J., 4, 65, 5; 11, 50, 2.   [12] C. J., 1, 3, 20.
[13] C. Th., 5, 10, 1, 2-4; C. J., 11, 48, 2, 7, 22, 23; but see C. J., 11, 48, 13.

THE STATE AND THE INDIVIDUAL

some oriental statutes allowed a man to escape from this condition by entering the priesthood or one of the religious orders with the consent of the master of the estate, and, until Justinian's time, the extinctive prescription of 30 or 40 years brought release from it.[1] When the Roman administration disappeared in the West and the condition of free and servile *adscripticii* tended to become the same, it is possible that enfranchisement also was allowed (*manumissio coloni*).[2] Some later statutes also attached to the soil the slaves who had been assigned to a holding.[3] The artisans and tradesmen of the estate, for whose payment of *capitatio* the owner was responsible and whose work was essential to the life of the *coloni*, were like them *adscripti* and subject to the same conditions of servitude.[4]

Over this plebs the great owner acquired a disciplinary authority—rights of arrest and corporal punishment, of supervision to insure fulfilment of the *functio*[5]—a kind of governmental power and, in the independent estates (*saltus* and *agri excepti*), a jurisdiction of which little is known.[6]

The illegal practice of *patrocinia* was superimposed upon or insinuated into this legal organization. The great owner (*possessor, potens, potentior*) was impelled by his own interest and that of his plebeians to react against the exactions of the State and the excesses of its soldiery or agents. If his own power or wealth was insufficient for this purpose, he and his *plebes* sometimes appealed for help to a more powerful owner.[7] Moreover, the surviving small owners who were similarly attached to the soil of their estates, at least in some districts, also placed themselves under the protection of these *potentes*. Thus the way was prepared for a new system of social organization, and it is impossible to say whether its development was delayed or still further hastened by the invasions. The ancient City had become a single imperial State; the single imperial State was broken up into a number of guilds and manors.

[1] C. Th., 5, 12, 19, 2; C. J., 1, 3, 16; 36-pr. Cf. *Nov. Val.* iii, 18, 8.
[2] Sid. Apoll., *Epist.*, V, 19.   [3] C. Th., 7, 1, 3; C. J., 11, 48, 1.
[4] CXXV, 380.   [5] C. Th., 5, 9, 1.   [6] CCXXXVIII, 10, 310.
[7] CXXV, 384 et seq ; CCXXXIX, 2, 28-76; XXVIII, 1, 41; XLIV, 2, 225-35.

CHAPTER II

JUSTICE AND PROCEDURE

I. JUDICIAL ORGANIZATION

FROM before the time of Diocletian and Maximian everything testifies to the disappearance of the formular system and of the old distinction between *jus* and *judicium*.[1] The conception of an authority from whose supervision no private interests should be exempt precipitated the reform of administrative procedure which had already begun to loom in the distance. Emanating from a sovereign who now monopolized the rôle of judge and peacemaker, justice was administered solely by his agents and their courts.

The judicial hierarchy was analogous to that of the imperial officials. At the top was the emperor and, in each prefecture, the prætorian prefect usually judging *vice principis*. The *cognitiones cæsarianæ* or proceedings by rescript increased in number for the same sort of reasons and with the same sort of disadvantages as our ancient appeals to the Council.[2] At Rome the special jurisdictions of the Præfectus Urbi, the Præfectus Annonæ and the Præfectus Vigilum were given a wider scope; and the degrees of this hierarchy were represented in the dioceses by the Vicarius, in the provinces by the governor (*præses* or *rector*) who, since the multiplication of these districts and the decrease in their area, had become the ordinary judge, so much so that *judex* was now his official and regular title. After the year 294 it was only exceptionally and in minor suits that the *præses* delegated his jurisdiction to the *judices pedanei*.[3] But in principle any judge could invest subordinate officials with authority to conduct inquiries, or even appoint a special delegate (*judex datus*) to take charge of a whole case.[4] The jurisdiction of the municipal magistrates was almost abolished, and that after-

---

[1] C. J., 3, 3, 2.—**XXXIII**, 7, 103 et seq.; **CXI**, 142 et seq.; **XIV**, 1923, 187 et seq.
[2] **CXVI**, 444; **XIII**, 23, 110; **LII**.   [3] C. J., 3, 3, 2.   [4] **LXXXII**.

wards assigned to the *defensores civitatum* varied in the fifth and sixth centuries from 50 to 500 *solidi*.[1] Constantine allowed a sort of jurisdiction to the bishops by making their arbitrament final and authorizing any litigant to bring his suit before the episcopal tribunal (*audientia episcopi*). This right was afterwards annulled—in the East in 398, in the West in 406—but Valentinian III allowed appeal from their sentences to the local judge, whose approval gave them finality; and then Majorian allowed a suit to be brought before the bishop in virtue of a mere agreement.[2]

II. GENERAL CHARACTER OF ADMINISTRATIVE PROCEDURE

Procedure seems at first sight to have been relieved of what remained of the old formal protections which were unnecessary now that the good will of the judicial administration was deemed the litigant's sole and sufficient guarantee. To have an action tended to become no more than the power to call upon public authority to secure the triumph of right. But the cases in which this was permitted remained few in number, and language retained the distinction between actions and kinds of actions. Until 342, when a constitution abolished the need of any kind of formula in any juridical act, and perhaps later still, the ancient formulas might serve as means whereby the judicial officials instructed the *judices dati* concerning their office and their duties;[3] and until 428 the plaintiff had to announce (*editio actionis*) and request from the judge (*impetratio actionis*) the action which he intended to bring.[4] As a result of statutes of 424 in the East and 449 in the West this right was extinguished, save in exceptional circumstances, in all the actions that used to be perpetual by failure to exercise it within thirty years.[5]

In the schools of the Orient a work of synthesis, which was destined to have important results in the legislation of Justinian, arrived at a classification of actions as general and particular.[6] The first were the forms of procedure adapted

[1] **CXXV**, 258-261, 293, 296, 301-304.
[2] *Const. Sirm.* (331), 1; C. Th., 16, 2, 47-1; C. J., 1, 4, 7, 8. Cf. *Nov. Val.* iii, 34.—**XIII**, 1898, 136-139.
[3] C. J., 2, 57, 1; cf. **XXV**, 28, 333; 34, 100; **XXXIII**, 15, 388; **XIV**, 1923, 189; **CX**, 142.
[4] *Cons. vet. cuj. jur.* (295): T. G., 627; C. J., 2, 57, 2; *Nov. Val.* iii, 35.
[5] C. J., 7, 39, 3; *Nov.* 111; I. J., 4, 12, pr.
[6] D., 12, 1, 9-pr.-3; 13, 5, 1, 6; I.J., 4, 6-28.—**CLVIII**, 1133, 2; **CI**, 200-210.

to the more or less numerous cases in which the form remained the same while the content of the action varied. It is clear that these procedures excluded what one might call the abstract action and required in every suit an announcement of the ground on which action was being taken.[1] They were empty forms ready to receive the particular concrete suits of the litigants, which became their content; with the result that they took the nature (*natura actionis*) of the particular case which they served to bring into court.[2] It was a first step in the direction of the modern doctrine that a man has an action whenever he has a legitimate interest to protect; but of this doctrine nothing was yet known in the West.

Certainly there was no longer any distinction between actions arising out of the Civil Law and those granted by the edict; but even in the Law of Justinian we still hear of *exceptiones*: peremptory, i.e. allegeable at any period in the suit, or dilatory, allegeable only at the beginning. These, however, were no more than counterclaims or means of defence derived from contravention of the rules of procedure.[3] Gradually, between the fourth and the sixth century, the interdicts were transformed into actions, the situations which used to give rise to them in the edict being now sanctioned by the ordinary means of procedure.[4]

All formality disappeared from procedure, and there were no longer public trials. The suits were prepared in writing in the courts where, in principle, only the litigants were admitted.[5] The considerable costs were borne by the losing party; and this, together with the penalties for perjury and the retention in certain actions of the condemnation in double the debt, took the place of the old checks on vexatious litigation.[6] But this administration of justice was slow and complicated and burdened by a multiplicity of regulations that were ever increasing in number.

III. THE SUIT. MODES OF EXECUTION. WAYS OF RECOURSE

The *in jus vocatio* was succeeded by a semi-official summons (*denuntiatio litis*) which replaced the *editio actionis* and in-

---

[1] LXXXVIII, 1, 115-124; 2, 446; XLVI,, 1, 439-464.
[2] XXIV, 17, 84-95; XLVIII, 1, 607-641.—Cf. XIV, 1923, 190, 1.
[3] I. J., 4, 13, 14.—Cf. C. J., 3, 10, 1; 4, 30, 14.   [4] I. J., 4, 15, 8; C. J., 8, 1.
[5] CXII, 887 et seq.   [6] I. J., 4, 16; C. J., 3, 13, 6.

JUSTICE AND PROCEDURE

formed the opposite party of the kind of action which it was proposed to bring against him. This was not altogether unknown to legal practice in the last days of the formular system, but from 322 onwards it had to be entered in the register and sent by the judge to the defendant together with a prescription of the term within which he had to appear in court.[1] Later, but before Justinian's time, a *libellus actionis* was sent by the judicial authority on request of the plaintiff who furnished a surety guaranteeing appearance within two months, and the opposite party had to reply to it with a *libellus conventionis* and the offer of a similar surety under pain of being arrested and kept under observation.[2] The new idea of administering justice without the personal activity of the litigants allowed judgment to go by default, first of all, after the formalities of the *eremodicium*,[3] against the defendant, who could then begin the suit anew by furnishing surety and paying the costs, the time allowed in which to defend the suit being only one year in real actions;[4] afterwards against the plaintiff, after three summonses and the expiry of one year's grace, according to *Nov.* 112.

When both parties were present the suit could be brought to an end by the *confessio* of the defendant, whether it concerned a *certum* or an *incertum*. The oath could be put without any restriction. The term *litis contestatio* was given to the moment when the parties stated their claims, within two months of being called upon to do so, and swore together with their advocates to plead in good faith; but its old effects were distributed among various other moments of the proceedings.[5] The period of three years for nonsuiting ran from the *litis contestatio*.[6] The extinctive effect seems to have disappeared.[7] The summons to appear in court made lifehold actions transmissible and temporary actions perpetual, and it was from that moment that the prescription of 30 years began to run.[8] In the procedure by rescript this effect was attached to the receipt of the summons (*libelli datio*). The plaintiff's claims could be modified until sentence had been

[1] C. Th., 2, 4, 2; 6, 1; SR., 75-76.—**VI,** 19; *BGU*, 228, 578; **LXXXIII,** 320 et seq.
[2] I. J., 4, 16, 24; *Nov.*, 96 pr.; 112, 2; 134, 9. Cf., for certain privileged persons, C. J., 12, 19, 12-pr. *Nov.* 112 also required a surety of the plaintiff.
[3] C. J., 3, 19, 2; 7, 43, 8, 9. [4] C. J., 7, 39, 8-3; 43, 8.
[5] C. J., 3, 9, 1, 14, 8. [6] C. J., 3, 1, 13-1; I. J., 4, 16, 1.—**XIV,** 1923, 194 et seq.
[7] **CCXLIV,** 3, 912; **XLIX,** 2, n° 785, 3*a*. [8] C. J., 7, 10, 1, 3.

given; but *plus petitio* was punished by a fine of thrice the debt, and prosecution before the due time by doubling the period of respite that still remained.[1] The judge enjoyed the widest powers both as regards weighing the evidence and giving sentence; but Constantine borrowed from Holy Writ the rule *testis unus, testis nullus ;* the oath of an *honestior* was preferred to that of an *humilior ;* and written evidence was strictly regulated and subjected to various complex distinctions.[2] The principle *omnia judicia sunt absolutoria* and the system of discretionary actions remained in force;[3] but the condemnation was no longer bound to be a sum of money; it might be the actual object in dispute. Moreover, the judge could take account of counterclaims and condemn the plaintiff.[4]

If execution in kind was possible, the judge proceeded to carry it out in virtue of his *officium* when the defendant had not executed within a period of two months, which was afterwards raised to four.[5] If it was not possible, or if a sum of money was at stake, the ways of execution were (i.) the *pignus ex causa judicati captum*, distress on goods belonging to the debtor which at the end of two months, failing payment, were sold by auction until the amount of the debt had been realized or, in the absence of bidders, were adjudged in payment to the creditor;[6] (ii.) *bonorum distractio*, at the request either of the creditor or of the debtor surrendering his property. In the former case it could be combined with imprisonment which, after Theodosius, had to be in a public prison.[7] Sale of separate items of property by the *curator* was no longer allowed except after a period of two years for persons present and four for persons absent, in order to give the creditors time to produce their titles.[8] Justinian restricted the privilege of *bonorum cessio* to cases of bankruptcy caused by force majeure, unless it was specially granted by the Emperor.[9]

The ways of recourse took different forms. An appeal could be renewed as long as there remained a higher judge, until

[1] C. J., 3, 10, 1, 2; I. J., 4, 6, 33-35.
[2] C. Th., 11, 39, 3; C. J., 4, 20, 8; 7, 52, 6; 20, 16; 9, 29, 21; *Nov.* 44, 11.
[3] I. J., 4, 6, 24; C. J., 12, 19, 12-pr ; *Nov.* 96; 112; 134, 9; 2-4; 90, 2; 73, 1. —**CXCV**, 1, 1001. [4] C. J., 3, 19, 2; 7, 43, 8, 9.
[5] C. Th., 11, 36, 25. [6] D., 42, 1, 31; C. J., 7, 53, 3.
[7] C. Th., 9, 11, 1, 11, 5, 1, 2; C. J., 7, 71; 7, 72, 10.
[8] C. J., 7, 10, 1, 3. [9] C. J., 4, 20, 8.

Justinian limited it to two successive jurisdictions. It had to be made immediately after the final judgment or by writing within ten days, and it was lodged by means of a dimissory letter delivered by the judge from whom the appeal was made or, on his refusal, by the appellant himself.[1] The appellant who failed was liable to heavy penalties.[2] In the case of judgments without appeal *retractatio* was possible at the request of the injured party within two years after the author of the judgment had left office.[3] *Consultatio* resulted in a rescript deciding the dispute between the judge and the appellant after examination of their written arguments.[4] This method was finally reserved for the sentences of judges who possessed the rank of *illustres*.[5]

[1] C. Th., 11, 30, 16; 36, 18; C. J., 7, 70, 1; cf. 11, 38, 1; *Nov.* 23, pr.-1.
[2] C. Th., 1, 5, 3; C. J., 7, 62, 64.
[3] C. J., 1, 19, 5; 7, 62; 35; 65, 5-5; *Nov. Th.* ii, 13.
[4] C. Th., 11, 30, 1, 8, 11; C. J., 1, 14, 2.
[5] C. J., 7, 62, 32.

CHAPTER III
THE FAMILY AND ITS DEPENDENCIES

Section I
THE ORGANIZATION OF THE " DOMUS "

I
THE FAMILY

I. RELATIONSHIP. THE " DOMUS "

THE development in favour of cognate relationship, which had begun in the classical period, was completed for the eastern half of the empire when Novels 118 and 127 based the Law of Inheritance solely on proximity in blood and on the degree of affection which that presupposes. This is the inorganic system of the modern inorganic family, and the gradual acceptance of Justinian's Law in the West caused it to triumph there too and obliterate the last remaining traces of agnate relationship. Henceforward *cognatio* was either natural, i.e. the result of birth, under whatever conditions so long as the filiation was established, or else purely legal, as in the case of adoption and sometimes of acknowledgment.[1]

On the other hand the *domus* became disunited. It is true that the *paterfamilias* is still surrounded by the same groups of persons, but their cohesion and solidarity among themselves is diminished, and their subjection to him is less complete. The quasi-sovereign autonomy of the family had disappeared. The absolutism of its head, which was the basis of this autonomy, had been limited in too many ways by the statutes. It was no longer the independent, aristocratic family that formed the essential element in and safeguard of the State, but the guild, the *collegium*, a passive machinery manipulated

---
[1] For *cognatio servilis* see C. J., 6, 4, 4, 9-13; 57, 6; *Nov. Valent.* iii, 24, 1; or acknowledgment, *Nov.* 117, 2.

from above by the socialistic and amorphous Empire into which the Roman world had developed. The family régime had become subordinate to public authority in the face of which there was no initiative left to it. The common patrimony of the *domus* was diminished: one after another almost all the acquisitions of the *filiifamilias* had been more or less detached from it.

II. THE WEAKENED " PATRIA POTESTAS "

Half reduced to impotence, the *paterfamilias* no longer held the powers that were left to him except as legal concessions. He no longer presided over the family cult which was now changed or extinct. Though the *patria potestas* remained always perpetual, it was nevertheless very anæmic, and the *manus* was no more than a memory. Exercise of the life and death power was regarded as parricide by Constantine and remained at least equivalent to homicide under Valentinian III.[1] Sale of a *filiusfamilias* had been forbidden by Diocletian and was only tolerated by Constantine in the case of a new-born child (*sanguinolentus*) and in circumstances of extreme poverty, with power of redemption.[2] The Law gave a choice between paternal and dominical power (under Justinian paternal power only) over an exposed child who had been taken up.[3] In a word, the *paterfamilias* no longer composed or ruled his *domus* according to his own taste. He himself only occupied the place assigned to him by statute.

Even the *potestas dominica* was not exempt from these restrictions. With the noxal surrender, suppressed by Justinian, the last *causa mancipii* disappeared; and although the *jura patronatus* were for a time reinforced, various constitutions provided the freedmen with means of escaping them.

The rights over persons *alieni juris* had long ceased to be assimilated to rights over things and to be estimated by the profit which the head of the *domus* derived from them. They concerned the political and social order and had become, in the sense in which we shall understand the term, questions of State.

[1] C. Th., 9, 15, 1; C. J., 9, 17, 1.—**XXXVIII**, s.v. *Infanticidium*.
[2] C. J., 4, 43, 1, 2.   [3] C. J., 8, 52, 3.

LAW OF THE LOWER EMPIRE

II

MARRIAGE

I. THE MARRIED WOMAN. MODIFICATIONS OF THE CONDITIONS AND EFFECTS OF MARRIAGE

Marriages were made solely by the consent of the spouses. All other formalities such as nuptial benediction, witnesses, certificate, were regarded by the Civil Law merely as evidential. Failing these, it was presumed from physical cohabitation between persons of equal rank or even between freeborn persons.[1] Justinian required a certificate in the case of *illustres*.[2]

But Christian thought had influenced the conditions of marriage: (i.) by adding new impediments, forbidding marriage between uncle and niece on pain of death, between brother-in-law and sister-in-law, at one time between first-cousins,[3] and also between Christians and Jews;[4] (ii.) by abolishing, at least under Justinian, the impediments founded on the social distinctions of the *Lex Julia*;[5] (iii.) by increasing the sanctions concerning impediments based on relationship, to which were added confiscation of property and incapacity to dispose of it or receive it gratuitously.[6] Justinian confirmed by legislation the Proculian system of determining attainment of puberty, on the ground that it was more decent. Parental consent was finally transformed into a measure of protection for the children. In the case of a son, the father's consent was dispensed with if he was in captivity or had been absent for 3 years, and the curator's consent was substituted for that of a lunatic father; in the case of a daughter, the father's place was taken by the mother, and hers by a council of cognate relatives.[7]

Still under the influence of Christianity, the rights and duties of the spouses tended to become equal. The idea of protection was substituted for that of the husband's power over his wife; and the duty of fidelity, regarded no longer from

---

[1] D., 25, 7, 3 (interpolated); 5, 4, 22, 23-7.—**XLIX**, 1, n° 81.
[2] *Nov.* 74, 4; cf. *Nov.* 117, 4.
[3] I. J., 1, 10; D., 23, 2, 9-1, 10, 11 (interpolated); C. J., 5, 4, 25.
[4] C. Th., 3, 12, 1, 2; I. J., 4, 18, 8; C.J., 1, 9, 6; 5, 4, 19.
[5] C. J., 5, 4, 23-1; *Nov.* 117, 6.
[6] C. J., 5, 4-6.   [7] C. J., 5, 4, 18, 19, 20, 25.

THE FAMILY AND ITS DEPENDENCIES 331

the social point of view but from that of the moral law, became reciprocal. Unless he restored the dowry without delay, the guilty husband lost the *donatio propter nuptias*; but he acquired them both in the case of his wife's adultery, which he alone could prosecute henceforward or, failing him, his wife's father, brother or uncles. The good name and position of families was no longer of public importance,[1] but the penalty for the wife and her paramour was death, and no appeal was allowed if guilt had been admitted or definitely proved.[2] Justinian suppressed the *actio de moribus* (528) and the *retentiones propter mores* (530),[3] and changed the wife's punishment from death to flogging and perpetual seclusion, failing the husband's forgiveness after a period of two years. Her property was assigned to a monastery, either wholly or partially according as she had or had not children or ascendants.[4]

Legislation inspired by the Church tended by a number of dispositions to make marriage indissoluble. It was dissolved by captivity only after 5 years and when the existence of the spouse was uncertain. Loss of citizenship left it intact if the other spouse agreed to its continuance.[5] Divorce was no longer allowed except on just grounds specified by statute and involving penal and civil sanctions, in particular loss of the *donatio propter nuptias* or the *lucra nuptialia*. Unjustified divorce involved the same penalties for its author.[6] Justinian suppressed divorce by mutual consent, though it is true that Justin re-established it.[7]

The widowed or divorced wife could not remarry for 12 months or, if the divorce was of her own making, for 5 years. Remarriage was forbidden altogether to the husband divorced through his own misconduct.[8] Moreover, the husband or wife who remarried could not bequeath to the new spouse more than a portion equal to that of the least favoured child of the first marriage; and a widow could not bequeath to her second husband any of the property received from the first.[9]

---

[1] C. Th., 9, 7, 2; C. J., 9, 9, 30-pr.—**CXLVI**, 162-169; **XXXVIII**, s.v. *Adulterium*.   [2] C. Th., 9, 40, 1, 11; 36, 1, 4.
[3] C. J., 5, 13, 1, 5; 17, 11-2.   [4] *Nov.* 117; 134, 10.—**CXLVI**, 163-169.
[5] D., 49, 15, 8 (interpolated); C. J., 5, 17, 1; *Nov.* 22, 12.—Cf. C. J., 5, 17, 8-pr.   [6] SR., 89-94; C. J., 5, 17, 11; *Nov.* 22.—**XXV**, 34, 105.
[7] *Nov.* 117; 140.   [8] C. J., 5, 7, 11; 9, 2.
[9] C. Th., 3, 8, 1; C. J., 5, 9, 2-5; *Nov.* 22, 21 to 26.

II. THE FINANCIAL AGREEMENTS IN REGARD TO MARRIAGE

The new conception of the family and also the influence of Greek and Egyptian legislation inspired some changes in the financial agreements between the spouses, which tended to place them both on the same level and to favour the interests of the children.

The old modes of settling the dowry continued in use, except that, for the eastern half of the empire, a constitution of 428 borrowed from Greek Law the *pactum de constituenda dote* for whose framing the lawyers seem to have made use of the formulas of the old contract of *dictio dotis* which thereupon disappeared in this part of the empire.[1]

As regards restitution of dowry the *Syro-Roman Law-Book* reveals in these regions a system that favoured the children and even the husband. If there were children living, the husband always retained the dowry in their interest, even when it was profectitious; if not, he retained more or less of the adventitious dowry according to the number of children he had had or the duration of the marriage, and the residue went to the wife's father. The Emperor Leo would have assigned half of it to the husband in all cases.[2]

On the other hand Justinian desired that the husband should always restore the dowry to the wife or to her heirs. Dominated by this idea he first of all reinforced the guarantees. In 529 he gave the wife the choice between an action for ownership and a privileged *actio hypothecaria* on the existing dotal property (the meaning of these latter terms is disputed);[3] in 530 he devised another mortgage, dating from the day of marriage, on the rest of the husband's property and prohibited alienation of the dowry even with the wife's consent; in 531 this new mortgage became privileged even in respect of creditors before the marriage, and it has been said with good reason that these two mortgages ruined the credit not only of married men but also of bachelors who might become married.[4] In the second place he substituted for the *actio rei uxoriæ* the action *ex stipulatu*, taking the stipulation for granted; but this became an action *bonæ fidei*.[5] It could not

---

[1] C. Th., 3, 13, 4.—**CI**, 291-305.
[2] SR., 1, 29; C. J., 5, 13, 1, 6.—**CCXXX**, 247-249. For the arrangements in case of divorce see p. 331.   [3] **CXII**, 196n, 3; **CCXLIV**, 3, 939.
[4] C. J., 5, 12, 30; 13, 1.—**CLVI**, 536.   [5] I. J., 4, 6, 37; C. J., 5, 13.

be brought for recovery of the profectitious dowry except by a father who still had the *patria potestas* and proceeded *adjecta filiæ persona* ; otherwise it belonged to the daughter. The husband had a respite of one year in which to restore the moveables and was granted the *beneficium competentiæ*.[1] The edict *de alterutro,* which obliged the wife to choose between the bequest of her dowry generally contained in the husband's will and the *actio rei uxoriæ,* was repealed. Roman Law had always transferred the ownership of the dowry to the husband; Greek Law had left it to the wife. Justinian's eclecticism thought to combine the advantages of both systems by saying that if by the subtlety of the statutes this ownership passed to the husband, it remained with the wife according to the Law of Nature: a statement which means nothing at all. All that has been written discussing the meaning of his reform is therefore quite idle. He never prided himself on being logical.[2] The receptitious dowry retained its old conditions. Further, it was allowed that agreements annexed to the adventitious dowry could determine to what extent and in what manner it should be returnable.[3]

The *donatio ante nuptias* was born of oriental practice but also of Roman usages. The gifts of the bridegroom elect to his future bride, which were subject to the ordinary regulations concerning gifts, or of the husband to his newly-wedded wife, which were in principle void, were generally confirmed by a legacy bequeathed by the husband to the wife who survived him.[4] Constantine made the first of these gifts, which seems to have become more important in the third century, dependent on the realization of the marriage, unless the breaking off was due to the man's fault or the kiss of betrothal had been exchanged. In the former case the girl kept the gift, in the latter she returned only half of it.[5] Fixed at one time at half the amount of the dowry, the *donatio ante nuptias* was affected in the same way as the latter in the children's interest, and various processes linked the two closely together. In the West, sometimes the wife added it to her dowry and the husband thus furnished an additional dowry or jointure, sometimes the latter confined himself to a promise on which execution could be levied on the dissolution of the marriage

[1] C. J., 5, 13, 1, 13c.; 7a, 3a.
[2] CCXXX, 242.
[3] C. J., 5, 13, 1, 13b.—CXLVI, 67.
[4] CXLVI, 59.
[5] C. Th., 3, 5, 2, 5; cf. SR., 91.

in cases when the dowry would have to be restored.¹ In the East, the amount of it which would remain with the wife was preferably determined by agreements, so that it took the form of an advantage of survivorship.² In 498 it was even laid down that the amount of the dowry kept by the surviving husband must be proportional to the amount of the *donatio ante nuptias* kept by the surviving wife.³ Justinian brought the system to completion by requiring that both should be of the same value. Giving the latter the name of *donatio propter nuptias*, he made it subject to regulations analogous to those of the dowry: the father was obliged to provide it for his son; if it was an immoveable, it was inalienable unless the wife consented to alienation and renewed her consent at the end of two years; it was guaranteed by a legal mortgage on the husband's property; registration in court was dispensed with; it could be settled or increased after marriage; it was exempt from the claims of creditors in case of the husband's bankruptcy.⁴

About the same time the importance of the *parapherna* was diminished. The husband administered them with full authority. At one time, according to Western practice, he even disposed of the property of his wife, if she was under 25, without having to render an account of the proceeds;⁵ while, in the East, he was only responsible for the fault *in concreto*, under the guarantee of a legal mortgage.⁶ There was a tendency to establish a sort of community of goods between the spouses under the husband's administration. Justinian had to forbid the custom, approved by a constitution of Anastasius, of renouncing for the wife the benefit of the Sc. Velleianum.⁷

III. FREE UNIONS; CONCUBINAGE

Under the influence of Christianity the imperial statutes showed their disapprobation of free unions by handicapping the children more or less in accordance with the degree of

[1] C. J., 5, 3, 20; 6, 61, 3.
[2] **CXLVI**, 67. This geographical division was not by any means absolute: **XXII**, 1, 341.
[3] C. J., 5, 14, 9. For the arrangements in case of divorce see p. 331.
[4] C. J., 5, 11, 7; 12, 29; 8, 12, 2; *Nov.* 61; 97, pr., 1; 119, 1; 127, 2.—**CXLVI**, 68-69. [5] C. Th., 3, 1, 3; C. J., 5, 14, 8.
[6] C. J., 5, 14, 11-2; *Nov. Val.* iii, 13, 1, 2. [7] C. J., 4, 29, 21; *Nov.* 134, 8.

blame which seemed to attach to their parents' relations. If they were the offspring of adulterous or incestuous unions, the children had not even a right to maintenance; if they were *spurii*, they no longer had the right to inherit from a mother of the highest rank; if they were born of a concubine, they could receive nothing from their father nor be adrogated by him.[1]

But under the Lower Empire concubinage became an *inæquale conjugium*, an inferior union of ill-defined significance, which was permitted by law so long as there was only one concubine, who must be a freewoman and live like a wife in the house.[2] The statutes allowed it but showed it little favour, their effect being to establish undoubted filiation between the concubine and the children born of this union. Under the name of natural children (*filii naturales*) Constantine penalized them as well as their mother with incapacity to receive anything from the father, but he urged their legitimization by subsequent marriage if the mother was freeborn.[3] Later on it was sufficient for her to be free. Justinian granted them a share in the father's inheritance, if there was no wife or legitimate child, and an annuity for aliment in the contrary case.[4]

III

THE CHILDREN

I. THE " FILIIFAMILIAS." MODES OF ACQUIRING " PATRIA POTESTAS "

The Law of the Lower Empire made no innovation on the imperial legislation of the second and third centuries concerning children born in wedlock,[5] except the dispositions in regard to sale and exposure to which we have already referred.[6]

Giving general application to certain earlier practices, Diocletian ruled that adrogation should no longer be possible except by an imperial rescript prompted by the childlessness

[1] C. J., 5, 5, 6; 27, 7-3; I. J., 3, 6, 10.
[2] C. J., 5, 27, 6; 6, 57-5; *Nov. Th. II*, 51, 22, 8.
[3] C. Th., 4, 6, 7.—CLVI, 573.   [4] *Nov.* 18, 5; 89, 4-5, 12.
[5] See p. 121 et seq.   [6] See p. 329.

of the adrogator and requiring registration in court.[1] Henceforward even women could adrogate in order to replace lost children, *in solatium amissorum filiorum*.[2] Children below the age of puberty could not be adrogated unless the approval of the family council had been notified to the prætor or the governor.[3] Justinian required the consent of all the curators to the *adrogatio* of persons less than 25 years old, and the consent of all the guardians to that of children below the age of puberty.[4] As a general rule the adrogator acquired no more than the usufruct of the patrimony of the adrogatus, who remained personally liable for its debts.[5] Nothing remained of the old political and religious interests which had once dictated the formalities of the proceeding. The consequences of the unity of the family patrimony were also set aside. For a long time past, in the East, an undertaking had been given by contract to treat each person adrogated as a son and to leave him a share in the inheritance.[6]

The complicated form of adoption seems to have been retained in Roman usage even in the East; but the Greek form: viz. declarations before the governor of the province, who caused them to be registered in his office, that the natural father resigned his *patria potestas* and the child submitted to that of the adoptive father, was alone authorized by Justinian, who also required a difference of 18 years between the ages of the adopter and the adoptee.[7] In this period the adoption of natural children by their father was prohibited, as well as that of slaves and aliens.[8] The traditional system was revolutionized by Justinian who regarded adoption only from the point of view of its advantages for the adoptee. In principle, the latter no longer left his family of origin but merely acquired a right of succession in that of the adopter, except in two cases: viz. when the adopter was one of his ascendants without power over him, and when the adoptee himself lacked the right of succession in his family of origin, being forestalled by one or two persons between himself and the *paterfamilias*, provided that this state of affairs existed at the latter's death. In these cases there was *adoptio plena*

---

[1] C. J., 8, 48, 2, 3, 6; I. J., 1, 11, 1.   [2] C. J., 8, 48, 5.
[3] C. J., 8, 48, 2.   [4] C. J., 5, 59, 5; 8, 48, 10.
[5] I. J., 3, 10, 2, 3.   [6] **IX**, 363; **VII**, 9, 1206.
[7] SR., 228; C. J., 8, 48, 11; I. J., 1, 4, 9; 12, 8.—**CI**, 52-54; **XXII**, 3, 173.
[8] I. J., 5, 27, 7; *Nov.* 27; 74, 2.

as of old. This complicated legislation continued the movement which, since the second century, had aimed at securing the rights of inheritance as far as possible for the adoptee and guarding him against the risks of premature emancipation.[1]

In order to improve the position of natural children born in concubinage and to induce their parents to marry, three successive modes of legitimization were devised which, as they brought the child hitherto *sui juris* under the *patria potestas*, required his consent. The first was legitimization by subsequent marriage, provided that no obstacle to marriage had existed at the time when the child was conceived. The ground for this is sufficiently obvious. An *instrumentum dotale* had to be drawn up.[2] This practice was introduced as a temporary measure, after various previous embodiments, and continued to be intermittent until it was permanently established by Justinian on condition that the mother was freeborn. He allowed the father to make use of it even if there were children by a previous marriage.[3] The second mode was legitimization by offer to the curia, established in 442 in order to procure recruits for the curias. The offer was either of a son provided with a sufficient patrimony to bear the expenses of the *consortium curiale*, or of a daughter married to a *curialis* with a sufficient dowry. Justinian took over this innovation and completed it by allowing the children to offer themselves to the curia after the father's death.[4] The third mode was legitimization by imperial rescript when marriage was impossible and there were no legitimate children. This was authorized by Nov. 74 when the father requested it either during his lifetime or by a clause in his will, and the child was then assimilated to a legitimate child.

II. THE JURIDICAL CAPACITY OF THE "FILIIFAMILIAS"

The Lower Empire saw an increase in the tendency to give an ever larger degree of independence to the personality of the *filiifamilias*. At some unknown date the daughters became capable of incurring obligations, subject to the reservations of the *Sc. Macedonianum* and *Velleianum*.[5] But this

[1] C. J., 8, 48, 10; I. J., 1, 11, 2.—**XLIX**, 1, n° 108; **CV**, 63.
[2] C. J., 5, 27, 5, 6, 7, 10, 11; Nov. 89, 11
[3] I. J., 1, 10, 13; Nov. 12, 4; 18, 11; 78, 3.
[4] I. J., 1, 10, 13; C. J., 5, 27, 3; Nov. 89, 2.—**CXXV**, 193.
[5] Cf. *Fr. vat.*, 99 and I. J., 4, 7, 7.

period was especially marked by the increase of the child's individual patrimony. It finally withdrew from the family patrimony all that the child, whether son or daughter, did not hold directly of the father. As early as 321 (or did it exist before for some inferior officials?)[1] the *peculium quasi castrense* had been established in the interest of the *palatini*, consisting of all the property they had acquired through the exercise of their profession and the Emperor's generosity. It was successively extended to advocates, public officials and clergy; and permission could be obtained as a special favour to dispose of this property by will. But besides the *peculium castrense* and *quasi castrense* two other classes of property came into being. The first was the *bona adventitia*, recognized in 319, which comprised property inherited from the mother, with the addition in 395 of gifts received from her and her ascendants gratuitously, in 426 of gifts received from spouse or affianced husband, in 429 of everything not derived from the father and not included in the *peculium castrense* or *quasi castrense*.[2] The *paterfamilias* had the administration of them and received their revenues, but he could not alienate them, except in rare cases, without the consent of the child who was their owner.[3] On the latter's death, however, he received them as a *peculium* (*jure peculii*); and if he emancipated the child, he retained one-third of them in full ownership and, after Justinian, one-half in usufruct only.[4] In the fifth century acquisitions by marriage, *lucra nuptialia*, were detached from this class of property and no longer went to the father unless the deceased titular had neither children nor brothers and sisters.[5] On the death of the *paterfamilias* the child deducted his *bona adventitia* before any division was made, in virtue of a right guaranteed by a mortgage. Hitherto he had not been able to dispose of them either *inter vivos* or in prospect of death.[6] The second class of property of which the *filiusfamilias* was full owner is thus described by Justinian: property given to the son on this condition; *bona adventitia* to which the father had renounced his rights; property inherited *ab intestato* from brothers and sisters. He could freely dispose of this *inter vivos*.[7] Further, the Law of Justinian

---

[1] **CXI**, 2, 125, 2.   [2] C. Th., 8, 18, 1; C. J., 6, 60, 2, 3; 61, 1, 6.
[3] C. J., 8, 61, 8-pr.-2-6.   [4] C. J., 6, 61, 6-3.   [5] C. J., 6, 61, 3, 4.
[6] C. J., 6, 61, 6-4.   [7] *Nov.* 118, 1, 2.

established the same testamentary succession for the two *peculia*, *castrense* or *quasi castrense*, and an intestate succession for these *peculia* and the *bona adventitia*, in which the descendants or, failing them, the brothers and sisters took precedence of the father, subject to his life-interest against the latter.[1]

III. GROUNDS FOR EXTINCTION OF "PATRIA POTESTAS"

Patria potestas was cancelled by very much the same processes as under the earlier Empire, except for some modifications in form and substance. Perhaps ἀποκήρυξις was in general use in Italian practice towards the beginning of the fourth century.[2] Since emancipation was always regarded as a favour, Constantine declared it to be revocable on the ground of ingratitude.[3] Its old forms were maintained; but Anastasius devised emancipation by imperial rescript, included among the *acta judicis*, at the father's request and with the son's consent,[4] and Justinian adopted in all cases the Greek form, i.e. an oral declaration before the judge, of which Theophilus has given us the purport.[5] A deed was drawn up for it as for the gifts made to the emancipated son. The *paterfamilias* retained the rights of guardianship and of succession over the latter; but on the other hand Anastasius allowed reservation to the child, in the deed, of his rights in his family of origin.[6]

For the religious grounds for cancelling or suspending *patria potestas*, which had disappeared with paganism, Justinian substituted attainment of the rank of patrician, consul, *præfectus prætorio*, *præfectus urbi*, bishop or *magister militum*.[7]

Deportation of father or son had the same effects as before, except for the *restitutio in integrum*.[8] A father who prostituted his daughter forfeited *patria potestas*. Sale or exposure of a newborn child either cancelled the *patria potestas* or merely suspended it for periods which varied several times between the fourth and the sixth century.[9]

[1] C. J., 3, 28, 37-pr.; 6, 59, 11; I. J., 4, 12-pr.; *Nov.* 123, 19.
[2] **CCXXV**, 101. See Aldo Albertoni *L' Ἀποκήρυξις*, Bologna, 1923, pp. 93-110.
[3] *Fr. vat.*, 246; C. J., 8, 49, 1. [4] C. J., 8, 49, 5, 6.
[5] SR., L, 3; R, 2, 21; I. J., 1, 12, 6; 3, 5, 1.—**CI**, 55-58.
[6] C. J., 6, 58, 15-1; cf. Th., 3, 5, 1.
[7] C. J., 12, 3, 5; I. J., 1, 12, 4; *Nov.* 85. [8] C. J., 9, 50, 13.
[9] C. J., 11, 40, 6.

IV

SLAVES AND FREEDMEN

I. The "Potestas Dominica." The Condition of Slaves

The number of slaves was beginning to decrease when the conflicts with the barbarians once more filled the markets and the private prisons. The population of slaves according to the Law of Nations was always kept up by war and birth; but the sources from which slaves according to the Civil Law had been derived were reduced to the senatusconsultum concerning fraudulent sale of false slaves, the Sc. Claudianum, the imperial constitutions concerning ungrateful freedmen, which remained in force under Justinian, and Constantine's enactment authorizing the *nutritor* of an exposed child to make it his slave, though this was repealed by Justinian.[1] The *servitus pœnæ* ceased to have any important effects.[2]

From the end of the third century, perhaps earlier in certain cases, the *causa liberalis* was decided, like every question of status, by means of a *præjudicium*. Justinian abolished the obligation to make use of an *assertor libertatis*, and the interested party pleaded henceforth in person; but the process could no longer be renewed as heretofore.[3] Slaves were thus taken out of the sphere of Rights *in rem* and clearly included in that of Rights *in personam*.

The actual condition of the servile population was more varied than ever. The Christian doctrine of the equality of all men in the sight of God helped to improve the lot of a great number of them, weakening the dominical power possessed by their masters and inspiring its limitation by statutes which assimilated to homicide the murder of a slave according to barbarian practice, and forbade the exposure of newborn slaves and the separation of *contubernales* from their children.[4] The Church refused to make a distinction between free persons and slaves in regard to marriage.[5]

---

[1] See pp. 127, 329 et seq.—C. Th., 5, 9, 1; I. J., 1, 3, 2-4.
[2] *Nov.* 22, 8.
[3] I. J., 4, 6, 13; C. J., 7, 17-1; D., 7, 16, 21.
[4] C. Th., 9, 12, 1, 2; 5, 7, 1, 2; C. J., 3, 38, 11.
[5] **LI**, 271-299.

II. The "Jura Patronatus." Enfranchisement and the Condition of Freedmen

The Church promoted an increase in the means of and grounds for enfranchisement, and its influence further tended to efface the distinctions admitted by Imperial Law between different freedmen and to assimilate them little by little to freeborn persons. Enfranchisement of slaves, often in a body, and ransom of slaves and captives became works of piety.

Enfranchisement took various forms: (i.) *per vindictam*, which had long been reduced to a declaration before the judge;[1] (ii.) *in sacrosanctis ecclesiis*, by a declaration made before the clergy in church at the great festivals, for which a verbal process was drawn up: an old ecclesiastical practice legalized by Constantine;[2] (iii.) by will, in the form of a legacy or trust, or in a codicil, whether confirmed or not;[3] (iv.) *inter amicos*, in the presence of five witnesses or by a written deed signed by the same number, or by any declaration made by a priest;[4] (v.) by express consent or, later on, tacit consent to the slave's engagement in military, clerical or monastic service; (vi.) by destruction before witnesses of the titles of ownership of the slave; (vii.) by giving the *ancilla* a dowry or appointing a slave as testamentary guardian; (viii.) by publicly calling the slave son or daughter, or by marrying the slave's mother, etc. Some enfranchisements of barbarian origin were recognized in practice.[5] The Church grew bolder and secured not only the admission of compulsory ransom of slaves who were priests or were ill-treated by their masters, but even the acquisition of liberty by the mere fact of holding clerical office or taking religious vows.[6] Compulsory prostitution of a slave was penalized by forfeiture of dominical power.[7] At one time liberty was acquired by a prescription of sixteen years.[8] Lack of full ownership of the slave was no longer a bar to enfranchisement which produced all the possible effects.[9]

[1] I. J., 1, 5, 1-5; C. J., 1, 13, 1; *Nov.* 78, 4; 123.
[2] C. Th., 4, 7, 1-2; C. J., 1, 8, 2; 13, 1; 7, 15, 2.
[3] I. J., 1, 5, 1. [4] C. Th., 4, 7, 1-1
[5] C. J., 7, 5, 1; 6, 1; *Nov.* 78, 1, 2.—CV, 149, 3.
[6] LI, 339-344. [7] C. Th., 5, 8, 1, 2; C. J., 1, 4, 14
[8] C. Th., 4, 8, 7. [9] I. J., 2, 24, 2; C. J., 7, 7, 1; 15, 1; *Nov.* 22, 8.

Justinian abolished the various categories of freedmen. All alike became citizens. The *Lex Junia* and the *Lex Fufia Caninia*, which had been almost forgotten, were repealed. The *Lex Ælia Sentia* was only enforced in so far as it required the *manumissor* to be twenty years old in cases of enfranchisement *inter vivos*.[1] Every enfranchisement included *ipso jure* the *jus aureorum annulorum*. The master could himself grant the *restitutio natalium*, either *inter vivos* or by will.[2]

Nevertheless families endeavoured to retain their freedmen and the descendants of their freedmen within their circle by various processes of which the testamentary trust *de nomine* was perhaps the most remarkable. The statutes themselves gave new strength to the bond of patronage by extending the power of revocation on ground of ingratitude in favour of the patron's heirs and against the freedman's children.[3] This was an important element in the reconstitution of the client system; but either through inconsistency or through fear of excessively powerful clientèles, the statutes limited the degree of succession to which the rights of patronage held good.[4]

Section II

PERSONS INCAPABLE " SUI JURIS "

I. Guardianship

Equality of juridical capacity was established between the sexes. Christianity and the relaxation of traditional rules both contributed to produce this result. In the fourth and fifth centuries we find no trace of the guardianship of women in Western practice. In the East there are still allusions to it in the sixth century, but without any clear distinction between the functions of the guardian and those of the κύριος.[5]

In accordance with the ideas of the time, the guardianship of children under puberty was made still further protective of the interests of the wards, for whom Justinian, following

[1] I. J., 1, 5, 3; 6, 7; 7 pr.; C. J., 7, 5, 1; 6, 1; *Nov.* 119, 2.—**CXI**, 2, 789.
[2] *Nov.* 78, 1, 2.
[3] C. Th., 2, 22, 1; 4, 10, 1; C. J., 6, 7, 3, 4.—**XLIII**, 151-153.
[4] *Nov. Val.* iii, 24.
[5] *Fr. vat.*, 225.—**XXII**, 1, 293-312; **XXXIII**, 25, 374; **CCXXX**, 155; cf. **CXII**, 221.

the advice of the Proculians, fixed the legal age of puberty at 14 and 12 respectively.[1] Nomination of the testamentary guardian or guardians could now precede as well as follow the appointment of an heir, or might even be contained in a mere codicil.[2] Statutory guardianship continued; but, by very free imitation of Greek guardianship, the mother over 25 years old was allowed by Theodosius (390) to claim the guardianship of her children in the absence of a testamentary or statutory guardian, on condition that she vowed not to marry again. If she broke her vow, an implied mortgage burdened the property of the second husband.[3] Justinian gave the mother or, failing her, the grandmother preference over the agnates on condition that she made the same promise, renounced the benefit of the *Sc. Velleianum* and furnished a general mortgage.[4] The guardianships of the patron and of the father who had emancipated the ward were maintained; but the latter disappeared with the ancient forms of emancipation. Finally Nov. 118 substituted cognates for agnates.

The *præfectus urbi*, the prætors, the provincial governors and later, in the case of poorer wards, the municipal magistrates appointed guardians for those who lacked them. In the case of children under puberty whose resources were less than 500 *solidi* Justinian charged the *defensor civitatis* to perform this duty with the assistance of the bishop and the duumvirs.[5] The system of disabilities and exemptions, brought up to date and extended to all guardianships alike, disqualified or exempted those who were rendered unfit to administer the property of others either by physical defects or by the duties of their office.[6]

Being suspicious of guardians, Byzantine Law increased the number of safeguards. The inventories at the beginning and during the period of guardianship, from which only testamentary guardians could be exempted by an express clause of the will, had to be made with the help of a *tabularius* and sometimes in the presence of witnesses, under pain of dismissal and ignominy. Justinian required, at the entry upon office, an oath to administer honourably and a declaration of the claims and debts outstanding between the guardian

[1] I. J., 1, 22, pr.; C. J., 5, 60, 3.   [2] I. J., 1, 21, 3.
[3] I. J., 1, 15; 21, 3; C. J., 5, 35, 2.
[4] C. J., 35, 3; *Nov.* 94; 118, 5.—**XXXIII**, 26, 449; 28, 305; 30, 173.
[5] I. J., 1, 20, 5.   [6] I. J., 1, 25, 13; *Nov.* 72, 1-14; 123, 4.

and the ward.¹ Constantine had enacted in 326 that the *oratio Severi* should apply to all the property of the *impubes* except useless animals and things on the point of perishing. Anxiety to make the ward's fortune consist principally of rural immoveables appears in a statute of 396, where investment of the capital at interest is regarded as a last resource, and the sequestration of imperishable property is held to be preferable in the long run, although unproductive. Justinian went still further in this direction.² Except the revenues of the estate, the guardian could no longer take the debts owed to the ward without the judge's authorization.³ All this is valuable evidence concerning the economic circumstances of the time. On the other hand, from 426, the guardian made *aditio hereditatis* on behalf of the ward who was *infans*, though his negligence or absence did not injure the latter's heirs.⁴

Justinian held that, if there were several guardians, the *auctoritas* of one alone sufficed for everything except adrogation, and limited to within five years after attainment of majority, at the age of 25, the right to plead the nullity of alienations made in violation of the *oratio Severi* and the complementary statutes.⁵ Constantine had transformed the classical *privilegium* of the ward into a general implied mortgage.⁶

II. CURATORSHIP

The Law of the Lower Empire made few changes in the system of curatorships; but it often employed curators to manage the patrimony of wards when the guardians were unfit or prevented from managing it, and even to administer *bona adventitia*, either permanently or temporarily, when the *paterfamilias* could not or would not do so.⁷

Justinian enacted that the testamentary and even the statutory curators of idiots should not enter upon their duties until they had appeared before the *præfectus urbi* or before the governor of the province supported by the bishop and three notables, whose duty it was to verify their fitness for the task, to receive their vow of honourable administration, to make

---

[1] C. J., 5, 37, 24; 51, 13-1-2; 53, 9; *Nov.* 11; 72, 2.
[2] C. J., 5, 37, 22. Cf. C. Th., 3, 30, 6; C. J., 5, 35, 24.
[3] C. J., 5, 37, 25, 27. [4] C. J., 6, 30, 18-2; cf. C. Th., 8, 15, 8.
[5] C. J., 5, 59, 5; 74, 3-1. [6] C. J., 5, 37, 20, 22. Cf. **CXCIII**, 425.
[7] I. J., 1, 23, 5, 6; *Nov.* 117, 1.

them draw up an inventory and, except in the case of testamentary curators or those whose credit was assured, provide the *satisdatio* and even a mortgage.[1] No innovation was made in the curatorship of spendthrifts[2] or of minors under 25 years of age.

The statutes of Constantine reinforcing the *oratio Severi* and that of Justinian concerning repayment of the incapable's capital were applied to all these curatorships. Justinian authorized the curator to claim *bonorum possessio* if an inheritance devolved upon the incapable.[3] The duties of the curator of a lunatic (*furiosus*) were suspended during the lucid intervals.[4] Contrary to the opinion of some Romanists,[5] the system of parallel administration and *consensus* does not seem to have been extended from the curatorship of the minor to that of the spendthrift, although Justinian granted the latter the right to make *aditio hereditatis*.[6] The period for claiming *restitutio in integrum* was increased to four continuous years.[7] Constantine had regulated the procedure for claiming *venia ætatis*.[8]

---

[1] C. J., 5, 70, 7.
[2] But the rubric of t. 70, bk. 5: *de curatore furiosi vel prodigi* suggests that the innovations applied to both alike.
[3] C. J., 5, 70, 7.   [4] *Ibid.*, 6.
[5] CCLVI, 136; XLIX, 1, n° 172; CCXCIX, 1, 871.
[6] LVII, 251-262; XIII, 13, 11-12; CCXLIV, 2.
[7] C. J., 2, 52, 7.   [8] C. J., 2, 44, 1.

CHAPTER IV

THE SYSTEM OF CORPORATIONS

WE know that at the end of the third century and during the fourth, when the State became weak and unreasonable in its demands, there was an increase in the number of associations of every kind. An outburst of syndicalism was then seen to affect every grade in the social scale. Administrative officials of all departments, soldiers and non-commissioned officers, artisans, workers in the national manufactures, devotees of the same cult, neighbouring proprietors, dwellers in the same ward or village, freedmen of the same patron, slaves of the Exchequer or of the same master, etc., formed associations in defence of their professional or social interests, their well-being and even their lives. In this inundation it is impossible to say how far the strict regulations of the earlier Empire concerning associations and *collegia* were respected and maintained by legal practice. The Digest and the Code prove that the statutes were not changed. At any rate we know that many *collegia* devoted to administrative and economic duties and incorporated by the State in its own administration or in those of the various cities had gradually absorbed the well-to-do population of the towns and submitted to the burdensome State-regulation which has been described above.[1]

New forms of artificial personality appeared at the same time, though there was no marked departure from the idea of corporation. Under Justinian a number of charitable foundations existed for special purposes with administrators of their own and a patrimony securing their existence. Although they had been founded under the bishop's supervision with the help of the Church's resources or of bounties bestowed upon the Church, they possessed legal autonomy, and it is a mistake to regard their civil personality as a mere reflection of that which was recognized as belonging to the

[1] See page 317 et seq.

THE SYSTEM OF CORPORATIONS 347

Church. Certain texts bear witness that there also the idea persisted of a corporation being formed by a collective body: viz. the group of persons in whose interest the foundation existed.[1]

This idea was still traceable, though but obscurely, when in the absence of any concrete foundation a patrimony was set apart for a definite object: e.g. for distribution to the poor or for ransoming captives. In reality there was a foundation, but one represented by physical beings, paupers or captives, to whom testamentary bequests could be made since they were allowed in favour of *personæ incertæ*.

[1] **CLVIII**, 248; **CXI** 2, 794-795; **XLIII**, 513-551, where all the references will be found.

CHAPTER V

THE SYSTEM OF PROPERTY AND REAL RIGHTS

I. THE CHATTELS AND THE PATRIMONY

THE characteristics of the family patrimony were not seriously changed under the Lower Empire except in two ways: (i.) by the constitution, within limits and under conditions which have already been described, of special patrimonies for the *filiifamilias* or of important personal rights over the property acquired by them, which was in like measure withdrawn from the common patrimony; (ii.) by the charges and the restrictions on freedom of disposal with which the social organization burdened the property of *curiales*, of *corporati* or *collegiati*, and of *coloni*.[1]

The distinctions formerly drawn between different kinds of chattels (*res*) still survived in the Law of Justinian, though he abolished the distinction between *res mancipi* and *res nec mancipi*, whose practical importance had long since been diminished and finally disappeared altogether.[2]

II. OWNERSHIP AND POSSESSION

The gradual obliteration of the distinction between Civil Law and Prætorian Law, and the power attached to *traditio* after the third century to transfer the ownership even of *res mancipi* impelled Justinian to abolish the distinction between quiritarian and bonitarian ownership.[3] The subjection of Italian estates to the land-tax by Maximianus Herculius, the new effect of *traditio* in regard to them, and the application of the provincial *transcriptio* to them by Justinian abolished every distinction between Italian and provincial estates.[4] There was a return to a single type of ownership, the *dominium*

---

[1] See pages 320, 336.—**CXXV**, 196-204.
[2] I. J., 2, 1, pr.-10; C. J., 7, 31, 1, 5.—**CI**, 233.   [3] C. J., 7, 25, 1.
[4] C. J., 7, 31, 1-pr.-4; I. J., 2, 1, 40.—**CI**, 234.

PROPERTY AND REAL RIGHTS

ex jure Quiritium, which was absolute and exclusive, notwithstanding the public charges and servitudes attached to it in the course of the centuries, and perpetual in spite of the fact that Justinian allowed transfers of ownership for a time (*ad tempus*) and armed the alienator, in case of a breach of contract, with a real action (*rei vindicatio utilis*) in addition to the *condictio*—an action founded not on the return of ownership to him *ipso jure*, but on a sort of natural right or power which would have remained with him.[1]

The sanctions of this *dominium* were always the action for ownership (though the mere occupier could now escape this by saying for whom he held the property) and the Publician action which was always available for the *bona fide* possessor in course of acquiring ownership by prescription.[2]

The disorder of the times caused possession to be more strictly safeguarded. From 389 violent dispossession involved, besides restitution, loss of ownership if the *dejiciens* was the owner, or else a fine equal in value to the property carried off. After Justinian the interdict *unde vi* was granted in this case without regard to flaws in the possession of the ejected party (*dejectus*).[3] The emperors ordered restitution of the property of absent persons in all cases, even when it had been acquired without violence, and framed for this purpose an interdict *momentariæ possessionis* which was open to anyone for 30 years and secured immediate restitution notwithstanding appeal. Moreover, after turning the *interdictum utrubi* into an interdict merely for retaining possession (*retinendæ possessionis causa*), Justinian framed an *actio spolii* as a means of recovering possession.[4]

III. THE MODES OF ACQUIRING OWNERSHIP

The *in jure cessio* fell into disuse in the fourth century as a result of the administrative procedure and the simplification of the other modes of transfer.[5] Mancipation had already lost all its practical values between 355, the date when it was last referred to in legislation, and the time of Justinian,

---

[1] D., 39, 6, 29; C. J., 5, 12, 30; 13, 1-5a; 8, 54-1 (interpolated).—**CI**, 174; **XXIII**, 36, 83 et seq.
[2] C. J., 3, 19, 3; I. J., 4, 15, 6, 4.—**XXIII**, 13, 175; **LIII**, 2, 317.
[3] C. Th., 4, 22, 3; C. J., 8, 4, 9; I. J., 4, 15, 6.
[4] C. Th., 4, 22, 1, 4, 6; C. J., 8, 4, 6, 8, 11.—**CLXXXIII**, 96, 129; **CCLXX**, 466.
[5] C. H., 7, 1; Cons. v. jur., 6, 10; T. G., 628.—**I**, 14, 715.

who obliterated the last traces of it in the eastern part of the Empire;[1] but adulterated forms of it continued to be used long afterwards in Italy, where it was converted into a written formula.[2] *Traditio* occupied the place thus left empty and was in fact applied to all kinds of property, moveables or immoveables, even before the constitution of 530. The *Institutes* preserve its classical form;[3] but as a matter of fact it was effected in two ways: (i.) by actual delivery of the moveable or public instalment (*solemnis introductio*) of the purchaser in the immoveable in the presence of neighbours or *curiales*, a *traditio* which however could be supplemented by a reserve of usufruct at least for several days; (ii.) by delivery of a written deed (*traditio cartæ*).[4] Registration (*transcriptio*) in the public registers[5] was also practised in the West, being sometimes optional and sometimes—as in the case of gifts—compulsory; but imperial legislation never extended to the whole Empire the very advanced system of registration of all real rights, though this had been known since before the Roman conquest in the Hellenistic kingdoms, above all in Egypt, and without it transfers could not be alleged against third parties.[6] Mere agreement, which remained inadmissible in transfers as late as the fifth century, was introduced by Justinian together with the agreements concerning dowry and gift.[7]

To usucapion and the *præscriptio longi temporis* the Lower Empire added a *longissimi temporis præscriptio* of 40 years under Constantine and of 30 years after Theodosius (who fixed this period for the extinction of actions), thanks to which the possessor of 30 years' standing could set aside an action for ownership. Justinian gave this possessor, when his possession was *bona fide*, the right of complete ownership; but Nov. 119 made it a condition that the owner should have known of the alienation.[8] Then, continuing his reforms, he extended the period for usucapion of moveables to 3 years and, while abolishing usucapion of immoveables, made the prescription of 10 years for persons present and 20 years for persons absent finally and universally applicable to them.

[1] C. Th., 8, 12, 7; C. J., 8, 47, 11; 48, 6.—**CI**, 223-249.
[2] **CI**, 252-269. [3] I. J., 2, 1, 40-46.
[4] T. G., 849; Fr at., 35; C. Th., 8, 12, 8, 9; 3, 2, 2; Marini, pp. 83, 86, 89, 107, 115.—**XC**, 1, 113; **XXVII**, 24, 162.
[5] C. Th., 2, 29, 2-2; 8, 12,! 8; Marini, pp. 86, 91-93, 112-123.
[6] **XXII**, 1, 183; **XXV**, 30, 592; **CXXXIX**; **CCXI**.
[7] C. J., 2, 3, 20. [8] C. J., 7. 39. 3-pr., 8-1; Nov. 119, 17.

PROPERTY AND REAL RIGHTS

Besides this general remodelling of the system there were many changes in detail: cessation of *bona fides* during the period of usucapion was no longer prejudicial to the person who acquired gratuitously; physical or civil interruptions were admitted in all cases, and the latter might be obtained by request; but summons to appear in court did not interrupt usucapion of moveables. Addition of possession was allowed in all cases of acquisition by singular succession, and the prescription was allegeable against the mortgagees as well as against the owner.[1] Property belonging to the Exchequer, to churches, pious foundations and, probably, minors could not be acquired by a prescription of less than 40 years.[2]

Among other dispositions concerning the modes of acquisition by legal grant the following should be mentioned: assignment of the fruits consumed to the *bona fide* possessor, excepting those in existence on the day of the suit;[3] assignment, under conditions which varied in different districts, of derelict land, *agri derelicti* or *deserti*, to anyone who was willing to cultivate it and pay the tax; some modification or clearer definition of the law concerning treasure-trove and accession of labour to moveables.[4]

IV. SERVITUDES

There was a growing tendency to attach usufruct, use, *habitatio*, etc. to the servitudes while terming them personal servitudes, though the compilations of Justinian have avoided this classification.

Apart from this, the only innovation made by the Lower Empire under this head was concerned with the modes of establishing servitudes. The ancient modes—legacy, *adjudicatio*, statute—were still in use;[5] but the prescription of 10 or 20 years was applied to them and also, *inter vivos*, the *quasi traditio*, though the pacts and stipulations borrowed from provincial Law by the Byzantine Civil Law were more usual.[6] In Italy the changed form of mancipation may also have been applied.[7] On the other hand the modes of extinction were

---

[1] C. J., 7, 40-2; 31, 1-3.   [2] I. J., 4, 17, 3.
[3] C. J., 7, 38-1; C. Th., 5, 15; C. J., 11, 59; *Nov.* 111, 1; 121, 6.
[4] C. J., 11, 59, 8.   [5] C. J., 7, 33, 12-4.
[6] D., 7, 1, 25-7 (interpolated); 8, 3, 33-pr. (interpolated); 8, 3, 1-4; I. J., 2, 3, 4; 4, 1.—CI, 161-173; XLIX, 1, no. 271, *in fine*, 278
[7] Marini, 86, 89, 93, 97, 123. Cf. C. Th., 8, 12, 9.

increased in number: renunciation by agreement; non-usage for 3 years in the case of moveables and for 10 to 20 years in the case of immoveables; death of the master or the *paterfamilias* in cases of usufruct in the interest of a slave or a *filiusfamilias*.[1]

V. EXTENSION OF CERTAIN NEW REAL RIGHTS

Progressive nationalization of the land or at any rate development of vast estates involved the creation of new real rights both over private domains and especially over those owned by the State.

The *jus perpetuum*, a sort of perpetual lease, was a continuation with certain modifications of the ancient *jus in agro vectigali* of the cities and temples, and was now closely connected with the *fundi rei privatæ*. The *perpetuarius*, a farmer on a very large scale, was not as a rule the owner of the estate, but enjoyed an hereditary right to it which was transmissible *inter vivos* and could only be taken away from him on certain conditions by an imperial decree, for example if he failed to pay the rent, *pensio*, for two consecutive years. Against other possessors he had the *actio Publiciana utilis*, but against the lessor, who was the Emperor, he could only make a petition.[2]

Emphyteusis, which was also a long lease, was used for exploitation of the *fundi patrimoniales* and by private individuals[3] with a view to bringing land under cultivation. By payment of a *pensio* or κανών the lessee acquired an hereditary right which in this case also was extinguished by failure to pay the rent for two years.[4] He disposed of it *inter vivos* with the consent of the lessor, who had a right of pre-emption for two months after the alienation and was entitled to charge the purchaser a sum of 2 per cent. on the purchase-money. *Utilitatis causa*, the emphyteuta had the benefit of the real actions: the action for ownership, the Publician action, the *actio confessoria* and the *actio negatoria*. Zeno made of this contract—half sale, half hire—a contract *sui generis* wherein the risks of total loss fell on the lessor and those of partial damage on the lessee.[5]

[1] C. J., 3, 34, 13; 37, 17.
[2] C. Th., 5, 13, 1, 4; C. J., 11, 61, 1.—**CLXXI**, 91 et seq.
[3] C .Th., 11, 62, 7; C. J., 5, 4, 16-2; I. J., 3, 24, 3; *Nov.* 7.
[4] GPB., 2, 323, *Nov.*, 7, 3-2; 120, 1, 2   [5] C. J., 4, 66, 1.

PROPERTY AND REAL RIGHTS

The *jus privatum salvo canone* was a right of ownership transferred by a sale, with reservation of a rent in perpetuity which was both hereditary and alienable. The holder of this right also had the benefit of the *actiones utiles*.[1] In contrast to it was the *jus privatum dempto canone* which resulted from a complete alienation.

VI. THE FATE OF MORTGAGE AND PLEDGE

Continued lack of publicity preserved the original defect in mortgage. A statute of 424, giving priority to those which were announced in a public deed or in a private deed signed by three witnesses, was a poor substitute for this.[2] It is strange that the Romans never gave general application, even in the East, to the Egyptian and Syrian systems of registration of real rights.

For security recourse was had to the practice, so fatal to credit, of general mortgages on property present and to come, and Justinian enacted that every general mortgage should be of this kind. In its passion for protecting the weak or those who posed as such, the Law of the Lower Empire misused the implied legal mortgages, all of which had this character: mortgages of wards, minors or idiots on the property of their guardians or curators, of legatees on the inheritance of the responsible heir, of wives on the property of their husbands in order to secure restitution of the dowry (a mortgage which, in the last resort, was given priority), of husbands to guarantee payment of the promised dowry, etc. Moreover, the mortgage of the lessor of city property was extended to the whole of the Empire, and a mortgage could be established by will.[3]

But sale became of the essence of mortgage, and the only effect of the clause to the contrary was to oblige the unpaid creditor to make three preliminary demands. The *lex commissoria* was prohibited. Third parties in occupation could claim the benefit of direct distress.[4] Justin enacted that the *actio hypothecaria* should only be extinguished after 40 years, when the principal action was itself extinguished in 30.[5]

[1] C. Th., 5, 13, 30, 38; C. J., 12, 62, 9.
[2] C. J., 8, 17, 9; 18, 11.   [3] C. J., 5, 9, 8-3-4; 13, 1-1.
[4] D., 13, 7, 4 (interpolated); C. J., 8, 34, 3; *Nov.* 4, 2.
[5] C. J., 7, 39, 7-1-2.

CHAPTER VI

OBLIGATIONS OR PERSONAL RIGHTS

I

DELICTS, CONTRACTS AND AGREEMENTS

I. THE SPIRIT OF THE IMPERIAL JURISPRUDENCE AND STATUTES

THE Law of the Lower Empire inherited its general idea of obligation from classical Law and borrowed from Gaius the classification (not a very happy one because incomplete and inexact) of obligations as delictual, contractual, quasi-delictual and quasi-contractual (*ex delicto, ex contractu, quasi ex delicto, quasi ex contractu*). In the amendments in detail which it introduced under this head it confined itself most often to a compromise between the more flexible and apparently more advanced methods of the Law of the Hellenistic countries and the logical and traditional ordinances of Roman Law. In fact the innovations were far more redolent than the ancient forms of the methods and subtleties of the schools. But the legislation of the Emperors was dominated above all by the anxiety, visible as early as the third century and remarkably exaggerated afterwards, to satisfy the requirements of humanitarianism, of a false and stupid sentimentality. Hence the continual digressions from the Common Law, which was so far superseded as to become in some matters the exception rather than the rule, owing to the gradual invasion of juridical antilogies and distortions, and to the demagogic bias of the constitutions, which were closely analogous in their object and result to what we in our time call the *lois sociales*.

II. THE LATER HISTORY OF PRIVATE DELICTS

There was an increase in the tendency of all delictual matter to fall within the sphere of Public Law.[1] In the course

[1] C. Th., 9, 34, 1; I. J., 4, 1, 4; 4, 10.

OBLIGATIONS OR PERSONAL RIGHTS

of time many penal actions had been eliminated. In accordance with tradition the Institutes and the Digest still devoted several chapters or titles to the private delicts of the old Law, but for a long time past legal practice had abandoned their old sanctions in favour of criminal prosecutions resulting in corporal punishments and only effective against the mass of insolvent delinquents. Perhaps, in cases when the financial advantage of actions for double or fourfold damages was particularly tempting and possible of attainment, there was a return for instance to the old actions *furti manifesti* or *nec manifesti*, the only ones still spoken of in connexion with theft;[1] but as a general rule criminal prosecution (*judicium publicum*) was chosen in preference.[2] Justinian abolished the noxal surrender, except of slaves, who were however allowed to claim enfranchisement after having repaired the damage by their labour: a system which in reality put a premium on law-breaking.[3] As for the penal actions which he maintained, this Emperor endeavoured above all to give prominence to their recuperatory or at any rate mixed character: e.g. in the case of the *Lex Aquilia*[4] or in the actions *vi bonorum raptorum, quod metus causa*.[5] The way in which the measures previously granted against fraud upon creditors (*fraus creditorum*) were amalgamated by the compilers is another proof of their desire to reduce these actions as far as possible to the level of claims for civil damages.[6]

III. THE LATER HISTORY OF CONTRACTS AND AGREEMENTS

The ancient formalism had disappeared as a result of the complexity of legal relations and the dominant anxiety to make the intention of the parties triumph, but there was no sign of the new formalism of more advanced legislations which tends to simplify proof and consists of various conventional symbols in the deeds which are the most widely used instruments of credit.

The only formal contract that survived was the stipulation required in all transactions for which the Law had framed

---

[1] D., 47, 2, 93; I. J., 4, 1, 4.—**XXXIII**, 47, 315; **CXXXII**, 340.
[2] D., 47, 10, 45; I. J., *l.c.*—**CCXLI**, 19, 775.   [3] I. J., 4, 8, 3-7.
[4] I. J., 4, 3, 9; 6, 19; D., 4, 2, 14-9-11.—Cf. G., 4, 8 (=I. J., 4, 2, pr.); P-L., 378, 904.—**CLVIII**, 440, 3.
[5] D., 42, 8; Ed.-P., 2, 177, 245.—**CXCV**, 2, 1400.
[6] I. J., 4, 6, 6.—**XLIX**, 2, n° 949.

neither a special contract with a name of its own nor a sanctioned agreement; but a statute of 472 declared this to be valid between persons present whatever terms might be employed in it. Justinian no longer allowed the presumptive evidence of a deed stating the existence of a stipulation to be otherwise disputed than by proving an alibi for one of the parties during the whole of the day on which it was dated, either by means of other deeds or by irrefragable witnesses. This was even extended to the engagement of sureties (*fidejussio*), and the importance which oriental practice attached to writing may have caused the general adoption of this solution.[1] The element of intention, acquiring increased importance with the disuse of forms, came to occupy a larger place in certain applications of the stipulation; thus for example the intention to novate (*animus novandi*), though it was not one of Justinian's innovations, became in his legislation the very basis of novation. It had to be expressly indicated and, subject to this condition, it resulted from any change not only in the accessories but also in the extent or nature of the object of the obligation.[2] Thus again, by interpreting the parties' intention, if a stipulation of penalty (*stipulatio pœnæ*) sanctioned the same obligation as an action *bonæ fidei*, the more advantageous action was granted after the other for the overplus;[3] and for the same reason certain exceptions were made to the principle that no man could stipulate or promise for another: viz. the gift burdened with a condition, which was excepted by Diocletian[4] and played a prominent part in the Middle Ages, and the stipulations or promises in favour of or at the expense of the contractor's heir which, together with some other kinds, were excepted by Justinian.[5]

In order to extend the protection of the *querela non numeratæ pecuniæ* to all contracts of loan for consumption that were in use in the Empire, Justinian gave a place in the Institutes to the contract *litteris* of Greek practice, the *chirographum* recording a loan; but unless the deed recognized a previous debt, the debtor could oppose the *exceptio non numeratæ pecuniæ* to it within two years and could make this perpetual

[1] C. J., 8, 37, 10, 14; I. J., 3, 19, 12; 20, 8; SR., 205.
[2] D., 45, 1, 8-5. Cf., P.-L., 715, 2929.—**XLIX**, 2, n° 696; **CLV**, 70, 79.
[3] D., 19, 1, 28.   [4] D., 24, 3, 45 (interpolated); C. J., 5, 14, 7.
[5] C. J., 3, 42, 8; 4, 11, 1; I. J., 3, 19, 3.—**CLVIII**, 449, 2.

OBLIGATIONS OR PERSONAL RIGHTS

by means of a declaration to the creditor or, in his absence, to the competent judge. It is true that if he failed in the *exceptio* he was condemned in double damages.[1]

The theory of consensual contracts was readjusted in some particulars. Almost all agreements were now drawn up in writing, and in the East most of them had to be written. The value of this note of hand was not always merely probative: in particular, Justinian enacted that when the parties had agreed on the drawing up of a deed for a contract of sale, they could retract so long as the deed had not been drawn up and completed by their signatures (*subscriptiones*).[2] The earnest, which in Roman tradition had been merely confirmatory, became under Greek influence a means of penal forfeiture, in sales *cum scriptura* when they had not been drawn up in writing, and probably in sales *sine scriptura* when they had already been made.[3] The contractual bond lost something of its strength. The vendor had already been authorized to claim annulment of sale when a thing had been sold for less than half its value, unless the vendee saved himself by making up the price to the full amount; but on the other hand Diocletian allowed the vendor to exact payment of the price, even when his ownership was being disputed (*quæstio dominii mota*), provided that he gave a surety.[4] In cases of hire Zeno allowed the lessor or lessee of rural property to renounce the lease in the first year of the contract.[5] Some authorities think that the right of lessor or lessee to give notice to quit *ad libitum* in leases for uncertain periods is not earlier than Justinian;[6] but it seems more probable that the innovation due to the compilers was the power given to the lessor of an immoveable for a fixed period to evict the lessee in certain circumstances.[7] The mechanism of commission was simplified. The third party who had contracted with a mandatary could always bring an action against the mandator; but on the other hand sureties acquired by the former profited the latter directly. Justinian held the commission *post mortem* to be lawful.[8]

[1] C. J., 4, 30, 13, 14; I. J., 3, 21; *Nov.* 18, 8.—CI, 60-84.
[2] SR., 205; I. J., 3, 23-pr.; C. J., 4, 21, 17.—CXI, 2, 110; CXCV, 1, 996.
[3] C. J., 4, 21, 17-2; I. J., 3, 23-pr.—CI, 1, 85-113; CLXVI, 1, 3, 81, 83.
[4] C. J., 4, 44, 2, 8; 8, 44, 24.—XXIII, 4, 49; CLVIII, 569 et seq.; CCXXXIX, 2, 89. [5] C. J., 4, 65, 34.—CCXXXIX, 2, 26
[6] XXIII, 10, 30; 22, 138. It is improbable: D., 43, 32, 1-24; CCXXXIX, 2, 114, 119. [7] C. J. 4, 65, 3.—CCXXXIX, 119. [8] C. J., 8, 37, 11; 4, 11, 1.

Of the contracts formed *re*, the *contractus fiduciæ* had gone out of use and no longer appears in the compilations of Justinian; the word had already changed its meaning in the Western texts.[1] Justinian deprived the *depositarius* of his previous rights to claim compensation and to retain the *depositum*.[2] To all intents and purposes he is regarded to-day as the true organizer of those contracts which the commentators call "innominate." Under the general title of *actio præscriptis verbis*, or sometimes *actio civilis in factum*, he extended the *actio civilis incerti* to all transactions of the type *do ut des, do ut facias, facio ut facias, facio ut des*, when one of the parties had executed, and thus reduced them all, as had already been done in some cases,[3] to synallagmatic agreements *bonæ fidei*.[4] The *actiones in factum* extolled by some classics were rejected and to this end many texts were revised or interpolated, while in others reference to the *actio præscriptis verbis* was inserted, e.g. in the cases of tenancy-at-will, compromise, division of an inheritance, restitution of a dowry, etc.[5] At the same time the *condictio* seems to have been made subject to the same conditions as regards its employment as the *actio præscriptis verbis*, and changed into a sort of action for dissolution of contract.[6]

The principal reform of Justinian in the matter of prætorian agreements was the amalgamation of the *pactum de constituto* with the *receptum argentarii*. Though in the West the latter probably continued to exist and occupy its own particular sphere, the legal and economic superiority of the Greek ἐγγύη had led to its rejection in the East.[7] A constitution of 531 merged the two institutions into one under the name of *constitutum debiti* for the recovery of a pre-existing debt, the period allowed for payment being 10 days if there was no fixed term. It was open to all, its object might be anything that could be the object of a stipulation, and it was provided with a perpetual and transmissible action for its sanction.[8]

[1] **CI**, 231, 262; cf. **CLVIII**, 545, 2.   [2] C. J., 4, 37, 11.
[3] D., 19, 5, 5-pr.; 2, 14, 7-2.—**CCLII**, 3, 221, 261, 302; **XXIII**, 9, 253; **CLXII**, 124, 131, 144 et seq.
[4] I. J., 3, 24, 1, 2; 4, 6, 28.—**XLIII**, 20-42; **XLVI**, 1, 37-58; **CLIV**, 122; **XXVIII**, 12, 70; **CLVII**, 623, 4.
[5] D., 9, 5, 13-1, 22, 24, 26; 43, 26, 2-2; C. J., 2, 3, 7; 4, 6.—**CCLII**, 89, 91, 278.
[6] **XIII**, 30, 774 et seq.; **CLVIII**, 625, 2, 3.   [7] **CI**, 1, 271-290.
[8] D., 13, 5, 21-1 (interpolated); C. J., 4, 18, 2-pr.-1; I. J., 4, 6, 8.—**CLIV**, 74.

Some agreements were confirmed by the imperial statutes and termed for that reason *pacta legitima*. In 428 Theodosius II and Valentinian III enacted that the mere agreement to give a dowry should be binding. Justinian did the same as regards the agreement to give a *donatio*, unless the parties had made its validity dependent on reduction to writing. If it was more than 500 *solidi* it had to be entered in the register. The agreement of compromise could be given binding force after it had been made, either by the oath of the arbiter and of the parties, though this was soon set aside, or by the express or tacit adherence of the parties to the arbiter's decision. These agreements were sanctioned by an action which the compilers called *condictio ex lege*.[1]

IV. GENERAL THEORY OF CONTRACT: INFLUENCE OF SOCIAL CONDITIONS

Thus the general theory of contract assumed a slightly different appearance in some particulars but was not seriously changed. We have been able to note in passing an extension of the purely consensual engagement (*pacta legitima*), a perceptible decrease in the use of formal procedure (suppression of the formulas), a larger place assigned to writing (sales, gifts, etc.), but also a diminution in the strength of and respect for the contractual bond, due in great measure to humanitarian and democratic prejudices. Starting with the idea that most contracts were made between a *potens* and a *humilior* who was deemed to be the victim of the former's manœuvres, the Emperors showed their desire to win popularity at the expense of the great by their constant endeavour to devise means for withdrawing from an agreement: annulment of sales, repudiation of leases and, above all, the right to change one's mind (*jus pœnitentiæ*), i.e. to go back on one's word, which was still very rare in the third century,[2] but was given ever wider scope after Diocletian, and was allowed by Justinian in all the innominate contracts and in some of the others.[3] The contractor who was legally authorized to change his mind was provided with a *condictio* tending to restore the

[1] C. Th., 3, 13, 4; C. J., 8, 54, 35-5, 36-3; I. J., 2, 7, 2; *Nov.* 82, 11.
[2] D., 12, 4, 3-2-3, 17-1, 27-1 (interpolated).—CLVIII, 625 et seq.; CCLVI, 415; CLXII, 146-179; CCLIII, 3, 261.
[3] C. J., 11, 54, 1-pr.—CXI, 2, 834; CCXXXIX, 2, 92-93, 103-123.

state of affairs existing before the contract. To this must be added the multiplication in Justinian's Law of *actiones utiles*, and the experiment to which we have already referred of allowing general actions such as the *condictio certæ pecuniæ* to be substituted without risk of *plus petitio* for any other action whatever.[1]

The doctrine of modality became more flexible. Suspensive terms and conditions, whether express or tacit, were accepted in all contracts. Justinian gave validity even to the *conditio præpostera*.[2] Contrary to classical tradition he attached a real effect to the *conditio resolutoria*, i.e. that its fulfilment should retransfer the real rights to the *tradens*, at least under certain conditions and sometimes with retroactive effect.[3]

The juridical relations labelled *quasi ex contractu* profited by the system of general actions (*actiones generales*) which was borrowed by the compilers from the oriental schools: *condictio certæ pecuniæ, condictio ex lege*.[4] Moreover Justinian reorganized the series of *condictiones* belonging to this category of obligations: the *condictio indebiti*, in which he modified the proof of excess payment in favour of the *tradens*, who was deemed to be more interesting socially than the *accipiens*;[5] the *condictiones causa data, causa non secuta* or *sine causa*, inspired by enrichments gained for a consideration that was not realized or did not exist;[6] the *conditiones ob turpem causam* and *ob injustam causam*, which he distinguished from one another. But the debtor was liable for all the loss occasioned and for risks to the object of the debt.[7] Justinian also recast the action for regulation of boundaries (*actio finium regundorum*), which was provided with an *adjudicatio* and made common to *controversiæ de fine* and *de loco*, though it was not possible to plead the thirty years' prescription against it.[8]

---

[1] D., 12, 1, 9 (interpolated).—**CXI**, 2, 833; **XIII**, 19, 416; **XXIII**, 13, 248; cf. **XLIX**, 2, n° 8, 875.

[2] C. J., 4, 37, 6; I. J., 3, 19, 14.   [3] **CLVIII**, 763-765 (and the references)

[4] D., 12, 1, 9-pr.; 13, 2, 1 (interpolated); C. J., 3, 31, 22; I. J., 4, 6, 24.—**LVIII**, 76 et seq.   [5] D., 22, 3, 25-pr.-2 (interpolated).

[6] D., 12, 1, 12-4; 5, 1 (interpolated); C. J., 4, 9, 2.   [7] C. Th., 2, 26-3.

[8] C. J., 7, 40, 1-1*d*.—**CLVIII**, 665; **CXCV**, 2, 459, 465; **CCLVI**, 2, 422, 445.

II

EFFECTS OF OBLIGATIONS

I. EFFECTS OF OBLIGATIONS: TRANSFER OF CLAIM AND REPRESENTATION

Without admitting that the transfer of a claim was implicitly allowed to all who had the right to demand it, Justinian granted *actiones utiles* to those (in particular the donee) who had concluded a juridical act whose object could not be attained in any other way.[1]

We have seen that from the time of the Severi it had become comparatively easy when explicitly stated, but later on humanitarian bias inspired a series of restrictions. First Diocletian forbade a *potens* to become the grantee of a right to an action, and in 380 the transfer of such a right was prohibited even in the form of a testamentary disposition. This principle was maintained by Justinian with certain exceptions.[2] Secondly Honorius extended the prohibition to every kind of claim under penalty of forfeiture. Thirdly Anastasius allowed the debtors in such cases, to whomsoever the claims had been transferred, to free themselves by mere repayment of the purchase price; and, fourthly, Justinian extended this legislation to the relations between guardians or curators and their former wards.[3]

Engagement by another's agency was widely recognized and strongly sanctioned. The Institutes reinforced the actions *quod jussu, exercitoria, institoria* with a *condictio* based on the *jussus* of the *paterfamilias*.[4] By means of interpolations an action *de in rem verso* was introduced against the principal even in cases of unratified administration or of acts exceeding the limits of the commission.[5] Mortgage granted to the mandatary or guardian benefited the mandator or ward directly.

On the other hand, there was no sign of progress in the direction of active representation.[6]

---

[1] C. J., 8, 53, 33.
[2] C. J., 2, 13, 1; 8, 30, 5
[3] C. J., 2, 13, 2; *Nov.* 72, 5.
[4] I. J., 4, 7, 8.
[5] C. J., 4, 26, 7-3 (interpolated).—**CLVIII**, 710, 3.
[6] **CLVIII**, 773 et seq.

II. EXECUTION AND EXTINCTION: IMPERIAL REFORMS

The same spirit inspired certain innovations in regard to the extinction of obligations: e.g. the necessary surrender in payment (*datio in solutum necessaria*) by which Justinian allowed the debtor to free himself by surrendering to the creditor on an estimate the property that he was unable to sell; the same Emperor's rule that in all cases where the object of the obligation would be determinable in kind and quantity (*qui certam habent quantitatem et naturam*),[1] the indemnification might not exceed twice the value of the object of the obligation; the judge's duty always to leave a means of livelihood to the condemned debtor, who enjoyed the *beneficium competentiæ*; the right of a debtor to free himself by proving that the object had perished, even after delivery and before the creditor had resold it, etc.[2]

In its anxiety to reduce the number of debts the imperial Legislature no longer required any formal act for their extinction. Justinian reformed the jurisprudence in regard to set-off. He required the defendant's counterclaim to be *liquidum* and forbade *depositarii*, *commodatarii* and *spoliatores* to avail themselves of the right; but he allowed its use both in real and in personal actions, and preserved its juridical character notwithstanding his statement that it operated *ipso jure*, i.e. without the need of an *exceptio*.[3] Certain constitutions had enacted that all the actions which had formerly been perpetual, and consequently the obligations which they sanctioned, should be extinguished after a period of thirty years from the date on which they fell due, except for suspension in favour of the *impubes*, interruption caused by a suit at law, or acknowledgment of the debt. The prescription for obligations to churches and pious foundations was extended by Justinian to 40 years.[4]

[1] *Nov.* 4, 3; C. J., 7, 47, 1-1; D., 50, 17, 173-pr.; 10, 4, 12-1 (interpolated). —**CCC**, 2, 138; **CXXX**, 2, n° 41.
[2] Functions preserved in the *acceptilatio*: I. J., 3, 29.
[3] C. J., 4, 31, 14-pr.-2; I. J., 4, 6, 30.—**CXII**, 631; **LIV**, 428-490.
[4] C. J., 3, 43, 1, 70; I. J., 4, 12-pr.; *Nov.* 111.

III

THE ORGANIZATION OF CREDIT

I. CREDIT: ITS PROCESSES

The Law of the Lower Empire gave very little attention to the problems of credit. Not only did it fail to profit by Greek practice, but sometimes the reforms of Justinian were retrogressive, as when he amalgamated the *pactum de constituto* with the *receptum argentarii* and thus substituted for them an institution of indeterminate character.[1] He has been given credit for the irregular deposit, but probably the compilers merely brought to perfection an adaptation of the oriental παρακαταθήκη which had been begun by Papinian.[2]

It is true that the Byzantine legislator confirmed mere agreement as to the interest on loans made by bankers, but this favour was not extended to any persons other than the *argentarii*.[3] Under the influence of his usual sentimentality Justinian impeded commerce by fixing a maximum rate for the *nauticum fœnus* (12 per cent.) and for the interest on loans of foodstuffs (5 per cent. instead of the 50 per cent. tolerated by Constantine).[4] He prohibited compound interest and formed the strange idea of making interest cease to run when the amount already paid equalled the capital. Finally he claimed, oddly enough, to make the interest on ordinary loans proportionate to the use which the contractors made of their capital and to their social rank: merchants (*negotiatores*) could lend at 8 per cent., *illustres* at 4 per cent. only, and mere tenants at 6 per cent. Agriculturists might not borrow at more than 4 to $4\frac{1}{2}$ per cent. But in his universal benevolence he reduced the penalties on usury to *infamia* and addition of the amount of the unlawful interest to the principal, or else to restitution of the interest unlawfully charged.[5]

II. PERSONAL AND REAL GUARANTEES

No less confusion was caused by Justinian's legislation in regard to personal guarantees. Contractual solidarity was

[1] See p. 358. [2] **XXVII**, 39, 59; **XXIV**, 18, 121.
[3] **CI**, 1, 114-123. [4] *Nov.* 136, 4.
[5] C. J., 4, 32, 26, 28; *Nov.* 13; 32; 121-2; cf. *Nov.* 106; 110.

retained, and also security, but only in the three forms of the *mandatum pecuniæ credendæ*, the amended *constitutum*, and the *fidejussio* that required employment of the words *fidejussio* or *satisdatio* in the written deed (*cautio*) declaring it. The creditor seemed to be favoured by the disappearance of the extinctive effect of the *litis contestatio*: joint-debtors and, in strict law, principal and accessory debtors could be sued successively until complete payment was obtained.[1] The interruption of one joint-debtor's prescription, or acknowledgment of the debt by one alone could be alleged against them all.[2]

The benefit of divided liability was granted to all sureties, even those bound by the *pactum de constituto*.[3] According to current doctrine Nov. 99 really destroyed all the advantages of solidarity by extending it to joint-debtors as well.[4] This seems so improbable that some would limit the application of the Novel to those who were bound in law for one another;[5] but it is better to admit that it does not concern Roman solidarity, in which this result was really obtained only by the *mutua fidejussio* or in consequence of an express clause, but has regard to the ἀλληλέγγυοι of oriental practice alone, whose solidarity depended on their being bound for one another, and among whom the divided liability that had formerly been optional was henceforward obligatory.[6]

In 535 Novel 4 conferred the benefit of distraint on all the sureties, except in the absence of the principal debtor; but the *argentarii* were subsequently authorized to require that the securities which they had received should be excluded from it.[7]

The real guarantees were pledge and mortgage which continued to be regarded almost as a single institution. We have already mentioned Justinian's reforms in both cases.[8]

---

[1] C. J., 6, 38, 3; 8, 40, 28. For active solidarity see D., 12, 2, 42-2 (interpolated). Cf. **CCXLIV**. 3, 825.   [2] C. J., 8, 39, 4.   [3] C, J., 4, 18, 3.
[4] **CVI**, 2, 845; **CLVIII**, 788 et seq.; **IX**, 2, 113; **CCXXX**, 115.
[5] **XLIX**, 2, no. 573.
[6] D., 19, 2, 47; 26, 7, 35 (interpolated).—**CI**, 1, 124-144.
[7] *Nov*. 136, 1.—**CCXLIV**, 38-49.—Cf. **CCXCIX**, 2, 471.   [8] See p. 353.

CHAPTER VII
THE LAW OF INHERITANCE AND GIFTS

I
INHERITANCE

I. WILLS AND CODICILS

UNDER the influence of Christianity and State Socialism the Law of Inheritance was developed along lines that diverged still more widely from the ideas of the ancient family. The presumed affection of the individual and the supreme right of the testator became its guiding principles.

There were still many forms of testation, though they were simplified and adapted for use in cases of physical disability: (i.) the nuncupative will in the presence of 7 witnesses (5 in the country);[1] (ii.) the tripartite will written by the testator or a third party (a *tabularius* if the testator was blind) and produced in the presence of 7 witnesses who then affixed their seals and signatures (439);[2] (iii.) the will *apud acta* recited in the presence of the provincial or municipal authorities, who drew up a memorandum thereof—a form borrowed from the East;[3] (iv.) the will addressed to the Emperor, who ordered it to be deposited among the archives; (v.) the holograph will.[4] After the abolition of testamentary formulas in 339, it was only necessary that the testator's wishes, expressed in any terms whatever, should be sufficiently clear. Wills in favour of descendants could not be disputed on the ground of any formal defect. Justinian limited the privileges of military testators to the duration of each campaign.[5]

Thanks to the codicil, freedom of disposal by will had become very great. Even oral dispositions were possible when it was

[1] C. J., 6, 23, 21-4, 31; I. J., 2, 10, 14.
[2] C. J., 6, 23, 21, 22-8; I. J., 2, 10, 21; T. G., 815.
[3] C. J., 6, 23, 19; *Nov.* 115.—**CCXXX**, 95; **XXV**, 34, 103; **VII**, 106, 107
[4] C. J., 6, 23, 19; *Nov.* 20, 1, 2-1.
[5] C. J., 6, 23, 15-pr.-2, 21, 3, 17; I. J., 2, 11, pr.-1; *Nov.* 107, pr., 2.

no longer required that the codicil should be confirmed by will. It could remain secret and any kind of proof was sufficient, until Constantine required the presence of 5 witnesses.[1] Although in principle the codicil could not contain the appointment of an heir, testation might be made *per relationem*, i.e. by referring to a codicil, whether written or confided by word of mouth to a third party, for the object of the inheritance or legacy or the designation of the heir.[2] But Justinian made codicils valid once more without witnesses or forms or confirmation by will, provided that those responsible for giving effect to them were notified.[3]

Factio testamenti in the active sense was extended by Justinian to the titular of a *peculium quasi castrense*, within the limits of the *peculium*,[4] and taken away from heretics and apostates.[5] In the passive sense it had already been granted to churches by Constantine, and it was extended successively to cities, *collegia* and *personæ incertæ*.[6]

Justinian finally determined the grounds for disinherison and required that it should be made by name in the case of daughters as well as of sons, on pain of annulment of the will.[7] Novel 118 increased the *legitima portio* to one-third of the share (*ab intestato*) if the deceased had only four children, to one-half if he had more than four; and, further, all ascendants and descendants had to be appointed at least for a share. But in addition to the bequests received by will, dowries and *donationes propter nuptias* were taken into account when reckoning the *legitima portio*.[8] The effect of the *querela inofficiosi testamenti* was merely to substitute the *querelans* for the heir appointed, and the will was maintained. After 361 the testator could set it aside by declaring that the incomplete *legitima portio* would be made perfect *arbitratu boni viri*, a condition that Justinian accepted implicitly in 528. A complementary action (*condictio ex lege*) was open to any statutory heir who had received a bounty.[9]

Under the name of *substitutio quasi pupillaris* Justinian allowed an ascendant to make a will in place of a lunatic descendant who had not made one when he was sane, pro-

[1] D., 29, 1, 3-2, 8-pr.; C. Th., 6, 4, 1. [2] D., 28, 5, 78; 85, 1, 38.
[3] C. J., 6, 42, ult.; I. J., 2, 23, 12. [4] I. J., 2, 12-pr.
[5] C. J., 1, 5, 4, 5; 7, 2, 4. [6] C. J., 1, 2, 1; 3, 48; I. J., 2, 20, 27.
[7] Nov. 115. [8] C. J., 3, 28, 29; Nov. 115, 3, 14.
[9] C. Th., 2, 19, 4; D., 5, 2, 25 (interpolated); I. J., 2, 18, 3.

vided that the latter was left his *legitima portio* and that his children were substituted for him or, if he had none, his brothers and sisters.¹

The laws of escheat were repealed by edicts of 320 and 410 and by Justinian. They had always been futile. Moreover, the *jus liberorum* disappeared bit by bit; and thus, after three centuries of failure, this system of coercion was brought to an end.²

II. THE NEW ORDER OF SUCCESSION " AB INTESTATO "

The spirit of the new Law was still better revealed in its provisions for intestate succession. Various reforms inspired by the wish to make cognate relationship prevail had marked the third and fourth centuries: admittance of the mother with the paternal uncles and their descendants to three-quarters of the inheritance, with agnates other than brothers and sisters to one-third of it;³ extension of the children's right of succession to ascendants on the female side; admittance to a brother's inheritance of the brothers and the sisters, whether agnates or emancipated, and of their descendants to the first degree, etc.⁴ Diffident and piecemeal legislation!

In 543 Novel 118 began a new era in intestate succession by enacting that property should devolve in accordance with the presumed affection of the deceased. There were four classes of heirs, with devolution from degree to degree in each. Failing one of them, the property devolved upon the next in proximity. To the first class belonged all descendants by the male or female line, who shared among themselves *per stirpes*, the nearest of kin in each *stirps* being preferred. To the second belonged all ascendants who, if of the same degree, shared *per capita* in the same line, after a preliminary division of the inheritance in equal shares between the two lines. Novel 127 (547) called to succeed along with these the brothers and sisters of the whole blood or their descendants as their representatives. The third class comprised the preferred collaterals, brothers and sisters of the whole blood and their children to the first degree; while the fourth class

---

[1] C. J., 6, 26, 9; I. J , 2, 16, 1.   [2] C. Th., 8, 16, 1; 17, 2; I. J., 6, 51, 1.
[3] C. Th., 5, 1, 1.   [4] C. Th., 5, 1, 4; C. J., 6, 55, 12.

consisted of the ordinary collaterals, the nearer in degree excluding the more remote *ad infinitum*.

Failing kinsmen, the *bonorum possessio unde vir et uxor* seems to have been maintained for the surviving spouse,[1] and Justinian appointed for a needy and childless spouse a share not exceeding 100 *solidi*, any legacy received by the spouse being reckoned as part of the share.[2] It could be reduced to an aliquot part—in full ownership if there were children of a previous marriage, in usufruct if there were children by the deceased spouse.[3] In the last resort natural children and their mother shared one-sixth of the inheritance between them.[4] Property in disinherison went to the Exchequer.

III. ACQUISITION AND DIVISION OF INHERITANCE

Acceptance of testamentary or intestate successions no longer required more than a declaration, often made *apud acta*, or an act of administration. Certain rescripts allowed the descendants of an heir who had died in the first year of his succession without making *aditio* to make it on their own account.[5] Heirs who had not availed themselves of the period of respite (*spatium deliberandi*) were deemed to have accepted.[6]

In order to facilitate acceptance Justinian created the benefit of inventory—a privilege which is still granted to-day. This inventory, which was made in the presence of a *tabularius* and of witnesses, after the creditors had been duly called, had to be begun within 30 days from the time when the heir learnt of his succession, finished within the 60 days following, certified correct under oath and signed by the heir. Then, after first deducting his due share of the inheritance, the heir paid the creditors in the order in which they presented themselves by sale of the inherited property, which cleared the mortgages, if there were any. But it was necessary to choose between the benefit of inventory and the old *jus deliberandi* which, in contrast to the former, lasted for nine months.[7]

The mode of dividing an inheritance was for the most part

---

[1] C. J., 6, 58, 14-6, 15-1-3.—**CXI**, 2, 850-852; **XLIX**, 2, n° 170a, 3rd.
[2] **XLIX**, 2, *l.c.*, 6th; **CXI**, 2, 853.   [3] *Nov.* 53, 6; 117, 5.
[4] *Nov.* 89, 4, 6.—**XLIX**, 2, n° 171a.
[5] C. J., 6, 30, 18-1; 19; 52, 1.—**CXI**, 2, 855; **CLVIII**, 920, 917, 921.
[6] C. J., 6, 30, 22-13-14.
[7] C. J., 6, 87, 21; I. J., 2, 20, 2.—**XLIX**, 1, n° 351, 1st; **CXI**, 877.

LAW OF INHERITANCE AND GIFTS

left unchanged, but that of bringing property into hotchpot (*collatio*) was absolutely transformed. This had been gradually limited to gifts received from the *paterfamilias* and savings made out of the revenue from property which, if the emancipated son had remained under paternal power, would have been *bona adventitia*.[1] A constitution of 472 made it obligatory, in the successions of ascendants, in respect of dowries and gifts received *propter nuptias* or at the moment of emancipation. Justinian added the costs of settlement, gifts to the brother or sister of children required to make *collatio*, and in principle every gift that could be reckoned as part of the *legitima portio*, for Novel 18 made *collatio* obligatory even in testamentary successions, in the absence of a clause to the contrary.[2] Gordian had already declared it to be applicable among all the *liberi*. After 472 it could be made in kind or by taking less. The object was to secure equality, for bounties bestowed on descendants were regarded merely as parts of the inheritance received in advance.

The sanctions of the heir's right remained the same: *petitio hereditatis*, *petitio possessoria*, which some regard as dating only from this period,[3] and the interdict *quorum bonorum* used even against possessors of individual things.[4] *Missio in possessionem* could still be claimed within 30 years by anyone producing a title to inherit which seemed worthy of consideration.[5]

II

LEGACIES AND TESTAMENTARY TRUSTS. THEIR AMALGAMATION UNDER JUSTINIAN

Legacies and testamentary trusts were gradually brought closer together, and at the same time the tendency became predominant to allow no obstacle to prevent fulfilment of the testator's wishes.

On the disuse of formulas in 339, distinction between different kinds of legacy became illusory, so Justinian reduced them all to a single species.[6] He freed their modalities from any kind of formalism, and gave validity to legacies with an

[1] I. J., 2, 20, 35, 36; C. J., 6, 57, 26.
[2] C. J., 6, 37, 21; I. J., 2, 20, 2, 35, 36.
[3] Cf. CXI, 762, 6.
[4] C. Th., 4, 21, 1.
[5] C. J., 6, 33, 3.
[6] C. J., 6, 37, 21; 43, 1; I. J., 2, 20, 2.

extinctive term or a resolutive condition or a suspensive term dated after the decease of the heir or the legatee, as well as to those left by way of penalty (*nomine pœnæ*).[1] He also simplified the modes of revocation, admitting a codicil unconfirmed by will, for which he no longer required witnesses.[2]

The right of accrual (*jus accrescendi*), in the form which it took after the *Leges Novæ*, disappeared with them. Henceforward accrual was compulsory and *sine onere* among *disjuncti*, optional and *cum onere* among *conjuncti*. The *dies cedens* was restored to the place in time which it had occupied before the *Lex Papia Poppæa*.[3]

Justinian's single species of legacy was strongly sanctioned: (i.) by an action for ownership when transfer of ownership was possible; (ii.) by a personal action *ex testamento*; (iii.) by an *actio hypothecaria* arising out of an implied mortgage on the inheritance, for which each heir was liable in proportion to the amount he had received. This mortgage, which was created by Justinian, dated from the day on which the inheritance vested.[4]

The imperial statutes made few innovations in the matter of testamentary trusts except for the witnesses required by Constantine and Theodosius, and the codicils, written or oral, failing which the *fideicommissarius* could administer an oath to the trustee. But Justinian put the universal *fideicommissarius* always *in loco heredis* and gave the fiduciary heir the right of claim, if he had surrendered too much, in all cases when he had made *aditio* of his own free will.[5] Moreover the latter could be deprived by the testator, either expressly or tacitly, of the Pegasian fourth, so that in most cases his function was merely instrumental and he was no more than an executive agent, a *minister purus*. Thus the trust served to oblige the *fiduciarius* to pay what the testator owed to the *fideicommissarius*, and also to constitute a deposit or an administration, in which case the *fiduciarius* need not have the *jus capiendi*.[6] But trusts addressed to incapables in secret form continued to be void.[7]

The main innovation was the amalgamation of legacies and trusts in a single institution by giving them the same

---

[1] C. J., 6, 57, 26; I. J., 2, 20, 35, 36.   [2] I. J., 2, 21-pr.
[3] C. J., 6, 51, 1.   [4] C. J., 6, 43, 1; I. J., 2, 20, 2.—**CXI**, 784.
[5] C. Th., 4, 4, 1; 7, 2; C. J., 6, 36, 8-2; I. J., 2, 33, 7.
[6] D., 35, 2, 57; 48, 36, 1.   [7] D., 49, 14, 3-pr., 40.—**CXLIX**, 312 et seq.

sanctions, i.e. the three actions mentioned above, and by enacting that the forms, extended modalities and various advantages allowed to either of them should be common to both.[1] The Novel completed these reforms. An heir who had not within one year obeyed the judge's decree ordering him to pay the amalgamated legacies and trusts was deprived, if he was statutory heir, of all except his *legitima portio* ; if he was not statutory heir, the succession was thereupon offered to a series of persons indicated in the Novel. The heir was denied his fourth if he did not make an inventory or if the testator had so willed.

Legacies and trusts continued to differ somewhat in freedom, since the latter were always indirect, and there were still some facilities of proof in favour of trusts.[2]

The practice of fideicommissary substitutions (*restitutiones post mortem*) was further developed, since they were strengthened by the real and hypothecary actions which armed subsequent *fideicommissarii* against the alienations agreed to by their predecessors; and this was also the case with family trusts to which the fourth did not apply. But Novel 108 limited substitution to four generations.[3]

III

GIFTS " INTER VIVOS " AND IN PROSPECT OF DEATH

Obsessed by the idea that gifts were generally extorted from the *humiliores* by the *potentes*, the emperors replaced the obsolescent system of the *Lex Cincia* by other protective formalities: the obligation of drawing up a written deed and gathering many witnesses from among the neighbours to be present at the *datio* ; the necessity of registration *apud acta* under pain of nullity which could be alleged by third parties and above all by the donor, for registration was at the same time an act of publicity and a guarantee of the freedom of the parties.[4] Constantine suppressed the second condition almost immediately for gifts in the direct line, and it only applied to those made with reservation of usufruct from 415 to 417. Theodosius II no longer required the written deed and

[1] C. J., 6, 43, 2, 3-2-3; I. J., 2, 23, 3.
[2] I. J., 2, 23, 12.   [3] *Nov.* 119, 11; 159.
[4] *Fr. vat.*, 249; C. Th., 8, 12, 3; 3, 5-1; C. J., 8, 53, 25.—CCXXXIX, 2, 85.

allowed the gift to be proved in any way, besides exempting gifts *ante nuptias* from registration when they were under 200 *solidi*.¹

Justinian made the gift an actionable agreement, sanctioned, whether it was written or oral, by the *condictio ex lege*. He no longer required its registration unless it exceeded 500 *solidi*, while gifts *propter nuptias* or for the ransom of captives, and some others as well, were exempted altogether. A gift exceeding 500 *solidi*, which had not been registered, was void as regards the overplus;² but a gift between spouses could be confirmed by the will of the donor.³

From the third century some statutes were used to subject gifts, like excessive dowries, to the *querela*.⁴ In 355 the revocation of a patron's gift to his freedman was limited to cases where a child appeared unexpectedly. Revocation on the ground of ingratitude was extended by Justinian to all gifts, and he finally determined the circumstances in which it was justifiable; the action available for this purpose, which however was not transmissible, being always the *condictio ex lege*.⁵

The gift in anticipation of death (*mortis causa*), whether oral or written, required under Justinian the presence of 5 witnesses, but no registration. It was revocable *ad nutum*, unless the donor had renounced it. After this emperor had made the gift an actionable agreement, it could be realized in that form with a contrary agreement annexed to it under two suspensive conditions: (i.) the predecease of the donee, a condition implied by the very nature of the operation and not needing to be expressed; (ii.) some other event, such as the donor's restoration to health or survival after a campaign or voyage, which had to be expressly stated.⁶ The fulfilment of the condition, which gave effect to the contrary agreement, thereby annulled the *pactum donationis* itself and, if it had already been executed, armed the donor with an *actio in rem*, a *vindicatio* apparently *utilitatis causa*, for recovery of the things given.⁷

¹ C. J., 8, 53, 29; C. Th., 3, 5, 13; 8, 12, 8, 9.—**CXII**, 522, 523.
² C. J., 8, 53, 34, 1; 35, 5b; I. J., 2, 7, 3.   ³ C. J., 5, 16, 25.
⁴ *Fr. vat.*, 270; D., 31, 87-3; C. J., 3, 19, 8-pr.   ⁵ C. J., 8, 55, 8, 10.
⁶ C. J., 8, 57, 4; 6, 35, 26-1; I. J., 2, 7, 2.—**XXXIII**, 12, 171; 13, 219; **CCXVII**, 23.   ⁷ D., 39, 6, 29.—**XIII**, 37, 199.

CONCLUSION

THE legal work of the Romans, covering almost a thousand years, provides instruction of several kinds for the historian and the jurist. In the face of such an achievement, whose whole course is now revealed to us in the pages of history—this mass of rules and institutions giving shape to men's private relations within the rigid framework of the City with its constant subsequent growth and development, the mind is at once fascinated by the strangeness of the methods used and of the advantages derived from them, and attracted by the study of that part which has survived as a permanent acquisition to constitute the legacy bequeathed by Rome for the profit of later ages.

The preceding chapters have made it clear that no *a priori* conception governed the creation of Rome's institutions of private Law. On the contrary they were simply organized one after the other in accordance with the vital process of the State to insure within its boundaries (gradually extended to include a vast empire) the rational development and at the same time the utilization for the common good of individual personalities that had originally been locked up in narrow and closed associations. It is possible however to distinguish two periods of unequal length in which, owing to a change in the political and social environment, the methods employed and at the same time the nature and worth of the results attained were widely different, although it is hard to fix the precise moment at which the paths began to diverge. Assuming that the first period covered the last centuries of the Republic and the early Empire until the last of the Severi—the times that are conventionally called classical—and that the second coincided with the Lower Empire, when the science and art of Law had already reached their climax with the jurists of the second and early third centuries, we find that the speculations of the moralists, an enfeebling philanthropy, the triumph of excessive sentimentality at the very centre of power, when everything was beginning to be dependent on the emperor alone, produced in him sudden vacillations of will which threatened to destroy that equilibrium between the interests of the community and of individuals which is essential to proper legislation.

The ancient and classical period was characterized on the one hand by the partial but gradually more complete liberation and the increased capacity of legal persons who had hitherto been lost or barely distinguished in the groups to which they belonged, first the clan and afterwards the family; and on the other by a marvellous enrichment and almost perfect adjustment of the legal apparatus required for the now more numerous and more varied relations between those groups or their representatives. In these two ways above all the State secured immediate contact with the individual and brought him under its own authority to an extent that had long been unknown; or, in other words, a system of private Law was organized within the framework of the City and in accordance with its wishes. Now what was altogether remarkable in this development was the reserve and moderation shown by the State authority and proved by the rarity, the discretion, if one may so put it, of legislative intervention. Fewer statutes contributed to the development of this vast body of Law during so long a period of time than are made with regard to the same matters in a single session of our legislative assemblies. If from the very first the Roman State had united the adult individuals with the *domus* on the definite political plane of their civic status, it long refrained from any intervention in the internal life of the secondary associations. Its rule seems to have been never to interfere unless they were insolvent or abdicated their authority. If the Twelve Tables gave the force of Law to certain customs that were essential to the maintenance of the *domus* and their patrimonies, it was because, after the dissolution of the *gens*, some superior authority had to be established to govern the relations of the patrician and plebeian houses, and its administrative and disciplinary power had to be extended to the country estates. So far from taking advantage of the disappearance of the *gentes* to usurp more power, the State confirmed the absolute authority of the *paterfamilias* and allowed it to increase, always respecting the independence

CONCLUSION 375

of the *domus* so long as the practices to which their heads devoted them served to advance its own ends. In the strength and prosperity of the families, the *seminarium reipublicæ* as Cicero called them, the City saw the best assurance of its own; so much so that the object of the first and most famous legislative interventions was their preservation.

By the mere fact of its existence, by the firm foundations on which it came at length to rest, by the security and amenities of life that it brought with it, by the new fields of activity which it thus laid open with their promise of pleasure and enrichment, the State gradually detached the individual from his ancestral customs and from the narrow associations whose benefits he began to relish less as greater advantages were offered in their stead. Hence, in the general conduct of life and more especially in testamentary dispositions, care to preserve continuity of line and cult was ever more seriously neglected. Now since it had associated its own prosperity with that of the *domus*, it was the State that led the reaction against this condition of affairs, although it was followed very soon and with surer methods by jurisprudence. We must refer to what has already been said about this mass of restrictions on freedom of bequest, on the institution of heirs, and on the making of gifts and loans. The statutes then voted were never meant to conflict with the traditional order. Such innovations as they made were intended to preserve it, as also were those of Augustus, who thought by using novel methods to restore the morals of his ancestors. His immediate successors had the same intention.

This control, exercised from above by a State authority whose interventions were only made to set right what was no longer in accord with the beneficial order which it administered, changed neither in nature nor in form when it was concerned no longer with the status of individuals but with the legal relations between members of different groups: a subject which embraced the whole field of contract and obligation, or in other words all that the jurists included under the title of *jus commercii*. It was only where public order was concerned or might be disturbed, in questions for example of *nova opera*, delict, loan at interest, restriction of the number or duration of debts, etc., that the statutes or, failing them, the edict intervened with sovereign authority.

But how small a sphere is that in comparison with the whole domain of Law!

During the Republic and the first century of the Empire the legislator intervened only on traditional lines, though elsewhere the stream of individualism began to show itself and in some matters gathered torrential force. Institutions originally devised in the interest of the family—guardianship, curatorship, adoption, emancipation—began to be used only in the interest of the child or the incapable. The legal personality of *filiifamilias* was precisely defined by a succession of amendments; the activity of persons *alieni juris*, either within or on the threshold of the *domus*, was legally organized; and all this was reflected even in the treatment of the slave. Simultaneously the Law of Property was complicated by the creation of new rights over things, for they too began to be distinguished individually. More numerous and more varied methods were devised for the enjoyment of property, and the administration of the patrimony became an art of more complexity and skill. Henceforward a whole apparatus of transfers and contracts was needed, whose nature and use we have already described, and also at least a rudimentary system of credit, though it is true that this was never developed very far. Thus on the old and still partially existent foundation of ancient Roman society—an aggregation of *domus* and family groups—the individual citizen, ever more carefully protected and provided for by the State, found within those secondary associations and in the intervals between them a field of activity which continually grew larger and more profitable, so that the Roman world seemed for a time to enjoy the advantages and conveniences of legal individualism while remaining shielded from its perils by the survival of the ancient institutions.

The process which had led to this result was peculiar and without parallel in the ancient world. In the slow and laborious development of a body of Law whose scope was already so vast and whose future was destined to be so remarkable, the statutes had served only as checks, whether they were used to maintain, with adjustments when necessary, the old spirit and customs of the race, or to establish order under a system of State control. On the other hand the outworn primitive customs, long since rendered obsolete, had been submerged by new creations, even when they had themselves caused them or suggested them. Thus it came about that the greater part of the Law and all that constituted its soul was the work of *interpretatio*, i.e. of the jurists. Now their method of teaching, which might vary in detail with the temperament of each jurist, admitted no *a priori* legal systems or constructions but only the study of individual cases, illuminated sometimes by their juxtaposition and comparison with one another, in order to arrive at solutions inspired by pure logic, common sense or analogy. On the one hand there was an analytic and logical method, sometimes subtle, always clear and practical; on the other a vast body of individual solutions which could be drawn upon like a legal arsenal. Thus the *interpretatio* was formed, unwittingly classifying the elements of latent combinations which gave it its inherent rationality and were destined to be brought to light long afterwards by our old French jurists. This Law, which in reality consisted simply of the best definitions that could be given of men's daily relations under Roman rule and the best solutions that could be found for their litigation, had and was destined to retain in all its future reincarnations an eminently realistic character. Until Augustus gave permanent authority to certain decisions of the jurists, or rather of some individuals among them, their teaching was of merely private significance, so that it was only by the way of procedure that Law received its form and became an integral part of the mechanism of the State. The result of this part played by procedure in standardizing legal rules was, at Rome, to reduce Law to a precise and vigorous technique, and almost to identify the rule with the means of procedure which gave it its correct form and force. If this was true in the time of the statutory processes, it was still truer in the time of the formulas. Hence the special service rendered by the edict; for the formulas devised by the Prætor imposed their form and plastic character upon the Law to such an extent that, after the system had been abandoned and the moulds broken up, it still retained their impression. Centuries afterwards the language of the Law Courts still sometimes uses Latin titles that once belonged to the forms of procedure wherein this Law was framed. These institutions, coined in the Roman mint and preserving its stamp, were begotten of practical experience and have survived to outlive a whole series of abstractions of metaphysical Law and jurisprudence to which they remain the best antidote. That is why they were so long accepted as the foundation of legal culture, before the strange idea arose of relegating their study to the sphere of archæological research and thus depriving them of their true value.

The second period, which coincides with that of the Lower Empire, was governed by different principles. If we can learn from the first how legal institutions and processes may promote the development of a people and contribute towards its civilization, from the second we can see how their rôle may be reversed and how, notwithstanding progress in detail, they may become one of the causes of decadence. When the other sources of Law have dried up, the initiative rests with the legislator alone who, under many different forms, constantly elaborates new conceptions or modifies the old ones. There is an abundance of statutes whose constant repetition and amendment prove their imperfection and inefficacy, and this is due to their abandonment of that inherent rationality which is required of them by the general order of society and the essential nature of Law itself. No longer interested in the old family or patronal systems which the statutes of the Republic and of the early Empire had striven to maintain, the new statutes hasten their disintegration by giving increased autonomy to the individuals comprised within them. This was a way to flatter the individual and at the same time bring him into subjection; for the State that frees as many descendants as it can from paternal power, weakens the husband's authority, releases freedmen from the bonds of patronage and indulges even slaves, binds all alike with the heavy chain of its socialistic organization, so that the advance of individualism proceeds *pari passu* with the establishment of the most extreme and the most cunningly devised system of State Socialism that our western world has ever known. Following the same tendency, the imperial constitutions, as we have seen, revolutionized the whole system of obligations and especially of contracts by rejecting reason and equity in the demagogue's zeal for popularity with the masses, whom it was thought to flatter by making a parade of weakness and partiality in their favour. In this department above all the rule of Law was audaciously set at naught by the subversion of legal presumptions and of the burden of proof, by allowing retraction of the plighted word, etc. But all this was accidental, the result of a decadence due to political causes which might have been avoided; and it is in the jurisprudence and doctrine of her classical period that the men of the Middle Ages and of modern times have recognized Rome's true legacy to posterity and her contribution towards the general civilization of mankind.

Very few nations have shared this civilization without drawing upon Rome's legacy, and there is hardly a legislation which has not been indebted to it for its guiding principles, if not for its most important chapters. The Byzantine Empire, which was at first merely the eastern part of the Roman Empire and, like it, endured for a thousand years, claims the credit for this; but in reality it adulterated Roman Law with an admixture of the various local systems which gradually became fused together within its boundaries. Thanks however to the Digest, a part of the Code, the Basilic constitutions and, above all, public instruction, classical Law continued to be the principal element in this compound. It was still further corrupted in the manuals or customaries which were scattered in various languages through the provinces and were drawn upon by the early doctors of Islam; for research will reveal those parts of the Koranic Law which were due to borrowings, whether disguised or open, from Byzantine Law, i.e. from Roman Law mixed with provincial customs and disfigured thereby. During this period the Church, which was not unaffected by certain innovations in the imperial Law, borrowed freely from it and owed to it the essentially legal character of its own organizations. But it was thanks to the compilations of Justinian that the Latin Church and the whole western world were once more given an entry, so to speak, on the mass of classical Law, and that this again became the foundation of legal culture from the twelfth century onwards. The considerable portions of it which they could derive from this source sufficed without any revision for the very practical purpose to which the succession of Romanists of various schools thought to devote it. The corruptions, then unsuspected, which it had undergone through contact with oriental Law or through the deliberate action of the compilers, had no perceptible consequences.

There needed the advent of humanism and the devotion to learning that it brought in its train to draw the attention of the historical school of the sixteenth century to these matters, and the critical or even hypercritical methods of the twentieth and later nineteenth centuries had to be developed before a serious attempt was made to distinguish between the true Roman creation on the one hand and, on the other, all that was derived from the legal magma of hellenistic origin by which the Eastern provinces used to live, or from the imagination and amendment of the compilers (interpolations and tribonianisms). So far as this work has been carried, and it has already advanced a long way, it does not seem likely to emerge from the region of historical curiosity. The importance of the influence of Roman Law on modern societies will not be diminished nor will the nature of its influence be changed. It has been established in different degrees in the different countries of Europe as an historical fact. But what in France might imperil our Roman heritage, or rather certain parts of the great legal structure raised by our jurists from the thirteenth to the nineteenth century on the basis of classical ideas and with the help of classical texts or texts deemed to be such, is a return to the practices which Rome also knew under the Lower Empire—practices which relate a considerable number of our more recent statutes to the imperial constitutions of the fourth and fifth centuries.

BIBLIOGRAPHY

N.B.—A complete bibliography must not be looked for here, but only a list of the general works and monographs that have been used and quoted in this volume. The reader will find abbreviated references to them in the footnotes. The *Bulletins bibliographiques* published in the *Nouvelle Revue historique de droit français et étranger*, 1876–1921, and continued by the *Revue historique de droit français et étranger*, 1922 et seq., may also be usefully consulted.

I.—SOURCES

I.—*Codex Theodosianus*, cum perpetuis commentariis Jacobi Gothofredi, edidit Ritter, 6 vol. in-f°, 1730–1750.

Theodosiani Libri XVI cum constitutionibus sirmondianis et leges Novellæ ad Theodosium pertinentes, recognoverunt Th. Mommsen et Paul-M. Meyer, 2 vol. in-4°, 1905. Abbreviated title: C. Th., 1 (book), 2 (title), 4-1 (constitution and paragraph). [We quote these two editions, the first on account of J. Godefroy's commentary, which, although written long ago, remains a monument of French learning, the second as the most recent critical edition. There is another widely used edition by Haenel (Leipzig, 1827).]

Corpus juris civilis in IV partes distinctum, eruditissimis Dyonysii Gothofredi I. C. clarissimi notis illustratum . . . diligenti studio et cura N. Antonii, jurium professoris, Lugduni, 2 vol. in-4°, 1682.

Corpus juris civilis, editio stereotypa: I. *Institutiones*, recognovit P. Krueger; *Digesta*, recognovit Th. Mommsen, 1872.—II. *Codex Justinianus*, recognovit P. Krueger, 1879.—III. *Novellæ*, recognovit E. Schœll, absolvit G. Krœll, 1880–1895, 3 vol. in-4°. Abbreviated titles: *Institutiones*: I. J., 1 (book), 2 (title), 5 (paragraph). *Digesta* and *Codex*: D. or C. J., 2 (book), 3 (title), 6-2 (fragment and paragraph). *Novellæ*: Nov. 50 (no. of the Novel), 6 (chapter). [We quote the first of these editions on account of the famous notes of Denys Godefroy; the second as critical and recent. There are many other editions of the *Corpus Juris Civilis*.]

Institutionum græca paraphrasis Theophilo antecessori vulgo attributa, recensuit E.-C. Ferrini, 1 vol. in-8°, 1884. Abbreviation: I. Th., 1 (book), 2 (title), 3 (paragraph).

Juliani epitome latina Novellarum Justiniani, instruxit Gustavus Hænel, 1 vol. in-4°, 1872.

Basilicarum libri LX, recensuit G. Ernestus Heimbach, Lipsiæ, 6 vol. in-f°, 1833–1870. An edition completed by Ferrini (1897).

II.—*Collectio librorum juris antejustiniani*, ediderunt P. Krueger, Th. Mommsen et Studmund, 1870–1906, 3 vol. in-8°.

Fontes juris romani antiqui, ediderunt Bruns et Gradenwitz, 7th edit., 1909.

Fontes juris romani antejustiniani, ediderunt Riccobono, Baviera, Ferrini, 1909.

Textes de droit romain, published by P. Frédéric Girard, 5th ed., Paris, 1923.

The texts of the period before Justinian are generally quoted from this collection: T. G. (page).

Syrisch-römisches Rechtsbuch aus dem fünften Jahrhundert mit Unterstützung der Akademie der Wissenschaften, aus orientalischen Quellen herausgegeben, übersetzt und erläutert von Dr Karl Georg Bruns und Dr Eduard Sachau. [M. Ferrini has given a latin translation of the syriac text in the *Fontes* of Riccobono, Baviera and Ferrini, p. 636 et seq.] Abbreviation: SR. n°.

III.—RECONSTRUCTIONS.—*Essai de reconstitution de l'Édit perpétuel*, translated into French by Frédéric Peltier from a text revised by the author (Otto Lenel), 2 vols., 8°, Paris, 1901–3; and *Das Edictum perpetuum. Ein Versuch zu seiner Wiederherstellung* von Otto Lenel, Zweite, verbesserte Auflage, Leipzig, 1907. Abbreviation: French edition, Ed.-P.; 2nd ed., in German, Ed.-L² and page.

Palingenesia juris civilis, von Otto Lenel, Lipsiæ, 2 vol. in-4°, 1889.

In this work, where the fragments of the jurists that have come down to us in the Digest or in sources other than the extant books of their own authorship have been rearranged in their original order, these texts are referred to by number only. Abbreviation: P.-L. (n°.).

Imperatoris Justiniani Institutionum palingenesia, per Zocco-Rosa, Catania, 1 vol. in-8°, 1911. Abbreviation: Z-R. (page).

OTHER ABBREVIATIONS

Aulus-Gellius	Aul. Gel.	Papinian	Pap.
Cicero	Cic.	Quintilian	Quint.
Dionysius of Halicarnassus	Dion.Hal.	Tacitus	Tac.
		Ulpian	Ulp.
Dion Cassius	D. Cass.	Valerius Maximus	Val. Max.
Gaius	G.	Varro	Var.
Festus	F.	Fragmenta vaticana	Fr. Vat.
Livy	L.	Collectio legum mosaïcarum	Col. leg. mos.
Pliny	Pl.		
Plutarch	Plut.		

EPIGRAPHICAL COLLECTIONS

Corpus inscriptionum latinarum, 1863 etc.	I
Inscriptionum latinarum amplissima collectio, ediderunt J.-C. Orellius et Henzen, 1828–1856, 3 vol. in-8°	II
Année épigraphique. Revue des publications épigraphiques relatives à l'antiquité romaine, publiée par R. Cagnat et Besnier, 27 vols., 1888–1914	III
Recueil des inscriptions juridiques grecques, publié par R. Dareste, B. Haussoulier et Th. Reinach, 2 vol. in-4°, 1891–1905	IV
Inscriptiones græcæ ad res romanas pertinentes, publiées par l'Académie des Inscriptions et Belles-Lettres (R. Cagnat, Lafaye, Toutain), 1901–1914	V
Corpus papyrorum Raineri, 1895	VI

BIBLIOGRAPHY

The Oxyrhynchus Papyri, edited with translations and notes by Bernard P. Grenfell and Arthur S. Hunt, in 4°, 1898–1904	VII
Papyri grœco-egizii, publicati dalla Accademia dei Lincei, 1905	VIII
Grundzuege und Chrestomathie der Papyruskunde, von Mitteis und Wilcken, 4 vol. in-8°, 1912	IX

FRENCH PERIODICALS

Comptes rendus de l'Académie des Inscriptions et Belles Lettres	X
Journal des Savants, 1665–1903–1924	XI
Mélanges d'archéologie et d'histoire publiés par l'Ecole française d'Athènes et de Rome, 1881 et suivantes	XII
Nouvelle Revue historique de droit français et étranger, Paris, 1877–1921	XIII
Revue historique de droit français et étranger, Paris, 1re série, 1855–1864; 2e série 1921 et suivantes	XIV
Revue archéologique, Paris, 1844 et suiv.	XV
Revue des études anciennes, Bordeaux, 1897 et suiv.	XVI
Revue générale du droit, de la législation et de la jurisprudence, Paris, 1873 et suiv.	XVII
Revue historique, Paris, 1876 et suiv.	XVIII
Revue de philologie, de littérature et d'histoire anciennes, Paris, 1877 et suiv.	XIX
Revue des questions historiques, Paris, 1866–1914, 1922 et suiv.	XX

FOREIGN PERIODICALS

Archivio giuridico, Bologna, 1867 etc. Modena, 1898 etc.	XXI
Archiv für die Papyrusforschung und verwandte Gebiete, Leipzig, 1900 etc.	XXII
Beiträge zur alten Geschichte, Berlin, 1906 etc.	XXIII
Bolletino dell'istituto di diritto romano, Roma, 1888 etc.	XXIV
Hermes, Berlin, 1866 etc.	XXV
Klio, Beiträge zur alten Geschichte, Leipzig, 1902 etc.	XXVI
Mnemosine, Bibliotheca philologica batava, Lugduni Batavorum	XXVII
Oxford studies in social and legal history, Oxford, 1909 etc.	XXVIII
Philologus, Stolberg, 1846 etc.	XXIX
Rivista italiana per la scienza giuridica, Roma, 1882 etc.	XXX
Rivista historica antiqua, Padova, 1896 etc.	XXXI

Tyjdschrift voor Rechtsgeschiedenis: Revue d'histoire de droit, Harlem, 1921 etc. XXXII
Zeitschrift der Savigny-Stiftung für Rechtsgeschichte, Röm. Abt., Weimar, 1880 etc. XXXIII
Zeitschrift für Geschichte der Rechtswissenschaft, 1815–1850 XXXIV
Zeitschrift für Rechtsgeschichte, 1861–1878 XXXV
Zeitschrift für privat und offentliches Recht, 1878 etc. XXXVI
Zeitschrift für vergleichende Rechtswissenschaft, Stuttgart, 1879 etc. XXXVII

DICTIONARIES AND MISCELLANIES

DAREMBERG, SAGLIO et POTTIER, *Dictionnaire des antiquités grecques et romaines*, Paris, 1897–1898 XXXVIII
PAULY-WISSOVA, *Realencyclopädie der klassischen Altertumwissenschaft* (1st ed., 1892 etc.) XXXIX
DI RUGGIERO, *Dizionario epigraphico di antiquita romana*, Roma (2 vol. already published) XL
SMITH, *Dictionary of greek and roman antiquities*, London, 1876 XLI
Mélanges Ch. Appleton, 2 vol., Lyon, 1903 XLII
Mélanges Gérardin, 1 vol., Paris, 1907 XLIII
Mélanges P. Frédéric Girard. Études de droit romain dédiées à M. P. Frédéric Girard, 2 vol., Paris, 1912 . XLIV
Études d'histoire juridique offertes à Paul-Frédéric Girard, 2 vol., in-4°, 1912 XLV
Mélanges Fitting, 2 vol. in-8°, Montpellier, 1907 XLVI
Studi giuridichi in onore di Carlo Fadda, 4 vol. in-8°, Napoli, 1906 XLVII
Studi in onore di Vitt. Scialoja, 2 vol., in-8°, Milano, 1905 XLVIII

GENERAL WORKS AND MONOGRAPHS

ACCARIAS, *Précis de droit romain* (4e édit., 2 vol., Paris, 1886–1891) XLIX
— *Théorie des contrats innommés*, Paris, 1866 L
ALLARD, *Les esclaves chrétiens*, Paris, 1900 LI
ANDT, *La procédure par rescrit*, Paris, 1920 LII
APPLETON (CH.), *Histoire de la propriété prétorienne et de l'action publicienne*, 2 vol., Paris, 1889 LIII
— *Histoire de la compensation en droit romain*, Paris, 1899 LIV
— *Le testament romain*. Paris, 1902 LV
APPLETON (H.), *Les interpolations dans les Pandectes*. Paris, 1895 LVI

BIBLIOGRAPHY

AUDIBERT, *Études sur l'histoire du droit romain. I. La prodigalité et la folie.* Paris, 1892 LVII

BARON, *Die Condictionen.* Berlin, 1881 LVIII
— *Abhandlungen aus dem römischen Zivilprozess. Das Denunciationsprozess.* Berlin, 1887 LIX
— *Zur legis actio postulationis judicis.* Berlin, 1873 . LX

BAVIERA, *Le due scuole dei giurisconsulti romani*, Roma, 1892 LXI

BEAUCHET, *Histoire du droit privé de la République athénienne*, 4 vol., Paris, 1897 LXII

BEAUDOUIN, *La limitation des fonds de terre.* Paris, 1894 LXIII
— *Les grands domaines dans l'empire romain.* Paris, 1899 LXIV

BECHMANN, *Der Kauf nach gemeinem Recht*, 2 vol., 1876 LXV
— *Das römische Dotalrecht*, 2 vol., 1863-1867 LXVI

BEKKER, *Die Actionen des römischen Privatrechts*, 2 vol., Berlin, 1871-1873 LXVII

BELOT, *Histoire des chevaliers romains, condidérée dans ses rapports avec les différentes constitutions de Rome depuis le temps des Gracques jusqu'à la division de l'Empire*, 2 vol., Paris, 1872 LXVIII

BERNÖFT, *Staat und Recht der römischen Königszeit*, Berlin, 1922 LXIX

BERTOLINI, *Appunti didattici di diritto romano*, 4 vol., Torino, 1905-1914 LXX
— *Giuramento nel diritto privato romano*, Torino, 1886. LXXI

BESELER, *Beiträge zur Kritik der römischen Rechtsquellen*, 4 vol., Tubingen, 1910-1920 LXXII

BETHMANN-HOLLWEGG, *Der Civilprozess des gemeinen Rechts in geschichtlicher Entwiklung*, 6 vol., Bonn, 1864-1874 LXXIII

BILLETER, *Geschichte des Zinsfusses im griechischrömischen Alterthum bis auf Justinian*, Berlin, 1898 LXXIV

BIONDO BIONDI, *Studi sulle actiones arbitrariæ e l'arbitrium judicis*, Roma, 1913 LXXV
— *Appunti intorno alla donatio mortis causa*, Roma, 1914 LXXVI

BONFANTE, *Storia di diritto romano*, Firenze, 1900 .. LXXVII
— *Scritti giuridichi*, 3 vol., Torino (s. d.) LXXVIII
— *Res mancipi e nec mancipi*, Torino, 1889 LXXIX
— *Istitutioni di diritto romano* (6ᵉ édit.), Roma, 1919 LXXX

BOULARD, *L. Salvius Julianus, son œuvre, ses doctrines sur la personnalité juridique*, 1902 LXXXI
— *Les instructions écrites du magistrat au juge commissaire dans l'Égypte romaine*, Paris, 1906 LXXXII

BOYÉ (A.-J.), *La denunciatio introductive d'instance sous le principat*, Bordeaux, 1922................. LXXXIII
BRASSLOFF, *Zur Kenntniss des Volksrechts in den romanisisten Ostprovinzen*, 1902 LXXXIV
BREZZO, *L'actio utilis nel diritto romano*, Torino, 1889 LXXXV
BRINI, *Matrimonio e divorzio in diritto romano*, 2 vol., Bologna, 1886 LXXXVI
BRINZ, *Lehrbuch der Pandecten*, 4 vol., Erlangen, 1871-1891 LXXXVII
BRUGI, *Istitutioni del diritto privato giustiniano* (2ᵉ édit., 2 vol.), Padova, 1910–1911 LXXXVIII
— *Le dottrine giuridiche degli agrimensores romani comparate a quelle del Digesto*, Verona, 1897 LXXXIX
BRUNNER, *Zur Rechtsgeschichte der römischen und germanischen Urkunde*, Berlin, 1880 XC
BRY, *Essai sur la vente dans les papyrus gréco-égyptiens*, Paris, 1909 XCI
BUCKLAND, *The roman law of Slavery. The condition of the slave in private law from Augustus to Justinian*, Cambridge, 1908 XCII
BUHL (E.), *Salvius Julianus*, 1886 XCIII
BUSZ, *Die Form der Litiscontestatio im klassischen römischen Recht*, Munster, 1908 XCIV

R. CAGNAT, *Cours d'épigraphie latine* (4ᵉ édit.), Paris 1913 XCV
CARLE, *Le origine del diritto romano*, Torino, 1888 .. XCVI
CHÉNON, *Études sur les controverses entre les Proculiens et les Sabiniens*, Paris, 1891 XCVII
— *La loi pérégrine à Rome*, Paris, 1891 XCVIII
CLARKE (L. D.), *History of roman private law*, 3 vol., Cambridge, 1914......................... XCIX
HUGO COLI, *Collegia e sodalitates*, Bologna, 1913...... C
COLLINET, *Études historiques sur le droit de Justinien.* I. *Le caractère oriental de l'œuvre de Justinien et les destinées des institutions classiques en Occident*, Paris, 1912. II. *Histoire de l'école de droit du Beyrouth*, Paris, 1925 CI
CORNIL, *Traité de la possession en droit romain*, Paris, 1905 CII
— *Debitum et obligatio*, Paris, 1912 CIII
— *Étude sur la publicité de la propriété en droit romain*, 1890 CIV
COSTA, *Storia del diritto romano privato d'alle origini alle compilazioni giustinianee*, Torino, 1925 CV
— *Storia delle fonti del diritto romano*, Torino, 1909 .. CVI
— *Papiniano. Studio di storia interna del diritto romano.* 4 vol., Bologna, 1894–1899 CVII
— *Il diritto romano nelle Comedie di Plauto*, Torino, 1890 CVIII

BIBLIOGRAPHY

Costa, *Cicero giurisconsulto*, 4 vol., Bologna, 1911-1919 CIX
— *Profilo storico del processo civile romano*, Roma, 1912 CX
Cuq (Ed.), *Les institutions juridiques des Romains :* I. *L'Ancien droit*. II. *Le droit classique et le droit du Bas-Empire*, Paris, 1891-1902 CXI
— *Manuel des institutions juridiques des Romains*, Paris, 1917 CXII
— *Recherches sur la possession à Rome sous la République et aux premiers siècles de l'Empire*, Paris, 1894 CXIII
— *L'édit publicien*, Paris, 1878 CXIV
— *Le colonat partiaire dans l'Afrique romaine*, Paris, 1897 CXV
— *Le Conseil des empereurs d'Auguste à Dioclétien*, Paris, 1884 CXVI
Czyhlarz, *Lehrbuch der Institutionen des römischen Rechts* (13ᵉ édit.), Wien, 1911 CXVII
— *Das römische Dotalrecht*, Giessen, 1870 CXVIII

Danz, *Die Forderungsüberweisung und die Verträge zu Gunsten*, Dritter, 1886 CXIX
— *Der sacrale Schutz im römischen Rechtsverkehr*, Iéna, 1857 CXX
Dareste (Rod.). *Études d'histoire du droit*, Paris, 1889 CXXI
— *Nouvelles études d'histoire du droit*, 2 vol., Paris, 1902-1906 CXXII
— *La science du droit en Grèce*, Paris, 1892 CXXIII
Declareuil, *La justice dans les coutumes primitives*, Paris, 1889 CXXIV
— *Quelques problèmes d'histoire des institutions municipales au temps de l'Empire romain*, Paris, 1911 CXXV
— *Paternité et Filiation. Contribution à l'histoire de la famille légale à Rome*, Paris, 1912 CXXVI
— *Notes sur quelques types de fidéicommis*, Paris, 1907 .. CXXVII
Démélius, *Die Confessio im römischen Civilprozess*, 1880 CXXVIII
— *Schiedeid und Beweiseid im römischen Civilprozess*, Leipzig, 1887 CXXIX
Dernburg, *System des römischen Rechts. Die Pandecten*, 2 vol., Berlin, 1911-1912 CXXX
— *Geschichte und Theorie der Compensation*, Berlin, 1869 CXXXI
Desjardin (Alb.), *Traité du vol dans les principales législations de l'antiquité et principalement en droit romain*, Paris, 1881 CXXXII
Desserteaux, *Études sur les effets de l'adrogatio*, Paris, 1892 CXXXIII

DESSERTEAUX, *Études sur la formation historique de la capitis deminutio*, 2 vol., Lyon, 1904; Paris, 1919 ... CXXXIV

DIEHL (CH.), *Justinien et la civilisation byzantine au VIe siècle*, Paris, 1901 CXXXV

DIENSTAG, *Die rechtliche Natur des Pignus ex causa judicati captum*, Berlin, 1900 CXXXVI

DIRKSEN, *Uebersicht der bisherigen Versuche zur Kritik und Herstellung des Textes der zwölf Tafelnfragmente*, 1824 CXXXVII

DUQUESNE, *La translatio judicii dans la procédure civile romaine*, Grenoble, 1910 CXXXVIII

EGGER, *Zum ægyptischen Grundbuchwesen in römischer Zeit*, Berlin, 1919 CXXXIX

EHRLICH (EUG.), *Beiträge zur Theorie der Rechtsquellen*, Berlin, 1902 CXL

EISELE (F.), *Abhandlungen zum romischen Civilprozess*, Freiburg, 1888–1891 CXLI

— *Beiträge zur römischen Rechtsgeschichte*, Freiburg, 1896 CXLII

— *Zur Geschichte der processual Verhandlung der Exceptionen*, 1875 CXLIII

— *Cognitur und Procuratur*, Freiburg, 1881 CXLIV

— *Die actiones utiles des Cessionnars*, Freiburg, 1887.. CXLV

ESMEIN (ADH.), *Mélanges d'histoire du droit et de critique. Droit romain*, Paris, 1886 CXLVI

FADDA, *Concetti fundamentali del diritto ereditario romano*, 2 vol., Napoli, 1901–1902 CXLVII

FERRINI, *Diritto pœnale romano*, Milano, 1899 CXLVIII

— *Theoria generale dei legati et dei fideicommessi*, Milano, 1889 CXLIX

FLINIAUX, *Le vadimonium*, Paris, 1908 CL

DE FRANCISCI, Συνάλλαγμα. *Storia e dottrina dei cosidetti contratti innominati*, 1916 CLI

FUSTEL DE COULANGES, *La cité antique* (9e édit.), Paris, 1920 CLII

— *La Gaule romaine*, Paris, 1891 CLIII

— *Recherches sur quelques problèmes d'histoire*, Paris, 1894 CLIV

GIDE (PAUL), *Études sur la novation et le transport des créances en droit romain*, Paris, 1885 CLV

— *Études sur la condition privée de la femme* (2e édit.), Paris, 1885 CLVI

GIFFARD (ANDRÉ). *De la confessio in jure. Étude d'histoire de la procédure romaine*, 1900 CLVII

GIRARD (P.-FR.), *Manuel élémentaire de droit romain* (7e édit.), Paris, 1924 CLVIII

BIBLIOGRAPHY

Girard, *Histoire de l'organisation judiciaire des Romains*.
1. *Les six premiers siècles de Rome*, Paris, 1901 ... CLIX
— *Mélanges du droit romain*, 2 vol., Paris, 1912–1923 CLX
Glasson, *Études sur Gaius*, Paris, 1885 CLXI
Gradenwitz, *Die Interpolationen in den Pandecten*, Berlin, 1887 CLXII
— *Zwangsvollstreckung und Urteilssicherung*, Berlin, 1888 CLXIII
— *Ungültigkeit obligatorischer Rechtsgeschäfte*, 1887 .. CLXIV
— *Natur und Sklave bei der naturalis obligatio*, Berlin, 1900 CLXV
— *Einführung in die Papyruskunde*, Leipzig, 1900.... CLXVI
Greenidge, *Infamia, its place in roman public and private law*, Oxford, 1894 CLXVII
— *The legal procedure of Cicero's time*, Oxford, 1901... CLXVIII

Heisterberg, *Die Entstehung des Kolonats*, Berlin, 1876 CLXIX
Herzen, *Études sur l'origine de l'hypothèque*, Lausanne 1899 CLXX
His, *Die Domänen der romischen Kaiserzeit*, Leipzig, 1896 CLXXI
Hitzig, *Beiträge zur Geschichte der Injuria im griechischen und römischen Recht*. Munschen, 1889 ... CLXXII
Holder, *Die römische Ehe*, Zurich, 1874 CLXXIII
— *Beiträge zur Geschichte des römischen Erbrechts*, Zurich, 1876 CLXXIV
Hoffmann, *Die Compilation der Digesten Justinians*, Berlin, 1900 CLXXV
Hruza, *Beiträge zur Geschichte des griechischen und römischen Familienrechts*, Leipzig, 1894 CLXXVI
— *Ueber das lege agere pro tutela*, Erlangen, 1887 CLXXVII
Huschke, *Die Multa und das Sacramentum*, Leipzig, 1874 CLXXVIII
— *Lehre des römischen Rechts vom Darlehn*, Leipzig, 1882 CLXXIX
Huvelin, *Études sur le furtum dans le très ancien droit romain*. I. *Les Sources*, Lyon-Paris, 1915 CLXXX
— *Les tablettes magiques et le droit romain*, Paris, 1901 CLXXXI

Jhering, *L'esprit du droit romain dans les diverses phases de son développement*, trad. franç. par C. de Meulenaere, 4 vol., 1875 CLXXXII
— *Du fondement de la protection possessoire*, trad. par le même, Gand, Paris (2ᵉ édit., 1882) CLXXXIII
— *Rôle de la volonté dans la possession*, trad. par le même, 1892 CLXXXIV
— *Actio injuriarum. Des lésions injurieuses en droit romain*, trad. du même, Paris, 1898 CLXXXV

JHERING, *L'évolution du droit*, trad. du même, 3º édit., 2 vol., Paris, 1901 CLXXXVI
— *Études complémentaires de l'esprit du droit romain*.— I. *De la faute en droit privé*.—II. *Fondement des interdits possessoires*, trad. du même, Paris, 1880, 1895 CLXXXVII
— *La lutte pour le droit*, trad. du même, Paris, 1890 CLXXXVIII
JAQUELIN, *De la fiducie*, Paris, 1891 CLXXXIX
JÉZES (G.), *Les registres de naissance à Rome*, Paris, 1894 CXC
JOBBÉ-DUVAL, *Études sur l'histoire de la procédure civile chez les Romains*. I. *Procédure par le pari. Agere per sponsionem*, Paris, 1896 CXCI
JOUGUET, *La vie municipale dans l'Égypte romaine*, Paris, 1911 CXCII
JOURDAN, *Études sur le droit romain. L'hypothèque*, Paris, 1876 CXCIII

KALB, *Die Jagd nach Interpolationenin den Digesten*, 1897 CXCIV
KARLOWA, *Römische Rechtsgeschichte*, 2 vol., Leipzig, 1885–1901 CXCV
— *Der römische Civilprozess zur Zeit der Legis Actionen*, Berlin, 1872 CXCVI
— *Die Formen der römischen Ehe und Manus*, Bonn, 1868 CXCVII
KNIEP, *Der Rechtsgelehrte Gaius und die Ediktscommentare*, Iéna, 1910 CXCVIII
KROELL, *Du rôle de l'écrit dans la preuve des contrats* CXCIX
KRUGER, *Geschichte der capitis deminutio*, 2 vol., Berlin, 1884 CC
— *Beiträge zur Lehre von der exceptio doli*, Berlin, 1892 CCI

LAMBERT (ED.), *La tradition romaine sur la succession des formes du testament devant l'histoire comparative*, Paris, 1901 CCII
LE BRAS, *L'évolution générale du procurator en droit privé romain des origines au IIIᵉ siècle*, Paris, 1922 CCIII
LEFÈVRE, *Du rôle des tribuns de la plèbe en procédure civile*, Paris, 1910 CCIV
LEIST, *Graeco-römische Rechtsgeschichte*, Iéna, 1884 .. CCV
— *Altarische jus gentium*, Iéna, 1889 CCVI
— *Altarische jus civile*, 2 vol., Iéna, 1892 CCVII
— *Mancipatio und Eigenthums traditio*, Iéna, 1865 .. CCVIII
LEMONNIER, *Étude historique sur la condition privée des affranchis*, Paris, 1887 CCIX
LENEL, *Ueber Ursprung und Wirkung der Exceptionen*, Leipzig, 1876 CCX
LEWALD, *Beiträge zur Kenntniss des römischen-aegyptischen Grundbuchrechts*, Berlin, 1909 CCXI

BIBLIOGRAPHY

LIEBMANN, *Zur Geschichte und Organisation des römischen Vereinswesens*, Liepzig, 1890	CCXII
MACHELARD, *Les interdits en droit romain*, Paris, 1864.	CCXIII
— *Des obligations naturelles en droit romain*, Paris, 1861	CCXIV
— *Dissertations sur le droit romain*, Paris, 1882	CCXV
— *Distinction des servitudes prédiales*, 1868	CCXVI
MANCALEONI, *Contributio alla storia della rei vindicatio utilis*, Sassari, 1901	CCXVII
— *Appunti sulla institutio ex re*, 1902	CCXVIII
MARCHI, *Actiones in bonum et æquum conceptæ*, Milano, 1898..	CCXIX
— *Le interpolazioni resultanti dal confronto tra il Gregoriano, il Ermogeniano, il Theodosiano, le Novelle posttheodosiane e il códice giustiniano*, Roma, 1906 ..	CCXX
MARIA, *Le vindex dans la legis actio per manus injectionem et dans l'in jus vocatio*, Paris, 1895	CCXXI
MARTIN (OLIVIER), *Le tribunal des Centumvirs*, Paris, 1904	CCXXII
MASCKLE (R.), *Die Persönlichkeitsrechte des römischen Injuriensystems*, 1903	CCXXIII
MAY (G.) et BECKER, *Précis des institutions du droit privé à Rome*, Paris, 1892	CCXXIV
G. MAY, *Eléments du droit romain*, 8ᵉ édit., Paris, 1920	CCXXV
MAYNZ, *Cours de droit romain*, 4ᵉ édit., 2 vol., 1876	CCXXVI
VON MAYR, *Die condictio des römischen Privatrechts*, 1900	CCXXVII
MEYER (P.) *Der römische Koncubinat nach den Rechtsquellen und den Inschriften*, Leipzig, 1895	CCXXVIII
MISPOULET, *Études d'institutions romaines*, Paris, 1887	CCXXIX
MITTEIS, *Reichs-und-Volksrecht in den östlichen Provinzen des römischen Kaiserreiches*, Leipzig, 1891	CCXXX
— *Römisches Privatrecht bis auf die Zeit Diocletians*, I., Leipzig, 1908	CCXXXI
— *Zur Geschichte der Erbpacht im Altertum*, Leipzig, 1901..	CCXXXII
— *Ueber drei neue Handschriften des syrisch-römischen Rechtsbuches*, 1905	CCXXXIII
MOMMSEN, TH., *Römische Geschichte*, 7ᵉ Aufl., Berlin, 1883	CCXXXIV
— *De collegiis et sodaliciis Romanorum*, Kiliac, 1843 ..	CCXXXV
— *Juristiche Schriften*, 4 vol., Berlin, 1905-1907......	CCXXXVI
— *Römische Forschungen*, 2 vol., Berlin, 1864-1879 ..	CCXXXVII

MOMMSEN (TH.) and MARQUARDT (J.), *Manuel des Antiquités romaines* traduit de l'allemand sous la direction de Gustave Humbert; T. I-VIII, *Le droit public romain*, par TH. MOMMSEN, trad. P.-Fr. Girard; T. IX-X, *Organisation de l'Empire romain*, par J. MARQUARDT, trad. A. Weiss et P.-L. Lucas; T. XII-XIII, *Le culte chez les Romains*, par J. MARQUARDT, trad. Brissaud; T. IX-XV, *La vie privée des Romains*, trad. V. Henry; T. XVI, *Histoire des sources du droit romain*, par P. KRUEGER, trad. Brissaud; T. XVII-XIX, *Le droit pénal romain*, par TH. MOMMSEN, trad. A. Duquesne, 19 vol., Paris, 1889-1907 CCXXXVIII

MONNIER (H.), *Études de droit byzantin* : I. De l' ἐπιβολή; II. *Méditation sur la constitution* Ἑκατέρωι *et le jus poenitendi*, Paris, 1895-1900 CCXXXIX

MONNIER (H.) et PATON, *La Meditatio de nudis pactis*, Paris, 1915 CCXL

MUIRHEAD, (J.), *Introduction historique au droit privé des Romains*, trad. franç. par BOURCART, Paris, 1889 .. CCXLI

NOAILLES, *Les collections grecques des Novelles de l'empereur Justinien*, Bordeaux, 1912 CCXLII

OBERZINER, *Origine della plebs romana*, Leipzig, 1901 CCXLIII

ORTOLAN, *Législation romaine* : I. *Histoire et généralisation*. II, III. *Explication historique des Institutes*, 12e édit., avec Appendices de Labbé, Paris, 1883-1884 CCXLIV

PAIS (ETTORE), *Storia di Roma*, 2 vol., Torino, 1898-1899 CCXLV

— *Storia critica di Roma durante i primi cinque secoli*, 2 vol., Roma, 1913 CCXLVI

PARTSCH, *Die Schriftformel im römischen Provinzialprocess*, Berlin, 1909 CCXLVII

— *Die longi temporis praescriptio im klassischen römischen Recht*. Leipzig, 1906 CCXLVIII

PELLAT, *Exposés généraux des principes généraux du droit romain sur la propriété et de l'usufruit suivi d'un Commentaire sur le livre VI des Pandectes*, 2e édit., Paris, 1853 CCXLIX

— *Textes du droit romain sur la dot*, traduits et comentés, 2e édit., Paris, 1853 CCL

— *Textes choisis des Pandectes*, traduits et documentés, Paris, 1866 CCLI

PERNICE, *Marcus Antistius Labeo. Das römische Privatrecht im ersten Jahrhunderte der Kaiserzeit*, 3 vol., Halle, 1878-1900 CCLII

PERROT, *L'appel dans la procédure de l'ordo judiciorum*, Paris, 1907 CCLIII

PERROZZI, *Istitutioni di diritto romano*, 2 vol., Firenze, 1908 CCLIV

BIBLIOGRAPHY

Perrozzi, *Sulla struttura di servitu prediali in diritto romano*, Roma, 1888 CCLV

Petit (Eug.), *Traité élémentaire de droit romain*, 6ᵉ édit., Paris, 1904 CCLVI

Petot, *Le défaut in judicio dans la procédure ordinaire romaine*, Paris, 1912 CCLVII

Pissard, *Les actions préjudicielles en droit romain*, Paris, 1907 CCLVIII

Plassard, *Le Concubinat romain sous le Haut-Empire*, Paris, 1921 CCLIX

Révillout, *Cours du droit égyptien*, 2 vol., 1887–1897 ... CCLX

Riccobono, *Lezione d'istitutioni del diritto romano*, 1907 ... CCLXI

— *Communio e comproprietà*, 1913 CCLXII

Rivier, *Précis du droit de famille romain*, Paris, 1891 ... CCLXIII

Roby, *Roman private law in the times of Cicero and of the Antonines*, 2 vol., Cambridge, 1902 CCLXIV

Rostowzew, *Studien zur Geschichte des römischen Kolonats*, Leipzig, 1910 CCLXV

Rudorff, Blume and Mommsen, *Die Schriften der römischen Feldmesser*, 2 vol., 1848–1852 CCLXVI

Saleilles, *Étude sur la théorie générale de l'obligation*, Paris, 1901 CCLXVII

Sanctis (de), *Storia dei Romani*, 4 vol., Roma, 1907–1917 CCLXVIII

Savigny (R.), *Traité de droit romain*, trad. franç. par Guenoux, 7 vol., Paris, 1851–1855 CCLXIX

— *Traité de la possession*, trad. franç. par Staedtler, Paris, 1864 CCLXX

— *Le droit des obligations*, trad. franç., par Ch. Gérardin et P. Jozon, 2 vol., Paris, 1863 CCLXXI

Schlossmann, *Nexum*, 1904 CCLXXII

— *Praescriptio und scripta verba*, Leipzig, 1907 CCLXXIII

— *In jure cessio und mancipatio*. Leipzig, 1904 CCLXXIV

— *Altrömisches Schuldrecht und Schuldverfahren*, 1904. CCLXXV

Schmidt, *Das Hauskind in mancipio*, Leipzig, 1879 CCLXXVI

Schoell, *Legis XII Tabularum reliquiæ*, 1866 CCLXXVII

Schulten, *Die römischen Grundherrschaften*, Weimar, 1896 CCLXXVIII

Senn, *Leges perfectæ, minus quam perfectæ et imperfectæ*, Paris, 1902 CCLXXIX

Sohm, *Institutionen des römischen Rechts*, 14ᵉ Aufl., Leipzig, 1911 CCLXXX

Solazzi, *La revoca degli atti fraudolenti*, 1902 CCLXXXI

— *La minore eta nel diritto romano*, Venezia, 1916 CCLXXXII

— *La restituzione della dote*, 1899 CCLXXXIII

394 BIBLIOGRAPHY

STINTZING, *Nexum mancipiumque und mancipatio*, Leipzig, 1907 CCLXXXIV
— *Beiträge zur römischen Rechtsgeschichte*, 1901 CCLXXXV

TALAMO, *Il concetto della schiavitu da Aristotele ai dottori scholastici*, Roma, 1908 CCLXXXVI
TISSET, *Contribution à l'histoire de la présomption de paternité*, Paris, 1921 CCLXXXVII

VERNAY, *Servius et son école*, Paris, 1909 CCLXXXVIII
VINCENT, *Le droit des Édiles*, Paris, 1922 CCLXXXIX
VOIGT, *Die XII Tafeln*, 2 Bde, Leipzig, 1883 CCXC
— *Die Lehre vom Jus naturale, aequum et bonum und jus gentium der Römer*, Leipzig, 1856–1876 CCXCI
— *Ueber die Banquiers, die Buchführung und die Litteralobligationen der Römer*, Leipzig, 1887 CCXCII

WALTZING, *Étude historique sur les corporations professionnelles chez les Romains*, 4 vol., Louvain, 1899 etc. CCXCIII
WEBER, *Die römische Agrargeschichte, bedeutung für das Staats und Privatrecht*, Stuttgart, 1891 CCXCIV
WENGER (LEON), *Zur Lehre von der actio judicati*, Graz, 1901 CCXCV
— *Papyrusforschung und Rechtswissenschaft*, Graz, 1902 CCXCVI
WEYMULLER, *Contribution à l'histoire de l'actio tutelæ. La cautio rem pupilli salvam fore*, Paris, 1901 CCXCVII
WILLEMS, *Le droit public romain*, 7e édit, Louvain, 1910 CCXCVIII
WINDSCHEID, *Lehrbuch des Pandectenrechts*, 3 Bde, Frankfurt, 1906 CCXCIX
WLASSAK, *Zur Geschichte der negotiorum gestio*, Iéna, 1890 CCC
— *Die Litiscontestation im Formularprocess*, Iéna, 1889 CCCI
— *Römische Processgesetze*, 2 Bde, Leipzig, 1897...... CCCII
— *Anklange und Streitbefestigung im Kriminalrecht der Römer*, Wien, 1917 CCCIII

ZOCCO-ROSA, *Li Istituti di Giustiniano secondo la critica moderna*, Palermo, 1896 CCCIV
— *L'Ius Flavianum e l'Ius Ælianum*, 2e édit., Palermo, 1915 CCCV

INDEX

ACCEPTANCE, 283
Acquisition, 302
Actio, 60, 63, 66-67, 73-74, 77, 111, 174, 233, 325
Ademptio, 301
Adgnatio, 93
Aditio, 284, 300, 302, 305, 370
Adjudicatio, 80, 171-72, 177, 245, 351
Adlectio, 315
Adoption, 93, 117, 119, 336
Adrogatio, 117, 335
Adstipulatio, 122, 241
Adultery, 105-06, 111, 113, 122, 330
Ager, 47, 56, 162, 175, 182, 319, 321, 351
Agnate Relationship, 93, 140
Agreement, 355-56
ALEXANDER, 4
ALEXANDRIA, 31
ALFENUS, 23
Aliens, 57
AMASIS, 9
ANASTASIUS, 339, 361
Animus, 167, 216, 356
ANTONINUS, 74, 116, 118, 154, 288
Appeal, 91
APPIAN, 53, 57, 119
Arbitrium, 68
Arca, 155
ARISTOTLE, 10
Ars, 25
Artisans, 44
Assignatio (*viritana*, 46, 51), 161
Association, 152
ASSYRIA, 5, 7
Auctoritas, 139, 145, 174
AUGUSTUS, 295
AULUS GELLIUS, 19, 39, 51, 55, 57, 73, 83, 86, 95, 97, 101, 110, 117, 119, 122, 130, 136, 139, 160, 179, 196, 200, 260, 275 280
AULUS OFILIUS, 23

BAILLY, 104
Basilic Constitutions, 379
BERYTUS, 31, 33

Betrothal, 102
BOCCHORIS, 5, 8
BRÉAL, 95
Byzantine Law, 15, 30, 171, 343

CÆSAR, 153
Capio, 310
CAPITOLINUS, 136, 150
Caput, 54, 81, 108, 138, 146, 188, 196, 198, 314
CATO, 196, 214, 229, 304
Cautio, 64, 74, 86, 88, 111, 207, 264, 284, 308, 364
Centumvirs, 63, 73, 127
Cession, 86, 175, 253
CHALDÆA, 5, 7, 8
Children, 52, 96-97, 114-26, 140, 208, 288, 291-92, 329, 332, 335-39, 343, 348, 367
Christianity, 330-31, 334, 346, 365
CICERO, *passim*
City, the, 10, 12, 42, 52, 96, 274, 314, 321, 373-75
Civis, 314
Claims, 252
Clarissimi, 315
CLAUDIUS, 166
Clients, 38, 136
Code, *Codex repetitæ prælectionis*, 33, 379
Code, Gregorian, 32
Code, Hermogenian, 32
Code, Theodosian, 32
Coemptio, 100-02
Cognate Relationship, 93, 289-90, 367
Cognatio, 120, 125, 128
Cognitio, 89, 127
Cognitor, 174
Collegium, 153, 315, 317, 348
Colonatus, 315, 319
Comitia, 19-20, 45, 57, 117, 274
Commercium, 43, 45, 56, 101, 127, 135, 175, 375
Commodatum, 231
Concilium, 45
Concubinage, 113, 334
Condemnatio, 80
Condictio, 177, 222, 242, 309-10, 360

395

396 INDEX

Conductio, 226
Confarreatio, 100
Confessio, 65, 325
Consecratio, 196
Consideration, 239
CONSTANTINE, 15, 329, 333, 339, 340, 341, 344, 345, 350
CONSTANTINOPLE, 33-34
Contestatio, 76-77, 86
Contumacy, 73
Contubernium, 104, 128, 138
Conubium, 43, 51, 56-57, 99, 120, 133, 135
Corporations, 152, 346
Corpus, 166, 200-01
CORUNCANIUS, 23
Credit, 258, 363
Cretio, 283
CUQ (ED.), 8
Curators, 118, 151, 344
Curatorship, 147, 249, 344
Curiales, 317, 348
Custodia, 224, 249
Custom, 17-20, 37, 44, 119, 277

Damnatio, 68, 210, 212, 301
Datio, 110
Debitum, 191, 358
Decemvirs, 48, 63, 127, 173
Decretales, 324
Decretum, 88
Decurions, 317
Deditio, 57
Deductio, 184
Defensio, 75
Delicts, 194, 354
Demonstratio, 78, 84, 233
Depopulation, 296-97
Deposit, 231
Dictio, 110
Digesta, 26, 31, 33, 181, 252, 298, 379
DIOCLETIAN, 356, 359
DION CASSIUS, 21, 53, 96, 152-53, 292, 296
DIONYSIUS OF HALICARNASSUS, 39, 41, 43, 44, 47, 62, 95, 126
DIRKSEN, 50
Divorce, 108, 295, 332
Dolus, 215
Dominium, 46, 51, 95, 97-98, 127, 131, 158, 161, 273, 349
Dominus, 126, 141
Domus, 39, 43-44, 46, 48, 93, 95-96, 98, 103, 114, 121, 129, 198, 273, 328, 374-75
DOROTHEUS, 34
Dowry, 109, 254, 332, 372

Earnest, 357
East, the, 151-52, 189, 323, 328, 332, 334, 336, 350, 357-58, 360, 363, 365
Edict, the Prætorian, 77, 206
Edictum, 21-24, 26, 30-31, 287
EGYPT, 5-9, 319
Emancipation, 98, 118, 125, 289
Emphyteusis, 189, 352
Emptor, 278
ERMAN, 129
ETRUSCANS, 12
Exceptio, 76-78, 82, 85, 102, 146, 234, 242, 250, 270, 301, 309, 324, 356, 362
Execution, 362
Expensum, 219
Extinction, 256, 362

Family, 93, 126, 314, 328-45
Fas, 39
Fasti, 49
FESTUS, 41, 43, 45, 47, 55-56, 63-67, 94, 98, 131, 160, 175, 196, 213, 273
Fideicommissum, 72, 305, 342, 369-70
Fidejussio, Fidepromissio, 264, 356, 364
Fides, 79, 141, 248
FITTING, 24
FLACCUS (GR.), 48
Flamen, 100
FLAVIUS (CN.), 49, 52
FLORENTINUS, 34
Fœdus, 57
Fœnus, 260, 363
Formalism, 172, 234
Formulas, 70, 84, 88, 164, 286
FRANCISCI (DE), 11
Freedmen, 39, 53, 96, 128, 130, 276, 296, 314, 340
Functio, 316

GAIUS, 14, 21, 24, 26, 29, 33, 49, 53, 55, 60-61, 64, 66, 70, 80, 89, 103, 111, 191, 284
Gens, 12, 17, 38, 100, 114, 117, 124, 274
Gentiles, 38, 93, 140, 276
Genus, 158, 238, 246
Gifts, 113, 272, 308-10, 331, 333, 356, 359, 369, 371
GIRARD, 174
Gods, 65, 94
GRANIUS FLACCUS, 48
GREECE, 5, 9, 13, 106, 124, 151, 201, 220, 260

INDEX

Guarantees, 262, 363
Guardianship, 137, 179, 243, 275, 342

Habitation, 185-87
HADRIAN, 22, 24, 72, 98, 123, 146, 178, 286, 290, 297, 302
HAMMOURABI, 8
Hereditas, 178, 281, 284, 287, 365-69
Heredium, 43
Heres, 115, 118-19, 273, 280-82
Hire, 226
HONORIUS, 361
HORACE, 259
HOREMHEB, 9
Hospitalitas, 56
HUVELIN, 210
HYGINUS, 162, 189

Idiocy, 147, 168, 208, 290, 353
IHERING, 166
Imperium, 88, 91
Incapable, 342
Indivision, 244
Infitiatio, 84, 86, 199, 265, 299
Ingenuus, 135, 296
Injectio (Manus), 60, 68
Institutes, 314, 355
Institutiones, 26, 34
Intentio, 78-80, 82, 87, 256
Interdicts, 168
Interpretatio, 20, 32, 52, 208
Intestato (*ab*), 273, 276, 288, 365-67

JOSEPHUS, 153
Judex, 322
Judicatum, 68, 86, 122, 165
Judicatus, 68, 75
Judicial organization, 70, 322
Judicium, 21, 62-63, 65, 71, 76-77, 80, 84-85, 89-90, 122, 169, 177, 196, 201, 322
JULIAN, 34, 121, 131, 191, 233, 249, 289
Juramentum, 217
Juridici, 72
Jurists, 5, 11-14, 21-25, 27-28, 51, 103, 121, 143, 157, 166, 172, 174, 179, 200, 233, 240, 243, 270, 274, 280, 374, 376-78
Jus, 62-63, 65, 72-73, 75, 85, 89-90, 95, 115, 121, 139, 156, 196, 234, 322
Jus Ælianum, 52, 62
Jus antiquum, 295

Jus civile, 28, 31, 49, 254
Jus dedititiorum, 57
Jus Flavianum, 52, 61
Jus gentilitatis, 41
Jus gentium, 11, 28-29, 31, 56
Jus honorarium, 28
Jus honorum, 48, 133, 135
Jus italicum, 162
Jus liberorum, 296
Jus militiæ, 276
Jus naturale, 28-29
Jus Papirianum, 48-49
Jus peregrinum, 57
Jus privatum, 27, 353
Jus publicum, 27
Jus reciperationis, 56, 63
Jus scriptum, 18
Jussus, 250, 261, 283, 361
Justice, 322
JUSTIN, 353
JUSTINIAN, 15, 31-32, 34, 80, 93, 204, 252, 313, 326, 328, 330-32, 336-39, 342-45, 353, 355-70, 372
Justus, 176, 179, 283
JUVENAL, 107, 136, 259

LABEO, 23, 49, 204
LACHMANN, 161
Lares, 94, 126
Latifundia, 162
Latinitas, 57, 131, 135, 284, 313
LATIUM, 53
Lease, 188, 357, 359
Legacy, 110, 275, 279, 290, 369
LENEL, 24
LEO, 332
Lex, 18-22, 27-29, 31, 33, 61, 67, 181, 297
Libellus, 325
Libertas, 127, 131, 179, 314
Lis, 68, 75-77, 85-86, 165, 181, 254, 324, 364
LIVY, 6, 20, 41, 47, 53, 97, 138-40, 142, 183
Loan, 258
LYCURGUS, 5

MACROBIUS, 126
MAJORIAN, 323
Maleficia, 194
Mancipatio, 101, 125, 139, 172, 278, 288
Mancipium, 95, 119, 125, 137, 156-58, 173, 329, 348
Mandatum, 222, 230, 264, 357
Manes, 94, 126
MANILIUS, 52

INDEX

Manus, 68, 93, 95, 97-102, 106, 108, 129, 131, 137, 212, 273, 329
MARCIAN, 34
MARINI, 350-51
Marriage, 39, 41, 52, 93, 98-114, 128, 330
MASPÉRO, 9
Merx, 242, 251
MINOS, 5
MODESTINUS, 24, 178
Money, 173
Mortgage, 268-71, 345, 353, 370
Municeps, 314, 317
Munus, 317
Mutatio, 221

NAMATIANUS, 4
Nationality, 313
Negotium, 205, 244
NEPOS (C.), 54, 219
Nexum, 212, 217-18, 220, 240, 259
NIEBUHR, 166, 260
Nobilitas, 315
Nomen, 37-38, 158, 210, 219, 342
Novæ (leges), 297, 303, 306, 310, 370
Novatio, 216
Novellæ, 15, 32, 34, 328, 350, 364, 367, 369, 371
Noxia, 197, 199
Nuptiæ, 52, 99, 101, 117, 121, 331, 369, 372

Obligatio, 190-94, 210, 242, 248, 253, 354, 361
Obsequium, 39, 114, 317, 319
Occupatio, 172
Onus, 281
OPPERT, 8
Oratio, 20
Ownership, 158, 348

PÆTUS, 23, 49, 52
PAIS (E.), 49
Pandectæ, 33
PAPINIAN, 14, 24, 30, 33, 230, 252, 262, 285, 363
Partnership, 222, 228
Pater, 41, 95
Paterfamilias, 43, 54, 93, 95-98, 100, 114, 120, 125, 277, 328, 339
Patricius, 38
Patronus, 38, 98
PAUL, 24, 75, 79, 84, 89, 94, 96, 98, 102, 113, 120, 124-25, 132, 147, 164, 167, 175, 185-88, 198-201, 204, 208, 214, 224-26, 259-60, 262, 270, 284, 294, 296, 299, 300, 305, 309
Pecunia, 158, 207, 243, 267, 275, 298
Penal Law, 207
Penates, 94
Peregrinus, 54, 57, 128, 161, 201, 313
Persecutio, 90
PERSIA, 5, 7
Personality, artificial, 154; juridical, 314
Personal guarantees, 262
Personal rights, 190, 354
Petitio, 84
Pietas, 293
Pignoris capio, 61, 70, 144
Pignus, 268, 326
PLATO, 10
PLAUTUS, 136, 150
Plebis scitum, 19
Plebs, 44, 50, 119, 316
Pledge, 231
PLINY, 43, 53, 125-26, 153, 162, 259, 294
PLUTARCH, 44
POMPONIUS, 26
Pœna, 193, 197, 204, 214, 301, 340, 356, 370
Populus, 44, 50, 119, 276
Possession, 165, 180, 286, 288, 320
Potestas, 95, 102, 124-26, 137, 140, 147, 161
Præscriptio, 46, 180
Prætor, 62, 72, 96, 111, 293
Prætorian (cf. Edict), 30, 170, 200, 202, 233, 252, 288
Preception, 300
Princeps, 41
PRISCUS, 24
Private justice, 39, 199, 209
Private Law, 208
Privilegia, 51
Procedure, 59, 322
PROCULIANS, PROCULUS, 23, 81, 105, 121, 300, 330
Procurator, 74
Promissio, 110
Property, 86-87, 154, 156, 285
Propinqui, 107
Puberty, 105, 121, 140, 168, 282, 330

Quarta legitimæ partis, 292, 294, 306

INDEX

Querela, 292, 366, 372
QUINTILIAN, 52, 69, 86, 200 282, 306
Quirites, 173

Real rights, 156, 182, 348
Reciperatio, 56, 63, 71
Recourse, 91
Regulæ, 26
Relatio, 20
Relationship, 93
Religion, 41, 94, 100-01
Religious brotherhoods, 44
Religious Law, 39
Repudiation, 283
Res, 156, 348
Responsibility, 198, 224
Restitutio, 89
RÉVILLOUT, 9
Rogatio, 117
ROSSI (DE), 153

SABINIANS, SABINUS, 23, 81, 105, 121, 193, 220, 232, 274, 280, 300
Sacra, 94, 98, 117, 276, 285
Sacramentum, 63, 65-66, 164, 286
Sale, 87, 98, 101, 110, 119, 125, 130, 173, 222, 353, 357, 359
SALVIAN, 320
SALVIUS JULIANUS, 29
Sanction, 283, 300-01
Sanguinis turbatio, 108
SAVIGNY, 166
SCÆVOLA, 23, 52, 79, 207, 262, 280
SCHEIL (L. P.), 8
Senate, 18, 20, 83, 116, 297, 315
SENECA, 31, 129, 136
Separatio bonorum, 285, 299
Servitudes, 182, 351
SERVIUS SULPICIUS, 14, 23, 49, 193, 204
SERVIUS TULLIUS, 12, 45
SICULUS FLACCUS, 161
SIDONIUS APOLLINARIS, 57, 321
Signum, 173
Slaves, 39, 55, 97, 126-30, 155, 173, 186, 201, 225, 282, 340, 352
Socialism, 32, 315, 318, 329, 365
Sodalitates, 44, 152
Solidarity, 263
Spatium, 284
Species, 158, 238, 246
Spectabiles, 315

Sponsio, 214, 265, 286
Sponsor, 210, 213, 255
Spurius, 113, 120
State, the, *passim*, 313-21, 373-75
Stipendium, 163
Stips, 213
Stipulatio, 214, 356
Stuprum, 104, 113
Successions, 272-310, 339, 365-68
SUETONIUS, 27, 95, 120, 136, 142, 153, 261, 296, 306
Suit, 324
Superficies, 188
Sureties, 268

Tables (the Twelve), 17, 23, 39, 48, 61, 64, 97, 101, 108, 125, 137-38, 140, 178, 195-96, 240, 245, 273-74, 285, 298-99
TACITUS, 20, 24, 101, 136, 297, 309
Tax, 163, 318
TERTULLIAN, 153
Theft, 141, 193, 202
THEODOSIUS, 33, 343, 350, 359, 371
THEOPHILUS, 34, 339
Trades, 44
Traditio, 172, 175-76, 184, 221, 224, 350-51
Transcriptio, 219-20
Translatio, 301
TRIBONIAN, 34
Tribunal, 94
Tributum, 163
Tripertita, 23, 52
TRYPHONINUS, 24

ULPIAN, 14, 24, 34, 53, 56, 96, 103, 105, 110-12, 117-18, 123-25, 127, 131-33, 135, 145, 147-48, 154, 158-59, 173, 175-78, 183, 186-87 200, 262, 275-80, 283-85, 295-303, 305-07, 309
ULPIUS MARCELLUS, 24
Universitas, 154
Urbs, 47
Use, 187, 351
Usucapio, 177, 277, 284, 350
Usufruct, 185, 351
Usus, 100, 108, 189
Uxor, 98, 128, 332, 368

Vades, 64
Vadimonium, 66, 73
VALENS, 24

VALENTINIAN, 24, 32, 323, 329, 359
VALERIUS MAXIMUS, 6, 95
Value, 158, 165, 252
VARRO, 38, 43, 56, 65, 102, 126, 174, 183, 212, 225, 237, 277
Vindex, 69, 73, 217
Vindicatio, 126, 134, 184, 188, 300, 303
Vindicta, 132, 341
Vis, 169
Vocatio, 73

Voluntas, 284
Vote, 19, 57

WENGER, 14
West, the, 323-24, 328, 358
Will, 56-57, 86, 119, 122, 135, 255, 273-74, 278, 284, 302, 366, 372
Women, 96, 98-103, 127-28, 131, 138, 150, 160, 179, 276, 280, 289, 296, 330-35, 342, 353

THE HISTORY OF CIVILIZATION

Titles in the series

Pre History	Language - A Linguistic Introduction to History	J Vendryes
	A Geographical Introduction to History	Lucien Febvre
	The Dawn of European Civilization	V Gordon Childe
	The Aryans	V Gordon Childe
	From Tribe to Empire	Moret & Davy
	Death Customs	Effie Bendann
	The Migration of Symbols	D Mackenzie
	The History of Witchcraft and Demonology	Montague Summers
	The History of Medicine	C G Cumston
	Money and Monetary Policy in Early Times	A R Burns
	Life and Work in Prehistoric Times	G Renard
	Social Organization	Rivers & Perry
Greek Civilization	The Ægean Civilization	G Glotz
	Ancient Greece at Work	G Glotz
	The Formation of the Greek People	A Jardé
	Art in Greece	de Ridder & Deonna
	Macedonian Imperialism	Pierre Jouguet
	Greek Thought and the Origins of the Scientific Spirit	Léon Robin
	The Greek City and its Institutions	G Glotz
Roman Civilization	Primitive Italy	Leon Homo
	Rome the Law-Giver	J Declareuil
	The Roman Spirit	Albert Grenier
	The Roman World	V Chapot
	Roman Political Institutions	Leon Homo
	The Economic Life of the Ancient World	J Toutain
Eastern Civilization	The Nile and Egyptian Civilization	A Moret
	The Peoples of Asia	L H Dudley Buxton
	Mesopotamia	L Delaporte
	A Thousand Years of the Tartars	E H Parker
	Ancient Persia and Iranian Civilization	Clement Huart
	Chinese Civilization	Marcel Granet
	The Life of Buddha	Edward J Thomas
	The History of Buddhist Thought	Edward J Thomas
	Ancient India and Indian Civilization	Masson-Oursel et al
	The Heroic Age of India	N K Sidhanta
Judaeo Christian Civilization		
	Israel	Adolphe Lods
	The Prophets and the Rise of Judaism	Adolphe Lods
	The Jewish World in the Time of Jesus	Charles Guignebert
	The History and Literature of Christianity	Pierre de Labriolle
European Civilization	The End of the Ancient World	Ferdinand Lot
	The Rise of the Celts	Henri Hubert
	The Greatness and Decline of the Celts	Henri Hubert
	Life and Work in Medieval Europe	P Boissonnade
	The Feudal Monarchy in France and England	C Petit-Dutaillis
	Travel and Travellers of the Middle Ages	Arthur Newton
	Chivalry	Edgar Prestage
	The Court of Burgundy	Otto Cartellieri
	Life and Work in Modern Europe	Renard & Weulersse
	China and Europe	Adolf Reichwein
	The American Indian Frontier	W Christie Macleod

For Product Safety Concerns and Information please contact our EU
representative GPSR@taylorandfrancis.com
Taylor & Francis Verlag GmbH, Kaufingerstraße 24, 80331 München, Germany

www.ingramcontent.com/pod-product-compliance
Lightning Source LLC
Chambersburg PA
CBHW051623230426
43669CB00013B/2162